THE MONOPOLY MAKERS

This book is printed on 100 percent recycled paper

THE MONOPOLY MAKERS

Ralph Nader's
Study Group Report
on Regulation
and Competition

Edited by Mark J. Green

WITHDRAWN

GROSSMAN PUBLISHERS
NEW YORK 1973

All royalties from the sale of this book will be given to the
Center for Study of Responsive Law, the organization established by Ralph Nader to conduct research into abuses of the
public interest by business and governmental groups. Contributions to further this work are tax deductible and may be
sent to the Center at P.O.B. 19367, Washington, D.C. 20036.

CONTRIBUTORS

Mark J. Green was the editor-in-chief of the *Harvard Civil Rights—Civil Liberties Law Review* and is currently the Director of the Corporate Accountability Research Group in Washington, D.C. He is the co-author of *Who Runs Congress?* and *The Closed Enterprise System,* and co-editor of *With Justice for Some* and *Corporate Power in America.*

Beverly C. Moore, Jr., is an attorney with the Corporate Accountability Research Group. He has contributed to *With Justice for Some,* co-authored *The Closed Enterprise System,* and is completing the forthcoming Nader study on the food industry.

Howard Saxner is an attorney in Boston, Massachusetts.

David Hemenway is a fourth-year graduate student at Harvard University, completing his doctoral dissertation on industry-wide voluntary product standards.

K. G. J. Pillai is the Executive Director of the Aviation Consumer Action Project in Washington, D.C. and the author of *The Air Net* (1969). He received his J. S. D. from the Yale Law School.

Marshall Beil clerked for Judge John F. Dooling, Jr. (Eastern District of New York), worked for Sen. George McGovern's presidential campaign, and is presently an attorney with Paul, Weiss, Rifkind, Wharton and Garrison in New York City.

Larry Ellsworth is a lawyer with the Institute for Public Interest Representation at the Georgetown University Law Center.

730809

Irene Till is an economist with the Corporate Accountability Research Group and author of Monograph #16, "Antitrust in Action," for the Temporary National Economic Committee (1941) and the co-author, with Sen. Estes Kefauver, of *In a Few Hands* (1965). She has worked for the Senate Antitrust and Monopoly Subcommittee and was the chief of the Division of Economic Reports at the Federal Trade Commission.

Howard Knee is a lawyer working for the Corporate Accountability Research Group.

CONTENTS

INTRODUCTION BY
RALPH NADER

The Monopoly Makers is the third in a series of studies on the political economy of Corporate America, on the ties between industry and Washington and their impact on consumer welfare.* This is a book about federal regulation, licensing, subsidies, procurement policies, and patent and import restrictions. It explores how government economic regulation has frustrated competitive efficiencies and has promoted monopolistic rigidities advocated by the regulatees themselves. It is, above all, a book about corporate socialism, a condition of federal statecraft wherein public agencies control much of the private economy on behalf of a designated corporate clientele.

Not that monopoly and unchecked corporate power are unusual in our economy. They are all too common. But when they are bred and nourished by the government itself in the guise of "the public interest," then it becomes time to question the purpose and goals of economic regulation. This is especially true when the intended beneficiary of the elaborate regulatory structure—the consumer—becomes its first victim. The consumer ultimately pays for the increased prices, encouraged waste, and retarded technology that economic regulation fosters.

In describing these patterns, *The Monopoly Makers* should not be misunderstood by adherents of various ideolo-

---

* The first two were *The Closed Enterprise System* (1972), by Mark J. Green, with Beverly C. Moore, Jr., and Bruce Wasserstein, and *Corporate Power in America* (1973), edited by Mark J. Green and myself.

gies. First, it does not discuss the "grants economy" of public assistance, Medicare, and so on. Second, the authors of the various chapters present their analyses and evaluations with a diversity that denies stereotypy. This book does not say that all government economic regulation is bad nor that only the market can satisfy every consumer need. Deregulation is suggested in some areas, such as private rate-making cartels condoned by the agencies in the transportation industries; but more consumer-oriented regulation is prescribed in the telephone and power areas, i.e., using improved utility practices where they are still needed. One underlying theme of these case studies, however, is that special economic interests can control a regulatory program unless the citizen-consumers supposedly served by it can have a systematic and continual role in decision-making through their experts and advocates. The verity is not novel except in its applications: there can be no good government without effective citizenship.

The evidence brought together in these pages points to more than episodic or even institutional debacles affecting various agencies. Certainly, patents have been used to stifle competition; taxpayers pay exorbitantly for the drugs purchased by the government for the military services and veterans hospitals; the Pentagon and a few giant prime defense industry contractors are expensively cozy; many trade restrictions, such as quotas and price-fixing, lock up markets for industries. But beyond these daily costs and injustices, there has emerged a fundamental change in our political economy. The arms-length relationship which must characterize any democratic government in its dealings with special interest groups has been replaced, and not just by *ad hoc* wheeling and dealing, which have been observed for generations. What is new is the institutionalized fusion of corporate desires with public bureaucracy—where the national security is synonymous with the state of Lockheed and Litton, where career roles are interchangeable along the industry-to-government-to-industry shuttle, where corporate risks and losses become taxpayer obligations. For the most part, the large unions do not object to this situation, having become modest co-partners, seeking derivative benefits from the governmental patrons of industry.

In an ironic, though not entirely unpredictable way, the predatory practices of the nineteenth-century "Robber

Barons" have become the accepted regulatory practices of today. It is so much easier and, above all, more stable to seize the legal and administrative apparatus than to fight it, turning government agencies into licensors of private monopolies and co-conspirators against the people. These truly are the kinds of quiet upheavals which require comprehensively fundamental responses. It is often said that political-economic dynamics have a way of generating their countervailing forces—populist-progressive movements, labor and producer cooperative organizations, and the like. But the corporation has succeeded in absorbing its challengers because it controls the most basic, fungible, motivating allocators of power in the society—wealth and income. And it controls them in an exceptionally concentrated, hierarchical manner with the fuller and detailed support of corporation laws and regulatory statutes, starting with that corporate Reno, the State of Delaware. Years ago, General Robert E. Wood, former chairman of the board, Sears, Roebuck & Company, put it succinctly:

> We stress the advantages of the free enterprise system, we complain about the totalitarian state, but in our individual organizations . . . we have created more or less of a totalitarian system in industry, particularly in large industry.

Those words are even more applicable today as the consequences of such concentrated power are more far-reaching and serious. Adverse corporate impacts on health and safety, a subject which this book does not discuss, are becoming more serious extensions of this power as new technologies breed new risks and traumas. But the economic costs, the central subject of these chapters, are also piling up and increasingly displaying a lock-step effect on one another. It is a phenomenon which can be discerned by large aggregate economic growth without commensurate growth in consumer value. This kind of economic growth cannot diminish the medical, transportation, and housing problems we suffer. It is based, in part, on sheer economic waste: an inefficient, imbalanced transportation system, for example, takes more out of the economic pie; modern, efficient mass transit would reduce the demand for gasoline, highways, repair parts, automobiles, auto insurance, and accident-injury expenditures, and they could help the economy use these savings to raise the quality of living standards. The enormous waste of energy resources also generates false economic growth—growth that is not needed to fulfill consumers' needs for energy. Those saved dollars—lower fuel and electricity charges from efficiently conserved and utilized energy—could go to meet other neglected needs of consumers.

Regulation that wastes scarce economic resources and inflates consumer prices, rewards inefficiency, and impairs service is a gross abuse. But when it assists in supressing highly beneficial technology because the entrenched companies do not wish to displace their outdated capital, a new, worse, dimension of corporate socialism appears. In the last two decades, spectacular new technology has been developed that can throw the challenge of abundance to older technologies of scarcity—satellite communications vs. AT&T's cables, CATV vs. the traditional limited TV spectrum, mass transit systems callable on demand vs. buses and automobiles. These are a few of many developments which the regulatory-industrial complex has succeeded in blocking, limiting, or delaying. What facilitates this resistance is the lack of specialists and resources within the regulatory agencies to integrate these new technical options in policies for the benefit of the public.

In December 1971, for example, the Federal Communications Commissions pathetically announced that it could not continue the study of AT&T's rate structure for lack of staff. A few weeks later, the FCC, under strong citizen and Congressional criticism relented, but more in form than fact. The handful of economists and accountants investigating this gigantic corporation is comparable to an ant surveying a movie mastodon. The FCC's entire $35 million budget is equivalent to about half a day's gross revenue of AT&T, and only a part of the FCC deals with the telephone industry. The total budget for the six major independent regulatory agencies for fiscal 1973 was $142 million—less than the Pentagon spends in one day and demonstratably inadequate to study and implement economic policies for the more than $125 billion of the gross national product which the commissions directly affect. And just as demonstrably, the subservience of these agencies to their client industries keeps them from using effectively the funds and staff that they do have.

Over the years there has been no dearth of recommendations to cure these regulatory problems. Earlier these focused on the need for policy changes; more recently there has been an emphasis on procedural revisions to streamline and open up the decision-making process. However, as with so many other deficiencies of the institutional condition, people must know how these agencies affect their daily lives and how in turn people can affect these agencies before any reforms of any kind will truly take hold. The instruments of civic action galvanizing governmental and non-governmental institutions, such as Congress and the media, will be forced when these linkages are made between regulators, industries and the public's plight, and translated into countervailing powers of response.

It should be stressed that *The Monopoly Makers* probes the world of *economic regulation*. There, the kinds of decisions classically within the competence and interest of private entrepreneurs—decisions affecting price, entry, and innovation—are made by public officials or by public officials in conjunction with producer cartels. But economic regulation is different from health and safety regulation, which seeks to complement, not replace, a market system incompetent or unwilling to fulfill certain social needs. This type of regulation properly understands that while competition may be an efficient and equitable allocator of some resources, it is still imperfect:

—*Safety regulation* explicitly assumes that the market will not adequately protect consumers against certain hazards. Such laws are based on the rationale that it is cost-effective to prevent consumer harm rather than to internalize the costs later, both because the harm inflicted may simply be unacceptable to society and the victim (deaths from dangerous drugs or crashed automobiles) or because assuming that a manufacturer will compensate all victims for damages is utterly unrealistic (one does not expend $1000 in court costs trying to recover $100 for product damages). Examples here include laws affecting food and drug safety, airline safety, auto crashworthiness, flammable fabrics, and radiation levels. Thus, the Federal Aviation Administration should continue to ensure the safe operation of airplanes, the Interstate Commerce Commission and Department of Transportation should keep dangerous trucks off the road, and the Food and Drug Administration should keep dangerous drugs off the market.

—*Non-market externalities* include damage caused to third parties who neither bought nor sold the product inflicting the damage. While dangerous cars and drugs go through the market system, nobody can be said to have "bought" auto pollution, or the risk of radiation poisoning from a nuclear reactor. Government standards here can protect all citizens from harms which producers lack a market incentive to contain.

—*Enabling Regulation* seeks to establish the necessary preconditions for competitive enterprise to succeed. Thus, antitrust law establishes the borders and rules for economic contest. Anti-discrimination laws, occupational health and safety requirements, and unemployment compensation establish minimal standards for protection of the individual in the production process. And corporate and product disclosure requirements are *sine qua nons* for investor knowledge and consumer sovereignty: the corporate balance sheet should be made public so the capital market can reward or sanction firms accordingly, while product information (like nutritional labeling, code dating, truth in lending provisions) can provide consumers with the intelligence which is a philosophic cornerstone of economic competitions.

—*Yardstick competition* might well have to be provided by the government when industry withdraws from a market because it is perceived as unprofitable. Such public enterprise could fulfill a public need and, if properly circumscribed and wisely deployed, set an example for private enterprise. For instance, railroads made it clear by their withdrawal petitions before the ICC and by their treatment of consumers that they did not want to provide passenger service; private insurance firms shied away from flood and crime insurance; and oil firms for years have not been interested in developing commercial processes for converting oil shale into oil because of oversupply. In such situations, government enterprise may be necessary—Amtrak to provide passenger rail service, government flood and crime insurance, or the creation of a federally chartered firm to explore and produce oil from oil shale. Yardstick enterprise should also include government-sponsored research and development in areas shunned by private industry. For example, government-sponsored programs to develop safety vehicles suitable for mass production will soon generate a technological push on a previously stagnant industry.

Since the competitive market can be a poor, long-range planner, government may have to step in. And such public enterprise can generate beneficial second-order effects. The TVA, by producing cheap power in the Tennessee Valley, induced much industry to develop there, and showed its competitors how to cut costs and prices while increasing profits; flood and crime insurance, mass transit, a non-addicting heroin substitute, and modular housing—none of which have been adequately developed and marketed by private enterprise—could revitalize the decaying inner city; the development of usable energy from the sun could make solar energy competitive with other forms. Government then opens avenues for other entrepreneurial enterprise, avoiding the discretion and drift which characterize economic regulation and fulfilling the role of a stimulator, not a suppressor, of competition.

The principal authors of this book have been researching the nature of corporate power since 1970 when they commenced a study project on the Antitrust Division of the Department of Justice, which was published as *The Closed Enterprise System* in 1972. As with *Corporate Power in America* (1973), the views of the contributors to the various chapters of this book are their own and not necessarily in agreement with those of their colleagues. *The Monopoly Makers* does, however, take as its operating framework the traditional economic system of market and regulatory behavior that prevails in this country. It does not, nor should it, prejudge alternate economic modes, existing or theoretical, for allocating economic resources and distributing economic justice.

Washington, D.C.
February, 1973

THE MONOPOLY MAKERS

1

Uncle Sam the Monopoly Man

MARK J. GREEN

Despite contrary speeches on the corporate hustings, the free enterprise economy embraced by laissez-faire purists is gone. Beginning with early regulatory laws in the 1880s and the antitrust laws of 1890, 1914, and 1950, to the acceptance of Keynesian economics by policymakers in the 1930s, through Truman's Employment Act of 1946 and right on to President Nixon's Phases I and II—it cannot be doubted that we have a mixed economy blending public control and private enterprise. Even beyond these pivotal changes are ongoing policies deeply woven into our economic tapestry: patent policy, tax write-offs, government procurement, the disposition of surplus property, import quotas, deficit spending, control of the money supply and interest rates. The list is lengthy. The question no longer is *what* the role of government should be but *how much.* Yet an even more basic question is *for what purpose?* Too often government programs have been launched in the name of competitive capitalism, only to find themselves having unintended effects. Subsidizing the maritime industry, guaranteeing Lockheed, underwriting the defense industry, and regulating the railroads, for example, have not surgically cured a slightly cancered capitalism. Rather, they have undermined competition and entrenched monopoly.

Which to many is a good thing. Instead of projecting pejorative images, some observers see corporate concentration resulting from the sophisticated utilization of new technology. Business is big in order to be good and it is good precisely because it is big. In an age of far-flung conglomerates and multi-national corporations, efficient production, distribution, and planning all militate against competition, they say. Vigorous antitrust action and competition are seen as inefficient, destructive, and irrational, philosophies swimming against the historical current. They are considered gospel only to populist prairie liberals and older industrial economists; but modern thinkers, if not Marxian, are at least Galbraithian. The prevalence of these views is a tribute to the influence and ability of their recent proponents—John Kenneth Galbraith, David Lilienthal, and the late A. A. Berle, among others.

Concentration over competition seems to have much going for it—except the facts. And lacking empirical evidence, adherents get stuck in the rut of their own arguments. The overwhelming weight of economic evidence supports the notion that a firm need not be gigantic to be efficient, that economies of scale are achieved in the plant and not the nation. In addition, huge size is not only unnecessary for technological advance, but it can be a retardant agent; while competition compels innovation for firms to stay ahead of or to stay even with their competitors, there is little incentive for shared monopolists with fixed market shares to change their ways. In fact, with a large investment in existing capital, there is a strong *disincentive* against retooling if new technology comes along. Further, industrial concentration can be associated with product hazards and pollution, racialism and inflation, and the kind of excessive political power that attends excessive economic power. The ties between the two, as well as elaboration of these other economic and social costs of monopoly, were discussed in our prior volume, *The Closed Enterprise System.*[1]

On the other hand, competition is to the economy what political freedom is to our polity: both oppose unchecked power and both value diversity in the contest for solutions. Economically, competition has the tendency to drive prices down and to deter inflation, to encourage innovation and penetration of new markets, and to give the consumer a diversity of buying choice. No one or few firms dominate the market, a market which is dynamic and self-regulating as all bid for the consumer's dollar. Competition will not work when enough government enforcers and industrial economists, blaming historical determinism, *say* it won't work. It is this premise—the efficacy of competition—which runs throughout this book.

The Monopoly Makers examines what is perhaps the most pernicious form of economic monopoly and hostility to competition—when it is promoted by the power and legitimacy of government itself. A variety of government policies as they impact on competition and concentration will be discussed in each of eleven chapters, including the procurement practices of the executive branch, and, especially, the historical habits of the independent regulatory agencies. The recurring theme was inspired by Walter Adams and Horace Gray in their 1955 book, *Monopoly in America: The Government as Promotor:* "Government today is, in many instances, a promoter of monopoly. It frequently puts together the power concentrates which the antitrust authorities are later called upon to break asunder. In short, government often supports, rather than countervails, the forces making for concentration and monopoly." It is an observation even more true today, a reality that damages consumers, taxpayers, and the integrity of government itself.

Take procurement policies, for example, where the economic stakes are quite high. Fully half of the defense budget, or $40 billion a year, goes to purchase military hardware. As Larry Ellsworth asserts in his chapter, only one firm is solicited in 60 percent of all contracts negotiated, despite the fact that prices are about 25 percent less under a system of competitive bidding. Not surprisingly, profits on defense contracts are excessive. According to the contractors themselves, replying to a Government Accounting Office (GAO) questionnaire, they made a pretax return on equity of 21.1 percent; but based on a GAO study of 146 actual defense contracts, the figure was 56.1 percent. Furthermore, the "cost-plus" mentality discourages efficiency, because the more one's costs, the more one's profits; this in turn leads to the huge "cost overruns" that have become part of our national language. The Pentagon's allegiance to the major firms simply increases economic concentration. In the late 1950s, when Senator John Sparkman complained that twenty big firms got one-half the defense contracts negotiated without competitive bidding, some Pentagon officials conceded that the system might create "some degree of concentration."[2] But it doesn't seem greatly to trouble the Defense Department, which has historically viewed antitrust principles as either irrelevant or even damaging to national security.

The story is similar with federal drug procurement. "The Federal Government currently spends about a billion and a half dollars a year for drugs," writes Dr. Irene Till, "usually on high-priced brand name products bought in the most costly manner." The lack of centralized procurement, the favoring of large drug firms over small, the lack of advertised bids, and the purchase of brand name rather than generic drugs have all greatly padded our public drug bills. Again, unsurprisingly, the industry is one of the most profitable, doubling the after-tax average return on investment of the economy's manufacturing sector.

Procurement policies in the defense and drug industries burden the taxpayer and deflect scarce public resources from far more important social needs than undergirding economic concentration. High officials and procurement bureaucrats must be made to comprehend the intimate connection between the principles of competition and inexpensive procurement. Yet even those who insist that competition is "irrelevant" to their tasks should be reminded that it is not uncommon for one public policy to nourish another. The revenue-raising function of tax policy goes hand-in-hand with encouraging or discouraging non-revenue issues, such as aiding the blind and working mothers via extra exemptions; and federal construction contracts cannot be given to firms or unions that discriminate on the basis of race, because racial equality is a nationally declared goal and policy. So, supposedly, is economic competition.

While government involvement in the economic system can take many forms, its most pervasive manifestation has been economic regulation by the so-called alphabet soup of regulatory agencies.*

The granddaddy, the Interstate Commerce Commission (ICC), was created in 1887 either to prevent rates abuses or to stabilize the railroads' revenues, depending on whether one holds to the traditional (I. L. Sharfman) or revisionist (Gabriel Kolko) view of its inception; ICC jurisdiction was extended to oil pipelines in 1906, motor carriers in 1935, and interstate water carriers in 1940. In 1920, the Federal Power Commission (FPC) was given regulatory power over interstate electric power and natural gas operations. The Federal Communications Commission (FCC), created in 1934, regulates radio and television broadcasting, interstate telephone services, and aspects of international telecommunications. Following the collapse of the securities market during the Depression, the Securities and Exchange Commission (SEC) was formed in 1934 to require disclosure of information pertaining to public offerings. The 1935 Public Utility Holding Company Act gave it authority to regulate the corporate structure and finances of electric and gas utility holding companies. The Civil Aeronautics Board (CAB), created in 1938, regulates domestic and (less directly) international airline operations. Transoceanic water carriers are regulated by the Federal Maritime Commission (FMC), reorganized in its present form in 1940. Finally, regulation of the American banking system is shared by the Comptroller of the Currency, the Federal Reserve System, the Federal Deposit Insurance Corporation (FDIC), as well as various state agencies. In all, according to the best estimates, regulated industries account for 9.2 percent of all wages,[3] 10.9 percent of the Gross National Product (or about $120 billion),[4] and 34.4 percent of all new plant and equipment expenditures.[5]

The governmental regulation of certain industries and markets did not suddenly erupt without precedent early in

* Generally excluded from this chapter is discussion of *welfare regulation*—such as involves fraudulent or unsafe commerce—as opposed to the *economic regulation* of actual market conditions. Ralph Nader's introduction elaborates upon this distinction, one the reader should keep in mind so that arguments against wasteful economic regulation are not misapplied to necessary welfare regulation.

our second century. Its roots reach historically deep. During the decline of the Roman Empire, the emperor issued an edict fixing the maximum prices for eight hundred articles of trade based on their cost. The church fathers of the Middle Ages, borrowing concepts of Saint Augustine, thought that legitimate trading implied a "just price" by the producer. "In most towns of the Middle Ages," says one authority, "there were regulations to secure fair prices, to maintain wages, to lay down standards of quality, and above all, to protect individual masters from competition."[6] Later English Common Law recognized certain trades as "common callings," which would require royal charters and would, therefore, be subject to official control. Lord Chief Justice Hale, in his *De Partibus Maris,* written in about 1670, wrote that when private property is "affected with a public interest, it ceased to be *juris privati* only. . . . Property does become clothed with a public interest when used in a manner to make it of public consequence, and affect the community at large." By the time of the American Revolution, eight of the original thirteen states passed laws fixing the price of almost every commodity in the market.[7] Soon after the Constitution was ratified, however, such government control ended.

Through the first two-thirds of the nineteenth century, American industrial enterprise reflected theories of Social Darwinism. Only the strong survive, it was thought, and government interference in the marketplace was unnecessary. It was a theory that served the strong well. But local corporate abuses, often but not always involving the railroads, led to successful citizen demands for public help. The earliest case establishing the constitutionality of rate regulation was *Munn* v. *Illinois* in 1877. The Supreme Court there said that the Illinois legislature, under the state and federal constitutions, could fix the maximum charge for the storage of grain in warehouses.[8] The court concluded: "When private property is devoted to a public use, it is subject to public regulation." And because the issue involved the greatest grain market in the country, and because this market "may be a 'virtual monopoly,' " the court found that "public use" was present. Yet the opinion qualified its reasoning, adding: "It is not everything that affects commerce that amounts to a regulation of it, within the meaning of the Constitution."

The next quantum leap in the legal definition of public regulation occurred in the 1934 case of *Nebbia* v. *New York*.[9] Mr. Justice Roberts upheld a New York law fixing the minimum and maximum retail prices for milk. While private contracts are the rule, he wrote, "neither property rights nor contract rights are absolute. . . . Equally fundamental with the private right is that of the public to regulate it in the common interest." Private rights must yield to public need if the rules are "accomplished by methods consistent with due process," and so long as the law was not "unreasonable, arbitrary or capricious." Although some critics still likened regulation to "communism and socialism" during the 1930s,[10] it had by then achieved a large measure of acceptance due largely to the lesson of the Depression that laissez-faire economics did not necessarily guarantee economic plenty.

State authority to regulate was based on the police power, which *Nebbia* interpreted as nearly unlimited. Federal authority was based on the Constitution's interstate commerce clause, which gives Congress the power "to regulate commerce . . . among the several states." It proved to be a power as extensive as the state equivalent. The Supreme Court said in 1945 that the federal authority to regulate commerce "is as broad as the economic needs of the nation."

The legal authority for regulation, therefore, is today quite clear. So is its administrative structure. For the most part, the regulatory agencies are collegial bodies (so that large discretionary power is shared), composed of "experts," appointed by the president for fixed five- to seven-year terms, and theoretically insulated from his control. No more than a majority of commissioners can be from the same political party; they are removable from office by the executive only for "inefficiency, neglect of duty, or malfeasance in office."[11] The commissions, among lesser chores, approve or fix rates, decide whether there will be new competitors in a given industry, and pass on mergers. Because of judicial deference to their "expertise," courts will not overturn an agency determination unless there is a mistake of law, unless all factors that legally should have been considered were not so considered, or unless the decision was clearly arbitrary.[12]

But while the legal authority and structure of regulation have been evident for decades, its economic rationale still is not. When and why is an industry put under public regulation? The most common justification for regulation is *natural monopoly,* when efficiency requires very large economies of scale; that is, because of large, fixed capital costs, unit costs decline as the scale of production increases. In such a situation competition would devolve into a monopoly because the largest firm would have the lowest costs and could, hence, drive out its rivals. Given the impotence of the market, protection for the consumer-public must then come from government. The laying down of telephone lines and water mains provide common examples.

There are problems, however, with the concept and its application.[13] It is not entirely clear what a natural monopoly is. Interstate telephoning has long been considered one, but microwave technology and satellite communications has challenged that concept. The Postal Service, long considered a natural monopoly, is now facing successful competition for the delivery of mail. Furthermore, in its application, the grasp of natural monopoly seems to exceed its reach. Even assuming AT&T *does* have a natural monopoly in interstate telephone communications, the manufacture of telephone *equipment* is decidedly not a natural monopoly; yet AT&T subsidiary Western Electric supplies its parent with all its telephones. While there are large economies of scale in the *generation* of electric power, they do not exist in its *distribution,* although the large scale of the first is used to justify large scale in the second. And although there may have been regional railroad monopolies in the late 1880s and 1890s, "the business of truck transportation" says David Hemenway, "would probably come about as close to the model of pure competition and ideal resource allocation as is possible in the real world"; yet trucking is as regulated by the ICC as railroads.[14]

Other justifications are offered for economic regulation. *Economic failure,* as in banking, may be judged too damaging to be publicly tolerated; yet Donald Turner, former head of the Antitrust Division, argues that we would be "better off with free entry and more bank failures," which would ultimately benefit the consumer as increased competition led to higher interest rates on deposits, more convenient locations, and more high-risk loans of the type over-cautious bank officials now shun. *Limited space,* affecting airlines and the broadcast spectrums, supposedly requires a government agency to allocate the scarcity; but satellite and cable technology have effectively ended the scarcity of broadcast space, and the limited airspace for airplanes leads to the need for safety regulation, not economic regulation. *Destructive competition,* sometimes loosely used by industrialists to refer simply to stiff competition, may lead to below-cost, predatory pricing and deterioration of quality in a capital-intensive industry; while this did occur around the turn of the century, it is considered highly unlikely by commentators today, especially since the Sherman Act already proscribes destructive competition when motivated by an attempt to monopolize. Finally, regulation may be necessary to *guarantee service* to small towns; but it is not clear why, via "cross-subsidization," people who travel between Miami and New York City should subsidize those who fly from Elmira to Ithaca, New York, or why such determinations are made secretly by agency action rather than openly in congressional hearings.

All these reasons for regulation are no longer convincing, if they ever were. They are at times irrational (misallocating resources by suppressing inter-modal transportation competition, for example) and at times contradictory: they sometimes seek to avoid excessive monopoly, other times excessive competition; sometimes price is regulated but entry is not (insurance) and sometimes entry is regulated but price is not (television and radio); some agencies have "primary jurisdiction" which effectively insulates their decisions from later court challenge (CAB, ICC), while others do not (FCC, FPC). These economic justifications fail to explain why certain industries are more "clothed with a public interest" than others. Lee Loevinger, once an FCC commissioner, complains that "we are wholly lacking any theory of regulation . . . [and] also have no notion when to regulate."[15] For example, why motor carriers and not automobile production? The latter involves far more commerce and has inflicted far more external costs (pollution, traffic fatalities) than trucking. In sum, one can generalize that the government will regulate an industry if there is a strong public feeling about it, if the legislature agrees, if a court does not think the action "unreasonable, arbitrary or capricious," and (usually) if the industry doesn't mind. Horace Gray argues that industry usually doesn't mind at all:

> The public utility status was to be the haven and refuge for all aspiring monopolists who found it too difficult, too costly, or too precarious to secure and maintain monopoly by private action alone. Their future prosperity would be assured if only they could induce the government to grant them monopoly power and to protect them against interlopers. . . . Just as in the days of the Empire all roads led to Rome so in a capitalist society all forms of social control lead ultimately to state protection of the dominant interest.[16]

The government regulatory presence imposes two kinds of costs: administrative and competitive. To set the context for the chapters that follow, both will be sketched here. But *The Monopoly Makers* is only very secondarily about the administrative or organizational design of the independent regulatory agencies. A number of official studies—the Hoover Commission Report of 1949, the Landis Report of 1960, and the Ash Council of 1970—have dealt with the *structure* more than the *substance* of regulation. Although the two are of course connected, this book focuses on the substance of economic regulation that leads to the vesting of public power in private hands and, hence, to domestic cartels.

With that caveat in mind, there are a number of administrative defects that cripple effective regulatory operations:

Delay. "The Achilles' heel of the regulatory process is delay," said the Landis Report.[17] Part of the problem is attributable to the Administrative Procedure Act of 1946, which tried to make regulatory procedures more fair and open. It did this—and more. For it also slowed proceedings down agonizingly, creating scenes seemingly out of *Bleak House*. Proceedings initiated by Southern Railway to prove that its proposed rates were not below its costs for its new "Big John" boxcars took four years, covered seventeen thousand pages of testimony, and damaged the health of the ICC examiner involved. Many determinations take far longer. The average age of dockets at the CAB in 1960 was thirty-two months. The Landis Report noted: "Only last September [1959], [the FPC] announced that it would take 13 years with its present staff to clear up its 2313 producer rate cases pending as of July 1, 1960, and that with the contemplated 6500 cases that would be filed during that 13 year period it would not become current until 2043 A.D. even if its staff were tripled."[18] Such delays and work loads can only sap even the most zealous agency from effectively conducting its task.

Inflexibility. Because decisions take so long to be made, they are often not made. Old ways become new ways, and the law of inertia—bureaucratic principle Number One—sets in. Although the arguments for deregulation of railroad rates and trucking are strong, both industry and ICC fear the unknown effects of disrupting established mechanisms. This inflexibility largely explains ICC concern over the far more efficient "Big John" boxcar and FCC discomfort over cable television (CATV). "Indeed, the regulatory process may have become frozen in the last half century," argues economist Paul MacAvoy, "while the regulated industries themselves grew and developed around the commissions."[19]

Lack of Information. In mid-1970, the FPC announced that the country would suffer an oil and gas shortage that winter. How did it know? Oil and gas trade associations told it so. In December, 1971, the FCC announced it simply could not determine AT&T's rate base and asked for "voluntary" cooperation from Ma Bell. (It later re-initiated the inquiry.) The regulatory agencies often lack the kind of data needed for effective regulation.[20] The reasons are multiple: the staff, especially economic staff, is usually inadequate; industry often has the only reliable data; and the 1942 Federal Reports Act has been used by industry advisory committees, attached to each commission, to restrict the collection of needed data.* But regulating with-

---

* One instance of such activity, not particularly unlike other examples, moved a usually mild Senator Lee Metcalf to remark:

> It is now 6 years since the Department of Health, Education and Welfare prodded by the House Natural Resources and Power Subcommittee, first attempted to inventory waste discharges. That inventory was stopped, year after year, by a business advisory committee. . . .
>
> Let us tell it like it is: The purpose of industry advisory committees to Government is to enhance corporate image, to create an illusion of action and to impede Government officials who are attempting to enforce law and order and gather the data upon which enforcement is based.[21]

out necessary information is like playing tennis blindfolded against a sighted opponent.

Inexpertness. Expertise is an agency's theoretical cornerstone, equipping it to decide complex economic issues unmanageable by judges and executive officials. As the Supreme Court said in 1934, the commissions are "specifically competent to deal with them [difficult issues] by reason of information, experience and careful study of the business and economic conditions of the industry affected."[22] The original hope of their New Deal creators was that agency administrators would be as intellectually endowed as their British counterparts, rather than political appointees without adequate resources. Instead, the latter became reality. The Landis Report concluded that the agencies had suffered "a deterioration in quality both at the top level and throughout the staff." Only three of eleven recent ICC commissioners had any transportation experience prior to their official tenure, while the rest were mostly former FBI agents and politicos. At his Senate confirmation hearing upon appointment to the FCC, one nominee was asked about his qualifications in the communications field. He replied, "Senator, I don't know anything about communications. I came to Washington expecting to be appointed to the Federal Power Commission."[23] But even beyond the obvious inexpertness of present commission hierarchies, "expertness' as a quantifiable value has been oversold anyway. Questions before the agencies are not ultimately technical but broadly economic and political, turning on value judgments rather than factual analysis. The analytic expertise of Robert McNamara and McGeorge Bundy did not solve the Vietnam war; it accelerated it. And in economics, it is proverbial that one can always find an economist on each side of every issue. In the FTC's *Cement Institute* case of 1948 one clutch of experts testified that delivered pricing was a form of perfect competition, while other economists argued as passionately that it was obviously monopolistic. Or as George Bernard Shaw reputedly said, if you laid all economists in the world end to end, they still wouldn't reach a conclusion.

Politics. While theoretically independent, the agencies operate in a decidedly political context. The president, of course, appoints an agency's commissioners and the Senate confirms them; but the regulator can be refused reappointment or refused confirmation. President Truman, for example, refused to reappoint James Landis, chairman of the CAB, in 1947, and the Senate refused to confirm Leland Olds to the FPC in 1949, allegedly because both had antagonized the business interests they aimed to regulate. Because it is known that presidents very often "clear" appointments with the relevant industry, a commissioner's vigor understandably can be chilled. Also, congressional testimony and budgetary requests must first be cleared by the Office of Management and Budget, an executive office to the president, which has been described as "the Cerberus at the gate of any program."[24]

Politics can play a more direct role as well. The White House in 1945 secretly asked that the SEC not adopt proposed rules that would have abolished "floor trading" on stock exchanges, and the SEC did not; Sherman Adams aided Bernard Goldfine with his regulatory problems; presidential candidate Richard Nixon vowed in 1968 to end "heavy-handed" regulation, making specific reference to the SEC; and Nixon aide Peter Flanigan met with members of the broadcast and CATV industries to work out a modus operandi between these warring factions *after* the FCC had ironed out a compromise. Louis Kohlmeier, a longtime observer of the Washington scene for the *Wall Street Journal,* says flatly (with perhaps only slight exaggeration): "There probably is no member of Congress who has not asked something of the regulators."[25] Kohlmeier quotes one FCC aide who told him: "We now have before us a matter concerning a television station here in the East. I've been informed that one of the Senators in whose state the station is located is interested in the matter. He's a member of the Commerce Committee and that's all I need to know."

Business Pressure. The Landis Report's observation on the influence a regulated industry exerts on "its" agency has, justifiably, been widely quoted. "[I]t is the daily machine-gun like impact on both agency and its staff of industry representation on the part of agencies." The crucial fact is that this impact is one-sided, exerted by a business sector with far more resources, access, and leverage than its consumer counterparts. Such lobbying can take the form of ex parte communications between industry lobbyists and commissioners. These contacts so violated one

peals' sense of fair play and due process that it
n issue back to the CAB in *Moss* v. *CAB*[*26]
it. To an extent this pressure seems built into
en Dr. Herbert Ley resigned as FDA commissioner in 1969, he lamented to the *New York Times* that
he had been under "consistent, tremendous, sometimes
unmerciful pressure" from the drug industry. "Some days I
spent as many as six hours fending off representatives of
the drug industry."[28] His problem had its predecessor in
FCC Commissioner Newton Minow's farewell memorandum to President Kennedy in 1963: "Those who make
policy and regulate must necessarily have frequent contact
with the industry in order to be well informed. Under the
present system, the possibility of improper influence or at
least of charges of such influence is always present."[29]

Business pressure is an atmosphere as well as an arm
twist. The dinners, junkets, and seminars thrown by industry for their regulators, noted in David Hemenway's chapter
"Railroading Antitrust at the ICC," can take its subcon-
scious toll. Further contributing to the indirect shaping of
a commissioner's views is the knowledge that he will most
likely retire to the industry he now oversees. Over half the
former FCC commissioners leaving in recent years are high
executives in the communications industry; all but two of
the ICC commissioners leaving that agency in the 1960s
have either gone into the transportation industry directly or
become "ICC practitioners" lawyering for the industry.[30]
This regulatory ambience leads to what Senator Paul
Douglas called "clientism," where in a spirit of sympathetic
camaraderie the regulators come to view themselves as
promoters of their regulatees.

These defects of process slide into errors of policy.
Economist Fritz Machlup once said: "Governments, apparently, have never been able to make up their minds as
to which they dislike more, competition or monopoly."[31]
He was being unduly generous, for the answer in America
is clear: competition.

An official in the Justice Department's Antitrust Divi-

* Joint interfirm lobbying was dealt a significant setback on January 13, 1972, when the Supreme Court, qualifying the so-called
Noerr doctrine, ruled that companies that combine in a "massive,
concerted and purposeful" campaign to utilize regulatory agencies
and courts for stifling competition are violating the antitrust laws.[27]

sion, sensitive over regulatory agencies' indifference to antitrust, used historic license to explain the problem.[32] The Charles River Bridge was built in 1786 by a private company given a seventy-year charter by the State of Massachusetts; but the state legislature, eager to encourage competition for lower fares, chartered a new bridge in 1828. The first company brought suit, and in 1837 the Supreme Court upheld the second charter, saying that while private property rights should be "sacredly guarded," the public interest must prevail.[33] Imagine, said Don Baker, this case coming before a modern regulatory agency. Squadrons of attorneys, economists, businessmen, engineers, and accountants would present volumes of briefs, statistics, charts, and multiple regression analyses showing why the second bridge was bad. They would argue that there is no public need for the new service, that it would lead to overcapacity, "cream skimming" and cutthroat pricing, that economies of scale require a bigger first bridge (not a second bridge), that the safety and quality of the second bridge was in doubt, and that an integrated and balanced transportation system, looking toward future needs, requires just one bridge run by one bridge authority. QED. Against this array of (speculative) horribles would be the idea of competition. But given the weight of evidence, the constitution of the regulators, and their fear of uncharted waters, it can be doubted whether today's decision would be the same as in 1837.

Competition depends on the built-in incentives of the marketplace; regulation turns to human decisions to license a new competitor or permit a price hike. Grammar reflects the difference: to compete is active, to be regulated is passive; at its best, regulation attempts to figure out the prices and conditions that *would* prevail if competition existed. But economist Clair Wilcox makes it clear that the substitute is no match for the original:

> Regulation, at best, is a pallid substitute for competition. It cannot prescribe quality, force efficiency, or require innovation, because such action would invade the sphere of management. But when it leaves these matters to the discretion of industry, it denies consumers the protection that competition would afford. Regulation cannot set prices below an industry's costs however excessive they may be. Competition does so, and the high-cost company is compelled to discover means whereby its costs can be reduced.

Regulation does not enlarge consumption by setting prices at the lowest level consistent with a fair return. Competition has this effect. Regulation fails to encourage performance in the public interest by offering rewards and penalties. Competition offers both.

Regulation is static, backward-looking, preoccupied with the problems of the past. It does nothing to stimulate change, seeking to maintain order on the basis of the old technology. It is slow to adapt to change; new problems appear, but regulatory thinking lags. Competition, by contrast, is dynamic.[34]

Some brave antitrust officials claim that the two systems are not really incompatible but complementary, for both work together to maximize the efficient use of resources. But in fact the two seek this mutual goal by quite different routes, and, as two objects cannot occupy the same place at the same time, the existence of one can preclude the other.

This does not mean, however, that once part of an industry is regulated, all of it must be. The bank agencies cannot permit the fixing of rates charged by banks for credit services nor can the CAB allow the Air Transport Association to instruct its member airlines to refuse to buy a newly manufactured plane. The current problem is how to define the borderline between competition and regulation. In the past, governing statutes made an attempt. The 1938 act creating the CAB ordered that agency to "consider the following among other things as being in the public interest . . . Competition to the extent necessary to assure the sound development of an air-transportation system."[35] The Reed-Bulwinkle Act of 1948, giving the ICC power to approve rate agreements between carriers, still required that the commission provide "to each party the free and unrestrained right to take independent action either before or after any determination arrived at through such procedure."[36]

In addition, some recent judicial decisions have stressed that the regulators must consider and respect economic competition. The 1963 Supreme Court decision in *United States* v. *Philadelphia National Bank* held that the antitrust laws applied to banks, the existence of the banking agencies notwithstanding.[37] In *Silver* v. *New York Stock Exchange,* decided the same year, the court said that "repeal [of the antitrust laws] is to be regarded as implied only if necessary to make the Securities Exchange Act work, and even then only to the minimum extent necessary."[38] Two 1968 cases continued this trend. In *Federal Maritime Commission* v. *Svenska Amerika Linien,* the Supreme Court permitted the FMC to disapprove of two anticompetitive shipping conference agreements under the "contrary to the public interest" standard in the 1916 Shipping Act.[39] And in the most lucid language to date, the District of Columbia Circuit Court of Appeals emphasized in the *Northern Natural Gas* case that "antitrust concepts are intimately involved in a determination of what action is in the public interest, and therefore the [Federal Power] Commission is obliged to weigh antitrust policy."[40] Because the FPC did not in this case, the issue was remanded to it for further consideration.

The usual agency standard of "public convenience and necessity," however, remains immensely broad. It permits great latitude on how much weight to give principles of competition. The Antitrust Division now increasingly intervenes in agency proceedings to advocate antitrust considerations, but, with certain exceptions (banking, communications), the final policy decision rests with neither the division nor the courts. The doctrine of "primary jurisdiction," deferring to the mystique of agency expertness, leaves such decisions up to the regulatory agencies themselves. Victories for antitrust do not result.

Rate Regulation. Professor F. M. Scherer at the University of Michigan eloquently protested: "The Supreme Power who conceived gravity, supply and demand, and double helix must have been absorbed elsewhere when public utility regulation was invented. The system is cumbersome, vulnerable to incompetence, and prone toward becoming ingrown and co-opted."[41] This pessimism applies both to rate *setting* in "natural monopolies," such as by state public utility commisions and the FCC's common carrier bureau, and to more general rate *regulation* in "natural oligopolies," as over airlines and maritime shipping. Rate setting involves the valuation of a company's assets ("rate base"), which is then multiplied by a "fair rate of return"—composed of interest payments to bondholders and the estimated cost of attracting equity capital —to arrive at the firm's permissible profits. This rate of return must not be so high as to exploit consumers nor so

low as to discourage investors. But as Felix Frankfurter
and Henry Hart pointed out in 1934, a fair and rational
determination of the rate base is nearly impossible to
make.[42] Commissions often lack the requisite data and staff
and therefore must depend for information on industry,
which can inflate asset worth by a variety of accounting
methods. Because it is in their interest to inflate assets to
yield higher returns, regulated firms may engage in a variety
of uneconomical activities or may pad their expenses with
emoluments for themselves. Firms can also emasculate any
profit ceilings by reducing the quality of service. Even if
the agency catches up to this cost cutting, there is always
some lag time during which the extra profits can be
earned.[43] One highly respected study, comparing the
differences in average electricity rates in regulated and
unregulated states betwen 1907 and 1937, concluded that
rate regulation had no measurable effect on utility rates,
discriminatory pricing, or the value of utility stocks.[44]
Other studies corroborate that "regulation has not significantly decreased the power of natural monopolies to practice extensive price discrimination."[45]

Agencies such as the ICC, CAB, and FMC depend on
industry collaboration in so-called rate conferences or
private cartels to set the prices firms can charge. Fears of
rate instability lead the agencies to approve docilely those
rates presented them. When an 1897 Supreme Court decision declared such railroad rate conferences illegal, the
ICC permitted them to continue;[46] they were again declared illegal by the court in 1945.[47] A 1948 law, passed
over President Truman's veto, finally gave them Congress's
legal blessings. Today an unmanageable 270,000 tariffs are
filed each year with the ICC (and 43 *trillion* rates are on
file there) and less than 3 percent of all proposed rate
changes by regulated common carriers are generally investigated by the commission. When truckers did try to
lower their prices, the ICC *discouraged* them, being suspi-
cious of any price cutting as a prelude to price wars.

Nor did the CAB have to acquiesce with the International Air Transport Association (IATA) when that world
cartel fixed prices in 1946. The agency lamely explained
that it felt pressured because of control by foreign governments over the right of American planes to land abroad.
But we had already secured, through bilateral agreements,

landing rights in most of the world. K. G. J. Pillai argues in his chapter on the CAB that domestic and international airline rates are 50 percent too high because of collusion by the airline trade associations (ATA domestically and IATA internationally). For example, while the 340 mile, unregulated (intrastate) Los Angeles–San Francisco plane trip costs $16.20, a trip of equivalent distance between Chicago and Minneapolis costs $33 and the New York City–Washington shuttle (230 miles) costs $26. The consumer overcharge is direct and costly. After carefully studying the effects of ICC and CAB rate regulation, William Jordan concluded the agencies served producers, not consumers:

> The available evidence regarding the effects of regulation on price levels for formerly oligopolistic industries is consistent and unambiguous. Regulatory actions and procedures have allowed the carriers in each industry to reach agreements regarding prices and to enforce adherence to these agreements. . . . Without regulation, *prices [for interstate airlines, freight motor carriers, and railroads] would be from 9 to 50 percent lower than they are with regulation with many reductions in the long-run exceeding 30 percent.**[48]

Entry. Most of the regulatory agencies restrict entry of new competitors into their regulated industries. An entrant must obtain a certificate of public convenience and necessity by showing that he is qualified to perform the service in question and that there is a public need for another firm. Instead of permitting competitive forces to determine whether a new venture can be profitable or not, the burden is shifted to the potential firm to prove its worth. It is both

---

* It must be stressed that high rates do not necessarily mean high profits. The "quiet life" of monopoly can lead to waste and inefficiency, dissipating the returns of monopoly-set prices. Recently, railroads and defense contractors exhibit this tendency. In addition, industries accorded cartel power by their regulators may inadvertently price themselves out of their markets, losing more in revenues than they recoup in high prices; the airlines seem victim to this syndrome. Their shortsightedness is not without precedent. Detroit watched for fifteen years while small, cheap imports climbed to 16 percent of all cars sold in this country before massively marketing their own versions; steel manufacturers insisted on continually raising prices even as demand was falling; it was only when southeastern electric power companies faced the competition of TVA that they realized that low rates could so increase volume as to increase profits.

expensive and difficult to assume this burden of proof, and competition is thereby discouraged. All is oriented toward stability of the existing lines, whose value is enhanced by this imposition of artificial scarcity.

The CAB has not certified a new trunk carrier since its creation in 1938. Yet within the confines of California, where CAB jurisdiction does not extend, sixteen intrastate carriers entered the market between 1946 and 1965. The ICC not only restricts new entrants into the potentially competitive trucking industry, but it also lays down a network of other controls: e.g., backhauls are limited, only certain commodities can be carried, specific routes must be taken. A trucking firm operating between Philadelphia and Montreal was required to travel through Reading, Pennsylvania. The company petitioned the ICC to take an alternate route that would reduce the distance by sixty-two miles. The ICC said no, prompting one of its commissioners to protest that "[i]nstead of preventing a monopoly, it helps to establish one, and once created, it becomes a case for the perpetuation of the monopoly."[49] Finally, the Food and Drug Administration thwarts competition in drugs by bureaucratic legerdemain of "New Drug Applications." The safety and efficacy of newly marketed drugs must be shown through extensive clinical studies—often costing $50,000 to $100,000—*for each successive applicant although the drug is already on the market*. This rule bars smaller competitors and entrenches the dominance of existing drugs.

Mergers. While new entrants must make an affirmative showing to earn their existence, mergers by statute are usually only limited by the requirement that the transition be "consistent with the public interest." (The CAB, as already noted, is something of a statutory exception.) Competition usually does not survive the kind of ad hoc arguments that can be used to justify nearly any merger: that there will be labor savings, that the managements complement each other, that there is overcapacity anyway, and so on. Thus, the FPC approved of the 1957 acquisition by El Paso Natural Gas of the Pacific Northwest Gas Company; but the Supreme Court has now said three times that the merger violated the antitrust laws and that the FPC should never have approved it. A consequence of the Penn-Central merger—the proponents convincing the ICC that there existed various economies and efficiencies in this corporate wedding—has been the biggest bankruptcy in American history; the commission approved 29 of 34 principal railroad mergers it considered between 1957 and 1967.

Technology. It is difficult to provide evidence of what innovations would have occurred without regulation; yet it is clear that technological lethargy logically inheres in the very structure of regulation.* For one specific example—AT&T sits on Comsat's board of directors and has an interest in its earth stations. More generally, a firm with a steady rate base and rate of return will not be overly eager to introduce innovations. In fact, because a firm's return depends on the extent of its capital investment, it is encouraged to retain older equipment long after obsolete in order to inflate the rate base,[50] as Beverly C. Moore subsequently notes. Not only the regulatees, but also the regulators are wary of technological change toppling carefully coordinated patterns. A report by the Brookings Institution notes: "No matter how beneficial an innovation, it has little chance of timely adoption in a regulated industry if it will lead to a substantial redistribution of wealth among the regulated that cannot be compensated through some clever regulatory device."[51] "Timely adoption" seems to be the operative phrase, for agencies have approved some innovations—but only after years of delay and pressure—such as widespread pipeline transportation, containerships, "piggyback" operations in rail transport, "foreign attachments to Bell telephones," and (shortly one hopes) cable TV.[52]

Efficiency. Competition compels cost cutting and the search for efficiencies; regulation does not. As noted, the opposite is true: because the bigger the rate base the bigger the return, public utilities are tempted to inflate the value of their rate base. This ploy leads to overcapitalization, a reluctance to lease from others, resistance to capital-saving technology, and bargaining over wholesale rates. The regulated industries know that their regulators are their pro-

---

* There is a long-standing dispute on whether large size is a prerequisite to innovation or a suppressant. Galbraith's *The New Industrial State* is premised on the former view; for the latter, see John Blair's *Economic Concentration* (chapters 5, 6, 9, and 10) as well as our earlier volume *The Closed Enterprise System* (chapter 1).

tectors as well, protectors who will not permit competing modes or new competitors to unsettle the system's homeostasis. This dissipation of competitive pressures quite naturally leads to managerial sloth and productive inefficiency, because the market penalty—loss of revenues—is absent. The Penn-Central debacle is but one, albeit the biggest, example.

All of these regulatory policies—on rates, entry, mergers, technology, and efficiency—exact a huge economic and social toll. Below is a partial list and the best guesstimate of the economic losses inflicted by this cartel management:*

Sector	Annual Economic Waste from Regulation
Transportation	
ICC Increased costs and shifting of traffic from low-cost to high-cost modes, involving railroads, trucks, water carriers	$4.02–$8.7 billion[54]
CAB and trade association price-fixing	$2–$4 billion[55]
Economic misallocation due to maritime regulation	$2–$3.5 billion[56]
Communications	
FCC "Additional value to consumers" if FCC reallocated TV channels so as to permit seven national networks instead of three	$8 billion[57]
Total:	$16.02–$24.2 billion

* Some of the most momentous economic losses inflicted by government activity are not included here. They involved both pure economic waste, and the transfer of income from one group to another —really from consumers to producers. Accurate data on the extent of Pentagon cost overruns due to negotiated rather than competitive bidding are not made available by either the Department of Defense or the aerospace industry. Nor is there reliable information on the precise competitive costs incurred by federal drug procurement programs or the SEC-tolerated minimum brokerage fees of $300,000. One cost of FCC restrictions—loss of viewing diversity and, hence, a discouragement of First Amendment speech—is not quantifiable. A recent study by C. Fred Bergsten put the total consumer cost of tariff and quota restrictions at between $10 billion and $15 billion annually. Finally, a 1972 report by Senator William Proxmire's Joint Economic Committee estimated that subsidies—cash, tax, and credit—cost the government a minimum of $63 billion in 1970.[53]

Uncle Sam need not inevitably be a monopoly man. The diseconomies of large size and gains from economic competition, once widely understood, could be profitably applied to rearrange the patterns of government involvement in industrial enterprise. Changes from the present way of doing things could range from the short-range and *procedural* to the long-range and *structural*.

First, the procedural. It should not require statutory and economic upheavals for federal procurement to become administratively more centralized (to exploit the efficiencies of centralized procurement) *and* more competitive (rewarding the able rather than the huge). There should be a prejudice for new and small competitors rather than for the aerospace giants, because competition ultimately saves the government and taxpayer money; negotiated single-source procurement does not. Nor is it writ on the mount that agency officials must be second-rate. Presidents should view regulatory officials as important guardians of our industrial welfare, and stop treating these positions as repositories for defeated politicians. It should not prove difficult to find able commissioners. In addition, there should be at least one economist as a commissioner in every agency; lawyers and politicians have abilities, to be sure, but not a monopoly on wise economic regulation. Better people will not automatically create better, or less, regulation, for much of the problem involves the structure of regulation itself. But at the same time, the fault is not entirely in the stars. The comptroller does not have to be so lenient toward bank mergers; the CAB need not be so tolerant of IATA; and the ICC is not compelled to be hostile to rate cutting. Some regulatory procedures revised in 1972—new CAB rules encouraging charter flights and FCC permission for domestic companies to launch communications satellites to compete with AT&T—underscore the fact that regulation need not be anti-competitive. Given the wide ambit of discretion provided by the regulatory statutes, better personnel can provide an important, though perhaps not a sufficient, improvement.

Again procedurally, there are roles to be played by courts, citizens, and the Justice Department to make economic regulation less monopolistic. Judicial authority is often concurrent with agency jurisdiction. It should not defer to a nonexistent expertise without even knowing the basis of the decision. Until such time as the regulatory commissions reveal a sensitivity to the antitrust laws, appeals courts should closely and independently review agency decisions, rather than rubber-stamping all under the calendar-clearing invocation of "primary jurisdiction." Courts could also go beyond the rationale of the *Northern Natural Gas* line of cases and declare that because antitrust is our dominant economic philosophy, the burden is on the agencies to show why they have departed from it when their statutes do not require it. (New legislation—which created just this burden regarding pollution in the National Environmental Policy Act of 1969—could achieve this same result.) Citizen suits—aided by more liberal "standing" rules and more access to agency data under the Freedom of Information Act—could provide the stimulus for such judicial creativity. Even the agencies themselves could be the stimulants if proposals for in-house "public interest" legal counsel, as has been suggested at the FCC, succeed.

Agency interventions by the Justice Department's Antitrust Division must also increase. Although treated as meddling interlopers, division attorneys force commissioners to consider the antitrust implications of their actions. Antitrust Division chiefs Robert Bicks in the late 1950s and Donald Turner in the 1960s each encouraged such participation, but budgetary constraints have limited this role. The budget of the Antitrust Division should therefore increase to permit the addition of new personnel to join those twenty-five division lawyers whose major job now is to oversee the agencies. Finally, congressional supervision must be more frequent and substantive than some questioning at closed-door budget hearings or than the occasional convening of hearings after a scandal.

Finally, the lines of agency authority should be seriously redesigned. The number of agencies, the scores of commissioners, the complexity of the subject matter have all combined to shield economic regulation from political and public scrutiny; for example, press coverage of the regulatory process is embarrassingly sparse. Different agencies promote different policies; general and consistent principles are not apparent. One cabinet-level presidential appointee should be responsible for the behavior and performance of all the regulatory agencies. In effect, the heads of the ICC, CAB, FCC, FMC, SEC, FPC, and banking authorities would be *his* cabinet, responsible to him. Such an arrangement would enable the public, the press, the Congress, and the president to focus attention on economic regulation. This regulation chairman would be publicly identifiable (try to name the eleven ICC commissioners) and hence accountable for the success or failure of central management, being lavished with kudos or criticism as is appropriate. His or her broad authority should make this person both less susceptible to the kind of specific industry pressure exerted on specific agencies and more of a focused target for consumer pressures—of the kind now largely absent from this process. An industry-inclined regulation chairman could hardly do worse than the present agencies have done. A strong-minded and independent one, however, could compel the regulatory authorities to pay heed to their raison d'être: protection of consumers, not producers. It would be a reorientation long overdue.

Beyond these changes of emphasis and personnel, more structural rearrangements are possible. New legislation could clarify the proper role and authority for many of the agencies, which now find themselves in the contradictory role of both regulating their industries and promoting them. The 1887 act creating the ICC emphasized regulation; the National Transportation Act of 1920 emphasized promotion. The 1938 CAB act does both. Even if public-spirited commissioners were appointed to the ICC or CAB, one could well understand their institutional schizophrenia.

A more pervasive antidote to excessive regulation is deregulation, one long discussed but never tried. Where there would be a viably competitive market but for economic regulation, that industry should be freed from regulatory restraint. By this standard, trucking, air and water transport, and radio, television, and some inter-city communications (perhaps with some maximum rate ceilings) could return to the open market. Whether natural gas field prices should be deregulated, which would undoubtedly result in higher consumer prices, is under intense present debate.[58] In addition, railroads, transoceanic shippers and airlines should no longer be able to price-fix with or without agency approval. Then they could compete on price and not so much on the color of their planes or their advertising jingles; then airlines and railroads might not price themselves out of their markets; and then we might begin to recoup some of that $16-$23 billion annual economic waste attributable to economic regulation.

But whatever the economic merits—and there are many —deregulation would be politically difficult to achieve. Industry and agency have often built up quite a benign interdependence, and more competition can only destabilize. President Kennedy's 1962 transportation message did call for the abandonment of minimum rate regulation in the shipment of bulk commodities on trucks, trains, and barges. The plan, however, was buried in Congress, opposed by the truckers and the barge operators *and* the ICC. In the 92nd Congress, a deregulation proposal entitled the "Regulatory Modernization Act of 1971" (S. 2842) was submitted by the Department of Transportation to Congress. The measure had been cleared by, but not endorsed by, the White House. The bill would give carrier management more freedom to price their services, discourage collective rate making, permit the abandonment of unprofitable operations, and allow greater freedom of entry. It never got reported out of its House Committee, being opposed by industry (railroads, truckers, and barges) as promoting "destructive" competition that would weaken the carriers financially. But the effort need not inevitably fail. History provides at least one clear example—the Public Utilities Holding Company Act of 1935—when an industry was restructured despite the protests of the firms and businessmen involved.

Deregulation, if it is to occur, has a number of necessary predicates. First, antitrust policy and competition must be vigorous to contain the kind of monopolistic abuses that bedeviled shippers in the late 1880s. While many railroads did have local or regional monopolies at that time, today there could be far more intermodal competition. Our earlier book, however, *The Closed Enterprise System,* argued that competition rarely exists in heavy industry. Not that it *could* not prevail, but that it *does* not. Any move toward deregulation, therefore, must be preceded by a serious commitment of resources and resolve by future administrations to make antitrust enforcement a reality. Second, the introduction of competition will transfer traffic to more efficient modes, causing shutdowns of inefficient facilities. A complementary program can make employees adversely affected eligible for relocation and re-training assistance. Third, there should be comparable insurance for customers damaged as a result of any re-structuring. Free entry into banking would probably in-crease bank failures, an event that traumatized earlier eras. To mitigate the harm from such occurrences, quite simply, federal insurance programs could underwrite any losses.

Another possible policy alternative, mentioned in both Larry Ellsworth's and Beverly Moore's chapters, is na-tionalization. Of course it is a historical hobgoblin in America, as politically taboo and radical, no doubt, as wage and price controls (were). The President's Task Force on Communications Policy, for example, omitted any discussion of public ownership (although we *already* theoretically "own" the airwaves) because, according to one realistic staff member, "Congress would not hear of it."[59] But it must be noted that, except for Germany, Spain, and the United States, all major countries publicly own, in some form or other, their public utilities. And besides Marxist economists, Henry Simons, the eminent conservative Chicago economist, once suggested the public takeover of certain public utilities because there existed the worst of two worlds: a monopoly that is privately owned yet effectively unregulated.[60] The collapse of domestic railroad passenger service, Penn-Central's troubles, and the creation of Amtrak (part public, part private), all make nationalization a very possible alterna-tive for that declining industry. "It's conceivable that we will propose some kind of nationalization," said Under-secretary of Transportation James Beggs, and ICC Chair-man George Stafford agrees.[61] Another candidate is the aerospace industry, where many firms are already depen-dent for their existence on government largess. If Lock-heed's losses can be socialized, one may well wonder why its profits must be untouchable. The FCC's vacillation on AT&T's rate base in 1972—first throwing in the towel and then, under public pressure, reluctantly reentering the ring—raises serious doubt about the capacity of public utility regulation. The public will not, and should not, tolerate an unregulated monopoly. Government ownership of AT&T would little change the complexities that so befuddled the FCC, but at least it could encourage more cooperation in the determination of what a fair and reasonable rate of return is and what AT&T's rate base is really made of.

There are many problems with public ownership. Not only does it not cure the difficulties of monopoly and bureaucracy, it can increase them; there are inadequate incentives for efficient operations and innovation; measures for economic performance are lacking; there is the danger of political interference; and the government monopolist can be successfully intolerant of *any* new competition. Perhaps the biggest problem is that we simply do not know enough about it. Few economists—William Shepherd and John Blair being two exceptions—have systematically studied the performance of public enterprise. Until such time, nationalization must remain a possibility in certain areas, but a far from problem-free possibility. It does however, pose the recurring conflict of our economy: controls or competition. Wendell Berge, former head of the Antitrust Division, said in 1949: "If we do not move toward vigorous termination of monopoly power over American industry, it seems to me inevitable that we shall find ourselves in less than another generation with some form of government controlled and socialized economy."[62] Berge's prediction has not yet materialized, but if the activities of federal monopoly makers continues unchecked, his forecast of socialism—albeit in the form of corporate socialism —may have been wrong only by a generation.

The verdict on the failure of economic regulation, discounting those who benefit from it, is nearly uniform. President Johnson's Antitrust Task Force reported in 1968: "In the regulated sector of the economy, the bias and its enforcement is overwhelmingly against competition. This bias manifests itself in more permissive policies toward mergers and exemption of mergers from antitrust standards. . . . We believe this bias is contrary to the public interest."[63] The Nixon Antitrust Group, headed by George Stigler, criticized regulatory restrictions on entrants and rates. It suggested: "The commissions should have the merits of competition pressed upon them. Competition is not a matter of all or none, and the fact of regulation should not exclude competition as a force at each of a hundred points where it is relevant and feasible."[64] The

Council of Economic Advisors 1970 report to the president comes to a similar conclusion:

> Regulated industries have been more progressive when the agencies have endeavored to confine regulation to a necessary minimum and have otherwise fostered competition. When regulation has stifled competition, performance has deteriorated. The clearest lesson of all, however, is that regulation should be narrowed or halted when it has outlived its original purpose.

Finally, law professor Ronald Coase summarized a Brookings Institution symposium on this subject with clarity: "What the regulatory commissions are trying to do is difficult to discover; what effect these commissions actually have is, to a large extent unknown; when it can be discovered, it is often absurd."[65]

In ten instances of government interplay with the market, the chapters in this book scrutinize what government is trying to do and what its effect is. True, the effect is often "absurd," but such an abstract conclusion fails to convey the extent and personalization of the harm. Excessive air rates mean that many middle-income consumers are overcharged while many poor citizens never get the opportunity to travel by air. Excessive truck and railroad rates for shippers are ultimately passed on to consumers in the form of higher prices for the finished product. Telephones cost more and telephone calls cost more because public telephone utilities inadequately monitor rates and rate bases. The complexity of the subject matter should not obscure the intimate consumer harm due to the public policy of favoring monopoly over competition. Nor should we ignore the problem because it has been so long with us. In fact, its longevity should encourage reappraisal rather than resignation. The problem of familiarity breeding acceptance may be one of the most serious roadblocks to reform in this complex terrain. What Alexander Pope observed about vice is as true for monopoly:

> Vice is a monster of so frightful mien,
> As, to be hated, needs but to be seen;
> Yet seen too oft, familiar with her face,
> We first endure, then pity, then embrace.

COMMUNICATIONS

2

The FCC: Competition and Communications

BEVERLY C. MOORE, JR.

> *The American people should be made aware of the trend toward the monopolization of the great public information vehicles and the concentration of more and more power over public opinion in fewer and fewer hands.*
>
> —*Vice-President Spiro T. Agnew*[1]

> Television Correspondent: *Do you envisage using antitrust laws as a weapon against the communications medium monopolies or near-monopolies which concern the Vice-President of late?*
>
> Former Attorney General John N. Mitchell: *No, that's the last thing in the world that we have under consideration.*[2]

The average household spent $417 in 1969 for "mass communications"—television, radio, newspapers, magazines, books, recordings, and theaters—plus $314 on postal and telephone services.[3] The significance of these purchases far surpasses the approximately 8 percent of consumer spending that they represent. For what these information machines tell us significantly shapes what we learn, value, and desire as individuals, as well as the growth and direction of our culture. The role of the mass media must be scrutinized, as the First Amendment implies, from the premise "that the widest possible dissemination of information *from diverse and antagonistic sources* is essential to the welfare of the public [emphasis supplied]."[4] Perhaps the single most important responsibility of antitrust enforcement is to structure the media to ensure the presence of many competing voices in the marketplace of ideas.

The availability of this diverse information is dependent upon technology, and we are on the threshold of a revolution in communications technology. Cablevision, microwave, satellites, lasers, video cassettes, and a burgeoning computer technology can offer the average citizen instant and low-cost access to vast amounts of information and entertainment. The promise of these new technologies will be realized only as fast as the Federal Communications Commission, which regulates broadcasting and cable television, and the Justice Department, which regulates the antitrust laws, dissipate the media monopolies.

Concentration and Ownership

The average citizen receives most of his information about the outside world from television and newspapers. But, as one commentator observes, "most local daily newspapers and television stations serve as little more than conduits of news, information, and entertainment prepared and produced in a few distant centers and utilized by local newspapers and television studios to fill in the blank spaces between advertising."[5] Of the 683 commercial television stations, 542 receive the bulk of their programs from one of three national networks. Over 70 percent of all daily newspapers are affiliated with only one of the two dominant wire services—AP (43.4 percent) or UPI (28 percent).[6]

Even if these information *sources* could be diversified, the number of local *outlets* would remain severely limited. The average citizen can view only three or four VHF television stations (channels 2–13). In 1880, 61 percent of urban places had more than one independently owned newspaper. By 1969 this was true of only thirty-nine cities.[7] Paris at the time of the Dreyfus Affair had twenty-five to thirty-five dailies.[8] Now New York and Chicago are the only cities in the United States with more than two. Monopoly newspapers tend to rely more heavily upon the cheapest news sources, particularly the wire services. A 1966 study of one monopoly newspaper found that when faced with new competition, it increased staff-written news by 24 percent.[9]

This small number of media outlets serving a given locality is made even smaller when the same company owns more than one of the media. Daily newspapers own at least one competing VHF television station in thirty of the fifty largest markets, the population centers containing 75 percent of the national television audience[10] Newspapers own 25 percent of all television stations, with 34 percent of the total audience,[11] and a majority of the stations affiliated with CBS and NBC, the largest networks.[12] When cable television and radio are included, seven out of every ten broadcast stations within the top fifty markets are commonly owned by another "voice" in the same market.[13] Such extensive interlocking control demeans the goal of diversity that is the touchstone of both the First Amendment and the antitrust laws.

Chain ownership of media further reduces the number of nationally or regionally available information outlets. In 1967, 871 of 1,767 daily newspapers were chain owned, including 19 of the 25 largest circulation papers; chains owned 73.6 percent of all television stations, and 81.3 percent of all VHF television stations were licensed either to chain broadcasters or newspaper publishers.[14] Twelve corporations own over one-third of all the VHF stations serving 75 percent of the nation's viewers.[15] And chain ownership of all media is rapidly accelerating. That degree of national or regional concentration would not be alarming in a manufacturing industry, where it is unusual to have as many as a dozen strong competitors producing a single, undifferentiated product. But where the mass media are concerned, there can only be a sufficient number of independent sources of information when existing outlets exhaust all shades of opinion and cover all subjects—which is far from the present situation.

Many media baronies are regionally oriented. In the West, the Mormon Church owns four television stations, twelve radio stations, numerous cable TV systems, the Salt

Lake City *Deseret News,* and 5 percent of the *Los Angeles Times.*[16] Typical of the nationally operating media combines is the E. W. Scripps Company. Its holdings include four television stations, three radio stations, *The World Almanac,* seventeen daily newspapers, United Press International, United Feature Syndicate, and the Newspaper Enterprise Association (two leading syndicators of newspaper columns and comics).[17] Time, Inc., in addition to the largest weekly news magazine, owns *Fortune, Sports Illustrated,* five VHF television stations in top markets, eight radio stations, MGM movies, thirteen cable television systems,[18] and has recently been acquiring newspapers. The NBC radio and television networks are owned by RCA, a major manufacturer of television sets. Like CBS, RCA is an important defense contractor with extensive foreign investments and owns, among other things, book publishers, record companies, and the maximum quota, as set by the FCC, of five VHF, two UHF, seven AM, and seven FM stations, all located in major cities. Using their hefty profits to finance acquisitions, such media moguls as RCA and CBS are intent upon consolidating and dominating a "knowledge industry," described by FCC Commissioner Nicholas Johnson as

> . . . corporate casserole dishes blending radio and television stations, networks, and programming; films, movie houses, and record companies; newspaper, magazine, and book publishing; advertising agencies; sports or other entertainment companies; and teaching machines and other profitable appurtenances of the $50 billion "education biz."[19]

One study observed the following economic consequences of media concentration: monopoly newspaper advertising rates are 15 percent higher than competitive rates; newspaper-television cross-ownership in the same market results in 10 percent higher newspaper rates on national advertising (the TV stations' rates are 15 percent higher); chain newspapers charge 7 percent more for national advertising than nonchain papers of comparable circulation.[20] The overcharges are, of course, passed on to consumers of the advertised products. Rate discrimination, by which newspapers and broadcast stations favor the larger advertisers, is almost universal.

Press critic Ben H. Bagdikian also warns against the media's outside corporate interests, which, in the case of the television networks, produces three times as much revenue as their broadcasting operations. Would financial interests in defense contracting, the New York Yankees (formerly), or auto-industry credit affiliates lead CBS to promote defense spending, "their" team, or car sales?[21] Or, more subtly, would the ownership of non-media enterprises foster a general pro-business orientation?

The media owners insist that their own views do not influence the news stories of editors, reporters, and commentators (whom they select). Because these professional journalists remain "independent," the argument goes, media concentration does not affect or diminish the diversity of media content.[22] Yet one study discovered that newspaper reporters clothed with normal journalistic autonomy learn and are guided by their publishers' policy preferences by "osmosis."[23] Another study revealed that publishers' attitudes affected reporters' treatment of Medicare news more than twelve other variables combined.[24] And in a 1960 experiment at the University of California, advanced journalism students were asked to write editorials about presidential candidate Richard Nixon's policy of opposing the admission of Communist China to the United Nations for a newspaper known to agree with Nixon. Not only did the students as a group write editorials tending to oppose admission of China, but those students who personally favored admission wrote the most one-sided editorials opposing it.[25]

One wonders why, if journalistic freedom is so unfettered, the media so rarely cover the issue of media concentration or criticize each other's coverage of news and events, or devote so few resources to investigative reporting. For example, viewers of station KRON-TV in San Francisco received no information concerning the 1965 price fixing and joint operating agreement of the local Chronicle and Hearst newspapers, although the story was widely covered by other local media. The reason: KRON-TV is owned by the Chronicle Publishing Company.[26] Why (with notable exceptions) are some of the most difficult to convey but fundamental economic issues of the day largely neglected—the distribution of wealth, the oligopolistic nature of the economy, the role of advertising in relation to consumer sovereignty, or the myriad government subsidies and favors to special interest groups?

Since 1968 the Antitrust Division of the Department of Justice has twice urged the FCC to reduce media concentration under the "public interest" standard of the Communications Act that the commission must apply in granting, renewing, or approving the transfer of any broadcast license. This "public interest" standard includes the interest in economic competition embodied in the antitrust laws as well as a broader "marketplace of ideas" concept fostered by media diversity.* In one case, a Beaumont, Texas, newspaper dropped its TV acquisition plans after the FCC announced that it would hold a hearing. In another, the Frontier Broadcasting Company was forced to divest after the Antitrust Division opposed the renewal of its license to the only television station in Cheyenne, Wyoming, because Frontier also owned Cheyenne's only two daily newspapers, its only cablevision system, and two of its six radio stations.

These sporadic achievements, however, are no substitute for the restructuring of the communications industry that Justice Department antitrust suits could attain. When asked why the Antitrust Division had not launched a vigorous media deconcentration program, its staff attorneys replied "no resources," "don't know," or "that's the FCC's job." Some suggested that the media are powerful in every congressional district. They remember the "Newspaper Preservation Act," a classic case of legislation prompted by special-interest lobbying, which allows newspapers in

---

* An FCC regulation that violates the antitrust laws will be upheld only on the rare occasion that the commission can make a specific "expert" finding that the broader public interest served by the regulation outweighs the benefits of competition. The Supreme Court has said that "although not charged with the duty of enforcing . . . [the antitrust laws, the FCC] should administer its regulatory powers with respect to broadcasting in the light of the purposes which the Sherman Act was designed to achieve."[27] Unlike most other regulatory agencies, the FCC does not have "primary jurisdiction" over media antitrust matters, meaning that the commission's approval of an anticompetitive act or combination does not immunize it from being attacked by the Justice Department under the antitrust laws, either on appeal from an FCC ruling or by independent lawsuit. However, the latter possibility has remained academic. The Antitrust Division has never independently challenged a newspaper's acquisition or renewal of a competing broadcast license.

twenty-three cities to fix prices.[28] Anticipatory politics, however, is not a valid criterion to be weighed by agencies duty bound to enforce existing laws.

The FCC finally began to deal with cross-media ownership on March 25, 1970, when by a vote of four Democrats to three Republicans it ruled that a single company's ownership of a VHF television station *and* an AM or FM radio station in the same market would no longer be permitted. But a grandfather clause exempted all existing combinations. The Justice Department, among the 4 out of 120 parties who submitted comments *favoring* this "one-to-a-market" proposal, urged divestiture not only of existing broadcast combinations but also of newspaper-broadcast combinations. The commission (which now has a Republican majority) will air these proposals in "further proceedings." Meanwhile, the American Newspaper Publishers Association, the same group responsible for passage of the "Newspaper Preservation Act," has launched a vigorous campaign against an important proposal now before the FCC that would force newspapers to sell their competing broadcast properties—some 476 radio and TV stations—within five years. "Wherever we have to fight the battle, we will fight it," says ANPA general manager Stanford Smith, noting that the publishers would again descend upon Congress if necessary.[29] The aroused publishers will probably have plenty of time to work their will, for the FCC is not inclined toward hasty decisions. It required fifteen years for the commission to permit a form of pay television, and it was laden with crippling restrictions. And as long as current cross-media rule-making proceedings continue, newspaper applications for renewals or acquisitions of competing broadcast licenses will be routinely granted.

Although the FCC's one-to-a-market proceedings have at least produced minimal results, the commission has not restricted other forms of media concentration. In 1964 it decided to consider a rule that would prohibit any corporation from acquiring more than two VHF television stations in the top fifty markets. During the pendency of the proceedings and "absent compelling circumstances," a hearing would be required for approval of any license acquisition request resulting in the applicant's exceeding the proposed maximum. But the hearing requirement was waived in all ten cases that arose before the commission decided in 1968 *not* to adopt the "top-fifty-market" rule.

The same pattern emerges with respect to the FCC's treatment of the "conglomerate problem." As mentioned, many of the larger media combines also have extensive nonmedia holdings, creating the possibility of various economic abuses. Suppose, for example, that a corporation owns a television station, a department store, and an apparel manufacturing company. The department store might place its advertisements on the parent's TV station when it would otherwise have chosen a competing station. The profits from the TV station might be used to subsidize below-cost pricing by the apparel manufacturer. Manufacturers wanting their product lines carried by the department store or retail clothing merchants wanting to carry the apparel manufacturer's fashions might feel obliged to advertise on the parent's TV station.

In 1969 the Justice Department charged the General Tire and Rubber Company with illegal reciprocal dealings involving advertising on television stations of RKO, its subsidiary. The commission promptly renewed four RKO licenses without a hearing. Five weeks earlier, the FCC had approved sales of several other licenses to conglomerates, also without hearings. At that time, the commission majority, in order to soothe dissenters Kenneth Cox and Nicholas Johnson, had tentatively authorized the first comprehensive staff study of more than fifty broadcast conglomerates. *Broadcasting* magazine reported that even that investigation would never have been allowed to go forward had not a pilot inquiry of six firms turned up advertising abuses in two of them.[30]

Thus, where fundamental media concentration issues are involved, a commission majority might (1) authorize an investigation or make a proposal but not adopt a rule (top-fifty proposal and conglomerate inquiry); (2) adopt a rule but not apply it retroactively (one-to-a-market rule); or (3) adopt a new policy but not enforce it. As an example of the latter, the one-to-a-market rule prohibited AM-FM radio combinations, except those that were "economically or technically interdependent." In practice, however, the commission automatically granted this waiver upon the bare allegations of AM-FM owners and without even holding hearings. Then it formally rescinded the AM-FM ban altogether.

That a conglomerate's nonmedia interests might improperly influence its broadcast stations' news content should be of ascendant FCC concern. It is precisely this kind of peril that the FCC's "public interest" or "marketplace of ideas" standards should be alert to, even without Antitrust Division pressure. But not so, as the events in 1966–67 surrounding the proposed ABC-ITT merger reveal.

International Telephone and Telegraph, the world's ninth largest industrial corporation in size of work force, received 60 percent of its revenues from operations in more than forty foreign nations, including electronic equipment sales to foreign governments and administration of many foreign telephone companies. Consequently, ITT had a large stake in the internal political and financial developments in these countries. In addition, half of this conglomerate's domestic income came from defense and space contracts. Its proposed partner, ABC, had 137 network affiliate stations reaching 93 percent of the fifty-three million TV homes. The ABC radio network, second largest of the big four, reached fifty-five million listeners. Furthermore, it produced and distributed films throughout the world, owned the largest domestic theater chain (399 theaters), and operated a major record business. What was wrong with the marriage of these two giants?

The Antitrust Division found at least four possible anticompetitive effects: (1) ITT, which had previously contemplated entry into the tightly oligopolistic broadcast industry by acquiring major market stations, had the resources to become a significant independent programming source or even a fourth TV network if the merger were disallowed; (2) ITT was engaged in communications satellite technology, had already entered the cable television field, and was considering pay-TV operations and a network linking whole areas of local cable franchises—an enormous competitive potential that would be negated by merger with ABC; (3) vertical integration of ITT's communications equipment technology with ABC's over-the-air broadcasting operations would reduce ITT's incentive to develop equipment for satellite, cable, and other competitive technologies; and (4) the merger would create a high probability of reciprocal advertising policies.

The FCC received Antitrust Division chief Donald Turner's letter listing these points on December 20, 1966, and was obviously unimpressed. For on December 21, the next day, it approved the merger by a 4–3 vote. Turner, however, practically invited the abrupt treatment he received by concluding in his letter that "the possibilities of such anticompetitive consequences seem sufficiently speculative that we are not presently contemplating an action under the antitrust laws."[31] In any event, the commission majority had already drafted its opinion approving the merger when Turner's letter arrived.

ABC was then at a competitive disadvantage because it had fewer affiliates, and thus reached a smaller audience, than NBC or CBS. Rather than eliminating the exclusive-dealing relationships between networks and their affiliate stations, the commission concluded that what ABC needed was an infusion of capital from ITT. The majority decision ignored the dissenters' contention that ABC could easily have borrowed additional capital and contained no reference to a spectacular disclosure in Turner's letter—that ITT anticipated a cash flow of $100 million *to it* from ABC's operations between 1966 and 1970. The Division's predictions of anticompetitive consequences were dismissed by the FCC majority as "speculative," the word Turner had unwisely used, in order to maintain the conclusion already reached.

After the Antitrust Division had asked for and had been granted a rehearing, much attention was focused upon whether ITT's far-flung economic interests would threaten the independent content of ABC news and public affairs programming. For example, would ITT's desire to negotiate a favorable telephone contract or to wrest tax concessions from some foreign regime become a factor in ABC's decision whether to produce a documentary film critical of that government? Would the mere awareness of ITT economic interests make it impossible for even the most conscientious ABC news officials to maintain their objectivity? ITT's conduct during the hearings gave credence to such fears.

The most flagrant incident involved *New York Times* reporter Eileen Shanahan. On one occasion she was approached by Edward G. Gerrity, senior ITT vice-president in charge of public relations, who indirectly asked to look at the story that she was then writing. He badgered her in an "accusatory and certainly nasty" tone, according to Ms. Shanahan in sworn FCC testimony, to print another story favorable to the merger's prospects. Gerrity then asked Ms. Shanahan whether she had been following the prices of ABC and ITT stocks and whether she did not feel "a responsibility to the shareholders who might lose money as a result of what [she wrote]." Gerrity was apparently unable to comprehend the significance of Ms. Shanahan's reply that "my responsibility was to find out the truth and print it." For he next asked whether she was aware that Commissioner Johnson and Senator Gaylord Nelson were collaborating on legislation that would forbid any newspaper from owning broadcast property. Gerrity felt that this information (which was false, because Johnson and Nelson had in fact never met) was something Ms. Shanahan "ought to pass on to [her] . . . publisher." One obvious implication was that since the *Times* owned some radio stations, it would want to consider its economic interests in deciding what to publish about broadcasting. Another implication was that ITT, as ABC's owner, would too.

"There is no greater political pressure brought against us than in the communications area," said Robert Baker, the attorney who did much of the Antitrust Division's work on the case. He was referring to the nearly three hundred letters received by the Antitrust Division from Capitol Hill opposed to halting the merger. Former Senator Thruston Morton (R.–Ky.), whose family holds a large interest in ABC's Louisville affiliate, urged the FCC to ignore Turner's efforts to have the merger approval overturned. Democratic Senator Russell Long attacked Turner after attending a ground-breaking ceremony for a new ITT manufacturing facility in Monroe, Louisiana. In the House, Fred Rooney (D.–Pa.) was promerger: an ITT electron tube division operates in his district. Thomas Pelly (R.–Wash.) also heard "a scream from my district," namely from ABC's Seattle affiliate. (ABC urged all of its affiliate stations to telegram their congressmen in support of the merger.)[32]

The commission majority was not impressed by numerous instances of ITT's lack of candor, its overt attempts to manipulate the press, or the testimony of many independent economists substantiating the Antitrust Division's economic arguments. But, surprisingly, the merger still failed. The Justice Department appealed the second 4–3 FCC decision. Before the appeals court reached a decision, ITT canceled the merger; its stock had increased in the interim, making it no longer profitable to exchange shares with ABC.

Over-the-Air Broadcasting: Network Dominance

In 1968, 97 percent of America's sixty million homes had at least one television set, and it was turned on for an average of six and one-half hours each day. The average adult watches television about twenty-five hours each week.[33] By the age of five, a child normally has spent more time watching TV than he will spend in college classrooms. "The average male viewer," says Commissioner Johnson, "between his second and sixty-fifth year, will watch television for over 3,000 entire days—roughly nine full years of his life."[34] Whatever the cause—whether the medium *is* the message or whether TV viewing is the electronic age surrogate for the caveman's sitting long hours before flickering fires—the magnitude of television's importance in shaping our national consciousness cannot be questioned. It should be of substantial concern, therefore, that the programs watched by 85 percent of the viewers during "prime time" (7:00 P.M. to 11:00 P.M.) emanate from only three large corporations—CBS, NBC, and ABC.

There are four ways to transmit television signals into the home: (1) by satellite, which the FCC has only recently authorized after seven years of delay; (2) by wire cable, as telephone conversations are transmitted; (3) by use of Ultra High Frequency (UHF) radio waves, or channels 14–83 on the 90 percent of television sets equipped with UHF tuners; and (4) by use of Very High Frequency (VHF) radio waves—i.e., the familiar channels 2–13. Which method is chosen determines how many channels will be available. Unlike the radio spectrum, satellites and cables have virtually limitless channel capacity. But satellites and cables were not around when television began, so the FCC carved out, first the VHF, then the

UHF portions of the radio spectrum and allocated them to television.

The FCC's initial and most damaging error was to allocate the UHF-VHF spectrum so as to minimize the number of channels available to the average viewer. Because VHF technology appeared first, most sets were not equipped to receive UHF signals. In addition, UHF signals do not range as far as VHF signals or survive interfering structures as well. It was too expensive for UHF operators to transmit at higher power to overcome these obstacles, so UHF audiences and advertising revenues fell. On the other hand, the spacious UHF spectrum permitted seventy channels in each locality, ten times more than VHF. CBS championed UHF against RCA, which had a firmer foothold in the new industry and preferred few-channel VHF. RCA won, although the FCC steadfastly predicted that all television would eventually be UHF.

In order to neutralize UHF's disadvantages, all channels in a given community should have been allocated *either* to UHF *or* to VHF. Otherwise, the UHF stations, being technologically inferior, could not establish themselves against VHF competition.* The FCC did adopt this either/or policy, called "deintermixture," in 1956, but abandoned it by 1962 at the behest of Congress, which then authorized a requirement that all new television sets be equipped to select UHF channels as easily as VHF channels. Because the commission relied for eight years on voluntary manufacturer cooperation, which did not materialize, it will be 1982 before virtually all TV sets are equipped with "click

---

* The valuable UHF spectrum would then be wasted. Indeed, another FCC mistake was to allocate the UHF-VHF spectrum arbitrarily to television. There are other, possibly more valuable, uses of the radio spectrum. For example, the amount of spectrum space that the FCC has reserved for "land mobile" communications—i.e., two-way dispatching used in providing police, fire, taxi, and other services—is by one estimate worth $8 to $11 billion to the national economy each year when compared to the next best alternative of replacing two-way radios with more cars and drivers. It would cost only an estimated $3.6 billion per year to replace over-the-air television with cablevision and free the UHF-VHF spectrum for land mobile and other uses. These figures tell little in themselves, for it is the *marginal* demand for more spectrum space by various users that is the important variable.[35] Competitive bidding for use of the spectrum, not arbitrary FCC allocations, would ensure the most efficient use of this very valuable natural resource.

stop" turning dials that select UHF channels as easily as VHF channels.[36] Competitively disadvantaged by agency indecision, UHF has suffered. Approximately 65 percent of the 169 UHF stations on the air lost money in 1969, including 96 percent of UHFs not affiliated with networks. On May 31, 1970, there were still 106 commercial and 65 educational UHF channels reserved for the top one hundred markets that no one wanted.[37]

The average television viewer would obviously be better off if his TV set picked up seven VHF channels instead of three; he would then have a greater variety of programs from which to choose. The FCC thought otherwise. It assigned a few VHF channels to each *locality* instead of more channels to each *region*. For example, rather than allocating four VHFs to Washington and three to Baltimore, the FCC could have licensed seven stations, with powerful transmitting facilities, *each serving the entire area*. Each channel could be programmed from a different city within the region. Such a system would also have the merit of providing most viewers access to an equal number of stations, whether they lived in large cities or rural areas.

Having decided to give each city its "own" stations—as if persons in different cities were not interested in watching the same types of programs—the FCC could still have allocated VHF channels on a population basis, to insure a relatively competitive, as opposed to a relatively oligopolistic, number of program choices for a majority of the national viewing audience. But the top 50 television markets, with 75 percent of the viewing population, have been allocated a total of 157 VHF channels, while the bottom 175 markets, containing only 11 percent of the viewing population, have been allocated 240 VHFs.

The FCC had hoped that this VHF allocation scheme would encourage locally originated programming. Instead, it has helped entrench the three national networks. Live local programming (primarily local news, weather, and sports) accounts for only 13 percent of all programming. During the other 87 percent of the time local stations "throw the network switch, or open a syndicated film package as they would a can of beans," said former FCC Chairman E. William Henry.[38] It is no wonder that many viewers shun locally originated programming. Advertising revenues from small local audiences are quite insufficient for supporting the type of prime-time program production that costs the networks an average of $90,000 per half hour.

Theoretically, a network is a broker, matching up advertisers, programs, and local stations. But national advertisers, who in 1969 provided 83 percent of the industry's $2.8 billion advertising revenues, are primarily interested in saturation coverage with a minimum of duplication. Therefore, the national advertiser seeks out a network that can line up at least one station to carry its ads in each of as many of the most densely populated markets as possible. In order to guarantee advertisers a mass audience, each network has entered into "affiliation" contracts—in practice, exclusive-dealing contracts—with a single station in each of the 127 markets that are served by at least three stations and which contain over 90 percent of the national television audience. As a result of the FCC's channel allocations, there are more than three VHFs in only 16 markets, providing access to but 34 percent of the total viewers. Therefore, it would be difficult if not impossible for a fourth network to line up a sufficient number of unaffiliated major market VHFs for advertising revenues to cover expenses and program costs.

What is the cost of the FCC's rejection of a channel allocation scheme that would have provided enough channels in every region for seven national networks? The term *cost* here does not refer to the foregone intangible educational or cultural benefits from documentaries, public affairs, and other more diverse types of programming that millions of people desire. It refers to how much more money consumers would be willing to pay for seven instead of three channels carrying the standard network fare of westerns, situation comedies, and so forth that even larger numbers of persons want more of. Calculations by Brookings Institution economists place the figure at *$8 billion annually.* Viewers would benefit by this amount at no extra cost to them, for the Brookings' analysis also demonstrates that advertising revenues would be sufficient to support a seven-network system.[39]

To overcome the handicaps imposed by the FCC's channel allocations a potential fourth network would have to persuade at least some of the major market network-affiliated stations to air its programs. Because of clauses in their affiliation contracts, these stations *had* to carry their own networks' offerings until 1963, when a Justice Department antitrust suit against CBS forced a defiant FCC to adopt the "option time" rules (after twice considering and rejecting them). Although the option time rules theoretically grant an affiliate the right to reject any network program, affiliates still "clear" over 95 percent of prime time with their own networks.[40] As a 1963 industry memorandum for investors explained:

> . . . networks attempt to achieve clearances through the use of several available levers, the least important of which is "option time." . . . The network is ultimately responsible for the determination of network rates, and this authority can be used to influence station cooperation on clearances. Clearances can also be a factor in the negotiation of compensation formulas between network and stations which are rewritten every 2 years. As a final and ultimate lever, the network may switch its station affiliation in a given market.[41]

Even the FCC agrees that the fourth network's disadvantage in gaining access to existing affiliates is "insurmountable." In the commission's recent "prime time access rule" opinion, it observed that:

> Not only is there the natural tendency of an affiliate to do more business with its dominant supplier, but the program distribution process is much simpler via a network. There is a semi-permanent affiliation agreement covering almost all programs. The syndicator is forced to make a new contract with each station for each program. Similarly, it is much simpler for an advertiser to make one arrangement for an entire network than to buy station by station.[42]

Yet suppose there were no affiliation contracts, and a new entrant could challenge the networks through competitive bidding for stations to air its programs. Still, CBS, NBC, and ABC each own five strategically located VHF stations, giving them immediate access to 32 percent of the national television audience. This vertical integration forecloses a fourth network from competition for program time on these stations. But, more seriously, the existing networks also have a tremendous head start in attracting advertisers. Because national advertisers are desirous of saturation coverage, and will pay a premium for it, even a small initial audience headstart due to network station ownership would cause fourth network advertising revenues to lag significantly, given present channel allocations.

Not surprisingly, the television business is enormously profitable. "What's wrong with that?" former Commissioner Robert Wells is said to have exclaimed upon learning that broadcast profits averaged 60 to 70 percent return on investment. (American business as a whole averages about a 10 percent return.) In 1969 the networks and their fifteen owned stations reaped a 127 percent return, before taxes, on the net tangible value of their broadcast assets. This amounted to 40 percent of the television industry's profits.[43]

The five major market stations that each network owns earn perhaps 200 to 300 percent on tangible investment, because their profits comprise 70 percent of total network profits. The 1969 network profits exceeded the average return on investment in manufacturing by about $375 million. Local network affiliate stations are somewhat less profitable than network-owned stations, due primarily to their location in less populous markets. Unaffiliated stations are least profitable of all, because they cannot bid for network programs and commensurate advertising revenues.[44]

How the networks have performed in earning their profits is another matter. Even without channel limitations, television programs must attract mass audiences or there will be no advertisers willing to finance programming costs. Although the smaller minority tastes might never be served, effective competition would drive each network to concentrate on appealing to segments of the population that had been relatively ignored by other networks' programs. In newscasting, for example, three competing networks might adopt "liberal," "moderate," and "conservative" editorial stances, thereby maximizing viewer preferences within the limitations of the mass audience requirement. Instead, the networks do not relish competition. All three try to appeal to the same 62.7 percent of the population who tune in to prime time on an average night. This audience consists of 31 percent men, 40 percent women, 11 percent teen-agers, and 18 percent children under twelve. As the viewer's socioeconomic class declines, the amount of time spent viewing accelerates markedly and the rate of acceleration does not level off toward the bottom of the social ladder.[45] It is, statistically speaking, a "lowest common denominator" audience.

"Competition" in network programming proceeds through imitation, not innovation. Network managers, it was once said, assume that if viewers like one domestic comedy or one adult western they will like twenty even better. *Variety* editor Les Brown describes the new programs in the 1971 season in his book, *Television:*

> Each network had its police: ABC, *Mod Squad;* CBS, *Hawaii Five-O;* NBC, *Adam 12.* Each had its father-centered situation comedy: CBS, Fred MacMurray's *My Three Sons;* ABC, Henry Fonda's *The Smith Family;* NBC, the new *James Stewart Show.* Each had its stylized Western: ABC, *Alias Smith and Jones;* CBS, *Cade's County* and *The Big Wheels;* NBC, *Nichols.* And each had its ninety-minute ersatz movie, begat of ABC's *Movie of the Week,* which predominantly were going to be mystery anthologies.
>
> As NBC had a successful series with a crippled police investigator in *Ironside,* ABC would have a new one with a blind detective, *Longstreet.* As ABC had a hit with federal crime-busters in *The FBI,* CBS added *O'Hara, U.S. Treasury.* As NBC had its winning barristers in *The Bold Ones,* ABC added *Owen Marshall: Counselor At Law* and NBC another to its roster, *The D.A.*
>
> Approximately 58 percent of network prime time would be given over to escapist adventure in the law-and-order motif and to movies. Some 40 percent would be made up of situation comedy, music and variety, and melodramas dealing with medicine and the occult.[46]

Indeed, imitation and adherence to the status quo is to be expected as long as there are only three networks. Innovation is especially risky because if it succeeds, it will be copied, and if it fails, audience ratings and advertising revenues will plummet. Of course, the networks claim that audience ratings prove that their programs are what the public desires. Yet, television being the captivating medium that it is, it is by no means self-evident that the programs that the public *will* watch are the same programs that the public *wants* to watch. What *is* self-evident, as Les Brown observes, is that "television is not so much interested in the business of communications as in the business of delivering people to advertisers. People are the merchandise, not the shows. The shows are merely bait."[47]

To that end, all network programs are subject, in CBS's

words, to "the continuing participation of the network's programming officials at every stage of the creative process from the initial script to the final broadcast."[48] New programs are tested before sample audiences, as the networks fashion programs "scientifically" calculated to appeal to that segment of the population that would constitute the largest single audience—an audience whose tastes have been molded, in part, by network programming of past years.

The corporate sponsors of the 1950s (e.g., *The Reynolds Hour, Armstrong Theatre*) also tried to control the content of "independently" produced programs, but at least they had different notions of what kinds of programs would sell their products and what types of audiences to appeal to than did the three networks. By 1968, however, only 3.3 percent of all network programs were independently sponsored. By moving to exert virtually absolute control over program content, the networks could take the easy road of programming for advertisers in general rather than for particular advertisers whose products had narrower, but more diverse, audience appeals. As the networks expanded their objectives from profit to power and status, their means of rivalry evolved to include the cultivating of a bland, non-controversial programming image pleasing to businessmen, politicians, and regulators.

To maintain their corporate images, the networks demand absolute and unaccountable control over the public's airwaves. For example, the networks have been vigorous in their smear campaign against the proposition that up to 20 percent of commercial air time be set aside for free "counter-advertising" by consumer- or public-interest groups. It has become increasingly apparent that the one-sided nature of television advertising is seriously misinforming consumers, resulting in significant diminution of their purchasing power. Too bad, say the networks and the FCC, who fear that counter-advertising might drive some effectively criticized advertisers off the air, possibly reducing network advertising revenues. One of the most frightening applications of the power of the networks (and their affiliated stations) to block public exposure to ideas has been their recent refusal even to *sell* time to (1) a labor union seeking to comment on the inflationary aspects of a wage settlement; (2) environmental groups seeking to contest the antipollution claims of televised gasoline commercials; (3) a group opposing the admission of Communist China to the United Nations; (4) groups opposing the Vietnam war; (5) the Democratic National Committee seeking contributions to finance its 1972 presidential campaign; (6) a Congressional Commission on Population Growth seeking to air its findings; and (7) the Allstate Insurance Company seeking to counter auto industry statements concerning the efficiency of air-bag safety devices. The FCC has steadfastly backed the networks' refusals, even though its decisions have been reversed by the courts in some cases.[49]

In an age in which controversial causes that do not strike a handful of network officials and commentators as "newsworthy" can no longer gain significant numbers of adherents through person-to-person contacts, the question must be repeatedly raised whether the First Amendment has been effectively subverted—not through government censorship but through the economic structure of the mass media.

Can it even be said that it is most "efficient" economically to have only three television networks? In 1954, the year in which the Dumont Television Network folded, Dr. Allen B. Dumont reminded Congress of "important facts which you members of the subcommittee should keep in mind as you weigh the testimony of those who would have you believe that it was their great wisdom and foresight which made them dominant in television broadcasting."[50] In addition to owning top stations and tying up the rest with exclusive affiliations, the networks have benefited from discriminatory AT&T tariffs for interconnections with affiliates. The FCC's 1958 Barrow Report found that the average hourly rate for a New York–Boston interconnection was $1,075.62 if the lines were leased for at least eight continuous hours (i.e., by established networks) but the per hour charge was $7,018.50 for occasional users (i.e., independent programmers or an infant fourth network). The AT&T "eight-hour" tariff remained in effect until 1966, when a still pending FCC proceeding rendered it somewhat less discriminatory.

The networks raised another barrier to a fourth network through flagrantly illegal advertising rate discriminations, which tended to "capture" the larger advertisers. Some of the devices used were "cumulative volume discounts" and rate packages that made it cheaper for advertisers to buy time on all affiliate stations than in selected markets served by a potential fourth network. While many of these practices were discontinued after critical 1966 congressional hearings, more subtle forms of discrimination may persist.[51]

The movement from sponsor to network domination over program production was not dictated by advertisers' desires. Rather, a dramatic increase in hour-long network programs during the 1959–60 season and a sellers' market, which the networks fully exploited, tended to render independent sponsorship prohibitively expensive. At the same time, the networks were busy coercing independent producers to give up valuable syndication rights as a condition of accepting their programs for network showing. (Syndicated network reruns are the largest single source of programming for the twenty top-market unaffiliated VHFs.) Despite what the networks insist are "grave financial risks,"[52] independent TV program producers would come forth with an ample supply of quality material if network control were eliminated. The American Association of Advertising Agencies recently estimated that there were enough advertisers interested in financing and sponsoring independently produced programs appealing to distinctive audiences to fill 25 percent of evening TV schedules. And in its recent "prime time access rule" decision, the FCC pointed out that in the 1959–60 television season *"between 225 and 250* 'completed' pilot films were offered in the network television program market. About 90 percent were 'new investments,' which means that 'someone had an idea, had gone to the script form, had gotten financing.' "[53]

"Copyright exclusivity" is another industry practice not dictated by "efficiency." Just as network programs are licensed to affiliates on an exclusive basis, so are network reruns, independently produced syndicated programs, and old movies. Once licensed to one unaffiliated station, these program materials are usually unavailable to all other stations and cable systems within the same market (and often outside of it), for periods ranging from up to two years for regular length programs to five or six years for movies. By 1971 the FCC had finally realized that "the present method of distributing non-network programming

obviously works markedly to the benefit of established
VHF broadcasters, and against the new, struggling UHF
stations [and cable systems]."[54] If these outlets could
obtain programming adequate merely to establish their
viability, they might form the basis for new networks and
greater program diversity.

A copyright, to the extent that it allows the copyright
holder to determine the price (or advertising costs) that
viewers must pay, serves the necessary purpose of enabling
program producers to profit from their labors. Generally,
the wider the program's circulation, the greater are its
advertising revenues and the profits of the program producer.[55] Exclusivity thus runs counter to the antitrust and
First Amendment interests in the widest possible dissemination of information. In most cases, it is not the program
producers, but their biggest and best customers, the VHF
broadcasters, who stand to increase their profits through
exclusivity by eliminating competition from other stations
or cable systems.[56]

The best of several alternative means of eliminating
exclusivity would be to require all program owners, including the networks, to license all stations and cable systems
willing to pay the same price per thousand viewers as is
charged the highest bidder. This could be accomplished
through FCC regulations, compulsory copyright legislation, or a landmark antitrust decision. The number of
actual viewers of each station's showing could be determined by audience surveys periodically conducted by the
rating services. The maximum allowable period of exclusivity or "clearance" for the first showing in a market should
be severely limited to a matter of a few days.

It is the exclusivity that exists between the networks and
their affiliates that is both the backbone and the Achilles'
heel of network domination of television. Network affiliates
have a "right of first call" on all network offerings. The
present network triumvirate might survive the loss of their
major market television stations and their control over
program procurement and content, but, said the FCC's
1958 Barrow Report, "if the right of first call were effectively prohibited, and as a result all stations in a community could bid, or otherwise contract, for the programs of
any network, networks would be in the same category as
any other program supplier."[57]

These changes would make networks true "brokers." There would be no artificial barriers to entry of additional networks. In order to survive, new networks would have to compete for different segments of the potential viewing audience by offering more diverse programming. For the first time there would be significant competition between local stations for quality network programming—competition that, in turn, would expropriate the monopoly profits of local stations to provide the financial base for new networks and more program production. Rather than each of three networks airing a program in all of the top fifty markets, through competitive bidding each of five or six networks would air one program in twenty-five or thirty of the top fifty markets, and another program in a different set of twenty-five or thirty of the top fifty markets. The twenty independent VHFs in the top fifty markets would become full-time quality program outlets. There would be more quality programming available to aid development of the UHF and cable markets on both first and second run bases.

The FCC's Barrow Report viewed such a development with alarm:

> It is this possibility of the undermining of the network system which argues against effective prohibition of the right of first refusal . . . [T]he network system is an integral and vital part of American broadcasting; . . . and loss of the programming and communication values associated with the network system would be adverse to the public interest.[58]

To the contrary, few changes in American business structure would be more in the public interest. Assuming, for the sake of argument, that a multi-network competitive method of marketing television advertising time would be more *expensive* than the present fixed distribution channels, paradoxically it would not be less *efficient*. For the primary "value" of network programming is measured by its diversity—by total viewer satisfaction—not by its distribution costs. The issue is efficiency for whom—advertisers or consumers?

Comparative cost-benefit analyses of retaining the present network system vs. restructuring it competitively must conclude that any benefits from less expensive advertising are far outweighed by the costs of sacrificing program diversity. What Judge Learned Hand said of the Associated Press monopoly in 1943 is particularly germane to what kind of antitrust policy should be adopted toward the existing network structure:

> . . . [N]either exclusively, nor even primarily, are the interests of the newspaper industry conclusive; for that industry serves one of the most vital of all general interests: the dissemination of news from as many different sources, and with as many different facets and colors as is possible. That interest is closely akin to, if indeed it is not the same as, the interest protected by the First Amendment; it presupposes that right conclusions are more likely to be gathered out of a multitude of tongues, than through any kind of authoritative selection . . .[59]

Over-the-Air Broadcasting:
The Government's Response

The situation in the television industry is not the first time that monopolistic control has been exercised over the production, distribution, and exhibition of information and artistic properties. But it is the first time that the government has failed to take substantial action to dissolve such concentrations. Previously, radio networks had sought to control talent through "artists' bureaus." That scheme was ended in 1941 by the FCC's Chain Broadcast Rules, patterned after a threatened Justice Department suit. ASCAP (American Society of Composers, Authors, and Publishers) and BMI (Broadcast Music, Incorporated), the copyright clearinghouse monopolies, were not abolished by government decree but were at least subjected to judicial regulation of licensing terms and royalties charged broadcast stations for music rights. In the movie industry vertical integration of production and exhibition was broken up by the Supreme Court's 1948 *Paramount* decision.

From the mid-1950s until early 1972, Antitrust Division lawyers unsuccessfully sought approval of a *Paramount*-type suit to divest the networks from ownership or production of network programs. The remedy might require network program procurement practices to operate somewhat along common carrier lines. Independent producers (and whoever might finance them) would determine program content and compete with each other for sponsors. Because the network could not purchase any "rights" in the program at all, the only way it could affect content would be to refuse to sell time to the sponsor, which would also raise serious antitrust and First Amendment doubts. Attorney General William Rogers vetoed a *"Paramount-network"* complaint recommended by his Antitrust chief Victor Hansen in the late 1950s. Then in 1964 Attorney General Nicholas Katzenbach refused to approve a case suggested by his Antitrust Division that would have attempted to divest the networks from programming, on the ground that the FCC was already looking into the same issue. But according to Ashbrook Bryant, then director of the FCC's Office of Network Study, he had *already* rejected the request of Robert Wright, a top Antitrust Division aide, for FCC action divesting the networks from programming. Bryant suggested that the Antitrust Division bring the *Paramount*-type suit itself if it desired such a remedy. The buck passed both ways.

By 1968 the networks either themselves produced or obtained syndicated distribution or profit-sharing rights in 96.7 percent of all network programs aired between 6:00 P.M. and 11:00 P.M. In 1957 the figure had been 67.2 percent. The FCC finally acted in 1970, six years after Katzenbach's veto. Then, in a 5–2 decision, it adopted the "prime time access rule," which prohibits network affiliates in the top fifty markets from accepting more than three hours of network programs between 7:00 P.M. and 11:00 P.M. Because the networks supplied only three and one-half hours of prime time programming anyway, the effect of the rule is to free an additional half hour for independently produced programs, hardly the opening for a fourth network—much less a fifth or sixth one.[60]

The FCC thus retreated from its original proposal, Bryant's "fifty-fifty rule," which would have freed ninety instead of thirty minutes of prime time from network dominance and would have gone half as far as a *Paramount*-network suit. The commission had earlier been "in no great hurry" to proceed with the fifty-fifty rule, according to Bryant, because it wanted to wait and see if the 1963 option time rules would "work." The FCC's investigation of network dominance began in 1955.

Then, in April, 1972, the Justice Department filed an

antitrust suit to prohibit the networks "from carrying network produced entertainment programs, including feature
films, and from obtaining financial interests in independently produced entertainment programs." The move was a
surprise. Some staff attorneys suggested that the suit had
been filed to bolster staff morale and the Justice Department's image in the wake of the ITT-Hartford consent
decree scandal. Many in press circles viewed the case as an
administration slap at the mass media's "Eastern Liberal
Establishment bias." Theoretically, the lawsuit's success
would have shifted the responsibility for determining program content from the networks to the advertiser-sponsors
of independent program producers, thereby increasing program diversity. But the government was quick to point out
in its press release that "the networks would continue to
exercise responsibility for programs they accept for broadcast." What this apparently means is that the networks
could continue to reject programs tendered by advertiser-
sponsors on grounds of "taste" or "controversy." Then,
advertiser-sponsored programs might still have to conform
to the same criteria that network programs presently
require.

The easiest step that the commission could take to
diminish network domination would be to refuse to renew
the fifteen network VHF licenses. The closest the FCC has
come to action in this area was its proposal to limit group
owners to two top-fifty-market VHFs. The rule was rejected in 1968 on the ground that its adoption would lessen
the chances of a fourth network succeeding. That was in
fact the case, but only because the proposal contained a
grandfather clause exempting the networks and existing
group owners from divestiture. After all, the FCC likes the
present network system. Its regulatory function in the
broadcast field since the early 1950s has been primarily to
insure the stability of that system—by providing the networks with guaranteed annual incomes from their major
market stations, guaranteed audience edges through the
stations they own, and exclusive affiliates to perpetuate
themselves. In return, the networks guarantee that constant, predictable, and homogenous TV "service" that
satisfies the commission. It is a symbiotic relationship in
the best tradition of private socialism. Many viewers never
realize what they have missed.

This regulatory-industry relationship tempts one to view the commissioners as "captured" by the industry that they purport to regulate. The process is more subtle. The regulator's perspective is limited to a narrow sector of the economy; his public policy goals must be achieved through the client industry or not at all. Power is further limited because the regulator has no funds at his disposal to fund objectives he deems in the public interest. As a result, the regulator protects and encourages the networks' monopoly profits, which can, in turn, be used to subsidize projects such as Sunday-afternoon public affairs programs that cannot sustain themselves in the marketplace as presently structured. Naturally, then, as economists William Comaner and Bridger Mitchell observe,

> Factors which restrict revenues, and thereby the scale of the regulated industries, are immediately suspect, while factors which increase the revenues and size of the sector are to be encouraged . . . A large sector gives rise to greater prospects for regulatory good works while a smaller sector does not. . . . *Planning by regulation* leads directly to actions which generally distort the allocation of resources between the regulated and the unregulated sectors of the economy.[61]

This "healthy industry" orientation provides the FCC's policy rationale for rejection of the counter-advertising and top-fifty-market group VHF ownership proposals, for the delay in requiring newspapers to divest same-market broadcasting stations, for the permissive attitude toward conglomerate ownership, and for the maintenance of the network-affiliate relationships through the "right of first call." As we shall see, the commission's discriminatory policies toward pay and cable television are similarly predicated.

Thus the peculiar vision of the most well motivated of regulators tends to be that whatever is good for the networks or the broadcasters is also good for the public. Not surprisingly, those with a less confined conception of the public interest view this regulatory attitude as prima facie evidence of "capture" by the purportedly regulated firms. The case for capture becomes even more obvious when it is noted that the broadcast industry's monopoly profits, which regulation has fostered, continue to go into corporate accounts instead of into "regulatory good works."

Cable Technology

With network hegemony over the minds and eyes of television viewers unlikely to be toppled by Antitrust Division or FCC action, the best alternative is a new communications technology that will outflank over-the-air broadcasting. At this moment one is being deployed that may rival the computer and electricity in its revolutionary impact upon civilization. *TV Guide* quotes an FCC staffer as musing:

> Think about it this way . . . There's this wire leading out from your television set, through a hole in the wall, and then down the street to a building we'll call the neighborhood program-distribution center—something like a telephone exchange. Inside the building are some computers and a small receiving station capable of picking up satellite signals.
> OK. I come home from work and I'm absolutely *dying* to see "Petticoat Junction." Do I sit around twiddling my thumbs until 8 o'clock when the program comes on? Nope. I pick up my program catalogue, look up the code number, punch my touch-tone buttons, and up pops the show on my TV screen. Suppose I want to read *Moby Dick*. I just tap out the right code number and there it is, page by page, on the screen.
> Maybe I want to take a college course, for credit; or settle an argument about the Franco-Prussian War; or learn more about the culture of India; or see a painting owned by the Louvre. It's all there, waiting for me to summon it up—thousands and thousands of bits of knowledge, guidance and entertainment stored in computers, awaiting my beck and call.[62]

Through "facsimile print-outs," newspapers and mail may be delivered to the home over wire. Two-way cable can facilitate, for example, the checkless society, meter reading, opinion polling, voting, security surveillance, and display and purchase of merchandise.

This so-called wired city is an offshoot of Community Antenna Television (CATV). CATV began in the late 1940s as a means of bringing broadcast signals by cable to areas in which there were no local stations or where topography caused poor reception. By 1972, about 7.5 percent of the nation's television homes are CATV subscribers, and this rapidly expanding industry has only recently sought to penetrate the major population centers. The President's Task Force on Telecommunications Policy estimated that by 1980 there will be 100 million households in the United States and that wiring the least expensive half of them would cost $5 billion. The Electronics Industries Association predicts a total hookup cost of $11 billion, but it forecasts a saving to the economy of *$50 billion each year*—in air travel ($6 billion) and highways ($6 billion), as cable communication supplants transportation needs, police ($3 billion) and fire ($1 billion) protection, postal service ($6 billion), and increased opportunities and leisure time for recreation ($28 billion).[63] Most observers agree that a nationwide cable system will become a reality in the near future if it is merely allowed to develop itself free of artificial restraints. But the politically powerful broadcast industry, threatened by CATV's virtually unlimited channel capacity, has found a willing protector in the FCC. "CATV competition can have a substantial negative effect upon station audience and revenues," declared an alarmed commission in 1965.

The regulatory controversy has focused upon whether, in addition to carrying local broadcast signals, local CATV operators may import "distant signals" from VHF independents in New York, Los Angeles, and other major cities. Without distant signals, only about one-sixth of television homes will subscribe to cable service. With distant signal importation, however, cable will penetrate more than half of the market, giving it a financial base to support new programming for its dormant channel capacity.[64] The cable entrepreneurs at first sought to import distant signals without paying copyright royalties. But in 1968 the FCC countered with a freeze on cable importation of distant signals into the top one hundred markets unless "retransmission consent" was first obtained from the imported stations. The problem, described by former National Cable Television Association (NCTA) general counsel Gary Christensen, was that if a New York independent VHF allowed a Philadelphia CATV to import its programs, Philadelphia independents would quickly retaliate by allowing New York CATVs to import their signals. The VHFs' refusal to sell retransmission consent to CATVs even at handsome prices is merely another variation of program copyright exclusivity.

Why should cable systems pay copyright royalties for imported signals anyway? In a community with only two local network broadcast stations, cable importation of the missing network signal would increase the imported network's total audience and advertising revenues. Likewise, the fragmentation of an independent VHF's local audience share due to cable importation of other independents into its own market would be more than offset by cable exportation of its signals to audiences in other markets. True, competition from nationwide signal importation would reduce the profits of networks and their affiliates, by perhaps $200 million annually, yet network affiliates would still be making after tax profits of 30 percent on tangible investment.* [65]

But let us assume that cable TV would severely damage or even destroy the viability of broadcast television. Ordinarily, that would be a simple case of an inferior technology giving way to a superior one in the public interest. Yet, FCC Chairman Dean Burch rationalized to the House Communications Subcommittee that

> we feel it would be in the public interest for cable to proceed. We also feel it would be in the public interest for over-the-air broadcasting not to be adversely affected. You can translate that into a shorthand of protectionism for over-the-air broadcasting, but we feel that is a public interest consideration as well.[66]

What is the commission's formal public interest rationale for protecting over-the-air broadcasting at all costs? One concern may be that up to 10 percent of the population lives in rural areas where the laying of cable is economically unfeasible. But rural areas can receive cable service via local microwave systems. And in any event,

* The FCC explicitly fears that cable's distant signal importation would siphon off local audiences from struggling UHF stations to an extent that would sound their final death knell. Because the FCC has invested so much hope for so long in UHF as the ultimate vehicle of television diversity, such an eventuality would be understandably unbearable. Yet it faces a dilemma. On the one hand, CATV carriage of local UHF signals would place UHF reception quality on a par with local VHF signals, thus overcoming UHF's most severe technological disadvantage. On the other hand, without importation of audience-fragmenting distant signals, cable systems will not exist to carry local UHF signals.

rural electrification programs, among others, provide ample (though not justifiable) precedent for 90 percent of the population directly subsidizing the rural 10 percent.

The FCC's most fundamental concern is expressed as a preference for "free" TV over "pay" TV. Most viewers would associate "pay" TV with a special charge for each program. But cable programming has thus far been primarily advertiser-sponsored. The only "pay" aspect of present cable systems is that subscribers are billed for basic monthly charges, which amount to about $60 annually. The commission worries that the $5 monthly CATV charge is "regressive" and that some lower-income viewers might not be able to afford it if over-the-air broadcasting were to lose out to market forces and no longer be available as a "free" service.

Of course, by that logic, the telephone, with *its* regressive monthly charges, and the postal service, with *its* regressive uniform rates, should never have been allowed to make inroads upon word-of-mouth communications. If "regressiveness" is the test, why focus upon CATV charges? Why not graduate the market prices of all goods and services—food, electricity, housing, ad infinitum—in order to equalize the utility of a dollar spent by consumers in each income class? The reason is that there is a better means than tampering with the market mechanism for enabling low-income citizens to afford television (or any other service). It is to provide persons of lesser incomes with the necessary purchasing funds out of general tax revenues. This could be accomplished through the present welfare system.

The FCC's favoritism toward existing broadcasting springs from the premise that its own regulatory duty is to "guarantee" television for all income groups. Yet the vital service it "guarantees" is television per se, not the diversity and total appeal of *programs* that would be maximized by multi-channel CATV. The commission's preference for "free" TV therefore subordinates the class of television viewers who would prefer CATV program diversity (including many poor persons such as racial minorities) to the class of persons who would not (including many non-poor). It should be emphasized that the term *diversity* does not refer only to the provision of highbrow programming for the intellectual classes. It refers as well, if not more so in the short run, to the provision of a greater variety of such program types as westerns, adventure stories, and situation comedies.

Over-the-air broadcasting is by no means "free" anyway. Each year the average TV home pays about $150 for "free" TV—for increased, but hidden, product costs from advertising expenditures, for electricity, for repairs, and for amortization of the cost of television sets and antennas.[67] For many, there is also a great deal of misery in having to watch annoying television commercials. CATV would not simply add $60 per year per TV home to these expenses. It has been estimated that if CATV coverage were to saturate all sixty million TV households, monthly subscriber's charges could be reduced to about $1.50, or $18 per year.[68] Moreover, CATV would eliminate antenna costs; cable television sets could ultimately be substantially less expensive than over-the-air receivers; CATV operators would have no transmitter and tower costs; the cable viewers' cost *per channel* would be a fraction of the per channel costs of "free" TV; and cable subscribers would also have access to cable radio, postal service, remote control shopping, and so forth. Indeed, the $50 billion annually that the Electronics Industries Association has estimated that cable services would save the economy would be enough to provide every family of four in the United States with a guaranteed annual income of $6,500; and the FCC purports to be concerned that lower-income viewers may suffer from CATV!

Were it not for the Antitrust Division's persistent interest in freeing CATV from competitive restraints, the future would probably be far more bleak than it now is. When broadcasters and newspapers realized the potential—and the threat—of CATV, they acted accordingly. Forty-six percent of the cable systems started in 1966 were broadcaster owned.[69] In 1968 newspapers had interests in 225 cable systems and were seeking another 300 franchises.[70] The FCC has at least adopted rules that the networks and same-market television stations cannot own cable interests, because the two modes would be obvious direct competitors. The commission is presently considering whether to ban radio-CATV cross-ownership, and it promises someday to get around to newspaper-CATV cross-ownership.

The FCC has also proposed to limit the number of CATV systems in the top markets a corporation can own, or, alternatively, the total number of subscribers. But no matter how competitively independent the CATV franchises become, they will be unable to compete as long as program exclusivity and signal importation restrictions remain.

The ultimate explanation of why restrictions remain traces to the ample political power of the broadcasting industry. The broadcasters' principal leverage is their power to alter the politician's news coverage in his district. Besides this threat, other factors make implementation of cable technology difficult. One is that the issues involved are sufficiently complex that too few congressmen or members of the public are aroused by their significance. Another is that, aside from a few public interest groups and the rather timid NCTA (which represents primarily the rural mom-and-pop cable systems), there is no well-heeled vested interest to oppose the broadcasters in the political arena. (This may be changing as large conglomerate corporations are now buying up CATV franchises.) The present debate is not over whether the signal importation and exclusivity restrictions should be removed. Rather, it revolves around narrow cartel-like compromises by which these restrictions can be relaxed to accommodate at least some growth of cable without "adversely affecting" broadcast profits and invoking that industry's political wrath. In May, 1969, a tentative compromise agreement was announced between NCTA and the National Association of Broadcasters (NAB). The broadcasters would agree to compulsory copyright licensing if the CATVs would agree: (1) to import distant signals only up to the point of "adequate service" within the CATV's own market, defined as three network and three independent signals; (2) to originate only one advertiser-sponsored or entertainment program channel; and (3) to renounce any intentions of forming an interconnected CATV network for the distribution of entertainment programs. FCC and congressional approval would have been necessary both to fix the amount of copyright royalties for imported signals and to immunize this cartel from the antitrust laws. Why was the cable industry willing to enter into such a flagrantly anticompetitive arrangement for so little gain? "When you're dying," said NCTA's Christensen, "you take crumbs." The NAB board, however, was not even willing to give crumbs. It rejected the proposal.

Then, in an August 5, 1971, letter, Chairman Burch outlined to Congress the FCC's long-awaited proposals for CATV. Focusing on the critical top fifty markets, the proposal would have allowed cable systems to import two— occasionally three—independent signals, in order to provide, in conjunction with local signals, at least three network and three independent channels. Again, that was too much for the broadcast industry, which communicated its displeasure to the appropriate persons. Tom Whitehead, chief of the White House Office of Telecommunications Policy (OTP), summoned the interested parties—the broadcast, cable, and movie industries (copyright holders) —to a series of meetings to work out a different compromise more acceptable to the broadcasters. Representatives of the general public, such as public interest law firms specializing in communications work, were not invited. At the outset Whitehead informed the cable interests that "whatever you come up with is not going to be what the FCC proposes." Peter Flanigan, Nixon aide and business advocate, who was present at one of the earlier meetings, is quoted by Christensen to have stated: "You may be assured that the FCC's recent announcement is not the position of the administration and it will be opposed."

The distinguishing feature of the new compromise, which NCTA had no choice but to accept, and which the FCC has now formally adopted, is that unlimited exclusivity rights are explicitly recognized in the top fifty markets. That is, a program cannot be imported if a local broadcaster has contracted for exclusive rights to it, no matter how long the period of exclusivity lasts. This provision will severely inhibit cable access to quality syndicated programming, especially in the sixteen markets served by at least one independent VHF, which contain 34 percent of the TV homes. Theoretically, FCC rulemaking could limit the length of exclusivity for the first two imported signals. But concerning any additional number of imported signals that the FCC might permit in the future, the exclusivity provisions are to be embodied in copyright legislation that the parties, as part of the compromise, have agreed to support. Because the pending copyright bill is the first major revision of copyright legislation since 1906, such a provision would be extremely difficult to repeal.

In an interview, the then OTP general counsel Antonin Scalia contended that the administration was in fact pro-cable and that the compromise had nothing to do with its long-range cable policy. It was simply a means of breaking the deadlock by lifting the total freeze on signal importation. But why was it necessary to alter the FCC proposals? Because the broadcasters had too much clout in Congress, Scalia responded, although he agreed that it was especially unhealthy for any segment of the press to wield such special interest political power. But if the administration is really pro-cable, will it not inevitably have to confront the broadcasters' power in Congress—if not now, then at some future date? To that question Scalia could only reply that President Nixon would have to temper his options in light of political reality.

There is no doubt that CATV faces formidable opposition in Congress. Scalia specifically mentioned Senator John Pastore (D.–R.I.), chairman of the Senate Communications Subcommittee, whom he dubbed "Mr. Communications." A firm ally of the broadcasters, Pastore introduced legislation to convince the FCC to defy court decisions by making it virtually impossible for local citizens' groups to challenge broadcast license renewals under the Communications Act's public interest standard. But congressional opposition to cable does seem to be diminishing. At least there were no public statements of outright opposition to the FCC proposals by key congressmen. In fact, after the FCC incorporated the OTP compromise into its own regulations, House Communications Subcommittee Chairman Torbert MacDonald (D.–Mass.) chastised Whitehead for White House interference with the "independent" FCC, echoing the dissenting opinion of Commissioner Johnson.

It is clear that the Nixon administration did not simply yield to inevitable political reality; it willingly acquiesced. One cable official quoted Peter Flanigan as saying: "I've done a whip study [head count] and it appears that CATV does not have as many votes on the Hill as the independent broadcasters [presumably referring to all local station owners, as distinguished from the networks themselves]. Now, I'm for cable on the merits, and I don't give a damn about the independent broadcasters, but it's a matter of

political expediency." It was pointed out to Scalia that
whenever the Nixon administration really wanted something from Congress, such as a Lockheed or SST bill, it
had been willing to mobilize its forces to obtain it. He
replied that such efforts applied only to priority items,
conceding that cable TV was not very high on the president's priority list.

"Stability" and "orderly growth" in the communications
industry are the politically loaded terms bandied about by
Nixon administration aides. Director of Communications
Herb Klein once told broadcasters:

> The real way to determine the Nixon Administration's at-
> titude toward broadcasters is from its appointments to the
> Federal Communications Commission, not its [Agnew's]
> speeches. . . . Aren't the Nixon appointees good men
> from the industry point of view?[71]

Yes, the Nixon Administration is for cable television. But
not today, thank you.

Pay Television

The broadcasters have elicited the most severe congressional opposition to cable by pointing to its probable trans-
formation into "pay cable," through which viewers would
be charged on a per program basis. While cable would no
doubt continue to provide a number of mass audience,
advertiser-sponsored channels, the development of pay
cable is essential if this new technology is to harness its full
potential for diversity of content and maximization of
viewer preferences. Economist J. R. Minasian explains
why:

> The fundamental character of commercial broadcasting,
> both television and radio . . . is that the nature and thus
> the value of programs . . . are determined by the pro-
> ductivity of advertisements. In contrast, under a subscrip-
> tion [pay] system the value of a program will depend upon
> the demand for the program in its entertainment or edu-
> cational sense. . . .
>   In an advertising-supported system voting is by response
> to the message, and the program results in an all-or-
> nothing type of voting, since votes take weights of either

one (viewer) or zero (non-viewer). In contrast, a subscription system allows proportional representation, since votes take different weights (different prices paid for different kinds of programs) and reveal the voters' subjective evaluations of the program.

Therefore, a subscription system can be expected to yield a more diversified program menu than an advertising system, because the former enables individuals, by concentrating their dollar votes, to overcome the "unpopularity" of their tastes.

To gain some perspective, note that programs which are currently discarded may have had as many as 15–20 million viewers. Network programs do not become "profitable" before passing the 20 million mark, and popular shows command 30–50 million viewers, according to the rating services. A nonpopular show by current standards, if viewers are willing to pay a quarter on subscription television, needs an audience of less than a million to compete with a current show with 30 million viewers on advertising-supported television.[72]

The point is that advertising is an inefficient means of financing the dissemination of information.[73] But advertising has been relied upon by the over-the-air media because it was prohibitively expensive to collect charges from those viewers who would be willing to pay to see a particular program. Now, however, cable television sets can be equipped with meters that automatically tabulate a subscriber's bill. Signal scrambling devices can do the same for over-the-air subscription television. Nevertheless, the 1962–1966 Zenith-Teco experiment with over-the-air subscription TV in Hartford, Connecticut, conducted with FCC permission, aroused strong congressional efforts to block any type of pay TV. The rules that the commission finally adopted in 1968, after fifteen years of opposition from House Commerce Committee Chairman Harley Staggers (D.–W. Va.), were highly restrictive. Pay television was prohibited from carrying the staples of over-the-air television—most sports events and movies and all "series" programs with interconnected plot and the same cast of principal characters. And unlike newspapers and magazines, cable systems were prohibited from supporting any programs partially through advertiser revenues and partially through specific viewer charges. Dissenting Commissioner Robert Bartley observed that the restrictions amounted to "complete strangulation of a potentially new economic base for program origination."[74] Even the Antitrust Division has raised no objections.

The pay TV controversy has most often focused upon sports programming and was rekindled most recently by the Ali-Frazier heavyweight title fight in 1971. It bypassed "free" TV altogether in the United States, where it was viewed by slightly over a million persons who paid $8 to $30 a head for closed circuit theater seats. The promoters grossed about $15 million. Many were alarmed that a nationwide pay cable network might enable promoters with rights to the Super Bowl or the World Series to exact exorbitant charges from millions of sports fans.

But suppose the Ali-Frazier fight promoters could have beamed the bout to a nationwide audience through pay cable. If fifty million homes tuned in—the same number that viewed the 1968 Democratic National Convention— and assuming two persons in each household actually watched the fight, the promoters could charge only thirty cents per set—fifteen cents per person—and *still* gross $15 million.

On the other hand, say the pay TV critics, what is to prevent the program owner from maintaining a high price and reaping even greater profits than he could through a closed circuit theater apparatus? First, the program charge cannot profitably be raised to a level higher than that which would induce a substantial portion of the audience to share their neighbors' television sets. Second, every pay program will have to keep its charges down in order to meet stiff competition from programs on the cable's many other channels. Then, if society is not solicitous of athletes' earnings, it has the option of placing a ceiling on pay cable charges for championship sports events.

Of course, a fifteen cent TV charge for "the fight of the century" would be quite atypical of charges that would be levied for less spectacular mass appeal programs. An hour-long program that cost $300,000 to produce (including profit, cable charges, and other expenses) and was viewed by forty million persons in twenty million homes would cost each pay TV viewer only three-fourths of a cent. This charge is less to viewers than the higher prices that consumers (including, of course, viewers) must presently pay for advertiser-supported programs, because the ad agency commissions, which eat up 15 percent of network advertising revenues, would be eliminated.

There are other ways in which pay TV is more beneficial than advertiser-supported TV. Most importantly, the enormous diversity of ideas generated by the ability of 0.5 percent of the American people to finance a $250,000 program by paying twenty-five cents each would maximize the objectives of the First Amendment—a mass culture whose direction is governed by a rational synthesis of divergent perspectives rather than being retarded by the overrepresented values of the preceding generation's majority.

Pay TV is also a cost saver for the individual viewer. He can view what he *wants* to see instead of what he is *willing* to see. Thus, the extent to which the average viewer might spend more on pay TV than on "free" TV would be more than counterbalanced by his increased satisfaction. Perhaps as important, placing a price tag on television viewing would enable persons to allocate their leisure time more efficiently. If the presently hidden costs of watching television were revealed, some people might decide that there are better things to do than to be pacified by the tube for twenty-five hours a week. Too bad our political-regulatory complex isn't about to let that happen.

3

AT&T: The Phony Monopoly

BEVERLY C. MOORE, JR.

The American Telephone and Telegraph Company is by far the world's largest corporation. It has assets approaching $60 billion, annual revenues of $20.5 billion, and profits of over $2.5 billion. It is also our largest monopoly, operating 85 percent of the local telephone service and 98 percent of all long-distance telephone facilities in the United States. Actually, AT&T is the parent of a holding company known as the Bell System. AT&T's "Long Lines Division" provides interstate telephone and other communications services; its "General Department" funnels technical and administrative assistance to the twenty-four Bell operating companies that furnish local and long-distance telephone service. Almost all of the system's communications equipment is purchased from Western Electric, which AT&T owns. Research and development, half of it government financed, is carried on at the Bell Telephone Laboratory.

Basics of Public Utility Regulation

Because it is a monopoly providing essential services to vast numbers of consumers, AT&T's interstate operations come under the purview of the Federal Communications Commission, with intrastate operations scrutinized by state utility commissions. In terms of plant investment, the FCC regulates about 25 percent of the Bell System and the states, 75 percent.

In simplest terms, regulators perform two tasks. The first is to determine the company's "overall revenue requirements." These must be sufficient to cover all costs (which include operating expenses, depreciation, interest, and taxes) and to yield a fair profit, or "rate of return," which enables the company to attract the necessary capital for maintenance and expansion of its services. The second task is to devise the appropriate rate structure, consisting of a schedule of charges which, when applied to the various services that the company provides, will satisfy the overall revenue requirements. For both of these steps it is necessary to determine the value of the "rate base"—the company's capital investment in plant and equipment used in providing each regulated service—because the amount of profit that the company is allowed to earn is expressed as a percentage of the rate base.

The appearance of simplicity in these regulatory steps is deceptive. Take the rate of return as a starting point. Assuming a rate base of $50 billion, a mere 1 percent difference in the after tax profit rate is $1 billion annually out of the pocketbooks of consumers.[1] The point is not merely theoretical. The difference between the 7.25 percent return, which the FCC had informally set for interstate operations during the 1960s, and the average 6 percent return allowed by the states translated into $325 million annually in consumer contributions to the profits of a monopoly facing virtually no risk of financial failure.[2] AT&T also consistently earns—and keeps—more than its allowable rate of return at both the state and federal levels. For example, notwithstanding the 7.25 percent limitation, AT&T's actual earnings in August, 1966, were 9.33 percent. The House Antitrust Subcommittee calculated that AT&T's earnings during the 1955–1961 period (when the rate base was much smaller than today) exceeded the 6.5 percent maximum set in 1953 by almost $1 billion.[3]

Nor has AT&T overlooked the profit opportunities inherent in various accounting strategies. The rate of return is computed on the company's net assets,* which derive from two sources: the funds put up by stockholders (equity capital) and debt put up by bondholders. Given a fixed overall rate of return, the profit rate *to the stockholders* depends upon the interest rate paid to bondholders and the relative proportions of debt and equity that comprise the rate base. Up to a point, it is cheaper to raise capital through debt than through the public sale of stock, especially for such a secure monopoly as AT&T. Given these circumstances, then, an increase in the ratio of debt to equity increases the stockholders' percentage return on their equity investment. For example, while electric utilities, with a debt-equity ratio of 2:1 and an average rate of return of 6.6 percent in 1968, earned 12.3 percent on stockholders' equity, AT&T, with a nearly opposite 2:3 debt-equity ratio, earned 7.5 percent on its total rate base but only 9.3 percent for its stockholders. The higher overall rate of return required by AT&T's overly conservative capital structure costs consumers additional hundreds of millions of dollars annually. FCC Commissioner Nicholas Johnson observes:

> It is a bit ironic and tragically costly for everyone involved that Bell is only *now* going to more debt financing —when it has to pay some of the highest interest rates in our nation's history (8.5 to 9 percent)—and that it failed to borrow during all those years when it could have borrowed in the 2 to 4 percent range [as the electric utilities did during the early 1950s].[4]

Or consider Bell's expenses—some $14 billion of them. In the absence of competition, regulators must scrutinize these expenditures to ensure against waste and extravagance. Are excessive salaries, fringe benefits, and expense accounts being paid to executives? Do advertising expenditures produce useful information or propaganda? Should Bell be allowed to contribute consumers' money to its favorite charities? "Is there a cheaper way of installing a telephone," Commissioner Johnson asks, "than sending a

---

* The rate base on which the profit is computed consists typically of the gross plant value less depreciation, but to this are often added allowances for materials and supplies, cash working capital, and plant under construction. Each of these additions is highly controversial and may represent significant windfall profits for the regulated monopoly.

man to take out the old phone one day and another man to put in an identical one in the same apartment two days later?"[5] All important questions, to be sure, but the FCC cannot answer them, for there has never been an FCC hearing examining AT&T expenses. The commission simply accepts the figures that AT&T supplies it.

The same picture emerges with AT&T's supposed $50 billion rate base. Again the issue has enormous consumer consequences. If the rate base were overvalued by $5 billion, and assuming a 7.5 percent after tax rate of return, consumers would be overcharged $750 million annually.[6] One accounting device operates to inflate the rate base by pretending that the assets depreciate more slowly than they actually do. This Bell has done. Long service lives, typically lasting twenty to seventy years, are assigned to equipment. The rationalization appears to be that the equipment will last until it physically wears out, rather than until it is replaced with newly developed, better technology.* Since the general absence of competition allows Bell to determine whether and when new technology will be introduced, the rationalization becomes a reality.[8]

Several states employ inflationary measures to value the rate base. New York Telephone's $3.5 billion rate base, revealed a General Services Administration lawyer in 1970, had been overstated by $800 million by using the "fair value" accounting method rather than the "original cost less depreciation" method. The cost of that to New York consumers was $56 million annually.[9] A further curiosity, which even AT&T now proposes to eliminate, is that the cost of turning on the telephone in an apartment when a new occupant moves in is included in the rate base (instead of being treated as an operating expense) although the price of the telephone, which AT&T has bought from itself (Western Electric), is *also* included in the rate base.[10]

---

* Depreciation is also an expense that offsets the corporate income taxes that AT&T passes on to telephone consumers through higher charges—like a regressive sales tax. Yet for rate-making purposes, AT&T uses the slow, straight-line method instead of the accelerated depreciation provisions of the 1954 Internal Revenue Code. During the period 1954–1967, AT&T's consumers were overcharged $4.2 billion because the giant monopoly failed to utilize accelerated depreciation.[7]

Some 65 percent of AT&T's net investment is the result of equipment purchases from Western Electric. Included in the prices that the wholly owned Western "charges" AT&T for equipment, and thus in the AT&T rate base, is Western's profit margin. Although Western is part of the AT&T monopoly, neither the FCC nor most state commissions regulate Western's profits or the reasonableness of its prices to AT&T. Western's 10.6 percent rate of return in 1970 would be quite modest if it faced the risks of competition. But lacking such risks, the California Supreme Court recently ruled, Western's profits should not exceed the substantially lower rate of return earned by the Bell operating companies. To the extent that Western's profits exceed a rate of return that is reasonable for the entire AT&T system as a regulated monopoly, ultimate consumers are forced to pay a rate of return (AT&T's) *on* a rate of return (Western's).[11]

Perhaps even more futile than policing all these accounting gimmicks is the fundamental objective of the regulatory enterprise: the effort to limit the rate of return while consumer demand and lack of competition guarantee a minimum profit on the rate base. This creates a powerful economic inducement for the monopolist to expand its rate base in a wasteful manner, one which would even be unprofitable to an unregulated monopolist.[12] The ways to accomplish this result are limited only by the ingenuity of the regulated monopolist. In addition to slow depreciation and lax procurement practices, AT&T can enlarge its rate base by (1) setting excessively high standards of performance, quality, and reliability, which pleases regulators and consumers who are unaware of the increased rates entailed; (2) building in excess capacity; (3) choosing more capital-intensive technology than necessary; and (4) owning equipment, vehicles, and buildings when leasing would be less costly.

Consider, for example, the Bell System's positions with respect to satellite communications. In the early 1960s AT&T championed the random-orbital technology that would have required a much larger capital investment (more satellites and more expensive ground stations) than the synchronous technology developed by Hughes Aircraft.[13] Later, AT&T vigorously sought to participate as an owner of ground stations, objecting to the alternative of leasing more satellite circuits for international communications unless a special rate base insertion was included as a quid pro quo. And in 1968 AT&T persuaded the FCC to approve an addition to its rate base for construction of a fifth transatlantic cable, despite evidence that satellites were less costly.[14]

FCC Regulation

These devices to expand the rate base complicate the regulator's task. He must scrutinize not only AT&T's accounting procedures but also the economic merits of its investment decisions. Yet the FCC's only formal, public examination of AT&T's rate base and expenses took place in 1935–1939. And although widespread abuses were uncovered, even then there was no systematic attempt to evaluate AT&T's investment decisions through comparison with technological alternatives. Since 1939 the FCC has followed a policy that it euphemistically calls "continuous surveillance." Instead of holding public hearings, the commissioners and AT&T's representatives sit down together in secret sessions and conduct an ad hoc bargaining session to determine, largely on the basis of data supplied by AT&T, what rates the public will pay.

Recent history confirms that the FCC is less than eager to regulate AT&T effectively. In 1965 the commission did announce that it would conduct the first public investigation in thirty years of AT&T's rate base, expenses, and internal rate structure. But those inquiries were to take place in "Phase II," after AT&T's fair rate of return had been determined in "Phase I." It may seem odd to tell AT&T its permissible rate of profit *before* investigating the validity of how the profits are computed, but that is the FCC way.

In 1967 the commission issued an interim Phase I determination maintaining the fair rate of return at 7.0–7.5 percent. Phase II was still in limbo when in 1971 the commission granted an interim rate increase of $250 million annually in long-distance charges, an 8.15 percent return. But as the Phase I hearings concluded, AT&T held out for 9.5 percent, which translates into a $545 million annual rate increase over the previous 7.25 percent. These developments should have stiffened the commission's resolve to push forward with Phase II. The Communications Act of 1934 specifically conditions the granting of rate increases upon a full public hearing "concerning the lawfulness thereof," in which "the burden of proof to show that the increased charge . . . is just and reasonable shall be upon the carrier." Moreover, the statute provides that "the Commission shall give to the hearing and decision of such questions [as those pending under Phase II] *preference over all other questions pending before it* and decide the same as speedily as possible [emphasis added]."

In late 1971, however, the FCC did precisely the opposite of what the statute commanded: it *dropped* Phase II. Despite the seeming importance of regulating the world's largest monopoly, the agency blamed an inadequate budget —yet they had not even requested the necessary funds. In fact, the Office of Management and Budget had to insist that the FCC take more than it had requested for its Common Carrier Bureau for fiscal year 1973.[15] Chairman Dean Burch refused comment on legislation introduced by Senator Fred Harris (D.–Okla.) and the late Representative William Ryan (D.–N.Y.), after the agency threw in the towel, to provide the FCC with $2 million to proceed with Phase II.

The public outcry was more than Burch had expected. The national organization of state regulatory commissioners branded the FCC's cancellation an "atrocity." The attorney general of Pennsylvania was "at a loss" to comprehend the sudden agency abdication. Numerous congressmen expressed their indignation, echoing Senator Harris's charge that the FCC had "surrendered to bigness." Senate Communications Subcommittee Chairman John Pastore (D.–R.I.) announced hearings. Commissioner Johnson labeled his agency "a leaning tower of Jello."

A sharp protest even emanated from the Department of Defense, on behalf of all the government's executive agencies, which purchase $400 million annually in AT&T services. In Senate testimony Curtis Wagner, chief of the Pentagon's Regulatory Law Office, offered the FCC use of DOD's thirty-two hundred experienced auditors for "a full-fledged investigation" of the AT&T rate base. The very next day, however, Wagner was forced to cancel the offer. This prompted Senator Lee Metcalf (D.–Mont.) to remark that "the Secretary [of Defense] or someone of that level

must have ordered this abrupt change in policy, and again
one can only conjecture where the pressure came from.
The greatest threat to AT&T were those 3,200 auditors
going through their books."* [16]

The FCC was finally chagrined into reinstating Phase II.
Yet one can only remain suspect about its resolve and
vigor. Based on its past, the agency seems a thin reed in a
corporate gale, being swayed by forces hostile both to it
and consumer interests.

Regulation by State Commissions

FCC deficiencies seem like successes by comparison with
state utility commissions, but *only* by comparison. Jack
Newfield and Jeff Greenfield, in *A Populist Manifesto,*
point to the pervasiveness of secrecy, exclusion of public
participation, conflict of interest, and pro-utility bias at the
state level—a regulatory level affecting a rate base three
times larger than its equivalent federal jurisdiction. Typical
examples include the State Corporation Commission's refusal to disclose the monthly revenue statements of the
Chesapeake and Potomac Telephone Company to Virginia
State Senator (now Lieutenant Governor) Henry Howell;
the barring of the Massachusetts and Pennsylvania state
consumer counsels from participation in rate cases; the
ruling of the Nevada Public Service Commission that the
rate base is "a matter beyond the comprehension of most
consumers [and] for the determination at the regulatory
level by commissioners who are the sole experts in a position to be adequately informed and to pass intelligent
judgments"; and the fact that a majority of the Arkansas
legislature "have at one time or another been retained by
Arkansas Power and Light."[17] Even when permitted to
challenge utility rate increases, consumer groups and
municipalities lack the finances for agency and court
battles, while the regulated utilities, via overcharges, draw
their litigation expense checks on consumers' accounts.

---

* On behalf of Ralph Nader, the author petitioned the FCC to open
its books to public inspection so that at least consumer advocates
and other public-spirited experts could complete Phase II themselves
if the FCC could not. The offer was rejected. Instead, a staff man
telephoned to ask whether Mr. Nader would still be willing to help
if the FCC did somehow manage to obtain the additional funds to
do the job by itself.

State commissions and their national lobby, the National Association of Regulatory Utility Commissioners (NARUC), rarely challenge the Bell operating companies. This passive ideology is certain to foster massive waste and abuse in the Bell system at the local level. For example, a public interest group with meager resources, the Independent Voters of Illinois (IVI), turned up numerous questionable practices of the Illinois Bell Telephone Company. Nearly $10 million had been spent on advertising and public relations. If this level of advertising per potential customer were projected nationwide, IVI's expert testified, Illinois Bell would rank as the twelfth largest advertiser in the nation. Yet most of the advertising was aimed not at providing useful information to consumers but at purchasing their good will to make them less resistant to rate increases. This was evidenced by the grossly wasteful and inefficient manner in which the advertising monies were spent. For example, ads were aired on television to viewers who had probably already seen the same ads in a newspaper. Other television ads, suggesting that the viewer send for a copy of a free booklet, "How to Save Money on Long Distance," produced 23 responses at an advertising cost of $325 per response.

IVI also discovered that Illinois Bell purchased its gasoline with credit cards at the regular price, averaging 39 cents per gallon, rather than at the bulk volume price of 24 cents per gallon. Moreover, Illinois Bell purchased its automobiles at dealer cost plus $50, whereas the federal government, for example, purchased in fleet volume directly from the lowest bidding manufacturer at 20 percent *below* dealer cost. And instead of purchasing all of one type vehicle for a particular use, in order to save on maintenance and replacement parts, Illinois Bell attempted to spread its purchases equally among local dealers of the major auto companies—apparently hoping to win influential friends at the expense of telephone consumers. These examples are merely representative.

Even if these problems were eliminated, state commissions are consigned to failure. For the lack of resources would remain a crippling handicap; you can't herd elephants with flyswatters. The one hundred professionals in the FCC's Common Carrier Bureau may feel helpless against the enormous resources of AT&T. But consider the chief accountant of the Massachusetts Department of Public Utilities, who must supervise the examination and audit of the accounting returns filed by 14 electric, 26 gas, 6 phone, and 63 water companies, plus 88 bus and street-car lines, 816 securities brokers, 2,599 moving firms, and 15,055 truck carriers. Partially relieved of his burdens by his staff of one other accountant and a clerk, he can be confident that after twenty-two years of service he is worth every penny of his $11,752 a year salary.[18]

The Mushrooming Rate Base

Going further, how could regulators cope with the likes of AT&T *even if* regulatory resources were ample? This task would appear so vast that effective regulation would border upon government control. The regulatory commission would have to actively manage the corporation—so powerful are the economic incentives to evade regulation. As already noted, rate of return regulation actually fuels the monopolist's drive to expand its rate base. As long as the regulated monopolist is guaranteed a minimum profit on its entire rate base, it can raise the prices charged for certain services far above cost in order to subsidize below-cost pricing of services otherwise unable to pay for themselves. Providing the "cross-subsidized" services expand the rate base. The prices raised are usually those of relatively essential services for which the monopolist faces little or no competition and for which consumers have no real purchasing alternatives. The prices that are subsidized are of services that face some degree of competition, or for which there are substitutes available, or which are not so essential that many consumers cannot do without them. This tendency conflicts directly with an essential purpose of regulation: to ensure that the prices of monopolized products are geared to cost, as would be the case under competition.

AT&T's own pricing practices illustrate this pattern. While AT&T's per mile costs for long-distance calls appear to be lower on high volume, high capacity routes, its rates for any one route are based not on that route's cost but on the national average of long-distance per mile costs. For example, the rates are the same between Boonesville, Indiana, and Big Stone Gap, Virginia, and between Chicago and Saint Louis, because the distances are equal. Consequently, the least costly calls are discouraged while the most costly calls are encouraged.[19]

National rate averaging is defended as a means of alleviating urban congestion by subsidizing living costs in less populous areas. But the right to dictate broad social policies of that nature has not been delegated to either AT&T or its regulators. Nor is the policy necessarily a wise one. Efforts to revitalize the central cities are clearly discouraged when low-income urban dwellers are forced to subsidize businesses and affluent residents who have fled to the suburbs. And it is inequitable to deny city dwellers the natural advantages of bulk communications while they must suffer the natural disadvantages of urban living, such as crime and congestion.

Another way to expand the rate base is the underutilization of existing facilities. Peak telephone usage has historically been concentrated in the four or five business hours around noon; during many other time periods, however, much of the AT&T plant lies idle. Instead of adding more and more costly new capacity as the level of peak use increases, AT&T could slash rates for calls made during the idle periods. "Peak load pricing," as this strategy is called, creates an economic incentive for the peak hour caller to place his call during off-peak hours instead. AT&T did grudgingly institute lower rates for night and weekend long-distance calls, resulting in a new peak in evening residential use. But these are only token advances compared with the radically greater capacity utilization that further peak pricing moves might bring were AT&T not inclined to balk at the whole idea.

Laggard Technology

As regulated monopolists artificially expand the rate base, they also injure consumers by distorting the process of technological innovation. There is, for example, the preference for the most capital intensive technology rather than the most productive technology. With assets three times greater than annual revenues, AT&T is top-heavy with capital expansion. In 1971 the Bell System alone accounted for 20 percent of all new capital raised from stocks and bonds by American industry.[20]

Unregulated monopolists, as well, are reluctant to introduce new technology until the old is fully amortized. "Step-by-step" central office equipment, the fundamental principle behind operator-less interconnection between caller and called, was first developed in the 1890s and prevails in the Bell System today, although introduction of new step-by-step equipment was finally halted by 1970. "Cross bar switching," a more efficient, flexible, and less costly alternative was developed in Sweden in the 1930s. It has been relatively ignored by Bell which, instead of replacing step-by-step with cross bar long ago, waited until recently to mount a crash changeover to electronic switching by the year 2000—when the $30 billion investment may be obsolete due to intervening advances in computer technology. Various AT&T critics, including the Justice Department, have pointed out that unattended automatic switching was introduced by a competitor fifteen years before Bell introduced it in 1919, that unattended dial control equipment for smaller offices was introduced by independent telephone companies thirteen years before Bell began marketing it in 1927, that modern telephone handsets were in use in Europe twenty-two years before Bell introduced them in 1927, and that European systems' pay phones provided direct operator access without a dime for years while Bell insisted that such an innovation was impossible.[21]

AT&T can afford continued lethargy as long as there are no innovative competitors to lure customers away from total reliance upon the Bell System. Bell's reaction to the competition that does exist is instructive. In the early 1960s entrepreneur Thomas Carter developed and marketed a simple device called the Carterfone. When placed next to a telephone handset, it could transmit a caller's conversation to a person in a boat or vehicle equipped with a private land-mobile radio. Not having emanated from Western Electric, this equipment was a "foreign attachment" to Bell, and therefore not to be tolerated. Although the availability of the Carterfone was likely to *increase* total usage of the Bell System, AT&T jealously contended that foreign attachments, not designed by it to "fit" into its system, would cause technical interference—which was itself a rather creative argument because the Carterfone was not electrically connected to the Bell telephone at all. Happily, an unexpected 1968 FCC decision sanctioned the

Carterfone attachment. Only then did Bell reveal that it had an inexpensive interfacing device capable of eliminating most interference problems with foreign attachments.[22] And even before *Carterfone,* Bell had in 1965 authorized foreign attachments to private leased lines. There resulted a greater variety of independently produced terminal equipment for private leased lines than for the public dial network.

After *Carterfone* AT&T Chairman H. I. Romnes declared that "Since customers now have more options in using [the AT&T] network, this should further increase usage and enhance the growth of our business. . . . We want to make the connection of such equipment as easy as possible." One wonders why this wasn't so apparent to AT&T while it was fighting *Carterfone.* As usual, however, company practice belied company rhetoric. AT&T is "trying every conceivable method to prevent implementation" of the FCC's ruling, charged Ronnie Harlow, president of an independent terminal equipment company in Chicago. Independent suppliers of equipment, identical to what Bell might supply, have to secure special connecting arrangements, and the Bell charge for an interfacing device is often prohibitive. Illinois Bell's harassing tactics, Harlow alleges, include deliberately faulty installation of interfacing devices and intimidation of prospective customers by suggesting that their names will not be listed in the telephone book if they use foreign equipment. One purchaser of Harlow's touch-tone phones is being forced to pay Illinois Bell a "special charge" of $4 per line per month, although no tariff authorizing any such charge had been filed with or approved by the Illinois Commerce Commission. The commission, however, has refused to initiate any action to correct this abuse.

"Bell's approach to this rapidly diversifying market is still one of trying to be all things to all people by fencing off all communications markets from others as best it can," observes former FCC economist William H. Melody.[23] And in the absence of competition, AT&T has been pricing its telephone equipment far above cost. Consider, for example, the extension phone. At ninety cents per month rental fee for the thirteen and a half years of the phone's useful life, the customer pays $145.80 exclusive of the initial installation charge. But if the Bell System did not require that extension phones be purchased from it alone, the customer could have the phone company install a wall jack for a one-time charge of less than $10 and then purchase his own reconverted extension phone from an independent company for $10. Total price (excluding future maintenance expense): $20. In his book, *Monopoly,* Joseph Goulden comments:

> My office in the National Press Building in Washington is equipped with . . . five desk telephones . . . each with six buttons, which bring a $3.50 monthly rental charge each. The hold mechanism on each of the instruments costs another $1.50. These rentals, multiplied by every business office in the nation and by every home that has anything other than the basic telephone instrument, produce quite a pile of money for the Bell System, and therefore AT&T protects its equipment monopoly with commensurate vigor.[24]

For another bilk there is the thirty-five cents per month the phone customer is charged for an extralong cord. The charge appears separately on the first bill only, thereafter being lumped into the monthly total. After ten years the consumer has paid $42 for a piece of cord he probably could have bought at the hardware store for thirty-five cents.

Many independent competitors have been lured by *Carterfone* to enter the equipment market—only to face the threat of their prices being undercut as AT&T reduces its own equipment charges while recouping the lost revenue through increased line charges. At the same time, AT&T continues to object to foreign equipment on the basis of alleged technical interference. The FCC has only recently convened a joint federal-state board to propose technical standards for interconnecting independent equipment. Yet NARUC, representing the states, is on record as still opposing *Carterfone* in principle, which is consistent with its promonopoly ideology. And as Melody points out, it is likely that the Bell-NARUC axis can substantially delay any adoption of standards.

This scenario is quite typical of AT&T's's reaction to other forms of competition. The transmission of long-distance messages and television signals via microwave radio is a case in point. This was another technology that AT&T failed to pioneer, although it is today a principal mode of intercity communication. Only when other companies had planned to connect major cities with microwave did AT&T institute a crash program in 1946 to create a nationwide microwave relay grid. By refusing to allow Western Union and others to interconnect their microwave systems with the Bell System, AT&T had by 1950 achieved a complete monopoly over this new technology. The FCC went along, meekly but unabashedly protecting the giant utility from competitive entry.[25]

It was not until 1968 that the FCC ruled that AT&T's "promotional prices" for the television market, in effect since 1948, were below cost and being subsidized by higher rates on other services. Yet, observes Melody, "Bell's own studies . . . showed that the television transmission market was still not paying its way. Nevertheless, Bell is now about ready to propose special rate reductions for the TV service . . . because of competitive developments in domestic satellites."

In 1959, the FCC allowed petitioning corporations and other large entities to construct their own private city-to-city microwave systems—primarily for specialized data transmission rather than for voice communications. But these served only as internal company intercom systems, again because AT&T refused their interconnection with the Bell System. Then, in a surprise 1969 move, the FCC indicated its willingness to allow tiny Microwave Communications, Inc. (MCI), to construct a publicly accessible common carrier microwave system between Chicago and Saint Louis that would duplicate and compete with existing AT&T facilities. Due to a combination of factors—the specialized nature of the services MCI's system would provide, its preference for economy over extravagant service quality, and the application of AT&T's nationwide average rates to the high-volume, low-unit-cost Saint Louis–Chicago route—MCI offered rates that were *less than half of AT&T's.* [26] Which is only one more example of how competition within regulation works. Thanks to the FCC's backing, MCI is now in operation and interconnected with the Bell system. Although the MCI decision was only to be an experiment, within a year the FCC had been flooded with new applications for the construction of one-third as many microwave stations as are in the entire Bell System.

The FCC staff argued that only 2 to 4 percent of AT&T's existing business would be subject to the new competition and that, as in the Carterfone situation, by tapping formerly unmet demands for these specialized communications services, the interconnection of the new systems with the Bell System might produce a net increase in AT&T revenues. But AT&T wanted it all. Following the 1959 authorization of private microwave systems, Bell introduced a number of private line services accompanied by drastic rate reductions. A 1964 FCC investigation confirmed that AT&T was subsidizing low rates for these competitive services out of the inflated profits from its captive monopoly services in an attempt to cripple the infant microwave competitors. For example, AT&T's rate of return on TELPAK (a bulk lease service that undercut previous private line rates by 51 to 85 percent) was only 0.3 percent, while its rate of return on regular long-distance calls was over 10 percent. Although the FCC later struck down some of the less objectionable aspects of the TELPAK rates—the most discriminatory price cuts are, after ten years, still being investigated—AT&T has more recently announced new services, again with deep price reductions, in response to the MCI threat.

The demand is growing for increasingly diverse and specialized types of communications services. But the supply remains static and unresponsive, consisting of existing AT&T technology. When a competitor appears to satisfy the new demand, AT&T's first reaction is to refuse interconnection with the Bell System. Indeed, after the expiration of the Bell patents in 1893, the refusal to interconnect with competing systems was a chief AT&T weapon in monopolizing both long-distance and local telephone service. The same tactic was used against microwave and terminal equipment competitors. And when refusal to interconnect fails to drive out competition, AT&T turns belatedly to cross-subsidized predatory pricing to capture the new technology for itself. Now on the horizon is the marriage of computer and communications technologies. Computers can operate as miniature communications systems linking their customers into a private communications subsystem that would operate independently of the AT&T switching apparatus. AT&T has long recognized the threat of such middlemen by its policies against customers' sharing or reselling its circuits.[27]

The Competition Alternative?

But what is all this talk about competition with AT&T? Isn't AT&T regulated on the theory that it is a "natural monopoly," i.e., that the economies of scale that characterize its operations are so great that only one firm can occupy the market at an efficient level of output? Isn't the prevention of wasteful duplication of facilities the precise rationale of regulatory commissions in prohibiting competitive entry into natural monopoly markets? If the market is really a natural monopoly, why would competitors want to enter it anyway?

Because a substantial segment of AT&T, particularly Western Electric and the high-volume intercity transmission facilities, is *not* a natural monopoly, for two reasons: first, in its preregulation acquisition days or in its quest for rate-base expansion, AT&T monopolized potentially competitive operations (equipment manufacturing); and second, advances in technology (microwave, satellites) have opened up long-presumed natural monopoly operations to possible competition.

In fact, AT&T's monopoly status predated the onset of regulation. And as Melody observes, there was nothing "natural" about how it was acquired:

> It was built on the following: the initial Bell patents; the purchase of the patents of others; the refusal to interconnect with independent companies; the refusal to sell telephone equipment to non-Bell companies; an aggressive program of acquiring some independent companies and destroying others; an extensive public relations and propaganda campaign [according to a recent poll, consumers believe that they receive more value from the telephone industry than from any other, except electric utilities]; and finally the promotion of regulation as a substitute for the rigors of competition. Bell's behavior in its flight from competition was really not much different from that of other corporations in other fields except . . . [that] instead of being subjected to the antitrust laws, the Company was

able to crawl behind the protective shield of regulation
which it had actively recruited for many years.[28]

There are three major levels of AT&T, and competition is
feasible in each of them.

Intercity. Apart from specialized communications services demanded by government and business, microwave[29]
and satellite technologies are viable competitive alternatives
to AT&T's presumed natural monopoly over ordinary long-
distance telephone calls. Consequently, there is no longer
any justification for regulatory control over intercity communications except for those routes where the volume of
usage is insufficient to support workable competition.
Divestiture and deregulation would eliminate the present
necessity for prospective competitors to obtain FCC permission to compete.*

Equipment Manufacturing. A 1949 Justice Department
antitrust suit sought just this result—divestiture—for
Western Electric. The complaint took aim at this $5 billion
a year unnatural monopoly over telephone equipment
manufacturing, and sought to break it up into three independent competitors; the Bell System's purchasers were to
have been allocated among them through competitive bidding. In 1956, however, an obviously weak and politically
scandalous consent decree left AT&T's ownership of Western fully intact.[30] The government's relief consisted primarily of a requirement that AT&T license its patents. But
because there was no telephone equipment market in which
would-be competitors of Western could exploit those
patents, this settlement was more form than content.

The consent decree in fact left matters worse than if no
case had been filed.[31] By its terms Western agreed to
confine its talents to manufacturing telephone equipment,
largely for the Bell System, thus depriving other segments
of the communications and electronics equipment industries of a potential competitor and innovator. Also, the

---

* Even on those intercity routes that remain regulated, competitive
entry should be completely unrestricted in the event that new technology or a growing volume of calls renders competition feasible.
AT&T could still be a competitor in intercity communications but
financial separation of its regulated and unregulated operations
would prevent it from relying upon a guaranteed overall rate of
return to subsidize predatory pricing as a means of destroying its
competitors, as in the TELPAK situation.

decree's precedent forced the Justice Department to stand by and watch acquisitions by General Telephone & Telegraph, the largest non-Bell company, cement its own vertically integrated structure.[32] As late as President Lyndon Johnson's administration, the Antitrust Division was recommending that the AT&T–Western Electric case be filed again and the attorney general was ignoring such recommendations.

AT&T, of course, insists that Western's performance would deteriorate rather than improve as a result of horizontal and vertical divestiture.[33] Western's superior performance is said to be reflected in a productivity rate twice that of the private economy. But several factors are overlooked here. The productivity rates of the electrical machinery industry, and even more so of the communications industry, exceed the rates for all manufacturing by a substantial margin. The opportunity within the Bell System to exploit economies of scale, plus the fact that Bell's rate of capital investment is higher than the communications and manufacturing sectors, provide ample explanation for Western's performance in that category. AT&T's greatest period of productivity was 1899–1909, when the original Bell System fought its toughest competition ever. The present question, which the Bell System fails to answer, is whether Western would be even *more* productive if it faced competition.[34]

AT&T also argues that Western's prices to the Bell System are substantially lower than other telephone equipment manufacturers' prices. But the items to which these prices refer are selected by AT&T. The prices themselves are internal bookkeeping entries determined by AT&T, which neither allows these prices to be submitted to competitive bidding (why not, if Western is so efficient?) nor informs us of their underlying costs. It would be rather surprising if Western's prices were *not* substantially lower than the small comparison companies. Having been shut out of the Bell market, these firms have not explored the technology and cannot begin to exploit the economies of scale available to Western from its captive Bell market.[35] Incidentally, Western's price advantages are not available to the 16 percent of the population served by non-Bell telephone companies.

It is important to note just who is being foreclosed from the Bell market by its exclusive relationship with Western: the electrical equipment, electronics, aerospace, communications, and computer industries; such companies as IBM, ITT, RCA, General Electric, and Raytheon. It is also noteworthy that the technological innovations that Western had neglected—synchronous satellites, terminal equipment such as the Carterfone, microwave, and computer modems and switching—were all developed and introduced through nonvertically integrated equipment suppliers. When Western claims "low prices," one response is "low prices for what technology?"

AT&T contends that Western's manufacturing activities comprise part of the Bell System's natural monopoly—"a web of millions of intricate and complicated mechanisms . . . an ever changing and delicately balanced machine." Under this concept all parts of the Bell System coalesce into a natural monopoly whose efficiencies derive from continuous and intimate collaboration, particularly between Western and Bell Labs in applied research. It is, at the least, an argument without precedent. Economist Alfred Kahn emphasizes that

> the defense of vertical integration in this industry is almost unique in its assertion of genuine managerial and technological benefits flowing from it. Not in petroleum, steel, cement, aluminum, motion pictures, or grocery distribution, in all of which integration has been both widely prevalent and strenuously debated, have its protagonists based their arguments so directly on technological grounds.[36]

Vertical integration, especially on the scale that it takes within the Bell System, is rarely found in the telephone systems of other countries; and it has proven unnecessary in other high technology sectors such as the aircraft and nuclear power industries.[37]

Local Telephone Service. The laying of local telephone lines has generally been assumed to be a natural monopoly enterprise. Yet the original grants of exclusive monopoly franchises by local governments were largely based not on any scientific finding of natural monopoly but on the desire to lure the new industry to the area.[38] There is no reason to foreclose, especially for all time, the possibility of competing technologies for local telephone transmission. But aside from telephone cables, many aspects of local telephone service—repair and installation, for example—are clearly not natural monopolies. So again, the objective should be to divest the local telephone monopolies of their unnatural monopoly components. In addition, economic efficiency does not require that a single holding company like AT&T, or even a single operating company such as Southern Bell, own the local telephone companies in different geographic areas.

A New Regulatory Framework

The divestiture from AT&T of major intercity routes, Western Electric, and the operations of local telephone companies should make regulation more manageable and competition more feasible. Depending on divestiture actions brought by the government's antitrust authorities (or private antitrust suits) and forbidding regulators to restrict competitive entry, the impulse of regulators to expand their jurisdiction and to protect their client regulatees can be substantially frustrated. These principles should be applied not just to AT&T, but to all industries subject to rate regulation—for example, the electric power industry, which is the nation's largest with over $100 billion in assets (see chapter 7).

But for the natural monopolies that remain, so too remain the inherent difficulties with existing rate regulation—wasteful expansion of rate base, cross-subsidization, retarded or distorted innovation, and internal inefficiency absent the stimulus of competition. Even if profits are held down, the public faces rising prices, often accompanied by deteriorating service. The recent crisis in New York City is but one example. By its own admission, AT&T blundered massively in failing to foresee a substantial increase in the demand for telephone service there, even cutting back its construction program for new facilities at one point. The situation became so bad that local businessmen began taking out full-page newspaper ads telling their customers that they were still there even though unreachable by telephone. A poor business judgment of that magnitude might have resulted in a well-deserved bankruptcy for an unregulated company. The New York Telephone Company simply asked for a rate increase.*

What can be done? Government ownership has often been proposed. But there is little reason to expect that simply making Richard Nixon chairman of the board would significantly improve AT&T's economic performance. Proponents of nationalization sometimes contend that a government-owned utility could reduce its rate of return to zero and thereby benefit consumers with lower prices. But this ignores the valuable role of profits and interest in allocating a limited amount of capital among competing uses. The government cannot magically create the utility's capital investment without paying for it. Whether through interest on government bonds, government stock purchases, credit subsidies, or direct appropriations, savings for consumers from zero government profits can only be gained at the expense of taxpayers—which is truly stealing from Peter to pay Paul.

The private managers of AT&T and other regulated monopolies are not necessarily evil men. The philosophies they espouse and the manner in which they operate their enterprises are largely the product of an environment that offers them prestige, power, security, and unaccountable economic discretion. Government managers are likely to be swayed by the same conditioners. Although their policy objectives might differ from those of private managers or regulatory commissioners, government managers are just as likely to view the expansion of their industry as a precondition to accomplishing whatever their goals might be. The larger the sector under government ownership, the more the government managers (or regulators) can claim to accomplish "in the public interest."

The fundamental issue is whether government-managed

* One type of inefficiency likely to characterize regulated monopolies is employment discrimination. Because profits are guaranteed whether or not employees are hired and promoted on the basis of their proficiency, regulated monopolies can afford the temptation of a disproportionately white, male work force. Indeed, AT&T has been the subject of by far the largest government employment discrimination suit ever filed, with damages potentially exceeding $1 billion. The EEOC charged that "the Bell monolith is without doubt the largest oppressor of women workers in the United States" and termed the discriminatory treatment of blacks a "national tragedy." The suit was settled for $15 million, under two cents on the dollar of potential damages.

corporations should seek out any policy goals for "the public interest" other than the optimum economic efficiency and innovation that would flow from competition if it were feasible. The response must be negative if nationalization is urged as a substitute for ineffective regulation that itself had been conceived to simulate competitive outcomes. The necessary expansion in the size of the nationalized industry in order to accomplish noncompetitive policy goals can only be accomplished by government managers unilaterally appropriating tax moneys that consumers might have preferred to spend elsewhere.

One suspects that "public interest" will often consist of government managers preferring one class of customers over another. The favored customers may often turn out to be those with the greatest political clout. Barring that, the government's cure may unwittingly be worse than the disease, as is characteristic of so many New Deal and present regulatory measures. For example, one can imagine that the government managers, to help the poor and the average citizen, might subsidize lower charges for residential telephone service out of higher rates to businesses. Overlooked, however, would be that businesses would pass on their higher charges to consumers in the form of higher, regressive prices for goods and services. The advocates of nationalization must concede that government managers are likely to engage in these kinds of strategies with only theoretical accountability to Congress or the president for the consequences. It is preferable to rely upon more direct and less costly means for the government to promote income redistribution and similar goals: for instance, general tax and welfare policies.

The reform of the regulatory process must therefore take other directions. Two of these are full corporate disclosure and the funding of a true adversary system in which the regulators would be exposed to a variety of consumer and economists' viewpoints from which the "public interest" could be more easily discerned. These outside advocates would have the same access to AT&T's internal books and records and the same capacity to present their case to the regulatory commission and to the public as would AT&T itself.

What is needed, in addition, is a radically different approach to public utility regulation—one that completely abandons reliance upon the rate of return and rate base criteria and focuses instead upon efficiency and innovation. This would entail a new set of economic incentives. Natural monopolies would be allowed to earn unlimited profits as long as they did so only by reducing rates while not allowing quality of service to deteriorate. These rate reductions could be achieved only through greater efficiency and innovation, not through wasteful expansion of the rate base. Consumers would be in no position to complain of excessive profits accompanied by lower rates, for the present alternative has not only failed to limit profits but has also led to higher rates and often declining service quality as well.

The mechanics of the new approach might be as follows.[39] A Natural Monopoly Contracting Agency (NMCA) would be established at the federal level. This agency would take over the functions of all state and federal agencies with jurisdiction over natural monopolies (and "natural oligopolies") affecting interstate commerce. The NMCA would be part of the executive branch and headed by a presidential appointee, although its operation would be decentralized through regional directors. To eliminate the inadequate resources problem, the NMCA would be self-financing through "user taxes" on all regulated corporations.

In contrast to the vast discretionary powers of existing regulatory agencies, the functions of the NMCA would be relatively ministerial. It would negotiate ten-year contracts for natural monopoly services. These contracts would contain two important elements: the maximum rates that could be charged for each natural monopoly service and the levels of quality that would have to be maintained for each type of service.

A third new feature is that there would be competitive bidding at contract negotiation time. The bidders would include the utility presently providing the natural monopoly services, other utilities or private corporations who think that they can offer a contract more advantageous to consumers, and a number of government-owned Federal Public Utility Corporations (FPUCs). The latter, while obtaining their equity capital from the government, would operate just as private corporations do: being chartered, raising capital, being sued, dealing with labor unions, and earning a reasonable profit for their (governmental) stock-holders. The FPUCs would function as yardsticks to en-sure that the NMCA's efforts to contract for the lowest possible rates were not thwarted by the inefficiency, re-tarded innovation, or collusion of the private bidders.

The NMCA and the various bidders would negotiate for contract rates without reference to a rate base. Instead, a "sliding scale" would provide for a maximum profit per unit sold at the maximum contract rate. Only as rates went down (on account of increased efficiency and innovation) would the company's allowed profit per unit go up.[40] The contract would specify a ceiling price for each service pro-vided by the same utility, in order to prevent cross-subsidi-zation, although peak load pricing could be built into the contract formula.

The rates would be adjusted during the period of the contract by a negotiated inflation factor that would vary according to the nature of the utility. For some utilities, such as a telephone company, the Cost of Living Index might suffice. But for other utilities, whose major operating costs are related to fuel costs, a different adjustment would be appropriate. In any case, the inflation adjustment should be less than 100 percent of the cost increase, perhaps 95 percent, in order to encourage hard bargaining in procure-ment by the regulated firm.

It is important that each rate be tied to a negotiated grade of service quality that must be maintained during the contract period. Otherwise, the regulated monopoly can lower its rates and increase its profits by allowing quality to deteriorate. To ensure compliance, every contract would set up a standard, statistically valid random sampling pro-cedure for testing the grade of service provided. For example, the factors tested would include, in the case of an electric power company, maintenance of the required volt-age and frequency, and in the case of a telephone com-pany, the length of time it takes to get a dial tone and what percentage of calls to nonbusy numbers do not get through. Predetermined fines would be automatically levied in amounts sufficient to make it prohibitively expensive for a utility to allow its service quality to fall below contract specifications.

Suppose that the existing utility is outbid by a private corporation or a FPUC. How does the new company take over the operations of the old? Each existing contract would contain a "buy back" provision by which the utility agreed, if its contract was not renewed, to sell its assets to the NMCA for transfer to the successful bidder at book value plus a negotiated factor representing good-will and reflecting the "going concern" status of the company. If a utility went bankrupt during the contract period, the guaranteed price in the "buy back" provision would not apply; the assets would simply be sold to the highest bidder willing to undertake the contract obligation. The geographic boundaries separating independently owned local telephone companies (and other local utility monopolies) would be defined to correspond with the minimum efficient scale of operations. This would facilitate entry into the bidding process by as many outside companies as possible.*

Finally, the statute creating this structure would set forth criteria to be applied in evaluating contract bids. Private citizens would be afforded the right to sue the NMCA for failure to award the contract to the bid most favorable to consumers—and to recover attorney fees, litigation costs, and a cash "incentive bonus" if the private suit was successful.

These proposals should prove far less complex and costly than the imbroglios of tariff, rate, and rate base determinations—which now mire regulation in archaic and unproductive ways. At the same time, they should help achieve what present practice discourages: efficiency and innovation. After over a half-century of unsuccessful utility regulation and dominance by AT&T, it is time to consider new approaches.

* Note that the higher profits available to natural monopolies under the proposed system are justified not only as rewards for efficiency, innovation, and lower rates, but also because periodic competitive bidding would provide a definite risk of business failure. Note also, in particular, that AT&T's arguments for "collaborative efficiency" as justifying its ownership of Western Electric now have even less force. For the new procedures would create strong economic incentives for the surviving natural monopoly portions of AT&T to seek out collaborative arrangements with equipment manufacturers, to press for (instead of against) interconnection agreements with competing carriers, and to promulgate reliable but cost-effective technical standards for repair and maintenance contractors and for independent terminal equipment suppliers in order to meet its own NMCA grade of service requirements.

TRANSPORTATION

4

On Troubled Waters: Subsidies, Cartels, and the Maritime Commission

HOWARD SAXNER

You do not revitalize an industry by flooding it with Federal dollars and imprisoning it within a wall of protection.
— Alan Boyd, Secretary of Transportation,
   before the Senate Commerce Committee
   in May, 1967

Subsidies for the American Merchant Marine

The clipper ship splashing ahead under billowed sail, the tramp steamer hoisting netfuls of American goods onto bustling foreign docks, the tramper braving enemy submarines in the North Atlantic during World War II—all represent our seagoing heritage. But the merchant marine also enjoys a less romantic and less publicized tradition: dependency upon government protectionism. Since subsidization of the fleet began in 1845, Congress has continually expanded the protections which shelter carriers from the workings of competition. To offset the industry's inefficiency, the government presently gives money to the industry to build ships, buy ships, operate ships, and retire ships. Congress also bestows unprecedented privileges upon carriers, in the form of tax advantages, monopolies on cargo, industry-wide research and development programs, exemptions from antitrust laws, and a government agency that usually acts as an industry lobbyist.

To catch a glimpse of the beneficiaries of our protectionism, one need only venture to the nearest Great Lakes port and watch encrusted hulks struggle in their way for just one more cargo. In the foreign trades, about three-fourths of our ships are over twenty years old. The 650 or so ships in the American fleet have watched their share of the world's commerce fall from 39 percent in 1950 to 5.6 percent in 1970. As a result, even old line shipping families appear anxious to abandon ship. United States Lines, recipient of over half a billion dollars in subsidies over the last three decades, recently went on the trading block for $65 million. The American Export firm is rumored to be $100 million in debt, with its stock plummeting from $70 to $5 per share. The subsidy program, according to a former Department of Transportation official who worked on maritime affairs for six years, has been "like pouring money down a drain."

The hard fortunes of the maritime industry have generated continuing pleas from labor and management for further economic protections. Presidents Kennedy, Johnson, and Nixon have all dutifully made campaign promises to formulate a new national policy. Only Nixon managed to enact a program, largely by allowing the industry to draft its own legislation. Consulting with labor and management on each phase of the legislation and relaying all interest-group vetoes to drafters of the legislation, the government formulated a program that satisfied the unions, management, the promotional agency, the president, and Congress. In contrast, LBJ's Secretary of Transportation, Alan Boyd, wrote in a private memorandum to his president on June 20, 1967, that one option was to "continue to seek full consensus from shipbuilders and unions. In my view, this is obtainable only by capitulation on major reform."[1]

Because the shipping industry lacks the "sex appeal" of an industry with direct effect upon passengers or consumers, and because the threat of foreign competitors provides a convenient justification for subsidies, the purposes of our maritime program have rarely been scrutinized. The defenses of the subsidies—providing for national security, strengthening our balance of payments, sustaining American jobs, and insuring the carriage of American cargo— have a certain ring of authority. When repeated for twenty years by Washington lobbyists and the Maritime Administrator, such slogans begin to take on the force of gospel. But piercing the veil of patriotic rationalizations, one uncovers a welter of economic and political mischief.

SUBSIDIES FOR SHIPBUILDERS

Under the Nixon program, the government currently pays shipyards up to 39 percent of the cost of building a ship. This sum represents the difference in costs between American and foreign ship builders. It goes largely to underwrite the inefficient American shipyard worker, who is one-half as productive as his foreign counterpart.[2] This government contribution, coupled with tax policies enabling some shipyards to amortize their investments over ten years and earn a 15 percent return on investment, has lured conglomerates such as Litton and Tenneco into the industry.[3] They stand to gain much from the current administration's plan to build three hundred new ships in the next decade; during this time the cost of the shipbuilding subsidy to the federal government will be $4 billion.

What justifications are offered for this public presence in private enterprise? First, proponents of the subsidy argue that by subsidizing commercial shipbuilding the U.S. keeps shipyards open in case they should be needed in a national emergency. But Navy and Coast Guard construction already make the United States the leading builder of ships in the world. Compared with nearly $3 billion in Navy and Coast Guard contracts, the subsidy of $400 million or so per year does little to purchase shipyard readiness.[4] A Department of Transportation memorandum of spring, 1967, concluded that "the private shipyard industry does not stand or fall on marginal changes made in the merchant ship construction program." Indeed, government business constitutes almost 90 percent of America's total shipyard business, and employs nearly 85 percent of all shipyard workers. One former planner for the Maritime Administration estimated that stopping shipbuilding subsidies entirely would drive "maybe one company" from business. A January 10, 1972, *New York Times* editorial asserted that "there is no compelling reason from the standpoint of national defense for using scarce funds to prop up this ailing industry."

Nor do the shipbuilding subsidies go for merchant ships that could be modified to help the Navy in time of war. It was only *after* committing itself to a program of subsidization that the Nixon administration undertook a thorough investigation of the nation's security needs. Moreover, as an official of the Department of Transportation explained in a personal interview, "the monster ships are not much good for defense . . . none of the new program ships could be used as an auxiliary of the Navy." In effect, commercial and defense needs no longer overlap. The Department of Defense wants small, mobile ships; commerce requires behemoth, specialized containerships and supertankers—and that is what rolls off the American shipyards and into the fleet.

Advocates of the subsidy also cite statistics on the balance of payments "savings" resulting from domestic shipbuilding. Certainly, construction at home rather than purchase abroad would, on its face, aid the balance of payments. But the program, viewed in its entirety, makes little sense. The same ship that costs $1 to build in a Japanese yard will cost nearly $2 to build in an American yard. Through the subsidy, the government pays 39 percent of this $2, or 78 cents, to keep American carriers from spending $1 in a Japanese yard. Bob Thorpe, an assistant to Nicholas Johnson, the former maritime administrator, bristled at this policy: "You don't spend $10 million to save $12 million. It's ridiculous."

If the government is interested in improving our trade and payments balance, expenditures in areas of comparative American economic advantage (such as sophisticated electronic equipment), rather than in areas of comparative American disadvantage (such as shipbuilding), would reap more balance of payments advantages and stimulate the international specialization of labor that ultimately benefits everyone. In addition, whatever the small savings which do occur, these subsidies inflict a larger economic and social cost. A subsidy is by definition a misallocation of resources. By pouring money into an inefficient industry that cannot otherwise compete, the government saddles more efficient sectors of the economy with the burden of supporting shipping.

A final defense of the construction subsidy focuses upon the jobs created by the industry. Although perhaps politically expedient, government subsidies to private enterprise contradict in principle the role of government in a free enterprise system. But even on practical grounds, government involvement lacks justification. Subsidies appear somewhat attractive in studies showing that each $1 million of shipbuilding creates one year of employment for forty-three shipyard workers and sixty-seven manufacturing employees.[5] This translates into government assistance of around $9,000 per shipyard worker per year, and almost $4,000 per year for every job created throughout the economy by shipbuilding subsidies. Small wonder that Alan Boyd, in an internal memorandum for President Johnson on April 8, 1967, commented that the shipbuilding subsidy was "an expensive way of providing jobs. The investment of these funds in other Federal programs would be much more productive in creating employment." Payments of $400 million a year to protect the jobs of around twenty thousand shipyard workers dependent on subsidized construction (or $20,000 per worker) is neither good business, good economics, nor good government.

The subsidization of ship construction also entails hidden public costs. To create a captive market for the ship builder's product, the government's operating subsidy program requires that ships flying the American flag must be American built, thus saddling U.S. shipping lines with more expensive ships. In addition, the government has paid much of the cost of shipbuilding labor, thereby lessening the builder's incentive to cut costs through automation or more efficient use of the work force. Perhaps as a result of this protectionism, shipbuilding payrolls in the late 1960s ran a high 40 to 50 percent of the value of the finished product.[6]

The requirement that U.S.-flag ships be purchased from American builders has stifled expansion of the fleet in a number of ways. Because of costly government imposed building standards, efficiency alone cannot reduce American ship prices to the level of a foreign builder. Consequently, American carriers forced to purchase domestically face the choice of paying higher prices for their ships or not expanding their fleet. In addition, according to Joe Curran, president of the National Maritime Union, "American shipyards have more than they can handle of Navy work and repair. Merchant ship construction in American yards now is subject to long delays."[7] These delays threaten to keep the American fleet from its best hope for survival, a speedy adjustment to changing shipping conditions. In recent years, the containership has replaced the slow loading by hoist of cargo with the highly automated loading by cranes of crated cargo. By requiring less labor and more capital, containerships substantially reduce, if not eliminate, the competitive disadvantages of the American carriers.

But such developments threaten to leave the Americans waiting at the docks. One American carrier ordered a new ship from an American yard in 1967, only to wait over three years for delivery. In ordering a second ship, the company forfeited its right to an operating subsidy by going to a Japanese yard, which produced the ship in fifteen months. American carriers seeking to modernize their fleets thus face the dilemma of foregoing subsidization by purchasing abroad or remaining eligible for the operating subsidy by ordering through the slower American yards.

Given this lagging productivity of the American shipyards, what can be said of the Nixon proposal to increase domestic building from ten to thirty ships a year? Many of our allies earn foreign exchange through exportation of shipping services. For instance, shipping constitutes 40 percent of Norway's exports. Such countries may take any measures necessary, including expansion of their own subsidies, to retain their share of the world's carriage. If so, America may have little cargo to carry on its new ships— unless the government guarantees U.S.-flag carriers yet more cargo.[8]

It is not clear that a thirty-ship program benefits anyone other than the ship builders. Explaining the Johnson administration's support of this proposal, Alan Boyd wrote the president on August 16, 1967, that "the reason for a program as large as thirty ships per year arose from a desire to buy industry and labor acceptance of the major policy reform of foreign construction [eliminating the requirement that U.S.-flag ships be U.S. built]. . . . A much smaller program would meet all national needs. Shultze, McNamara, and I agree on this."

An alternative does exist. The government can rid itself of the albatross of subsidization by freeing American carriers to purchase ships abroad. American operators can then renew and expand their fleets, passing on the savings and generated income to exporters and the public. To minimize potential economic dislocation, the government can offer reemployment programs and maintain a level of shipbuilding commensurate with defense needs. Such advances constituted the heart of the reform measures that President Johnson brought forward in 1968—all in a losing gamble.

The attempt began with Lyndon Johnson's election promise to create a fresh maritime program. In the wake of this commitment, the Interagency Maritime Task Force undertook an examination of maritime policy. It recommended, among other things, that the government permit foreign building when defense needs, via domestic construction, had been satisfied. According to an early 1967 Cabinet Committee report, a proposed program based on the Interagency report "would meet national security needs at the lowest direct cost to the Federal Government and includes most of the policy objectives being sought by the administration. However: it would be unacceptable to maritime labor, to most of industry management, and to Congress."

Nicholas Johnson, at that time maritime administrator, had tried to convince the ship operators and their unions that buying foreign would spur carrier expansion and employment. But the unions would not bite at such speculative gains. So the administration proposed the construction of thirty ships a year in American yards, after which time American operators could purchase ships abroad.

There remained one unknown variable—Paul Hall, president of the tightly organized and politically active Seafarers International Union. He had pyramided his strength by gaining the presidency of the seven-million-member Maritime Trades Department of the AFL-CIO, a coalition of forty-one unions loosely connected with the maritime industry and often dominated by the wealthy and politically active Seafarers Union. Hall, therefore, held great sway over George Meany, who in turn was influential with

President Johnson. In addition, the administration feared that an unacceptable maritime program would precipitate an alliance between maritime labor and the Republicans in the 1968 election—a fear reflected in several Department of Transportation memorandums on the subject.

But Hall had committed himself to a maritime program that included provisions for thirty American-built ships, no foreign shipbuilding, and the removal of the Maritime Administration from the Department of Commerce.[9] As explained in a 1967 memorandum for Johnson adviser Joe Califano, the "key problem is how Paul Hall can find a basis for publicly moving away from opposition to construction abroad by U.S. operators." Hall's struggle for an independent Maritime Administration had driven him into an alliance with the shipbuilding unions and management, who adamantly opposed the administration's plan to permit foreign construction. Thus, the program hinged on Hall, whose decision in turn hinged on the internal politics of the AFL-CIO. Boyd summed up the situation for Hubert Humphrey in April, 1967. "Without their [Hall and the Seafarers Union] acquiescence, the AFL-CIO Maritime Trades Department will oppose any program which the President transmits to the Congress that contains foreign construction. Without the foreign construction provision, I cannot advise the President to go ahead with this program." The infighting continued. Finally, on August 16, 1967, Boyd sent word to the president: "We met with Paul Hall this afternoon; *he will not accept foreign construction* [emphasis in original]." Boyd continued, "The issue is entirely political."

The Johnson administration faced the decision of withdrawing its foreign construction measure and obtaining passage of the remainder of the bill, withdrawing the measure entirely, or pressing on. The program had won over nearly 80 percent of the shipping unions, including Joe Curran's National Maritime Union, as well as several of the newer shipbuilding companies, such as General Dynamics and Litton. More important, the administration realized that, in the words of one of Boyd's assistants, "a program without foreign construction will underwrite Paul Hall as major arbiter on maritime policy, in spite of the fact that he has been the primary opponent of reform."[10] Nevertheless, President Johnson, preoccupied with the

Vietnam war and unwilling to incur another political battle, decided to withdraw the measure. In contrast, the proposal of the Nixon administration called for 30 ships, without provision for foreign construction.

SUBSIDIES FOR SHIP OPERATORS

Beyond the ship*building* subsidy, which goes to protect American shipyards, the government offers ship-*operating* subsidies: tax deferred earnings, and monopolies on government cargoes to operators of American-flag vessels. Former Senator Stephen Young, in a speech to the Maritime Trades Department of the AFL-CIO on July 10, 1968, complained that "we have made the entire industry a captive, not of subsidies, but to the concept of subsidies, and in the process we have stifled private initiative throughout the maritime fleet." Although every subsidized line maintains a lobbyist in Washington, only one company in recent years has supported its own research department, and even that effort folded. Containerships, the most significant development in shipping, arose from innovations by trucking magnate Malcomb McLean in running his unsubsidized shipping line. Protectionism, then, can undermine the very competitive vigor that the government supposedly seeks to instill.

The operating subsidy. The principal transfusion is injected by the operating subsidy. It works on the same parity principle as the construction subsidy, granting American operators an amount equal to the difference between domestic and foreign labor and insurance costs. Consequently, the government pays around 70 percent of a ship's labor costs, or nearly $700,000 per ship per year. For example, Lykes Gulf-Orient in 1969 received $1 in subsidies for every seventy-four cents of revenue earned.[11] In return for this investment, the government requires the subsidized carrier to set up a replacement fund for its ships and to operate the ships on specific routes, within a prescribed maximum and minimum of sailings. For such privileges, and the security of a merchant marine, Americans will pay about $1.8 billion in operating subsidies over the coming decade.

The operating subsidy has encouraged the carriers to use labor-intensive ships, rather than more efficient, automated ships, because the government foots much of the bill for labor. So shipping avoided a capital-intensive structure, unlike most American industries seeking to compete internationally. Perhaps this explains the assessment of one Department of Transportation planner in an interview that "the industry is rife with featherbedding." If unions fight for forty-eight men on a ship, instead of twenty-eight, the present program gives carriers little incentive to resist their demands.

Until recently, the same principle led the carriers to accede to ever-rising wage demands by the unions. Government payments enabled the unions to get through subsidization what they could not get through the market. Between 1965 and 1967, the industry's employment costs rose 30 percent.[12] In part, these raises stemmed from the "me too" clauses in each maritime union's contract, by which a union could reopen its contract if any other maritime union received a more favorable settlement. And each reopening and resettlement meant higher government payments. Although recent reforms set a ceiling on the government's percentage contribution, the salaries of the seafarers will reflect neither their productivity nor their bargaining strength, but only their allotted share of the subsidy.

Prominent among the many restrictions coupled to the operating subsidy is the requirement that subsidized operators stick to an allotted trade route, within a minimum and maximum number of sailings. If a carrier desires to service another trade route, he must make a showing to the Maritime Administration of a transportation need. Because such a showing requires a hearing that may take years, the requirement creates a barrier to entry for carriers seeking to service new areas, particularly when established lines use the hearings to block the entrance of a newcomer onto the route. Department of Defense Working Papers of June, 1968, note that "because of the rigidity, the system acts as a device whereby a large portion of U.S. government cargoes is parcelled out among the subsidized lines, i.e., each operator is virtually guaranteed the government business on his route." This rigidity stifles the American carriers' responsiveness to market changes. An inquiry into ocean freight rates by the Joint Economic Committee, chaired by Senator Paul Douglas, found one subsidy contract requiring 150 sailings per year between Venezuela and North Atlantic ports. Although trade with Venezuela dropped 58 percent after the contract was negotiated, the contract was not changed.[13]

The tax reserve fund. Perhaps the greatest gift given to ship operators is the tax reserve fund, by which operators place a set portion of their profits into a ship replacement fund, tax deferred. Money from this fund—if going toward the purchase of new ships or meeting waiver requirements —escapes all taxation. The *New York Times* complained in 1970 that "at a time when the administration has re-pealed the 7 per cent investment tax credit for other indus-tries, shipping firms are permitted, in effect, to have a 100 per cent investment tax credit."[14] By fulfilling waiver requirements, Lykes Lines recently pulled out $35 million at tax rates under 30 percent, and Grace Lines withdrew $10 million, tax-free.

As a steamship company representative stated in a per-sonal interview, "taxes are the things that the boys have been hiding." Carriers can depreciate their full share of the ships, although the government, as part of the replacement program, has repurchased the ships since World War II at an average of 66 percent of their original value.[15] In addi-tion, government financing programs enable ship operators to buy new ships while paying as little as 12.5 percent of the purchase price with their own funds (the rest is bor-rowed from the government at very low interest rates). Finally, one tax-deferred dollar may effectively equal two earned dollars in terms of future earning power.[16] As a result, a lawyer representing several carriers placed the subsidized carriers' average tax rate at slightly above 20 percent, compared with the corporate tax rate of 48 per-cent. As of December, 1968, subsidized carriers possessed a net worth of $896 million, of which $403 million, or 45 percent, came from taxes saved since 1943. Of the United States Lines' total ship equity of $64 million in 1968, $60 million, or 94 percent, arose from tax savings.[17] Neverthe-less, the Nixon bill extended a modified version of the reserve fund to segments of the industry that had not previously enjoyed it. Senator John Williams cast the only dissenting vote, protesting that the bill "exempts a whole industry from taxes with one sweep."[18]

Cargo preference. Because payments for operating ex-penses and unprecedented tax breaks have not sufficiently protected the American fleet against its own inefficiencies, the government has offered further protections. The most prominent of these, cargo preference, reserves government-generated cargo for U.S.-flag ships. American carriers by law must carry all Department of Defense shipments and 50 percent of all foreign aid and subsidized food export shipments. Except for the Department of Defense carriage, the government pays "premium rates" that run well above the world market prices. For example, Lykes Lines in 1970 carried rice from the Gulf of Mexico to Vietnam at a price of $42 per ton, compared with the world rate of $23 per ton.[19] The Department of Defense Working Papers from June, 1968, estimate that cargo preference could cost the government an *additional* $1.3 billion in the next ten years.

The profitability of cargo preference has often protected inefficient tramp steamers, many of whom can no longer receive an operating subsidy. The government pledge to pay "fair and reasonable" rates has even been stretched to provide a reasonable rate of return for World War II ships, characterized by smallness, slowness, excessive maintenance costs, and exorbitant manpower requirements. Wheat hauled from the Pacific Northwest to Korea, for example, costs the government $21 per ton, compared with a foreign-flag rate of $8.25 per ton. In 1964, the four major unsubsidized lines, in the outbound trade, earned only $35 million in commercial carriage, while obtaining $128 million from government cargoes.[20] Returning home, many of these ships found it more profitable to return quickly empty than to compete with foreign ships for inbound cargo.[21] Thus, cargo preference has kept alive many valueless ships that offer no competitive leverage and little basis for revitalizing the fleet.

Even carriers receiving an operating subsidy may use their subsidy to compete, not with foreign lines, but with American unsubsidized carriers for the carriage of government cargo. The Lykes Gulf-Orient line in 1969 received an operating subsidy of $11,248,000, given in order that Lykes could compete with foreign liners on that route. Yet 94 percent of its export business came from cargo preference carriage.[22] American Mail Lines, recipient of $8.3 million in subsidies for 1969, carried 984 tons of commercial cargo and 118,215 tons of cargo preference on its outbound run to Korea. Such carriage contradicts the requirement of the Merchant Marine Act of 1936, which established the subsidy program, that "no such [operating subsidy] application shall be approved unless . . . required to meet foreign flag competition."

Cargo preference has also taught developing nations a lesson in protectionism. Following the American model, Brazil and several other South American countries have tried to promote their own merchant marines by imposing limits on the amount of their exports that foreign vessels may carry. So far, the American carriers and the Maritime Administration have endorsed such "bilateral agreements," which undermine competition and contradict the four-hundred-year-old tradition of freedom of the seas.

Fringe subsidies. As the final concessions, the government provides health care for seamen, virtually all of the industry's research and development work, and merchant marine training programs, at a ten-year cost of approximately $200 million. Additionally, by the Jones Act, Congress created a monopoly for American-flag ships in the domestic and intercoastal (between Hawaii, Alaska, Puerto Rico, and the mainland) trades. The use of more costly American ships will add another $2.4 billion onto the merchant marine price tag for the coming decade,[23] which indirectly compels impoverished Puerto Ricans to bear a disproportionate burden of support. Such subsidization, coupled with the costs of the operating subsidy, tax breaks, and cargo preference, means that the government in the next decade may contribute almost $6 billion to privately owned lines in addition to the $4 billion given to privately owned shipyards to operate in what has been termed the free enterprise system.

In endorsing this complex scheme of subsidization, Congresses have debated only the levels of assistance or the effectiveness of a particular subsidy. But in focusing on the methods rather than the objectives of support, Congress and the American public have bypassed the question of whether America should be in the shipping business at all, and if so, for what purposes. As a Department of Transportation economist asked, "What do we need a merchant marine *for,* anyway?"

For many proponents, the United State merchant marine offers self-reliance in time of international conflict. Should

a major conflagration break out, however, our NATO
allies, representing the majority of the world's seagoing
powers, would give the United States access to the world's
largest combined fleet. If necessary, the United States can
also seize the ships in its ports and territorial waters, providing it with an immediate collection of perhaps one-half
of the world's vessels. The United States can also call upon
the sizable flotilla of ships owned by American companies
or their affiliates, but registered under foreign flags. As
then Secretary of Defense Robert McNamara wrote Joe
Curran on June 16, 1967, "In a full scale national emergency, we believe 'effective U.S. controlled' ships will be as
available to DOD as U.S. flag ships."

In less than a total conflagration, cargo preference laws
prevent the Department of Defense from using foreign
shipping except in unique circumstances. Nevertheless, the
Department of Defense Working Papers assert that "when
we have been forced to turn to this market, there have
aways been enough foreign flag ships offered to meet our
needs." In the early days of the Vietnam war, a request for
dry cargo carriage netted 39 more positive responses from
foreign carriers than from American carriers. Shortly before the 1967 Arab-Israeli War, a Department of Defense
solicitation for tankers produced 138 foreign offers, although the government could use only 6.[24]

In contrast, U.S.-flag carriers often irritated the Department of Defense with their slowness to respond to American needs. Secretary McNamara complained to Joe Curran
that "the U.S. operators, primarily the subsidized operators,
have preferred to remain in the commercial trades." Additionally, "shipping American" has meant exorbitant prices
for the carriage of government cargo. When chartering its
own ships, the Department of Defense paid an average of
$52 per ton. When hiring United States liners, the Depart-
ment of Defense paid an average of $70 per ton.[25] Despite
competitive bidding, American liners have charged more
than the world rate for carrying United States military
cargoes. Although the military may need an auxiliary fleet,
then, little evidence exists that the U.S.-flag ships have
provided it any better or any cheaper than alternative
means.[26]

To augment the plea for defense, maritime interests have
recently conjured up the ghost of Soviet supremacy of the

seas. Yet our needs for cargo carriage have little to do with matching the Russians commercial ship for commercial ship. Moreover, the U.S.S.R.'s fleet of slow and small ships stands at about 5 percent of the world's fleet, far below the sum total of NATO. The Department of Defense papers flatly assert that "the Soviet Union's merchant fleet is not now, nor will it ever become a threat to our commerce or the dominant force in world shipping."

To justify subsidies for carriers, the industry also points to the economic value of the merchant marine. But the government pays ship owners as much as $1 in subsidies to generate $1 of foreign exchange, and contributes roughly *$7,000 per year* for each seafarer's job.[27] Yet American-flag carriers do not promote our commerce any more effectively than their foreign counterparts. Following the shipping axiom that "shipping follows and does not lead trade,"[28] American lines have rarely built up trade routes or protected smaller ports. According to the Department of Defense Working Papers, the smaller United States ports are predominantly serviced by foreign-flag carriers. Less than 7.5 percent of the voyages undertaken by American subsidized operators touch ports not served by foreign-flag lines. Nor have American operators kept down the commercial shipping rates. Many U.S.-flag operators in the competitive trades have joined international shipping cartels, which generally charge what the traffic will bear. Weighing this and the other economic arguments, economist Allen Ferguson concluded in *The Economic Value of the U.S. Merchant Marine* that "there appears to be little net economic contribution to the U.S. by the subsidized liner firms or deriving from the subsidy program."[29]

GUARDIANS OF THE MARITIME FIEFDOM

Although the public may have been unaware of the fallacies underlying our commitment to the merchant marine, those familiar with the industry should have known better. Why have they not acted?

Most prominently, Congress should closely scrutinize subsidy expenditures. But in 1970 the appropriation of the House Merchant Marine and Fisheries Committee exceeded the administration's budget request by $124.3 million. Yet not one member protested. According to Jerry Landauer, writing in the *Washington Monthly,* ten of the thirteen congressmen who spoke in favor of the appropriation receive regular campaign contributions from the Seafarers International Union.[30] In addition, many congressmen enjoy not only the usual mailing privileges, fundraising barbecues, and doorbell ringing that mark SIU campaigns, but also the honorariums of $1,000 or so for reading an SIU-prepared speech at events such as the regular "SIU breakfasts." In a recent twelve-month period, the Maritime Trades Department awarded fifty-five such honorariums.[31]

The Seafarers' generosity becomes even more evident around election time. For example, Landauer reported that in the first three months of 1968, each of six committees working for the reelection of Senator Warren Magnuson received a check for $5,000. It was after a similar contribution of $28,000 to the GOP Congressional Campaign Committee that Gerald Ford, at a July, 1968, Seafarers' banquet promised that there would be no Republican foreign shipbuilding program. Such devices enabled the Seafarers Union to obtain maximum political mileage from its 1968 campaign kitty of $1,028,458.[32]

The steamship companies complement the SIU's lobbying for higher subsidies.[33] In fact, American President Lines and Pacific Far East Lines, recipients of $43 million in subsidies in 1968, were recently fined the maximum penalty of $50,000 under the Corrupt Practices Act, for illegal campaign contributions. Their tactics were wonderfully simple; as one of the lobbyists explained, "I'd have a Congressman to lunch and present him with a contribution."[34] In like fashion, Albert Bonner, the former chairman of the House Merchant Marine Committee, often boasted that he rarely lost when playing gin rummy with several steamship company vice-presidents. His successor, Ed Garmatz, raised a 1968 campaign fund of $37,000, although running unopposed in both the primary and the election. Ninety percent of his contributions came from "shipping donations" or "maritime receptions."[35]

Attendance at industry receptions indicated the broad-based coalition of maritime interests. One $50-a-ticket affair was attended by the chairwoman of the Federal Maritime Commission, the number two man in the Maritime Administration, Seafarers' officials, executives from shipping companies, a former shipping lobbyist now serving on the House Committee, and a Coast Guard admiral.[36] These diversified representatives, rather than countering each other, have collaborated in support of escalating subsidies for the American fleet. The *New York Times* commented that President Nixon's subsidy program "is regarded as another triumph not only for labor, but also for the coalition of disparate but tightly allied interests in ship construction and seagoing operations, both labor and management"[37] as well as the maritime interests in government.

Congress also created a federal agency, the Maritime Administration, to dole out subsidies and to promote the privately owned merchant marine. Broadly interpreting this mandate, the Maritime Administrator has generally been quite responsive to industry suggestions for shoring up the fleet. When Hoyt Haddock, executive director of the AFL-CIO Maritime Committee, said, "We won't get the cargo unless the Maritime Administrator gets off his keester and goes after some bilateral trade agreements with other nations," Andy Gibson, the former maritime administrator, responded, "We will have bilaterals in the North Atlantic by the end of the year, if the Justice Department doesn't stop them, and in the Pacific within 18 months."[38] When the maritime administrator decided that a merger of the country's two largest containership lines would benefit the fleet, he applied great pressure to the Maritime Commission (a separate regulatory agency, which oversees anti-competitive agreements) to give cursory approval to this overtly monopolistic scheme. Gibson has even lobbied for legislation that would overturn the Supreme Court's holding against El Paso Natural Gas, in return for El Paso's promise to build its tankers in American yards—with American subsidies. Immersed in a world of shipping lobbyists, the maritime administration has viewed promotion of the fleet in terms of industry demands, rather than a healthy, competitive fleet, or the best interests of the nation.

Regardless of the consequences, the coalition of maritime interests clamors for more. George Hearn, a Maritime Commissioner, recently wrote: "Congress has confirmed as recently as last year that a strong and modern merchant marine is vital to the country. Efforts to achieve this goal will be wasted, however, if there is insufficient potential cargo to warrant investment by operators in new ship construction or if the new ships are without cargo."[39] Under this pretext, Hearn urged economic incentives for "shipping American." To insure cargo for the ships, Paul Hall and others have advocated more bilateral agreements or an expansion of cargo preference to 75 percent of American carriage. To make more money on cargoes that they do carry, carriers, aided by the maritime administrator and the chairman of the Maritime Commission, have begun a campaign to overturn the Department of Defense's policy of requiring competitive bidding from shippers. Finally, as the *National Journal* reported in July, 1971, "Maritime Administration officials say they are concerned about the impact on the industry of proposed Navy plans to acquire up to 10 new cargo ships. They believe that while the U.S. is building up its commercial tonnage, U.S. flag ships will need all the military cargo they can get."[40] Thus, the "Port of Washington," as Nicholas Johnson called the maritime lobby, continues to seek shelter from government, rather than face the competitive challenges of the market.

To stop this upward spiral of protectionism, the government must determine the size and type of commercial fleet that the U.S. needs in relation to the amount that the government is willing to invest. Ideally, the provision of shipping services should be left to market forces. But if the political facts of life should call for subsidization, the visible and quantifiable operating subsidy, with its direct payouts, seems to be the best means of support. At the same time, elimination of cargo preference would force inefficient, subsidy-dependent operators to meet competitive standards or get out. To further slow the bleeding of the American taxpayer, Congress should eliminate all the special reserve funds, tax breaks, and other forms of covert monetary transfusions that artificially buoy up our fleet. If America must pay for its merchant marine, it should know the cost. To protect those harmed by the termination of other forms of assistance, the government should permit all U.S.-flag operators, including tramp steamers, to enjoy the direct aid.[41] The redrawn subsidy program should also include incentives for innovation and automation, as well as freedom to respond to market conditions.[42] The philosophy of dependency and politics of expediency should no longer dictate our maritime policy.

International Shipping Cartels and the Federal Maritime Commission

All subsidized U.S.-flag carriers belong to shipping conferences, in which regularly scheduled American and foreign liners servicing a particular trade route came together to fix rates and, less frequently, to divide the revenues or the number of sailings on the route. Government funds that supposedly insure a competitive fleet thus go to ships that have agreed with foreign lines to limit competition. More importantly, through the control of rates, conferences may determine life and death for an American company, raise or lower American exports, and nurture or smother international commerce and specialization. In other words, the flow of American commerce rests in the hands of an international cartel.

CONGRESS AND CONFERENCES

The legislators who bestowed their benediction upon the conference system foresaw its dangers. But they apparently feared more the effects of ocean-going competition. By permitting conferences, they hoped to stabilize rates, fix sailing schedules, spread the costs of serving undesirable locations, end cutthroat competition that might drive American companies from the seas, and prevent carriers from discriminating against smaller shippers. In so doing, Congress overruled a Supreme Court holding that "the defendants were common carriers and it was their duty to compete, not combine."[43] With the Shipping Act of 1916, Congress sanctioned the anticompetitive international shipping cartel.

Congress permitted an end to competition only after satisfying itself that regulation could offer sufficient protection to American shippers and carriers. As the Alexander Commission of 1914 concluded, "The Commission believes that the disadvantages and abuses connected with steamship agreements and conferences as now conducted are inherent, and can only be eliminated by effective government control."[44] So the government, by the same Shipping Act of 1916, conditioned the grant of conference antitrust immunity upon approval of rates and agreements by the predecessor to the Federal Maritime Commission (FMC).

Although styling the regulation after the Interstate Commerce Commission, Congress could not provide the public with the protections it supposedly offered against the railroads. Rather, it stumbled upon the paradox of one nation attempting to control international trade unilaterally. Because shipping takes place between two countries and often involves foreign ships, how could the Federal Maritime Commission presume to tightly regulate the world's freight rates? Congress thus settled for a system of regulation that, while mollifying internationalists, offered the Maritime Commission fewer powers than any other federal regulatory agency. Congress denied the FMC the power to certify carriers, set reasonable rates, or suspend tariffs filed with the commission. In fact, a major thrust of the regulation centered around the conferences policing themselves. According to the 1965 report of the Joint Economic Committee, "Steamship conferences receive antitrust immunity if approved by the F.M.C. In the few instances where Congress permits monopolistic practices, it has imposed controls designed to approximate the conditions of free competition. Shipping is the exception."[45]

The regulatory framework suffers from international limitations and internal inconsistencies. For example, the commission has little power to obtain records or documents from foreign companies. Many European governments have seconded England's policy of forbidding their liners to obey American information requirements. Without such information, the commission cannot effectively look into the costs or profits of foreign companies; yet the statute envisions inquiry into carrier rates. As Senator Claire Engel of California said in a 1961 debate on the maritime program, "We provide that if any conference establishes a system of rates which is discriminatory, unfair, against the public interest, or detrimental to the U.S. commerce, the Federal Maritime Commission will disapprove of that conference. So the conference must work within the framework of reasonable rates and reasonable procedures."[46]

The commission similarly possesses no express mandate to consider its impact upon the allocation of the nation's overall resources or upon international relations, despite the potential domestic and international consequences of maritime regulation. For instance, the Shipping Act empowers the FMC to close American ports to foreign liners not complying with its regulations. But how does the commission balance the use of this remedy (even if it were inclined to use it) against the international hostility and retaliation that such actions might evoke? The legislation also permits conference members to pool all of their revenues and sailings and then apportion them according to a set formula. Such a "pooling agreement" lessens the incentive to carry more cargo, thereby ending the service competition also envisioned by the Shipping Act.

The unwillingness of Congress to provide the commission with an effective regulatory scheme reveals itself in the legislative history of the 1961 amendments to the Shipping Act. In 1958 the Supreme Court in effect outlawed a device known as a dual rate contract by which shippers pledging all of their transportation business to the conference would receive a reduction of up to 15 percent in their freight rates.[47] By tying shippers to a conference, the members hoped to discourage the use of independent liners. The court decision came about despite a rate war apparently staged by the carriers to show the ill effects of terminating the dual rate. An investigation of the ocean freight industry by House Representative Emanuel Celler's House Committee on the Judiciary revealed that during the so-called rate war, the Pacific Far East Line realized a 19.8 percent return.[48] The justification for the dual rate, then, did not lie in economic terms.

Failing to sway the court, the carriers organized a dual rate lobby. They carefully hid the interest of the foreign companies in order to make the potential beneficiaries appear to be the American companies. Donald Webster became the lobby's secretary, treasurer, and chief lobbyist.[49] After the House of Representatives passed a tough bill containing close checks on the use of the dual rate, however, Webster turned up as the chief counsel of the Senate Merchant Marine Committee. In that capacity, he took charge of drafting the final dual rate legislation, which effectively undermined the House version.

During the ensuing hearings, Webster and Senator Engel of California ignored testimony such as Chairman Clarence Morse's that "I personally feel and believe that the purpose and intent of a dual rate system is to drive out non-conference competition."[50] Instead, they sought to legalize a system having much the same effect as the deferred rebate outlawed in 1916.[51] Only Estes Kefauver protested: "H.R. 6775, if enacted as it now stands, will so inflate the power of steamship and conference lines that U.S. shippers and exporters, independent steamship operators, and the foreign commerce of the United States will be at the mercy of the conference system."[52] In the face of intensive industry lobbying, Congress chose to support Webster and the steamship companies.

But the conference system has not worked well. Because of the carriers' rebating techniques, neither the commission nor the conferences themselves can adequately police conference agreements on rates. As a result, the deferred rebate is as alive as it was when outlawed in 1916. A major rate war plagued the North Atlantic throughout the late 1960s and early 1970s, and threatens to break out again. Thus, although the Shipping Act envisions conferences as a means of handling overcapacity on a route, the appearance of overtonnaging has often led to rate wars and rebating.[53] These occurrences tarnish the myths of rate stability and protection of small shippers.

By setting rates high enough to protect their most inefficient members, conferences reduce the incentive to innovate and, hence, productivity lags. Perhaps this explains why an outsider introduced containerships, employing them first on the conference-free Puerto Rican run. Conferences also set tariffs according to their monopoly power against shippers, rather than by the free play of supply and demand. According to one estimate, the economic waste arising from such distortions of the market may run as high as $2 to $3.5 billion a year.[54]

European and foreign interests reap the greatest benefits from the conference system. The "rate umbrella" of high tariffs, often set to protect high-cost American operators, provides lower-cost foreign liners with hefty profits; these, in turn, provide funds and incentives for foreign expansion, damaging U.S. carriers in the long run. Additionally, foreign liners in conference meetings have been known to vote as a bloc against American liners and American shippers[55] —to the detriment of United States commerce. Foreign liners also appear to gain the most from rebating and malpractices.[56] To the extent that our tolerance of the conference system represents a hidden subsidy to support American carriers, a direct subsidy would save most of the expense borne by the American public, in the form of high rates, from going to foreign liners.

Through its failure, the conference system encourages further protectionism. The distorted profits of the conference members lure more entrants into the business than market forces would permit. When overtonnaging results, carriers swoop down on Congress and the Maritime Commission seeking pooling agreements, expanded cargo preference, mergers, and the like. But such measures, although favored by government officials because they provide a short-term solution, further remove the industry from the market pressures that stimulate productivity and responsiveness to demand.

THE COMMISSION: REGULATION? DIALOGUE? PROMOTION?

The abuses of the conference system stem in part from a lack of regulation by the Federal Maritime Commission. In the view of the Joint Economic Committee, "failure to enforce the law for 50 years has established that which Congress sought to outlaw. Neither the protection of free competition in the market place nor the protection of government regulation has been provided the public."[57]

Despite international limitations and statutory ambiguities, as noted above, Congress gave the commission what the Celler Committee termed "a veritable arsenal of weapons." Yet the commission has failed to exercise its full regulatory powers, backing away from the gray areas of its regulatory authority. Internationally, it has avoided disputes by approving bilateral agreements, refraining from even attempting to obtain information from foreign lines, exempting foreign lines from restrictions such as President Nixon's price hike guidelines, and refusing to disapprove conference rates. Domestically, it has rejected any regulation that might burden the struggling American fleet, approving mergers, pooling agreements, and other types of anticompetitive schemes. The commissioners fear that a part of its regulated industry may go under, as reflected in the statement of its present managing director that "we don't like Penn Central situations." So the FMC has chosen a narrow framework and minimal standards for its regulation.

The complexities of maritime regulation call for forceful handling by skillful regulators. But in appointing commissioners, presidents have often yielded to an industry veto. Consequently, the present commissioners on this quasi-judicial body on maritime affairs bring little legal and less economic background to their jobs. The chairman of the commissioners, Helen Bentley, was a proindustry newspaperwoman for the *Baltimore Sun*. She holds a reputation for colorful language and personal involvement. Displaying this enthusiasm, Mrs. Bentley recently disregarded the Hatch Act in advising officials of shipping companies that Vice-President Agnew would like to see C. Stanley Blair elected governor of Maryland and suggesting that they "help in any way they could."[58] As for the other commissioners, James Day, a friend of Senator Margaret Chase Smith, was a public relations man for the American Legion in Maine. James Fanseen practiced law very briefly before becoming police commissioner in Baltimore. George Hearn practiced law in New York before being hired as an assistant to a Civil Aeronautics Board member. Finally, Ashton Barrett, a longtime friend of Senator James Eastland, ran a dry cleaning establishment in Mississippi. Clarence Morse, with the dual virtue of being both a lawyer and a maritime specialist, was recently appointed. Morse was chairman of the old Federal Maritime Board, whose regulatory diligence sparked Rep. Celler to fume, "The chair would be less than candid if he did not state that this record of regulatory neglect by the FMB is unparalleled."[59]

Plagued by its fear of international ramifications and its own limitations, the commission has settled comfortably into the role of an ombudsman. The handling of complaints has thus captured much of the commission's attention. As Helen Bentley noted, "It's very difficult for us to go out . . . and get information. We almost have to wait for complaints." Many of the commissioners have adopted George Hearn's image of the commission as the "cop on the beat," intervening between squabbling contestants. As an adjunct of this ombudsman role, the FMC has often substituted jawboning for formal regulation. Aaron Reese, the managing director, commented that "we engage in a lot of dialogue."

Chairwoman Bentley has similarly expressed pride in her "open door" policy, which brings countless industry representatives to the commissioners' doors. In contrast, the commissioners have rarely consulted with the Antitrust Division of the Justice Department or the Department of Transportation, except when forced to communicate about a pending case. This steady flow of industry officials to the FMC seems to blur the lines between the regulators and the regulated. One officer in the agreements section of the commission admitted to the author that much of his information about conference activities came from industry cocktail parties. Former Commissioner James Fanseen, however, felt that his duty to regulate required him to "try to keep as far away as I can" from the carriers.

In recent years, the commissioners have exhibited a promotional side of their work. They have traveled to Hawaii, Japan, England, and across the country, to give speeches usually focusing upon the health of the American fleet, rather than the regulation of shipping. Ex-Commissioner Fanseen, however, noted: "We sit here as an international court. I can't wave the flag and have the Germans feel that they are getting a fair shake." Translating promotional talk into action, Mrs. Bentley encouraged North Atlantic carriers engaged in a rate war to collaborate on an anticompetitive agreement, and took an active hand in seeking to overturn Department of Defense competitive bidding. One lawyer for several steamship companies felt that such activity placed her "in competition with the maritime administrator to see who can do more for the American fleet."

The conflicting roles of the commissioners reflect their lack of a regulatory philosophy. James Day and his assistant stressed that "the watchword of our regulation is fairness." George Hearn emphasized that "we want to land our commerce on foreign lands." Commissioner Barrett felt that "the major problem is to keep our ships sailing." Robert Hope, the "confidential assistant to the chairman," commented: "We were created to grant exemption from the antitrust laws to shipping. That was and is the only reason for our existence."[60] Apparently, the commissioners have failed to sort out either those parties most in need of protection or those areas requiring the closest scrutiny. The watchword of the commission's regulation may be aimlessness.

Commission scrutiny of agreements. The same disabilities that keep the commission from setting goals also keep it from erecting guidelines for carrier agreements.[61] As the Douglas Committee warned, "In the absence of general standards based on national policy, the tendency becomes irresistible to permit what was on the one hand adroitly advocated by special interests and on the other hand was not condemned under articulated guidelines."[62] The FMC has often interpreted its ambiguous test of a "serious transportation need" in light of the industry's needs, rather than the primacy of the market.[63]

Reflecting the commission's tolerance of anticompetitive schemes, Helen Bentley and Robert Hope have actively participated in discussions by North Atlantic carriers seeking a pooling agreement. Although Chairwoman Bentley denies any intent other than to "put some teeth" into the conference's self-policing, one participant in the discussions felt that "in effect, she was saying, 'fix rates.' " According to the chairwoman, who must eventually pass on any agreement made by the carriers, the pooling discussions are a "good concrete step."[64]

But a pooling agreement, by limiting the share that each company can obtain, kills much intraconference competition. The agreement therefore conflicts with both the protections envisioned by the Shipping Act and the intent of the American subsidy program to foster competition between American and foreign carriers. As a former maritime official described it, "Pooling agreements are bald efforts to substitute monopoly for competition."[65] According to a lawyer for several independents, the institution of a pooling agreement on the "WINAC" route (between Italy and the U.S.) drove freight rates up nearly 200 percent. An attorney for a North Atlantic carrier claimed that "it isn't any worse than the Bell system." That, of course, is the problem.

The FMC has similarly approved blatantly anticompetitive bilateral trade agreements, such as the recent dividing up of 80 percent of Brazil's trade between United States and Brazilian carriers. Not only does the agreement curtail freedom of the seas and cripple the economic position of countries earning foreign exchange from such trade, but it also virtually guarantees higher rates between the United States and Brazil. In accepting lessened competition, the commission no doubt sought to avoid the international stress that might accompany its disapproval of the agreement. But a lawyer representing one of the involved American companies confessed that American, not Brazilian, liners had conceived of the plan and used foreign liners to pressure the commission into accepting the agreements.

The commission has also ignored the anticompetitive effects of mergers. In 1961, it approved the merger of American Export and Isbrandtsen Lines, one of the largest consolidation transactions in the industry's history. By that merger, three groups owned 134 of 420 American liners, with the eight largest carriers owning 79 percent of the American liner fleet.[66] Later, only the courts prevented the commission from approving the merger—before the actual merger had even been filed—of American President Lines, Mail Lines, and Pacific Far East Lines. Finally, the commission in 1972 approved a consolidation between the nation's two biggest containership operators, Sea-Land and United States Lines, possessing nearly 70 percent of the country's containership tonnage. Joint ownership of the lines was sanctioned by the FMC—although five companies presently control 90 percent of America's containership capacity and near 50 percent of the world's containership fleet.

In approving anticompetitive agreements, the FMC has disregarded not only the growing concentration within the industry, but also the erosion of the protections offered by the independent liner. The Celler Report cautioned that "in the absence of control of rates by some Federal or International agency, the independent is virtually the most effective deterrent against the assessment of freight charges by the conference."[67] Even in the early 1960s, however, independents were carrying less than 1 percent of the world's traffic. Today, the tremendous capital requirements of starting a containership service, perhaps nearing $100 million, raise a nearly insuperable barrier to entry. Consequently, the number of independents and their ability to respond to demand by entering or exiting a trade route continues to decline.[68]

The commission professes an unswerving commitment to the principle of open entry into conferences and onto routes. But Allen Ferguson, in his study on the economic value of the merchant marine, wrote that "it is . . . not clear that the so-called free entry policy of the Maritime Commission has significantly altered entry at all."[69] In fact, although James Fanseen admitted that barriers to entry "surely exist," the commission has never inquired into the matter. But the commission recently demonstrated its attitude toward independents and low rates by seizing upon a technicality to prevent a Russian independent from entering a Pacific route at prices 10 percent below those of the conference. As for independents facing discrimination by conference members, assistant professor of law James Gordon concluded in a 1970 article that "if, as appears plain, the purpose of outlawing 'unreasonably low' rates is to protect independent carriers from predatory conference pricing, the Commission has gutted the statute."[70]

Conference rate setting and the Commission. The Shipping Act also looks to the Maritime Commission as a bulwark against rate setting abuses by the cartels. Shippers need protection against the conference because rates are set according to the cartel's power over shippers rather than by the interplay of supply and demand. The carriers give each commodity its own rate, based on many ill-defined factors having little to do with costs or space taken. Studies for the commission in the mid-1960s, conducted by its former economist Daniel Mater, showed that nearly five out of every six pricing decisions made by the cartels served to stifle, rather than foster, commerce. In fact, the only touchstone of conference rate making seems to be short-term profit. Although general rate levels have risen continuously in almost all trades, the Puerto Rican run, with no conference and close scrutiny of rates by the commission's domestic section, went ten years without a price rise. Likewise, the entrance of an independent on one trade route forced down the rates on one commodity from $80 to $40 a ton, without eliminating the carrier's profits.[71] As the president of American President Lines confessed to the Celler Committee, "It is felt by the majority of the memberlines [sic] if we did not have this agreement the present level of rates would be some 25% or more lower than they are today."[72]

Contrary to the access that shipping lobbyists have to the commission, a representative for an exporter felt that "there's no place for the little shipper to go" about high rates. The FMC's informal docket, set up to expedite the handling of shipper's complaints on smaller matters, reveals that major companies such as Exxon and Colgate-Palmolive brought nearly 80 percent of the claims; nearly every dispute centered around overcharges on the bill of lading. Although complaints usually go to the conference first, so that "many complaints never reach us," the majority of high rates and rate increases appear to be borne in silence. "No one wants to go to the commission," said a lawyer with many shipping clients. "It's a waste of time and money and red tape. When a client calls up complaining about a rate increase and asks what we can do, I tell him 'nothing.' "

The frustrations of dealing with the commission can be seen in its handling of a complaint by the Weis-Fricker Mahogany Company. This floundering company informed the commission on January 15, 1971, of a South American conference's exorbitant freight rates on lumber. Helen Bentley responded by suggesting that the company take up the matter with the conference. After informing the conference and failing to get a response, the president of the company sent a detailed letter to the FMC showing that his freight rates ranged from 17.3 to 60.6 percent of the value of his product, clearly violating the commission's own approximate guidelines that the tariff should not exceed 10 to 15 percent of the value of the product. The company also documented instances in which the carriers refused to load previously booked cargo, in order to carry more profitable coffee cargoes. Hence, the complaint pointed out not only exorbitant rates that had kept the company in the red for four years running, but also carrier discrimination against a shipper, clearly prohibited by the Shipping Act.

Ignoring the question of discrimination, the commission one month later responded that "because of the importance of this matter to you, we are again writing to the conference requesting that the matter receive prompt attention." Perhaps the agency thought that a conference transmission of March 2, stating that the conference had initiated a special conference committee to study the rate, would resolve the problem. However, four months later, on July 13, Ashton Barrett was still writing interested congressmen that "we have been informed by that conference that the matter of ocean freight rates is under active study by a designated committee." Almost concurrently, the president received a letter from the FMC's director of compliance suggesting: "If you believe the conference or any common carrier acts in violation of our shipping statutes you may, of course, initiate a formal proceeding." Finally, in September, without any objection or any attempt to disapprove the rate, the commission approved new conference rates offering no relief to the company. Rather than exercise its authority to hold a rate hearing, the commission left the company to bear the high costs of a drawn-out proceeding. The president again wrote the FMC: "The Federal Maritime Commission has a 'rule of thumb' on rates and the Head of the Conference Lines has stated in his letter that the rates were out of line and too high—yet you tell us that we should hire an attorney in order to procure lower rates. What are my taxes being paid for?"

It was therefore understandable why James Fanseen talked about the "little man" who might be "afraid to come" before the commission. First, the smaller shipper, by complaining to the commission, risks conference retaliation in the form of rate increases or an inability to find space on board a conference ship. The subtlety of the discrimination makes it impossible for the commission to protect the complaining shipper. According to Fanseen, retaliation "is not a matter for the FMC to get involved. . . . I'd like to wipe it from my vocabulary." If small shippers dare not provoke the conference, what about presenting grievances to the FMC? "They're scared to open their mouths,"[73] the president of Weis-Fricker replied.

Usually, only large shippers such as Kodak and DuPont can risk conference retaliation or afford a commission proceeding. And only large shippers can support a staff to assess the effect of conference charges upon business. But large shippers often obtain rates 5 to 10 percent below the dual rate contract rate,[74] using their high volume of freight as a bargaining lever against the carriers. Thus, those companies that need protection cannot afford it, while those companies in a position to seek relief have little incentive to do so.

Second, many small shippers have hesitated to press their complaints lest they become ensnarled in the long and costly commission proceedings. One lawyer for a steamship company termed these proceedings a "WPA for lawyers and accountants." For example, the *Sapphire* case, brought in 1965 by an independent liner charging the conference with predatory practices, still lingers on in the Maritime Administration—although the company long ago was driven out of business. In the *Consolo* case, a shipper seeking reparations went through two agency hearings, two reports by examiners, three arguments before the agency, three arguments to the Court of Appeals, and a Supreme Court review, before the company could take the case to the District Court for collection.[75] With transcript fees running eighty cents per page, the transcript alone may cost up to $10,000. In addition, lawyers often charge $75 to $100 per hour so that legal fees may outstrip even a medium-sized claim.

But high prices do not guarantee a high quality of justice before the FMC. With little legal or economic background, the commissioners often depend on the attorneys in a case to do their homework and thinking for them. Perhaps as a result, after fifty-six years of supposedly looking for unreasonable rates, the commission confessed in its Puerto Rican trade study that "there are no specific criteria for determining the reasonableness of a rate." Expediency and inexpertise loom large in determining rate cases. As a result, commission proceedings leave an aura of injudiciousness about them, while the absence of guidelines prevents the commission's isolated rate cases from having any impact on the overall level of ocean freight rates.

Unfortunately, the commission's scrutiny of conference tariffs offers the shipper little more protection than its complaint process. A former Maritime Commission official noted: "In 16 years, there have probably been no more than 10 rates that the Commission found unlawful. And on most of these, nothing moved." Of 200,000 new rates and 260,000 rate changes filed in fiscal year 1970, 22 rates were voluntarily adjusted and none were formally disapproved. Several years ago, the FMC not only allowed containership operators in the North Atlantic, operating at one-third to one-half the cost of regular liners, to quote the same tariffs as other carriers, but even upheld an additional charge of 10 percent for better service. This failure to detect exorbitant rates stems from hiring tariff filing clerks with no economic background to go through 125,000 pages of tariffs per year; they lack criteria to determine what prices are so unreasonably high as to be detrimental to American commerce. When asked by what standard a tariff might be rejected, Commissioner Barrett responded, "Say, if an independent was undercutting [the conference rate] by 50 to 60 percent." A lawyer for several conference carriers remarked that the commission "gives unlimited power to fix rates without any supervision. It's just a filing bank."

The commission possesses ample authority to review the general rate structure prevailing in each trade route and to reject any rate that it finds to be "unjustly discriminatory" or "detrimental to our foreign commerce." But this power has gone unexercised, perhaps because of the paltriness of the commission's twenty-one-man analytic staff, the smallest of any federal regulatory agency. The commission's failure may also be one of attitude. Despite the Nixon price-hike guideline ot 5.5 percent, the commission has approved tariff increases of as much as 30 percent on the North Atlantic. Such hikes, according to the *New York Times,* "will inevitably translate into increases in the *Consumer Price Index.*" On the other hand, the commission responded within a day to one carrier's demand that the FMC investigate the low rates obtained through competitive bidding by another government agency, the Military Sealift Command.

The commission *has* asserted its jurisdiction in investigating claims that conferences charge American exporters more to ship from the United States than they charge foreign competitors to ship to the United States. But after two years of inquiry by Senator Paul Douglas's Joint Economic Committee, and a multi-volumed investigation by the commission, the commission found only seven rarely used rates unlawful.[76] In recent years, the FMC has undertaken similar studies of many routes. But two years after finding sixty-two unreasonably high rates on the Far East and North Atlantic–French Atlantic trades, the commission has yet to reject formally the forty rates that have not been voluntarily altered. James Gordon concludes: "In terms of rates actually lowered, the costs of the Commission's proceedings far exceed their benefits and in terms of the regulatory doctrine developed and the results which this doctrine have thus far produced, the entire exercise has been an intellectual debacle."[77]

The Commission in Action. Unable or unwilling to tackle key conference abuses, the commission immerses itself in minor tasks that are essentially harmless. A staff of nine reads and files the minutes sent in by the conferences of their meetings. The managing director asserted that such minutes are "very carefully" scrutinized for evidence of unfiled agreements and the like—despite the fact that conferences frequently omit key matters from their minutes. The chief of the agreements office admitted that the commission does not know if the minutes are complete or honest. The FMC employs twenty-four people to file rates and fifteen people to file agreements, with no noticeable effects. The commission also hires twenty-three investigators to insure that carriers do not circumvent the tariff structure by offering cheaper prices through the mislabeling of cargo. Yet conference rebates achieve the same effect.

Looking only for the occasional outrageous abuse, the commission has piled up a regulatory record that is unsurpassed for toothlessness. "To get voluntary jurisdiction," said George Hearn, "we might round a corner here and there . . . We're not in business to make criminal penalties." Consequently, the commission has only once sought to fine a carrier for an unlawful rate or agreement by referring the case to the Justice Department for prosecution. It has never used its power to close a port to a foreign liner engaged in discriminatory practices. It has on its own initiative only once in fifty-six years attempted to formally disapprove a basic conference agreement. It has rarely disapproved of a dual rate contract for anything other than a failure to meet technical requirements. It has never made a finding of a discriminatory contract based on the volume of freight. It has used its authority to make rules and regulations to handle foreign conflicts twice since 1920. Little has changed, then, since the Celler Committee charged in 1961 that "for a period of almost 45 years, lethargy and indifference have characterized its attitude, laxity and inefficiency its procedures, and frustration and ineffectiveness its administration of the regulatory features of the Shipping Act.[78]

The commission cannot be judged entirely on its formal record. The emphasis of the FMC on informal negotiation and voluntary compliance makes it difficult to evaluate its success in regulating ocean shipping. Nevertheless, it is clear that carriers use their antitrust immunity to build huge complexes in order to drive up rates. Conferences are perforated by secret rebating that usually benefits only the large shippers. Conferences ignore commission requests for rate reductions. In the words of the chairman of a North Atlantic conference, "Our ability to make a buck or our being forced to lose a buck, by and large is not determined by the FMC."[79] President Nixon's injunction—"you cannot have jawboning that is effective, without teeth"—has apparently gone unheeded at the Federal Maritime Commission. As a result, commission activity offers only the pretense of regulation, while collective monopolies continue to dictate world freight rates.

Alternatives to Dialogue. The failures of the commission point up the need to reexamine the conference system. According to a drafter of the 1961 legislation, "There could scarcely have been a worse condition if there had been no Shipping Act at all." Without cartels, America may face oligopolistic abuses, international tensions, and heightened protectionism. But these risks threaten to become realities under the conference system anyway. On the other hand, the advent of containerships offers the United States a fresh opportunity to experiment with competition by withdrawing American liners from the conferences, perhaps on one or two routes at a time, and revoking the cartels' antitrust immunity.

Competition will more closely adjust carrier supply to shippers' demands than will a system of regulated rates and services. If it pays, carriers will provide regular sailings, uniform handling, service of ports, and levels of service that vary with the shippers' needs. Market conditions may also lessen discriminations between shippers based on factors other than cost savings to the carrier.[80] Shippers have successfully used tramp steamers and tankers on a supply and demand basis for years. The liner trade need not be different.

Nor will abolition of the conference system drive American ships from the seas. According to a Department of Transportation official, "The U.S. companies that are going to go out of business will go out anyway." For the new American containerships, competition imposes no hardships other than forcing them to be efficient. Antitrust protections and perhaps a modified form of regulation by the Maritime Commission could mitigate the danger of predatory practices against American lines by foreign cartels. As Ferguson writes that "there is no evidence that competition would be ruinous in a social sense . . . Although the terms 'ruinous' and 'cut-throat' are popular, they are not often defined. Some mean by them only that competition erodes or retains capital values."[81] Unsubsidized and nonconference American carriers pioneered the containership. With the skillful management and technological innovation that arise from competitive pressure, they can maintain a leading position.

If political pressures prohibit competition, however, a revitalized commission could still provide some assistance to beleaguered shippers. Congress could clarify the aims and authority of the commission, and the president could appoint competent commissioners. The commission should divert energy from superfluous tasks into economic analysis and broad-scale investigation. It should complement case by case adjudication with a search for an overview and a willingness to set standards. In this vein, the FMC should undertake an inquiry into the stifling effect of unreasonable rates upon American business, actively recruit complainants, and engage in interagency dialogue on intermodal transportation, antitrust responsibilities, and international limitations.[82] The commission should also refuse to approve bilateral agreements, agreements between conferences, and dual rate contracts that seriously erode competition, and refuse to extend antitrust immunity to mergers and intermodal transportation. Finally, the commission should seek the information on carrier costs and profits it needs to regulate intelligently. But if nothing comes of rate hearings, if complainants still do not come forth, if agency differences curtail broad approaches to problems, if small shippers cannot be protected, then either the commission must be given heightened authority or the present system of cartels and regulation must be abandoned.

The alternative consists of a never-ending escalation of international protectionism. Already the U.S. government faces demands for bilateral agreements, pooling agreements, mergers, agreements between conferences, increased shipbuilding subsidies, expanded cargo preference, an end to the Department of Defense's competitive bidding, widened operating subsidies, and broadened tax benefits. The government agencies overseeing maritime affairs appear ever willing to endorse these costly and anticompetitive schemes. They disdain antitrust while breeding noncompetitiveness and dependency on government. They ignore their mandate from the public and exaggerate their accountability to the maritime community. Consequently, the protections grow and the subsidies go up and up.

5

Railroading Antitrust at the ICC

DAVID HEMENWAY

The Interstate Commerce Commission, the oldest federal regulatory agency, was born in 1887 at a time when the railroads held a virtual monopoly on the intercity movement of passengers and freight in the United States. Public dissatisfaction with the railroads probably stemmed less from high monopolistic rates than from the uneven rates caused in part by "cutthroat competition" in this high-fixed-cost industry. Thus the railroads, rather than protest the creation of the ICC, gave it their support and blessing. They hoped the commission could stabilize rates by successfully cartelizing an industry where private attempts had previously failed.[1]

The transportation picture has changed sharply in the last eighty years, with improved water transport and the increasing importance of automobiles, airplanes, and trucks. Although the nineteenth century rationale for regulation has become largely obsolete, the lawyer-dominated commission has remained true to its original purposes, i.e., the stability of the system rather than the welfare of society. It is illustrative that Antitrust Division personnel unanimously regard this commission as the unmatched worst of all government agencies in terms of antitrust sensitivity.

The focus of this chapter is on the anticompetitive aspects of regulation by the ICC and the enormous costs such regulation imposes on consumers. The first part describes the commission and its intimate relationship with industry—a prerequisite to understanding the agency's record on antitrust and competition. The large economic losses, and the severe misallocation of resources caused by current regulatory policies, are discussed in the second section. The final portion of the chapter deals with the ICC's role in the merger wave that is dramatically, and irreversibly, reshaping the transportation industry.

The Commission

The ICC is headed by eleven commissioners, whose very numbers and rotating chairmanship are not conducive to efficient regulation. These commissioners are selected less for their knowledge and experience than their political contacts and acceptance to industry groups. The recent Nader Report on the ICC revealed that, in 1969, only three of the commissioners had had any previous experience related to transportation and only one any experience in the area of public regulation of private industry. Virtually all had significant political connections. "That," stated the report, "is the only area in which all Commissioners are similarly well qualified."[2] Industry consent is also an important criterion for selection. As *Wall Street Journal* reporter Louis M. Kohlmeier, Jr., writes: "The test of competence to which a candidate for initial appointment is subjected consists of the submission by the White House of his or her name to industry executives before sending it on to the Senate for confirmation. . . . ICC appointees [are cleared] with railroad officials, and usually truckers too."[3]

Industry also controls the future career of ICC commissioners, partly through its influence via Congress, but more importantly with the lucrative positions it can offer officials upon retirement. The Nader ICC Study compiled an illuminating list of the "fate" of the then last eleven commissioners to leave the ICC. Those not retiring to the railroad industry itself became either high-ranking railroad executives or lawyers specializing in practicing before the ICC; one became the president of the National Association of Motor Bus Operators. This movement from commission to industry is also prevalent in the middle staff levels. One recent ICC job applicant told the editor of this volume, Mark Green, that his ICC interviewer said, "Listen, I can't guarantee you'll be doing very exciting work here, but I can assure you that you'll end up with a good industry job."

In addition, industry provides the commissioners a variety of small favors on a cumulative basis. One such favor is the opportunity to travel to speak at various industry gatherings. Commissioner Virginia Mae Brown, for example, has visited her home state on nineteen separate occasions at government expense (on "official business") since fiscal year 1966. In wintry February and March, 1970, Commissioner George Stafford made successive five- and four-day trips to Hawaii to attend industry meetings. By mid-November he had already spent thirty-three days of 1970 attending or traveling to and from industry gatherings.[4] Many such official trips are paid for by the private transportation companies themselves, an assumption of expenses not conducive to impartial policy making. Commissioner Rupert Murphy, for example, seemed proud that "no more than 25 percent" of his past travel expenses had been paid by industry groups. Murphy told the *New York Times,* which exposed this situation in a front-page story, that he "never did feel too sure about it, but . . . knew it was the practice"[5]—a practice that has supposedly now been changed.

More important than the job interchange and small favors performed by industry are the pervasive informal (and even formal) commission-industry contacts, from luncheons and golf dates to industry functions and commission business. The commissioners' argument that they need extensive personal contact with industry for information-collecting purposes is not entirely persuasive, because they are seldom seen soliciting consumer views, labor or truck drivers' views, the views of small shippers, and the like. It is, in fact, this continual one-sided contact that keeps the regulator's interests in conformity with those of the businessmen he supposedly regulates.

Controversies before the ICC are resolved by means of an adversary system, with interests clearly identified. It is extraordinarily expensive to present a case, costs including attorneys' fees, witnesses' expenses, consulting fees, and printing. Even the simplest cases run into the thousands of dollars. The commission fails to provide for a consumer or public interest representative in adjudication, yet a consumer or public interest representative cannot afford to enter the ICC arena.* Nor is it often worthwhile for the shipper, whose interest in low transportation prices approximates that of the consuming public, to enter into the proceedings because transportation is not so large a part of his costs that he can afford to spend the time and money to appear before a commission already biased in favor of the carriers. With the Departments of Transportation and Justice only rarely entering the fray, the consuming public has virtually no representative. The very fact that the commission has not created formal procedural mechanisms for public representation, nor used its rule-making function to any significant degree, indicates clearly the role the ICC has chosen is servant not of consumer but of business interests.

That the commission does not make extensive use of its rule-making power (little more than 1 percent of ICC proceedings are rule-making hearings) reflects its failure to make affirmative transportation policy. One commission observer, for example, has discussed the various historic and institutional factors that have produced "a timid and unimaginative approach," and made the commission "passive, backward-looking, and resistant to change. . . . It drifts along, responding to the most urgent pressures as they arise and perpetuates, for the most part, regulatory patterns which were created in the past to meet different problems."[7] When the writer wrote eminent economists to ask which antitrust issues seemed to them most pressing, one responded by suggesting instead we intensively examine "the doddering Interstate Commerce Commission . . .

---

* While hundreds of thousands of schedules and tariffs are annually filed with the commission (270,000 in fiscal 1969), 1969 was seemingly the first time that a consumer organization had ever protested rate increases. Washington lawyer Benny Kass, a representative for the Ad Hoc Committee on Consumer Protection, a coalition of more than forty local organizations, reported his incredible difficulties to the Senate Commerce Committee in March, 1970. Xeroxing costs alone (eighty-five cents a page) were exorbitant. Kass stated, among other things: "In the absence of public counsel assigned to help consumer organizations adequately participate in rate cases, the cost of such participation is prohibitive."[6]

the tendency for regulation to become negative, protective, slow-acting and lost in legalisms. . . . [T]he Commission has had no serious proposals for the railroads' situation but that this crisis was coming has been evident for 20 years."[8] Because the ICC has jurisdiction over only a part of our transportation system, to say that it is industry oriented is not to say enough; the concern of the commission is principally with the welfare of the transportation companies that it regulates.[9] But many of its policies have not even benefited these companies, the railroads and common carrier truckers. In the first place, trucks and railroads can be quite competitive with each other, and the ICC is forced to preside over their often internecine struggles. Second, the commission is usually concerned with the "stability" of the system, and the preservation and continued short-run prosperity of *existing* businesses, to the detriment of the long-run health of the system. Thus we have the paradox of a producer-interested agency, whose policies at times hurt not only the businesses it regulates, but also the consumers it should have been created to protect.

Economic Costs of Regulation

The economic costs of present ICC regulation are vast. Economist Thomas Gale Moore, for example, has estimated that the economic losses resulting from all aspects of ICC regulation are probably not lower than $4 billion per year, and may be as high as $8.7 billion.[10] In 1966 the Council of Economic Advisors stated that if the ICC allowed "rates to be appropriately geared to costs . . . on *railroad transportation alone* savings from possible rate reductions would come to more than $400 million a year [emphasis supplied]."[11] A recent Brookings Institution study estimated the direct social losses resulting from ICC policies in regard to freight transport to be on the order of $500 million a year.[12] Because the transportation price structure enters into all production costs, the secondary effects of this misallocation are considerable. Location, production, and consumption decisions become distorted. Moreover, as was generally agreed at the Brookings conference, the dynamic costs of regulation are probably far more important than these short-run allocation losses. In particular, regulation was thought to contribute to poor investment decisions, excess capacity, and very high costs of service.[13]

Social and economic losses are incurred by the commission's various operating restrictions, such as its limitation on entry, its minimum rate control and its support of value-of-service pricing. Freed of regulation, the business of truck transportation would probably come about as close to the model of pure competition and ideal resource allocation as is possible in the real world. In 1935, however, Congress passed the Motor Carrier Act for the regulation of the young trucking industry. It was threatening the viability of the pricing structure of the once powerful railroads that had been under federal regulatory control since 1887. Following passage of the 1935 act, the ICC gave immediate approval to truck rates and classifications that closely paralleled those for the railways.

Classifications and other restrictions become commission techniques to limit both inter- and intramodal competition. As the ICC puts it: "From the beginning of federal motor carrier regulation, restrictions generally have been imposed to protect already authorized carriers from unintended and unwarranted competition. . . ."[14] Competition thus becomes a contagion to be avoided rather than a policy to be pursued. Commission restrictions are often quite stringent, and may specify the type of vehicle, point of origin, point of destination (even the specific route), area served, and particular commodity to be carried. Virtually all the regulated motor carriers are restricted in one way or another, with the commodity restrictions imposing the most significant limitation on operating authority.

The efficiency losses caused by such commission restrictions appear to be substantial. Carriers with limited commodity authority or restricted routings and delivery points are unable to fill their trucks with authorized commodities. Partially loaded trucks and empty backhauls account for a great deal of the present excess capacity in trucking. In a study of the New England transportation system, motor carriers reported that on the average 17.2 percent of total miles operated were empty in 1954.[15] Ten years later, the ICC's own unpublished Inventory of Motor Carriers confirmed the substantial underutilization of capacity, finding, for example, "that backhaul movement [retracing one's route] has not been *authorized* for 19% of grants."[16] That study also supported the proposition that the more stringent the Commission's operating restrictions, the more the likelihood of empty or partially empty hauls.

Another inefficiency imposed by ICC restrictions is unnecessary added mileage due to gateway restrictions, restricted use of interstate highways, and circuitous regular routes. For example, a carrier providing service between eastern Pennsylvania and eastern Virginia is forced to observe a gateway restriction and travel an indirect route through *western* Virginia. As a result, mileage and traveltime costs have more than doubled.[17] The reason for this patent inefficiency is clear: to prevent that carrier from winning traffic from carriers who already hold direct route authority.

These restrictions have led to higher transport costs through the imposition of unnecessary mileage, increased excess capacity, and burdensome administrative costs. Higher transportation costs mean higher prices for virtually every item the consumer purchases. Rather than follow a competitive model that produces low prices and efficient allocation, the summum bonum becomes the protection of existing and inefficient modes. The constant battle among carriers at the ICC to guarantee that potential competitors do not intrude upon their respective jurisdictional grants comprises over 70 percent of the commission case load.

The commission's direct control of entry into the industry is crucial in its attempt to limit competition. By law, in order to obtain a required certificate of "public convenience and necessity," an applicant must first show specific shipper need for its services, i.e., that existing carriers cannot provide "adequate service." The ICC's criterion for "adequate service" is whether existing carriers have enough equipment to carry the freight load. Whether the applicant can profitably provide better service at lower rates does not seem to be an important consideration. Indeed, in *Wellspeak Common Carrier Application,* the ICC held evidence that a prospective carrier could and would charge lower rates to be inadmissible as irrelevant.[18]

The ICC's various operating restrictions, combined with strict entry control and a liberal policy regarding motor carrier mergers, has led to a pronounced decrease in the number of trucking concerns.[19] As a result, the commission has increased the market power of various firms without any corresponding benefit, because "in the trucking industry the small and large firms are on a cost parity."[20] Fewness of competitors can enhance the possibilities of parallel behavior and price-fixing, leading to higher and more inflexible prices. For truckers (and railways), where there are already institutional arrangements for price-fixing —the rate bureaus—fewness decreases the possibility of deviation from these agreements not to compete. As economist James C. Nelson wrote: "With fewer and larger firms, the rate suspension and minimum rate procedures can be utilized more effectively to thwart independent action." He found that the number of rate adjustments protested (usually by other carriers) had risen markedly from 567 in 1946 to 5,170 in 1962. "The number of the protested rate adjustments involving rate decreases, i.e., protests by carriers *against rate competition,* has risen even more rapidly—from 227 in 1946 to 4,712 in 1962, or from 40% to more than *90% of the total* [emphasis supplied]."[21]

The 1948 Reed-Bulwinkle Act legalized those price-fixing agreements of the rail, water, or motor carrier rate bureaus, which the ICC thought furthered "the national transportation policy." While the act cautioned that every carrier should have the unrestrained right to take independent action, economist Walter Adams comments: "In practice, this right is little more than a sterile gesture. . . . Independent action is not to be encouraged, but tolerated— tolerated so long as it falls short of promoting genuine rate competition."[22] He further argues that not only has the ICC failed to encourage independent rate setting, but it has also taken an active role in its suppression. The net effect of this price-fixing is, of course, higher prices than would prevail under competition, and a consequent misallocation of resources. Former Assistant Attorney General Richard McLaren has estimated that unregulated motor carriers rates have been from *20 to 30 percent lower* than in markets where rates are regulated.

As detrimental as price-fixing is the type of price structure allowed and enforced by the ICC, a form of substantial price discrimination that can be roughly called "value of service pricing." This pricing describes the present pattern of commodity-based discrimination that permits low-value bulk and agricultural commodities to travel at low rates while high rates are charged for manufactured goods. The rates differ even when the *costs* of transporting these different commodities are similar. When faced only with water competition as suitable for carrying bulk items, this policy made profit-maximizing sense for the railroads. But with the subsequent development of other modes of transportation, particularly highway transport, value-of-service price discrimination found lower-cost railways losing high-value traffic to higher-cost trucks. A respected text on transportation economics concludes that "value of service rate-making . . . has, on the basis of the historical evidence, failed miserably as an allocator of transportation resources."[23]

Price-fixing and the value-of-service pricing structure serve to misallocate resources. So too does the cost concept used by the ICC to determine the low-cost carrier. There is consensus among economists that the appropriate standard for pricing is long-run marginal cost—which is the *extra* cost of transporting an *additional* unit of a commodity. The commission, however, persists in using average or fully distributed cost (marginal cost plus an allocated portion of the fixed or overhead cost). This distinction is crucial for railroads where overhead costs (traffic structures, rights-of-way, roadbeds, and the like) form a substantial portion of total cost. Marginal cost pricing accepts these costs as "sunk," which they are, and sets prices according to out-of-pocket expenses. The *additional* cost to a railroad (and thus to society) of transporting an *extra* unit of a commodity is often much less than it is to a trucker. Yet the ICC's insistence on average cost pricing often prevents the railways from carrying this traffic.

A simple example will help illustrate the problem. Assume the out-of-pocket costs of shipping an additional ton of carpets from New York to Miami by rail is $15, by truck $20. The economist would argue that the carpet should go by rail, the cheaper mode. But the ICC insists that the cost of some of the existing fixed capital be included in the calculated cost, say some $10. The railroad "cost" then becomes $25, and the additional carpet is shipped by truck, with both the railroad and society the loser.

Merton Peck sums up the problem:

> Thus, the ICC rate policy (1) denied the shipper the advantages of lower-cost transportation by rail, (2) diverted resources toward the high cost carrier, (3) added capacity to the nonrail sectors of transportation at a time when railroads had substantial excess capacity, and (4) encouraged the growth of private truckers as a way for a shipper of higher rate commodities to escape the consequences of value-of-service rate-making. Surely this is almost a prima facie case of resource misallocation.[24]

Great harm is also done to the consumer by the more dynamic effect of regulation on the transport companies themselves. "Dynamic effect" means the commission's influence on ordinary costs, on excess capacity, and on technical change. While the rigors of competition compel efficiencies, the comparative "softness" of regulation often has a stultifying effect on management. There are indications, for example, that the "ordinary costs" (e.g., line-haul costs, labor costs, costs of terminals and buildings, and sales costs) of regulated traffic are higher than they need be.[25] The argument that managerial lassitude is a cause of many of the railroads' present problems has much merit. In addition, the cost of the excess capacity caused by regulation for the railroads alone has recently been estimated to be in the neighborhood of $3 billion annually.[26]

As regards technical change, there are a number of striking examples of the ICC deliberately obstructing the introduction of cost-saving innovations. One case involved the introduction of the "Big John" grain car by the Southern Railway; it was a mammoth car, cheaper to maintain and faster to load and unload than the old boxcar. It took a long and bitter battle before Southern was allowed to let these cost savings be reflected in price, thereby enabling it to compete effectively for the growing grain shipments to the Southeast. The case was four years at the ICC, nine times in lower federal courts, and twice before the Supreme Court. The opposition to Southern included a number of barge lines and truck interests, as well as others whose interests were in keeping grain traffic patterns and privileges as they were. It took those four years, and a Supreme Court order, before Southern was able to use the "Big John" cars freely.[27] Another case of commission obstructionism involved unit coal trains. Their introduction in the East was delayed at least five years by the regulatory process.[28] A recent study on regulation and innovation concludes that the "ICC has done the poorest job of all regulatory agencies,"[29] that the desire to preserve the inherent advantage of each mode practically requires the commission to rule against any innovative activity.

While ICC regulation imposes these huge costs on society, are there any offsetting benefits? There are a very few, but they are hardly "offsetting":

(1) "Common carrier" service, service for those whom unregulated carriers might find it uneconomical to provide, is undoubtedly increased. (But it is not easy to explain why the subsidization of Westchester County, New York, commuters by shippers of freight on the Penn-Central railroad should necessarily be regarded as a good thing.) Moreover, "common carrier" service under present regulation has been far from ideal. Witness the home moving situation.[30]

(2) Decreasing rate competition may mean increasing service competition. While this may be a theoretical possibility, it does not seem valid for transportation in the United States. Economist Walter Miklius conducted a thorough study of the exempt agricultural transport and concluded that in this competitive sector, the quality of service was superior to that in the regulated sector.[31] As James C. Nelson wrote: "There is little clear evidence that the economies to shippers from regulated services justify the higher rates. Where alternatives exist, the shippers voluntarily resort to private, exempt, and gray area types of carriage."[32]

(3) Regulation can avoid the chaotic conditions of excessive competition. In the motor carrier industry, however, fears of "chaotic conditions" appear ungrounded. The Miklius study concluded that "the available evidence from the competitive sector [agricultural transport], conclusions of studies, foreign evidence with non-regulated trucking [Canada and Australia] are all inconsistent with the hypothesis of 'excessive competition.' "[33] No study contradicts Miklius's findings. R. N. Farmer, using figures from a study of exempt agricultural traffic in the three-state area around Washington, D.C., similarly concluded that the exempt industry is not excessively unstable.[34] In its 1972 report, the Council of Economic Advisors asserts that "there is little danger that competition, once established,

could not remain viable." Furthermore, regulation has not eliminated the fly-by-night operators; indeed, high regulated rates probably encourage their entrance.

Why then does the ICC persist in its present regulatory policies? Most critics agree it is because the agency is "timid," "unimaginative," and "backward looking." This in turn is largely due to the fact that the ICC is not primarily concerned with promoting efficient operations, but apparently sees the protection of existing carriers as its true raison d'être. Any major policy shift would undoubtedly be severely detrimental to many common carriers, some dependent on the present perverse structure for their very existence. The ICC acts as if it prefers to do great harm to the nebulous and impotent consumer than inflict visible injury on any of its vocal and fraternal clientele.

The evidence leads one to argue for deregulation: an end to minimum and maximum rate control, an end to commodity and geographic restrictions on truckers, and an end to ICC entry control. Such, indeed, is the recommendation of a recent report by economist George Hilton prepared for the Council of Economic Advisors.[35] Because many people are dependent on the present distorted transportation structure, regulation should perhaps be phased out rather than abruptly abandoned.

We would conclude along with Hilton, Fellmeth, and Meyer that elimination of rate-bureau price-fixing for the railroads would prove beneficial to society. It is doubtful that price discrimination and excess capacity would be as great in a more competitive environment. For motor transport, there are a number of indications that substantial deregulation (there should still be minimum insurance and safety standards) would be equally cost saving and price reducing. The Miklius study, for example, found not only that competitive rates were generally lower than regulated rates, but that the competitive rate structure seemed to be patterned more closely to the cost of providing services. Department of Agriculture studies also documented a substantial price drop in several agricultural commodities when deregulated, as well as a significant increase when the same commodities were placed back under regulation.

The case for substantial deregulation is quite strong, as are some of its new backers. The Council of Economic

Advisors and former Antitrust Division chief Richard Mc-Laren have publicly urged the deregulation of surface transportation. The *Wall Street Journal* and even *Fortune* editorially approve, and former Transportation Secretary John Volpe was known to be sympathetic. Yet the prospects for reform are uncertain. In the early sixties a proposal by President Kennedy himself for a modest move toward transportation deregulation was soundly defeated. But given the poor performance of the ICC as a substitute for the market mechanism, and given the even worse record of railroads in this country, the commission must place greater reliance on the free marketplace and less on detailed restrictions. As the Council of Economic Advisors argues: "A policy of permitting and encouraging competition of all kinds would, if general economic experience is any guide, make the industry more efficient as well as benefit the public."[36]

Mergers and Competition

The most important development in American transportation in the past fifteen years has been the profound reorganization of the railroad industry. The recent railway merger movement is significant because it is largely irreversible, rapidly closing out the major policy options, and increasingly making the discussion of deregulation academic.

Railroad mergers require ICC approval, and this approval provides near immunity from antitrust prosecution. Some of the most scathing criticism of the commission's role in the recent merger movement has been its passive attitude toward mergers, its lack of any plan to assure a coordinated national system, its adamant refusal to consider mergers on other than a case-by-case basis. The commission argues that merger proposals must be started by the carriers, and that it "can't give a single case national consideration."[37] (After all, the Penn-Central merger only accounted for 51 percent of the assets, 50 percent of the trackage, 52 percent of the operating revenues, 75 percent of the revenue passenger miles, and almost 53 percent of the railroad employees in the eastern United States.)

Justices Brennan and Douglas have criticized this restrictive interpretation of the 1940 Transportation Act.

Brennan, for example, has written: "[T]he agency has wide latitude in fashioning procedures and a broad power to condition its approval of proposals. In other words, the ICC is not the prisoner of the parties' submissions."[38] A recent Ph.D. dissertation has concluded: "An examination of the consolidation decisions rendered by the Commission discloses adequate reason for serious doubt that the current manner of dealing with railroad consolidations will produce results consistent with the public interest. The major problems apparently arise from the practice of the case-by-case approach and the practice of making decisions from limited data."[39] The "limited data" refers principally to the fact that the commission restricts decisions solely to an evaluation of the data placed before it by the carriers! It is therefore not surprising that between 1957 and 1967 the commission approved twenty-nine of the thirty-four principal railroad mergers it considered.

The ICC's abnegation of its planning functions, combined with its narrow case-by-case approach, are especially serious because the commission itself is the principal representative of the public interest in merger proceedings. And, as usual, its thinking is industry oriented. The Justice Department, in its exceptions to the *Northern Lines* merger, stated, in remarkably strong terms: "The affidavits disclose a shocking, extreme, and undisciplined personal bias in favor of the merger." While the examiner's attitude toward the public was "clearly hostile and impatient, [he] betrayed] a dismaying gullibility" to the applicant's presentation. "This basic attitude—that industry sponsored witnesses are all-knowing and wise and that others are naive or ill-informed—most certainly account for the examiner's unfair conduct of the hearing. . . . The public trust was not given to the Commission to be handed over bodily to the carriers."[40] Justice Douglas thought that commission's action suggested "a subservience of the Commission to the railroad's estimates, the railroads' proposals, the railroads' evaluation, the railroads' prophecies of the future."[41]

The role of the Antitrust Division in railroad mergers is largely confined to appearances before the ICC to raise competitive issues. If the Justice Department is dissatisfied with the commission's determination, it can seek court review, as can other dissatisfied parties. Unlike the case of bank or natural gas pipeline mergers, however, the department is not free to bring a Section 7 Clayton Act case against a railroad merger after ICC approval.

The Antitrust Division became increasingly involved in agency proceedings in the 1960s, due principally to the recent merger wave. But the odds are overwhelmingly weighted against the division, because the ICC has "primary jurisdiction" in its area and because the division has the equivalent of two or three full-time attorneys concerned with ICC actions. The ICC sees the division as being "obsessed with the antitrust laws," according to the legal assistant of an ICC commissioner. The commission's limitation on discovery rights concerning carrier-alleged labor savings in the *Northern Lines* case aptly illustrates this hostility. The merger, originally turned down, was being reconsidered on the basis of a claim by the railroads that substantial cost saving would accrue to them if the merger were allowed. The Antitrust Division argued that a study was necessary to determine whether many of the savings in labor costs cited would have occurred *anyway* with advancing technology. The ICC gave the division an imminent deadline, then refused to compel the railroads to cooperate when the companies claimed not to possess a complete list of *their own employees*. The division fortuitously obtained such a "nonexistent" list from a different source, and primary investigations revealed that much of the claimed merger savings had already been realized by the firms operating separately. The Antitrust Division then filed an affidavit in the ICC claiming that the agency had been given false information. The ICC never ruled on this prior to the hearing, nor even following it. The merger was, of course, approved. In fact, it is highly probable that the commission would have reversed its earlier 6–5 decision and approved the merger without any hearings had not Washington columnist Jack Anderson unearthed evidence of ex parte communications between railroad representatives and commissioners. His probes encouraged the ICC to hold a hearing, according to division section chief Joseph Saunders, in order to approve the merger formally rather than approve it sub rosa.

The Antitrust Division's attempts to influence the ICC, or the courts for that matter, have been largely ineffectual. The division opposed such important mergers as Seaboard

Air Line–Atlantic Coast Line, the Great Northern–Northern Pacific–CB&Q, the C&O-B&O (acquisition of control),
and, initially, the Penn-Central—all without success. It
earlier urged the consolidation of Eastern District Railroad
Proceedings, to no avail. Its only "victory" came in the
Western Pacific acquisition case, but that was mainly due
to the fact of conflicting railroads; both the Santa Fe and
Southern Pacific wanted to acquire the Western Pacific.
And the division did help to divest the Pennsylvania stock
interest (and include the Erie-Lackawanna) in the Norfolk
& Western–Nickel Plate–Wabash consolidation.

The railroad merger pattern actually began with the
approval of the Norfolk and Western–Virginia consolidation in 1959. A significant and subsequent case was the
Seaboard and Atlantic Coast Line merger, of which a dissenting commissioner said: "In no prior case has the
Commission destroyed so much competition with so little
justification."[42] The two most important and recent consolidations are the Penn-Central, and the Northern Lines, each
merger creating substantial monopoly power.

In the Northeast there were four major railroads before
the merger of the Pennsylvania and New York Central
railroads. They were the Pennsylvania railroad, the New
York Central, the Norfolk & Western, and the B&O-C&O.
The former two were principal competitors, with most of
the relatively unprofitable passenger service. The latter two
were also principal competitors, possessing much of the
profitable coal routes. If mergers *had* to occur in the
Northeast, a result far from proven, a more optimal
pattern would have resulted from Penn–Norfolk & Western, and New York Central–B&O-C&O consolidations,
thereby maintaining much of the intramodal competition
and distributing the profitable and unprofitable carriage
more equally. This was the preferred pattern for most
Justice Department officials, including Attorney General
Ramsey Clark, Antitrust Chief Donald Turner and Antitrust Division official Joseph Saunders.

Stuart T. Saunders, "the man behind the Penn-Central
merger," was honored with the William Penn award in
Philadelphia in 1968, and in 1969 with *Saturday Review*'s
"Businessman of the Year" title. A year earlier, upon final
approval of the merger, *Time* magazine lauded him:

It was Saunders, as chairman and chief executive of the Pennsylvania, who planned the tactics and organized the arguments that led to one of the largest mergers in corporate history. It was Saunders who held the pieces together during the frequent assaults from competitors concerned about Penn-Central power. . . . Above all, it was Saunders, the lawyer-turned-railroader, who convinced the Interstate Commerce Commission and the Justice Department that both public interest and private good would be helped if two troubled rivals were allowed to operate as a unit, instead of continuing costly and wasteful competition.[43]

Yet more realistically, as described previously in *The Closed Enterprise System,* it was Saunders who arm-twisted Attorneys General Kennedy and Katzenbach into a blatant political *compromise* of the public interest, not an affirmation of it. The administration, however, did generally favor the merger. Katzenbach told us that when Justice was opposed to the merger (a position later reversed), the department was constantly embarrassed by the official statements of other high officials, as when Vice-President Humphrey said in Philadelphia that he thought the merger was a great thing.* Later in 1967, the night the Supreme Court had upheld the ICC's decision to approve the merger, Saunders received a personal telephone call from President Johnson congratulating him on the successful merger.

It proved to be a brief and pyrrhic victory. The cost of merging the two Goliaths (Stuart Saunders estimated this at $75 million),[44] the incompatibility of their computer systems (for example, thousands of freight cars were "lost" and many were delayed), the managerial civil war, the cost of "buying the opposition," and the very fact that there were few if any substantial economies to be gained from merging—all contributed to the Penn-Central's downfall. The immediate cause of the collapse was the company's lack of liquid capital. The economic slowdown, tight

* Penn-Central's agreement to take over the ailing New Haven was crucial to assuring the support of New York and New England political leaders. The ICC used the New Haven as a major justification for approving the merger. Penn-Central, has, of course, been unable to support this declining passenger service. So the public will be stuck not only with financing the New Haven, but also with the Penn-Central bankruptcy itself.

money, a chaotic bond market, and the collapse of its commercial paper all were contributing factors. On June 21, 1970, some two and one-half years after final approval of the merger, the Penn-Central Railroad became the biggest bankrupt in American history. This huge corporation, with $4.7 billion in assets, lost over $430 million in 1970 alone. It was a failure that, to Ramsey Clark and Edwin Zimmerman (Antitrust Chief after Turner) viewing the wreckage in 1970, disproved the companies' claims of merger efficiencies.

The *Northern Lines* merger involved three western railroads: the Great Northern, the Northern Pacific, and the Chicago, Burlington & Quincy. These railways had attempted to merge a number of times, the most notable attempt some sixty years previous when the Justice Department, in the famed 1904 *Northern Securities* case, succeeded in dissolving their holding company. The Antitrust Division again opposed the consolidation in the 1960s. The second and third largest lines between Chicago and the Northwest were involved. They were relatively healthy and there was great doubt whether any "efficiencies" could offset the resultant loss of competition. We have already briefly described how the ICC first denied the merger, and then reversed itself. The division fought approval both before the ICC and the Supreme Court, without success in either forum.

The principal danger from this recent railroad merger wave is, of course, the growth of market power. The Penn-Central merger, for example, resulted in the loss of interrail competition in *thirty-two* urban areas. Even if the rate bureaus had previously been successful in eliminating all intramodal price competition, such mergers would still have harmful effects. For railroads also compete with each other in terms of service, and rivalry may spur innovation and efficiency, as well as check some forms of discrimination. Further, the irreversibility of these mergers may have eliminated those benefits for all time, as well as any possibility for future intramodal price competition between the now monopolized areas.

The major gain from these mergers were supposed cost savings for the railroads. But the railroads' postmerger performances have grossly failed to attain their premerger

claims. A recent Ph.D. dissertation by Robert E. Gallamore, now with the Department of Transportation, provides the principal evidence on this subject. Gallamore did
statistical studies on nine consolidations and concluded:

> In most circumstances there have been difficulties in
> achieving merger savings. Merger is not a panacea. The
> summary picture is that the larger, more recent, and more
> complex mergers have produced the least favorable re-
> sults. . . . The particular configuration of routes involved
> does not seem to make as much difference as the overall
> size of consolidation. . . . The overwhelming evidence is
> that size and complexity of a merger plan are the qualities
> that can lead to extra costs, rather than savings, in the
> wake of consolidation.[45]

A correlation analysis by Kent Healy for nineteen western
railroads revealed a positive relationship between smaller-
sized firms and a high rate of return. In other words, there
were indications that diseconomies resulted from size
above a certain level.[46] Reviewing this evidence, a staff
study by the Department of Transportation argued: "The
conclusion of the economic evidence is that the cost savings arguments for large railroad mergers have to be very
largely discounted, and must be applied to individual cases
with very great circumspection."[47]

The consensus of economic wisdom, however, has yet to
be understood or accepted by the ICC. Its indifference to
antitrust and economic studies, and its pandering to politics and powerful interests, has produced a chaotic transportation industry. A more policy-oriented, rather than ad
hoc, approach by the commission will help it recover from
its self-created status of disrepute among government attorneys and industrial economists. Substantively, widespread deregulation and more competition must be sought
out. The public benefits would be many. Gallamore emphasized that "the risks and uncertainties of mounting a
planned outcome based on competitive transcontinental
systems should be painless by comparison with the costs to
the public, and the industry, of allowing present trends to
continue."[48] These are costs that unhappily, have flowed
directly from the very reason the ICC was created in 1887:
to guarantee stability and profits for a growing railroad
industry. In a sense the ICC has been all *too* true to its

original mandate, failing to change as the conditions leading to its creation have changed. As a result, notes economist George Hilton, "So undersirable is the Interstate
Commerce Commission that virtually no one who becomes
thoroughly familiar with the body defends it, unless he has
something to gain from its existence."[49]

6

The CAB as Travel Regulator

K. G. J. PILLAI

One of the odd things about statements on civil air transport is that they very rarely talk about the customer in simple language. So let us say that in our view the primary long-term objective of a national policy towards commercial flying should be to see that each customer, be it for personal travel or freight, gets what he wants—not what somebody else thinks he ought to want—at the minimum economic price that can be contrived.
                                    —Edwards Committee Report to
                                    the British Parliament, 1969

The freedom to travel is an important aspect of a citizen's liberty, deeply rooted in the American heritage. Travel within and across frontiers may be necessary for a livelihood. It may be as important personally as what an individual eats, wears, or reads. The Supreme Court has therefore said that a citizen cannot constitutionally be deprived of his freedom of movement by the arbitrary fiat of government or any of its instrumentalities.[1] But the free exercise of the right to travel depends largely on the availability of reasonable facilities for transportation. In the

United States, the airlines are the prime mode of common carrier transportation. More than 70 percent of the domestic intercity passengers who use common carrier facilities travel by air. About 96 percent of the passengers who travel between the United States and the rest of the world use the airlines.[2] The existence of reasonable facilities for air travel is an indispensable condition for the full exercise of the right to travel, and the absence of such facilities may well constitute a deprivation of that right.

The task of fostering "adequate economical and efficient services by air carriers at reasonable charges" is entrusted to the Civil Aeronautics Board (CAB) by the Federal Aviation Act.[3] Created at the urging of the airlines in 1938, the CAB is endowed with enormous powers to shape the destiny of the American air transportation system, and, consequently, to protect the public's right to travel. Unfortunately, the CAB behaves, according to two observers, as a "far-sighted trade association operated by a group of oligopolistic carriers"[4] and as an "imperfect cartel"[5] bent upon satisfying air carriers to the detriment of the traveling public.

The Closed Air Transportation System

DOMESTIC AIR FARES

The dominant factor preventing most Americans from traveling by air is the high level of fares promoted and perpetuated by CAB regulation. Although the CAB possesses unqualified rate-making powers in domestic air transportation,[6] such powers have not been utilized to hold domestic fares to a reasonable level. Instead, the CAB has invariably followed the simple expedient of adopting carrier-made rates without the independent evaluation it is legally required to undertake. Often CAB decisions on fares have been made in ex parte meetings with representatives of the airline industry.[7] For instance, in 1969 the CAB approved a 6 percent increase in airline revenues from passenger fares. The fare increase was developed in a private meeting of CAB members and airline representatives, from which the public and certain interested congressmen were excluded. Upon review, a Federal Court of Appeals in *Moss* v. *CAB* abrogated the CAB fare determination on the ground that "the procedure used by the Board is contrary to the statutory rate-making plan in that it fences the public out of the rate-making process and tends to frustrate judicial review."[8]

The disparity between the prices of the CAB-regulated carriers and the prices of intrastate carriers that are not regulated by the CAB underscores the effects of the agency's collusive rate regulation. The prices charged by the Pacific Southwest Airlines (PSA), for example, which operates wholly within California, are considerably less than the prices charged by CAB-regulated carriers for comparable services. A coach flight from Los Angeles to San Francisco costs $16.20. The CAB-set fares for flights of equivalent distance are $33 between Chicago and Minneapolis, $34 between Cleveland and Philadelphia, and $33 between Los Angeles and Phoenix. Economist William Jordan has estimated that, based on the PSA fare between Los Angeles and San Francisco, the standard economy fare for New York–Los Angeles should be less than $81.[9] However, the present New York–Los Angeles one-way economy fare of the CAB-regulated trunk carriers is $163, or double the projected reasonable fare. That the present domestic air fares could be reduced by at least 50 percent was indicated by the unsuccessful attempt of World Airways (a certificated supplemental airline) to get CAB approval for nonstop scheduled service between the East Coast and California at a "thrift service" fare of $79.50.[10]

Pressed by the adverse decision in the *Moss* case, the CAB conducted a general domestic passenger fare investigation in early 1970 in order to set reasonable fares in accordance with the statutory rate-making standards. The board later issued a tentative decision granting "interim fare relief" on the ground "that the carriers require an increase in yield of 12 percent over the fare levels which existed on October 15, 1970."[11] The whole investigation, then, seemed a springboard to justify existing fare levels and future fare *increases*. The board merely rearranged the cost and revenue figures supplied by the airlines; it did *not* examine the reasonableness of those figures themselves. Crucial questions, such as reducing airline costs by eliminating unnecessary promotional expenses, lowering the price of air travel to attract traffic adequate to fill empty seats, and examining the effect of the misuse of airline resources for nontransportation purposes were outside the purview of the investigation.

The market response to this fare increase was striking. Domestic airline traffic went down 1.5 percent in 1970,[12] while world scheduled passenger traffic increased 11 percent in 1970. The U.S. airlines recorded a loss of $180 million in 1970, as compared with an operating profit of $989 million made in the same year by the airlines of member states of the International Civil Aviation Organization (ICAO), the highest profit in the last 10 years.[13] Since the CAB granted the massive "fare relief," the situation has deteriorated rapidly. The eleven U.S. domestic trunk airlines' load factor (the percentage of seats filled with passengers) for the year ended June 30, 1971, decreased by 2.4 percent from the load factor of the comparable period in 1970.[14] TWA reported a loss of $34.8 million in the first half of 1971, and United lost $9.4 million during the same period. In 1970, the U.S. domestic trunk and regional airlines flew 305 million seats and filled 149 million with passengers, leaving 156 million seats empty. These empty seats are equivalent to the seats of 1.1 million Boeing 707 flights for the year, or 3,098 empty flights per day.[15] The eleven domestic carriers operating on international routes flew 16.5 million passengers but had more than 14 million empty seats in 1970. The CAB should have required the airlines to reduce the price of their tickets to fill the empty seats, thereby extending the benefits of technological progress in aviation to the lower-income segments of the public. Instead the CAB, like any cartel, recently allowed the major trunk carriers to reduce the number of flights up to 30 percent in the major domestic routes. This move will encourage poor and uneconomic utilization of equipment by keeping it idle on the ground; at the same time, the reduction in the flight schedules will inconvenience the traveling public. The waste of airline resources thus continues unabated, but in a different form.

THE CAB AS A MERGER BROKER

The present malaise of the air transport industry stems mostly from the market concentration of a few airline corporations. Since the period immediately following the passage of the Civil Aeronautics Act, no new trunk carrier has been certificated; since 1946, mergers and acquisitions have caused the disappearance of five trunk carriers, reducing their number from sixteen to eleven. In the same period, the merger of eight local service carriers with other certificated carriers has reduced the number of local service carriers to nine. These mergers were approved by the CAB without consideration of the competitive impact of the mergers as the board simply allowed larger airlines to take over relatively weak ones.[16]

The basic statutory framework of aviation regulation does not contemplate excessive concentration in the airline industry. In fact, the legislative history of the 1938 Civil Aeronautics Act strongly indicates that Congress intended strict and comprehensive control over airline mergers, consolidations, and acquisitions that tended to affect competition. The original bill, which would have forbidden mergers that "unduly restrained competition" or "unreasonably" created monopolies, was changed in debate to the present, stricter version, which says that

> . . . the Board shall not approve any consolidation, merger [etc.] . . . which would result in creating a monopoly or monopolies and thereby restrain competition or jeopardize another air carrier not a party to the consolidation, merger.[17]

But it has been an unheeded mandate.[18]

The Federal Aviation Act requires the CAB to maintain "competition to the extent necessary to assure sound development of an air transportation system." In order to maintain such competition, section 408 of the act gives the CAB the power to veto mergers that would restrain competition. In 1940, the board recognized that the policies behind the antitrust laws, as articulated and applied by the courts, should govern CAB merger proceedings.[19] Thereafter the CAB stated that if a merger would have substantial anticompetitive effects under established antitrust principles, it should not be approved unless approval is the only way to meet a serious transportation need or to secure important public benefits.[20] Even though the CAB occasionally adhered to this principle in deciding certain intercarrier agreements, the board's merger cases have generally been governed by considerations extraneous and contrary to antitrust principles, such as financial need, favorable route structure, and profits.

The airlines freely negotiate mergers for the purpose of eliminating competition or for acquiring route authority previously denied them. They seem to consider mergers the natural order of things, the lawful means to achieve illegal ends. For instance, a memorandum of discussions held between National Airlines and Eastern Airlines, concerning the possible acquisition of Northeast Airlines, contains the following brazen assertion:

> National and Eastern are presented with a rare opportunity to eliminate a third carrier on the East Coast–Florida market by agreeing on a plan for the acquisition of Northeast and termination of its competitive operations. . . . Elimination of Northeast should result in an additional 70 million dollars annually of revenues being available to the two remaining carriers on the East Coast–Florida route and a very high percentage of this revenue, perhaps as much as 60–75 percent, should flow through to operating profit.[21]

Airlines consider that the time is now ripe to look out for a merger partner. Since June, 1970, the CAB has approved four mergers: American Airlines with Trans Caribbean Airways; Universal Airlines with American Flyers Airlines; Allegheny Airlines with Mohawk Airlines; and Delta Airlines with Northeast Airlines. As of this writing, the CAB has pending before it a proposed merger between Eastern Airlines and Caribbair Atlanta Airlines. In addition, it did reject the American–Western proposed merger. It is publicly known that Pan American and TWA are negotiating possible mergers with certain trunk carriers, including Eastern and Braniff. Unless the CAB changes its prevailing attitude toward mergers, the number of trunk carriers could be reduced to four or five within the next couple of years.

The failure of the CAB to apply substantive statutory standards to merger decisions results, at least partially, from its disregard of the procedural requirements stipulated by the statute for merger proceedings. Section 408 of the Federal Aviation Act requires that "any person seeking approval of a consolidation, merger [etc.] . . . shall present an application to the Board" and thereupon the board shall consider the application in a "public hearing." The members of the board, however, hear the representatives of merger parties in ex parte meetings prior to the filing of merger applications, and then decide the merits of the merger in a formal hearing according to the members' predispositions. The board's private dealings in the American-Western merger case is an example of this sort of practice.

On November 5, 1970, the presidents of American and Western airlines, at their request, held an ex parte meeting with four board members and a few top members of the CAB staff, to discuss the proposed merger between American and Western. The airline presidents presented in detail the merits of the proposed merger—such as the economic aspects, public interest, size and competitive impact—although the merger agreement had not then been filed. That the participants in the meeting themselves were aware of problems concerning the impropriety of the airlines' ex parte presentation is evident from the following discussion:

> MR. SPATER (president of American): I might say this, that I would regard what we said here as in the nature of pleadings, and . . .
>
> MR. GILLILLAND (CAB vice-chairman): Perhaps that is the way we will regard them.
>
> MR. SPATER: So we have an intention, I mean everything I said . . .
>
> MR. GILLILLAND: I don't want to imply that we think of anyone having been guilty of an impropriety here.
>
> MR. SPATER: Of course not. But we would not have come before the Board except in the nature of submitting preliminarily our pleadings. One of the things that worried us was that you can't avoid reading the papers.
>
> MR. GILLILLAND: Surely.[22]

Airline efforts to influence CAB officials charged with deciding contested issues in open proceedings conflict with concepts of fair regulatory proceedings.[23] The CAB's ex parte meetings with the airlines not only undermine the public's confidence in the integrity of the regulatory process but also diminish the chances of impartial decision. For another prominent example, the representatives of American and Western recently met in private with the officials of the Departments of Transportation, Justice, and Treasury, as well as with an advisor to the president, Peter Flanigan, to solicit their support in a merger case then pending before the CAB.[24]

Although the effects of these meetings on the CAB's decision-making process are not readily discernible, they did inhibit active participation of the executive departments in the merger proceeding. The Department of Transportation even reversed its long-standing opposition to airline mergers and became an active supporter of the American-Western merger. It argued that the merger would not "produce significant diseconomies,"[25] while CAB staff economists predicted at least $20 million annual loss as a result of diseconomies of scale of the merged firm. And contrary to its "airline merger policy criteria" that "a policy of increased concentration would not be justified either on the basis of policy precedent or on economic grounds,"[26] the department asserted that the American-Western merger "would not create a precedent for other mergers nor would it foster any defensive mergers."[27] Within a week after the department announced its merger stance, TWA declared that it was evaluating the department's "merger guidelines" to explore the prospects of a TWA–Pan Am matrimony, and National and Northwest Airlines expressed confidence that their merger proposal would pass the test in Washington. The department, like the merging airlines, did not spell out why the well-managed and profitable Western Airlines should be absorbed by American Airlines, which is one of the biggest airlines in the country.

The board's merger proceedings, dominated by carrier influence and ex parte briefing, are inappropriate for adjudicating issues of competition and monopoly. The current airline merger mania, consequently, has a direct relationship with the CAB's incompetence to administer the antitrust principles and the mandate of the Federal Aviation Act.

International Fares

In the regulation of international air fares also, the CAB has been delinquent both in implementing general antitrust principles as well as in administering the specific mandate of the Federal Aviation Act. The act grants the CAB only indirect authority over international air fares, an authority inferred from the power to disapprove air carrier agreements under section 412 and to remove "discriminatory, preferential or prejudicial" rates under section 1002. Acting under these implied powers, the board could approve or disapprove the air fares set by intercarrier agreements. In the event of disapproval of such agreements, however, the board could not prescribe the fares it might deem just and reasonable.

IMMUNITY FOR CARTEL PRICING

Presumably safely ensconced in the CAB's limited jurisdiction, the airlines proceeded to set up their own rate-making machinery. In 1945, the U.S. international air carriers, acting in concert with certain European airlines, created the International Air Transport Association (IATA). The CAB approved the articles of association of the IATA even before all the U.S. air carriers had accepted the document or filed their concurrence with the board.[28] Thereafter, the IATA members established traffic conferences in order to "consider and act upon all traffic matters of concern" to the IATA members. In February, 1946, the CAB approved the "Provisions for the Regulation and Conduct of the Traffic Conferences of IATA" for an experimental period of one year. The board then successively renewed its approval of the traffic conference machinery on a temporary basis until such approval was made permanent in 1955.

Since 1946 all the rates, fares, and conditions for the carriage of international air passengers and cargo have been determined by the traffic conferences of the IATA cartel. All IATA member airlines are required to become members of the traffic conferences. For rate-making purposes IATA divides the world into three areas or conferences, each of which holds periodic rate negotiations separately or in joint sessions with other conferences or areas. All rate decisions are made by the unanimous consent of participating airlines. The rate agreements are, in theory, subject to the approval of the various interested governments; in reality, the consent of an airline constitutes de facto consent of its government, which usually acts at the pleasure of its national airline. In this regard the CAB is similar to other foreign governments or governmental agencies.

The initial CAB decision to approve the IATA rate-making conference was not determined by an adversary proceeding of the regulatory process. In the pro forma hearing that did precede the decision, only the architects and proponents of the IATA conferences participated; neither the Justice Department nor various affected parties, such as consumers and travel agents, were represented. Further, the board repeatedly renewed its temporary approval, and finally accorded its permanent approval, solely on the basis of the recommendations of the board's staff, who had been influenced by private, off-the-record communications made by the airlines and IATA officials.

Subsequent events, however, undercut some of the board's fundamental assumptions that had led it to sanction IATA's rate-making conferences. The board anticipated that it would exercise effective supervision over conference actions by securing congressional approval for its rate-making authority over foreign air transportation. The CAB argued that the limited power to disapprove the rate agreements formulated by IATA conferences would be "quite inadequate . . . to meet with full effectiveness the rate problems that will arise in international air transportation."[29] Therefore, the board requested that the Congress "amend the Civil Aeronautics Act to give the board the same authority over rates, fares and charges of our air carriers in foreign air transportation that it now possesses over such rates, fares and charges in interstate air transportation." But all attempts of the board to secure the requisite power were thwarted by the joint lobbying efforts of the airlines. Still, the board continuously approved the IATA rate agreements as faits accomplis, instead of disclaiming jurisdiction over them, and thereby leaving the matter to appropriate congressional or executive action.

Another basis for the board's approval was the proposition that IATA rate agreements, subject to "investigation and judgment" by regulatory agencies, would be unlike "those secret price-fixing agreements to which certain industrialists have at times resorted for the purpose of fixing and maintaining prices at exorbitant levels at the expense of the public."[30] At least one member of the board understood that the IATA rate-making conferences would not be secret.[31] In fact, all IATA conferences have been held behind an impenetrable cloak of secrecy; the representatives of consumer organizations, travel agents, the press, and even of the CAB have been denied admission. The CAB never exercised the alleged power of investigation and judgment of government agencies, cited as a built-in safeguard against capricious conference action. The minutes and reports of the IATA conferences filed with the board were nothing more than truncated versions of the conference proceedings, being useless for the determination of the reasonableness of conference rates. In addition, IATA consistently refused to make available to the CAB all the reports, studies, and other pertinent documents that supposedly justified the conference rates.

Would the conference system of rate making produce economically sound rate levels, properly related to the reasonably attainable costs of efficient air carriers? This was the crucial issue confronting the board. But the agency in 1946 conveniently deferred its decision on the issue for the following reason:

> Nor are we disposed to declare *without proof* that the full benefits of competition, including the gearing of rates in international air transportation to the costs of the most efficient operator, will be realized under the procedure of consultation and agreement between the international air carriers. We refrain therefore from prejudging on this ground a proposal that is both assailed and supported by only theoretical considerations.[32]

And despite its later experience with the IATA conference system, the board has *never* acted on the issue. In fact, the CAB was incapacitated from judging the relationship of IATA rates with airline costs because IATA consistently denied the CAB access to cost figures available only to the "competing airlines" of the IATA club.

Misinterpretation as to both law and fact has further blemished CAB approval of the IATA system. The board emphatically believed that "the alternative to rate agreement in the traffic conference . . . would be to provoke unilateral control by other governments of the rates charged by our carriers."[33] This was illogical. No single government can arbitrarily dictate the rates to be charged by a foreign airline. The bilateral air transport agreements between nations invariably provide the method and procedure to avoid unilateral control of rates. They stipulate that "the rates to be agreed . . . shall be fixed at reasonable levels, due regard being paid to all relevant factors, such as cost of operation, reasonable profit and the rates charged by any other air carrier." This and other provisions of the agreements permit a government to disapprove only those rates that are demonstrably unreasonable. If a foreign government ventures to disapprove the rates proposed by the American carriers, the U.S. government cannot only take retaliatory action against the airline of that foreign government, but can also initiate governmental consultations with respect to the disputed fares.

The board also incorrectly concluded that, in the event of disapproval of the rate conference procedure, "neither the antitrust laws nor any other laws of the United States would prohibit our air carriers from being forced to agree with other governments on the rates to be charged."[34] If the prices charged by American carriers were so exorbitant as to produce an anticompetitive restraint on air commerce, the antitrust laws could effectively prevent the continuance of such prices, regardless of the source of means by which such prices are established.[35] Anticompetitive, prohibitive, and predatory prices would not be immune from the thrust of antitrust laws by the mere reason that they are agreed upon by the air carriers and foreign governments, or in foreign territories.[36] All air carrier activities and practices outside the jurisdiction of the CAB or not approved by the CAB are properly within the coverage of the antitrust laws, and therefore within the normal jurisdiction of the courts.

The CAB approved the IATA rate machinery under the unfounded apprehension that otherwise the airlines would engage in rate wars and destructive competition. But the prospects of rate wars are remote in an industry operating in a context of reciprocity and retaliation among various governments, where routes and traffic rights are carefully allocated between airlines. For instance, the airlines operated the transpacific routes without IATA rate agreements from 1963 to 1970. During the 1960s there were many instances in which IATA failed to reach agreements for the Latin American, Caribbean, and intra-European routes. On such occasions the airlines and interested governments avoided rate wars and other acts of self-destruction. Although the airlines frequently threaten rate wars for bargaining purposes, they ultimately charge uniform prices and conditions of service. In early 1970 Alitalia threatened a rate war on the North Atlantic for two months and then joined the other transatlantic carriers to agree on identical price levels. Similarly, Lufthansa held up the specter of a rate war on the North Atlantic routes in 1972; then, under pressure from foreign governments and other airlines, it backed down and agreed on a price level acceptable to all the other airlines.

Misgivings that disapproval by the IATA conferences would strip the board of its "only jurisdiction" over international fares is also unjustifiable. Under the regime of bilateral agreements, there can be no international fare not agreed on between the airlines. Therefore, the international fares could properly be considered as "agreements" subject to the board's jurisdiction. Alternatively, the board could include in the domestics' certificates of public convenience and necessity and in foreign air carrier permits "reasonable terms, conditions and limitations [concerning international fares] as the public interest may require."[37] In addition to this broad power, the board can "investigate and determine" whether any domestic or foreign air carrier is engaged in unfair practices or methods of competition. The Federal Aviation Act grants the CAB enormous power to control international fares without seeking aid from the airline cartel; however, there is no provision in the act that would penalize the CAB for not exercising its powers.

THE IATA BARONY

Under the board's normal practices, carriers are required to file formal application for CAB permission prior to engaging in any inter-carrier discussion concerning matters affecting competition or "fraught with antitrust considerations." To name a few of the most recent instances of the application of this regulatory procedure, the carriers sought and obtained prior CAB approval for discussions on air freight claims and liability rules and practices, reduction of capacity, passenger no-show problem, and on cargo security, traffic, and shortage problems of the New York airports. The requirement for prior permission enables the board to limit the scope of inter-carrier discussions and to impose procedural safeguards preventing secret understandings among the carriers. The carriers are often advised to file with the board "complete and accurate" minutes or transcripts of all discussions,[38] and to permit representatives of the board and "of any trade, shipping, or consumer association or group" to participate in the discussions.[39]

But the U.S. air carriers, apparently in defiance of the

board's procedural requirements, participated in the IATA
rate-making conferences without seeking prior permission
for inter-carrier discussion. The carriers construed CAB
approval of the traffic conference machinery as a blanket
and perpetual authorization for inter-carrier discussion
with respect to all matters affecting foreign air transportation. As a result, the board has been ignorant of the
matters discussed in the IATA conferences, and sometimes
even unaware of the conferences themselves.[40] The United
States carriers' rate proposals and agenda of the conferences
are filed with the CAB on the eve of the conferences by the
IATA as "IATA documents." The rate proposals are not
justified by any supporting documents, and the CAB is not
expected, and it never gets an opportunity, to evaluate the
proposals. The rate agreements ultimately formulated by
the conferences rarely bear any resemblance to the rate
proposals originally filed by the U.S. carriers with the board.
"The problem of obtaining adequate information on IATA
actions is an ever present one" the CAB confessed in
1966.[41]

The board's futile attempts to procure the documents
pertinent to IATA rate conferences started soon after its
approval of the traffic conference machinery. In 1946 the
board suggested that

> it will be of great value if the conference in reaching rate
> agreements hereafter will make a record of the data con-
> sidered by it and of the considerations which resulted in its
> conclusion that the rates fixed by it meet the required
> standards of economic soundness, and will make that
> record available to the Board, and the appropriate aero-
> nautical agencies of other nations which may undertake to
> review the conference action on rates.[42]

The carriers and the IATA ignored this request. The board
then transformed its request in 1955 into a "condition" for
the approval of the conferences. Because the carriers continued to disregard the condition, the CAB initiated a
"show cause proceeding" for modifying the approval of
traffic conferences. The proceedings contemplated the imposition of stringent requirements for filing IATA documents, including recommendations, reports, studies, and
surveys of IATA committees and working groups, and
statements showing reasons underlying the adoption of any
conference resolution. Faced with strenuous carrier opposi-

tion, the CAB quietly retreated from its initial position; it instead adopted an order requiring the carriers to "file with the Board such documents and other data as the Board may require." Thereafter, the board's staff privately met with the carriers and agreed that all the important documents filed with the board would be considered "confidential."[43]

The air carriers and IATA have consistently refused to furnish documents indispensable to the discharge of the CAB's regulatory functions. Even documents such as summary minutes, which the carriers choose to file with the board for the sake of formality, are carefully precensored accounts of discussions by anonymous carriers.[44] The IATA documents filed with the CAB do not contain any trade information to warrant their public suppression by the CAB. For instance, the IATA Cost Committee Reports show only arbitrary figures and conclusions concerning costs of airline groups. These figures and conclusions are not supported by data of any kind whatsoever.

Although preventing "rate wars" in international air transportation provided the initial basis for CAB approval of IATA traffic conferences, the carriers and the IATA conferences soon transgressed the scope and limits of their granted authority. The IATA carriers engaged in discussions and agreements on matters unrelated to rates and unnecessary to achieving the alleged rate stability. The U.S. carriers participated in IATA agreements designed to undermine the competitive potential of strong air carriers. The United States carriers are parties to IATA agreements prescribing uniform rules and conditions for customer and inflight services, reservations, confirmations and refunds, passenger en route expenses, stopover privileges and charges, density and pitch of aircraft seats, minimum free baggage allowance, baggage excess weight charges, construction of passenger fares and charges, free and reduced rate transportation, and circulation of schedule information among carriers. These restrictive agreements have dissipated the competitive strength of the U.S. carriers. Why have these carriers, for example, hesitated to offer competitive service by reconfiguring their six-abreast seating to the more commodious five-abreast seating, especially when most of their planes are flying half-empty every day?

IATA has also established absolute control over American travel agents and tour operators engaged in the marketing and sale of air transportation. These business entities are prohibited from doing business without an IATA license. IATA imposes penalties on the airlines for breach of this and other IATA regulations. In all, it has collected nearly $7 million in fines. The fares and rates are tabulated according to the special currency exchange rates determined by IATA; the airline revenues are channeled to the IATA Clearing House, which receives the commissions for handling revenues and accounts. IATA has already established its own insurance company, and the work for the establishment of an IATA subsidiary to control the airlines' hotel businesses is nearing completion.

Neither bilateral agreements nor CAB approval have granted IATA traffic conferences the authority to intrude into the American domestic air transportation system. Yet the IATA conferences set and enforce air fares for domestic transportation through the instrumentality of the so-called proportional fares. These are fares for the domestic segments of international routes, and as such they substitute for domestic fares in computing the fares for international travel that includes travel between domestic points. For instance, the one-way basic economy fare for Los Angeles–London is calculated by combining the fare for New York–London with the proportional fare for New York–Los Angeles, instead of the applicable domestic fare for New York–Los Angeles.

The most recent IATA resolution on "North American Proportional Fares" prescribes fares for more than five hundred domestic city-pairs of the United States. These fares are set substantially below the current domestic air fares. Thus, the proportional economy fare for New York–Los Angeles is $126, as compared with the effective domestic fare of $163. The term *proportional fare* suggests that these fares are proportional to the associated international fares, while in fact they bear no relation to those fares. If the New York–Los Angeles proportional fare were set in proportion to the New York–London fare, it would be $170.[45] Conversely, if the New York–London normal economy fare were set in proportion to the IATA's New York–Los Angeles proportional fare, the New York–London fare would not exceed $167. Although the IATA proportional fares undercut the high domestic air fares, such IATA fares discriminate between persons traveling between domestic points.[46]

THE REASONABLENESS OF INTERNATIONAL FARES

Only 5.3 million Americans (or less than 3 percent of the population) traveled to overseas countries in 1970. They spent $6.2 billion for passenger fares and related expenses abroad. But 2.3 million visitors from overseas spent only $2.7 billion in the United States. The "travel deficit" created by the uneven travel spending of Americans vis-à-vis the foreigners has been a constant drain on the balance of payments of the United States. The total U.S. balance of payments deficit attributable to foreign travel rose from $1.23 billion in 1961 to a record-breaking level of $2.46 billion in 1970.[47] The 1970 travel deficit alone was enough to cancel out the year's favorable trade balance of the United States.

The IATA fare levels play a decisive role in increasing and perpetuating the travel deficit. High IATA fares inhibit the free flow of tourists to and from the United States, and at the same time the arbitrary fare structure compels Americans traveling abroad to stay longer and spend more in foreign countries. The IATA "promotional fares," such as excursion fares and group inclusive tour fares, require passengers to stay at a foreign destination for a minimum period ranging from ten days to twenty-nine days. These discount fares are used by more than 65 percent of the air passengers. A Department of Commerce survey shows that the Americans who traveled to Europe and Mediterranean countries in 1970 stayed in those countries for twenty-seven days and spent $18.15 per day on the average.[48]

The IATA fares on the North Atlantic and Pacific routes do not bear any relation to the actual costs of operation of the international airlines. According to the unit cost estimates of the Bureau of Economics of the CAB (Bureau), the total economic cost of domestic trunk carriers operating wide-bodied four-engine turbofan jets on long-haul routes would be 3.7 cents per revenue coach passenger mile during the year ending December 31, 1971.[49] The following table would show how much higher are the IATA fares:

THE DISPARITY BETWEEN THE EXISTING IATA FARES AND THE
REASONABLE FARES BASED ON BUREAU'S ESTIMATED UNIT COST[51]

	Distance (miles)	IATA Economy* Basic	IATA Economy* Peak	Fares based on 3.7 cents per mile*
NYC–London	3456	$484	$590	$254
NYC–Paris	3628	504	636	268
NYC–Rome	4980	640	746	316
NYC–Athens	4925	756	872	364

* All fares shown in the table are round-trip fares.

IATA fares should be reduced by half in order to bring them to the reasonable level that approximates the actual costs of operation. Even the IATA excursion fares, which are fenced with minimum-stay requirements and surcharges for weekend travel, are set above the reasonably attainable cost level. For example, the New York–Tokyo fourteen to twenty-one day excursion fare is $868 or 6.4 cents per mile, the Seattle-Tokyo fourteen to twenty-one day excursion fare is $630 or 6.5 cents per mile, and the New York–Paris seventeen to twenty-eight day excursion fare is $353 or 4.8 cents per passenger mile.*

* Because the bureau's estimated unit cost of 3.7 cents is based purely on the cost characteristics of domestic airline operations, it does not adequately reflect the numerous cost advantages that are inherent in international operations. For example, in contrast with the bureau's assumption of 45 percent load factor, the average international traffic seldom drops below 50 percent load factor. Similarly, while the bureau's costing program is limited to a maximum distance of twenty-eight hundred miles, the distance of major international routes exceeds thirty-five hundred miles. The marked difference between the costs of domestic and international operations is apparent from the following figures:

AIRCRAFT OPERATING EXPENSES FOR B-747, TURBOFAN,
4-ENGINE, PASSENGER CABIN CONFIGURATION—
12 MONTHS ENDED 12/31/70[50]

(In U.S. cents)

	Domestic Operations Trunks	International & Territorial Operations
Per Revenue ton-mile	26.933	14.815
Per Available ton-mile	7.834	6.245
Per Revenue Passenger mile	3.122	1.847

The CAB should either be aware of the excessive nature of IATA fares or should use its investigative authority to become aware of it. Yet the CAB has approved three IATA fare increases since 1963. In 1971 the CAB rubber-stamped the IATA compromise agreement that increased the international fares across-the-board throughout the world.[52] For giving its perfunctory approval, the CAB relied on IATA's cost figures and their unsubstantiated arguments for higher revenues.[53] The fact that each dollar increase approved by the CAB would cost Americans $6 million in additional fares did not seem to worry the board.

IATA fares are not only exorbitant but are discriminatory as well. Most of them taper upward (i.e., higher unit price for more distant destinations) contrary to the elementary dictates of transportation economics. For example, the basic economy fare for New York–London (3,456 miles) is 6.56 cents per mile while the same fare for New York–Athens (4,925 miles) is 7.5 cents per mile, or for New York–Tokyo (10,170 miles via Moscow) is 8.6 cents per mile. Similarly, certain classes of passengers are accorded preferential treatment over others using comparable services. A passenger traveling from New York to London on a fourteen to twenty-eight day excursion fare pays $170 less than his counterpart who is traveling on the peak season economy fare. The only difference between these two fares is that the user of excursion fare is forbidden from making his return trip before two weeks from the date of his onward trip. But the airline does not save anything by inconveniencing the excursionist, and the stay requirement has nothing to do with the airline's cost.

Recently IATA agreed on a $200 round-trip "youth fare" for travel between Europe and North America. These

---

The aircraft operating expenses per revenue passenger-mile in international operations is 59 percent less than the comparable expenses in domestic operations. The aircraft operating expenses, which includes flying operations, maintenance, depreciation, and rentals, constitute almost 50 percent of the airline cost.[51] Therefore the bureau's domestic unit cost estimate of 3.7 cents should be reduced at least to 2.7 cents in order to reflect properly the intrinsic cost advantages of international operations. If this conclusion is valid, the New York–London round-trip economy fare should be around $186, and any excursion fare should be below $150—which means that even current youth fares to Europe (New York–London is $200) are unreasonably high.

fares are available to youths between the ages of twelve and twenty-six. Both the arbitrarily fixed age range and fare level have no justifiable relationship with the other existing fares. For instance, while a twenty-six-year-old passenger pays $200 for his New York–London round trip, a six-year-old child using the 50 percent peak season economy fare pays $276 for the same trip. Similarly, a senior citizen with limited sources of income is compelled to pay twice the price that is paid by a twenty-six-year-old youth having a well-paying job. The CAB did not utilize its powers under section 404(b) of the Federal Aviation Act to prevent the continuance of the discriminatory youth fare. (In early 1973, however, the CAB proposed to end *domestic* discount fares, including youth fares.)

Between March, 1971, and April, 1972, the CAB granted a more than 15 percent increase in international fares. For instance, the basic season economy round-trip fare for New York–London was increased from $420 to $484. The CAB justified its approval of higher fares on the ground that the U.S. carriers, primarily Pan American and TWA, were losing money. But the board paid no attention to the fact that during the twelve months ending March 31, 1972, Pan American and TWA have flown 55 percent of their seats empty. Had the carriers generated more traffic with lower fares to fill the empty seats, they could have made reasonable profits. Remember, the aircraft operating expenses do not vary according to the number of seats occupied by passengers. Say it costs $25,000 to fly a DC-8 aircraft (250 seat capacity) from X to Y. If the fare is $200, and the plane is half full, it will cover the costs, with $25,000 in revenue. If the fare is reduced to $150, and the plane is three-fourths full, it will generate $28,050 in revenue—making a profit for the airline while at the same time saving money for the customers. The only issue here is whether the lower fare would attract enough passengers to fill more empty seats. A recent CAB study shows that reduced fares would certainly increase the traffic of U.S. international airlines. It estimates that with an annual average 2.5 percent reduction in air fares, the revenue passenger miles flown by U.S. international carriers would increase from 43 billion in 1972 to 134 billion in 1980, as against an increase to 96 billion in 1980, with the fares remaining at the present level.[54]

Americans paid more than $1.8 billion as passenger fares to the international airlines in 1970.[55] By the most conservative estimate they could have traveled for less than one-half of the amount they paid but for the IATA cartel prices and the CAB's complicity in such prices. The CAB apparently nurtured the cartel pricing for the purpose of promoting the well-being of the U.S. international carriers. But the board both prevented Americans from traveling abroad at economical transportation prices, and at the same time it damaged the competitive strength of the U.S. carriers. Under the IATA regime, the competitive strength of the U.S. air carriers does not have much relevance; they are permitted to offer the same price and same service as the smaller, foreign and more inefficient airlines do. Pan American's share of international scheduled traffic dwindled from 19.8 percent in 1960 to 13.0 percent in 1970 in terms of "tonnekilometres" performed. Within the ten years from 1960 to 1970, Northwest was relegated from fourteenth to nineteenth position among the ranking international airlines. In the past decade no U.S. international carrier matched the annual growth rate of 22.5 percent for Lufthansa, 22 percent for Alitalia, or 29 percent for Japan Airlines. The situation will not improve until the CAB abandons its regulation that censures Americans' freedom to travel rather than the airlines' freedom to fix monopoly prices.

Domestic Private Regulation

THE AIR TRANSPORT ASSOCIATION OF AMERICA

There is hardly any aspect of commercial aviation in the United States that escapes the collective evaluation and scrutiny of the airlines. The CAB and FAA are invariably confronted with unified positions and joint presentations of air carriers in all rule-making proceedings. The airlines decide in concert the type and quantity of information to be given to regulatory agencies and the desirability of taking industry positions on regulatory or legislative issues. The terms for the carriage of passengers and cargo, and the amount of compensation to be paid for lost baggage or shipments, are seldom stipulated by individual air carriers. All these and other activities by the domestic airlines are initiated by and consummated under the auspices of the Air Transport Association of America (ATA).

ATA is the domestic industry association of certificated route air carriers.[56] The membership of the ATA is closed to supplemental air carriers and other potential competitors operating pursuant to certificates of public convenience and necessity or foreign air carrier permits issued by the CAB. An air carrier not a member of ATA or IATA will be denied the technical and engineering services of ATA, and even participation in the most harmless cooperative arrangements sponsored by the ATA, such as the standardized ticket plan.[57]

In 1940 the CAB quietly approved the articles of association of the ATA without exploring through open hearings the antitrust implications of the projected activities of the ATA combine. The board's approval, however, did not constitute the approval or disapproval of "any subsequent contract or agreement entered into, or any specific action taken pursuant to said articles of association." From its very inception ATA apparently disregarded the restrictions contained in the board's order. Not only did ATA fail to file with the board the minutes of ATA meetings, but it also refused to submit for CAB approval many of its agreements, bylaws, and resolutions. The ATA engaged in a large spectrum of activities, ranging from influencing the members of the CAB to freezing the actions of legislators and public officials. The anticompetitive impact of the ATA activities led the Antitrust Subcommittee of the House of Representatives, after extensive investigation, to recommend in 1957 the immediate withdrawal of CAB approval from the ATA articles of association.[58] The subcommittee seriously doubted the CAB's power to approve ATA operations and recommended that the air carrier agreements be approved on an individual basis according to their merits.

Some of the assailed ATA activities involved active lobbying of the CAB. ATA activities calculated "to bring pressure on the Board to obtain favorable decisions" had been so intense and disturbing that Welch Pogue, then chairman of the CAB, wrote directly to ATA in 1945 urging cessation of those activities. The letter contained the following plea:

> We cannot urge too strongly the necessity for discontinuance of these improper activities on the part of the airlines. The implication of these activities are so serious and sinister that it seems to the Board the airline industry should be so concerned that it would seek every possible means of promptly bringing them to an end.[59]

But the CAB chairman's secret communication failed to have any appreciable impact on the ATA's actions. An ATA internal memorandum dated February 18, 1948, indicates the continuing trend of ATA activities:

> One CAB man felt that perhaps more rather than less competition is needed in the international field and that this might well come from nonscheduled operations. As this person is ready to find a ready ear in the Board itself, it would seem to me that some missionary work might be advisable.[60]

Even the hard-hitting congressional investigation did not dissuade the ATA from chasing the CAB members and staff. In 1957 the ATA launched an "educational program" to "thoroughly indoctrinate the Civil Aeronautics Board and staff." The program included arranging field trips with board and key staff members and starting an organized campaign to find out who has influence on the individual members of the board. ATA hoped that the educational program would ultimately turn the CAB members and staff into "protagonists instead of antagonists."[61]

ATA's interests in the air transportation system extend far beyond the conventional arena of other trade associations. Apart from manipulating the regulatory process, the ATA functions as an instrument of monopoly for the air carriers. ATA has established special committees to arrange for the pooling of surplus aircraft parts and materials, and for negotiating the sale of such parts and materials with prospective purchasers. Likewise, the ATA meets with "selected suppliers" to apprise them of the needs of the airlines and to discuss the desired prices.[62] In 1968, the ATA supply committee even drew up the specifications for the ground equipment to be purchased by the airlines, and received bids from suppliers with a view to facilitating joint purchase of such equipment by the airlines.[63]

The ATA has also long established its monopolistic control over the travel agency business of this country.

One of ATA's subsidiaries, the Air Traffic Conference (ATC), regulates the travel agents by issuing and revoking licenses, by imposing dues and penalties, and by requiring them to abide by arbitrary conditions.* The ATC constitution and bylaws have never been approved by the CAB; nevertheless, the air carriers frequently assemble under the aegis of the ATC, discuss and conclude agreements affecting air transportation, and transact business involving millions of dollars without the prior approval of the CAB.

The ATC was created for the ostensible purpose of facilitating "joint and coordinated action" in the "traffic, sales and advertising problems" of air carriers. But the supplemental air carriers are excluded from the ATA establishment, and only ATA members are eligible to join ATC. Moreover, if any member ceases to be a member of the association (ATA), its membership in the ATC automatically terminates. A member which has withdrawn or has been expelled from ATC can be readmitted only "upon the unanimous approval of, and subject to such terms and conditions as may be imposed by a unanimous vote of, the regular members of the ATC." These closed and tie-in membership arrangements are designed to enlarge and fortify the monopolistic influence of the ATA dynasty over the air transportation system. No air carrier can afford to keep away from the ATC; yet many small air carriers would dissociate themselves from the "trunk-dominated" ATA if ATA were deprived of its jurisdiction over the travel agents.[65]

The ATC consistently propagandizes that its regime of travel agents brings beneficial results to the air transport consumers. This is not true. The ATC sales agency agreement and other regulations require the agents to furnish bonds in the amount of $10,000 in order to secure and protect the airlines' interests. There is no provision, however, in the ATC statutes to safeguard the interests of consumers in the event of fraudulent sales or misrepre-

---

* Practically no travel agent can enter the business of selling air tickets and services without the licenses from the ATA and the IATA. The ATC regulation stipulates that no air carrier shall "appoint or retain any person as its Agent, or any place of business as an authorized agency location, unless such person and such location appear on the Agency List then in effect."[64] Any person who desires to be included in the list shall make written application to the ATC, which may approve or disapprove such application.

sentation of agency status. When a passenger is cheated by the ATC appointed agent, the air carriers escape liability by attributing a form of principal-agent relationship between the passenger and agent concerned.[66]

INVESTIGATION AND AFTERMATH

Prompted mostly by public and congressional discontent, the CAB instituted an investigation in 1959 into the alleged misdoings of the ATA. The CAB ordered the ATA to make available for inspection all minutes, documents, and other ATA records and to show cause why they should not be filed with the board. The board rejected the ATA assertion that it lacked authority to conduct the investigation and obtain certain documents. Before the investigative staff examined the files, the ATA withdrew 509 documents on the ground that they were protected under the attorney-client privilege. The ATA also refused to yield to a CAB subpoena that called for the production of the allegedly "privileged" documents.

The board sued the ATA to enforce the subpoena. The court, rendering a partial summary judgment, found that the attorney-client privilege could be asserted by the ATA for the purposes of the proceedings involved in the case.[67] To the contrary, however, was section 407 (e) of the Federal Aviation Act, empowering the board to inspect and examine at all times "all documents, records and memoranda, including all documents, papers and correspondence, now or hereafter existing, and kept or required to be kept by air carriers."[68] If the air carriers are permitted to deposit their documents in the archives of their trade association, which claims attorney-client privilege, the purpose of section 407 (e) could be defeated by concerted carrier action.

The determination and enthusiasm for an in-depth investigation of the ATA, as expressed in the initial CAB order, evaporated within a few weeks. As soon as the ATA raised the privilege issue, the CAB suspended the inspection of ATA records; it was never resumed. The successive tactics of the ATA were designed to sidetrack the CAB from substantive to procedural issues; it largely succeeded by making the subpoena a major contest. The CAB seemed to be searching desperately for an honorable end to the investigation. In July, 1962, the ATA filed an "offer of settlement" with the CAB. It included the recognition of the CAB's right to "reasonable" inspection of the ATA files, an undertaking to file the resolutions, agreements, and conference bylaws with the CAB, and certain suggestions to amend the articles of association of the ATA. The CAB seized this opportunity to threaten disapproval of the ATA articles of association unless certain additional conditions were included in the ATA's offer. In the ensuing hearing the ATA reiterated the conditions articulated in its original offer. The resulting order[69] terminating the investigation did no more than to repeat the ATA's offer of settlement, which also included the claim for withholding documents on the basis of attorney-client privilege.

The CAB ultimately abdicated its responsibility by discarding the central purpose of the investigation: the prevention of the illegal and improper activities of a trade association created by the CAB. Neither its investigation nor the congressional hearing changed the pattern of the ATA activities; but the CAB's toothless proceeding and final order have accorded a new legitimacy to such activities. The ATA continues to engage in a wide variety of industry discussions, charts out action programs, and arrives at definite conclusions and understandings. The minutes of these discussions are invariably truncated and elliptical. Incredibly, no one at the CAB has ever perused these minutes; some members of the board are even ignorant of the existence of these minutes in the board's files.[70]

As of December 31, 1970, the ATA still withholds 239 of its documents under its so-called attorney-client privilege.[71] The CAB staff concedes that even those documents filed at the discretion of the ATA are not properly acted upon by the board. The ATA never filed the bylaws and other basic documents concerning the establishment and functioning of the various conferences, as required by the CAB order terminating the ATA investigation.[72] The bylaws of the Air Traffic Conference, which exercises absolute monopoly control over the travel agency business, have never been approved by the CAB. Similarly the budgets of ATA and its conferences, involving the joint spending of airline resources in millions, have also never been sanctioned by the CAB.

ATA seldom sought and received the permission of the board prior to discussions dealing with matters "fraught with antitrust considerations."[73] Yet such discussions develop often in ATA meetings. During the 1970 passenger fare investigation the ATA directors decided that "the ATA will constitute the machinery for industry co-operation in the rate investigation" and that "the ATA will provide or arrange for any joint studies the airline members may decide on."[74] Pursuant to this decision, the ATA convened in April, 1970, a meeting of the airlines for the purpose of reaching general agreement on areas of joint development of materials and courses of action. In the course of the investigation, the ATA Planning Committee decided to develop position papers covering rates, schedules, airports, labor, and the charter carriers.[75] Recently the ATA prepared the blueprints of a scheme to eliminate the CAB's authority on rates and fares and to establish in its place a "freight and passenger rate conference machinery."[76]

Some of the ATA activities have the direct effect of muting competition. ATA opposed at all times the granting of increased charter authority to the supplemental airlines by the Congress, CAB, or the Department of Defense.[77] ATA lobbied against the legislation that proposed the establishment of a third-level air carrier class, air taxi operators. And it recently prepared draft legislation for bringing the intrastate air carriers within the regulatory jurisdiction of the CAB, thereby eradicating their price competition with ATA member carriers.

The committees and departments of the ATA advise the airlines how they should assign costs and how to "eliminate discrepancies" in the airlines' rate-of-return reports to the CAB. The ATA also formulates the accounting procedures with regard to investment base, capitalization of interest, equipment purchase deposits, and depreciation of operating property and equipment. In short, the ATA intercedes in the free flow of economic information from individual airlines to the CAB; the reported statistical information is tailored to conform to "industry positions" and "accounting methods" formulated by the ATA machinery, the ultimate arbiter.

ATA has been instrumental in defeating all CAB efforts

to elicit reasonable statistical information from the airlines. For instance, when the CAB proposed a regulation in 1964 concerning the carrier reporting of long-term and short-term debt and major lease obligations, ATA held a private conference with the CAB staff to discuss the merits of that regulation. When the regulation was finally adopted, the ATA reported to its constituents that the information required on long- and short-term debt was "watered down" to a point where it was "no longer objectionable."[78]

In 1968 the CAB proposed to revise and modernize its traffic and capacity-data collection system. The proposed rule contemplated the collection of traffic and capacity data on a "flight stage" basis and passenger data broken down by fare category. According to the CAB, this information was crucially important for "regulating fares or determining the adequacy of existing service in particular markets."[79] The ATA, however, thought that the new rules would constitute "CAB's interference with the airline management decisions"; it expressed the "fear that the CAB will become a decision-making body instead of a regulatory agency."[80] ATA filed comments on behalf of 24 carriers objecting to the adoption of the rules, and two carriers filed independent comments favoring the rules. Because of the ATA objection, the CAB finally decided not to require data concerning passengers traveling on special and discount fares; the CAB still does not have this information.

Similarly, the CAB never instituted a comprehensive investigation into the accounting practices of the airlines, despite frequent complaints about the inadequacy of reported data. In 1965 one member of the CAB told the Management Conference Transportation Center of Northwestern University that "the main target of a new investigation will be more likely the diverse, and in some cases, bizarre and erratic accounting practices of the carriers." In a subsequent meeting of the ATA, the executive secretary of the Airline Financial and Accounting Conference (AFAC) had made the following remark: "It would be my thought that, if the erroneous opinion of the speaker could be corrected without embroiling ourselves into a controversy, it should be done."[81] The promised investigation never took place.

ATA "EDUCATES" THE REGULATORY AGENCIES

The exact amount or source of expenditures for manipulation of the regulatory process is not discernible from the ATA's public documents. Most such expenses are collected from the individual airlines as "unbudgeted" contributions. However, substantial amounts are spent each year to influence public officials, to prepare "presentations" to regulatory agencies, and to arrange "contacts" with regulatory personnel. In the ATA parlance, all such activities are known as public relations or educational programs.

In 1971 the ATA launched a massive "economic education program" with the avowed purpose of removing "public misconceptions" about airlines and to "build a pyramid of support [by] educating . . . members of Senate and House of Representatives and their aides, staff personnel of key committees of both Houses, members and staff of the CAB. . . ."[82] At least $1 million is assigned for combating "consumerism."[83] In 1969, ATA sponsored a radio advertising campaign aimed at the "very top level of Washington influentials," and in 1970, ATA ran an additional twenty-six-week, one-half hour syndicated television program.

Between November, 1967, and June, 1969, the ATA made three ex parte presentations to the CAB regarding the financial situation of the major airlines. Transcripts of these meetings were not taken or kept by the CAB, even though these presentations apparently persuaded the CAB to grant fare increases.[84] But the ATA was forced to discontinue the practice by the ruling of the D.C. Circuit Court in the earlier mentioned *Moss* v. *CAB,* which strongly condemned CAB rate making based on ex parte hearings. In November, 1970, the ATA acknowledged the *Moss* case to be an impediment to its private dealings with the CAB.[85] Despite the *Moss* decision, however, and the pendency of the domestic passenger fare investigation, the directors of the ATA instructed the staff to "develop and implement industry coordinated programs designed to convince the CAB that rate decisions should be based on strict observance of the Act."[86]

The CAB is not alone in its obedience to the ATA line. ATA influence on the Federal Aviation Administration

(FAA) is so significant that an informed official of the National Transportation Safety Board recently stated that the ATA "controls" the issuance of FAA regulations.[87] According to the ATA, its activities and existence are "now well accepted by the FAA."[88] Most of the ATA accomplishments, such as preventing the issuance or reducing the number of FAA's mandatory directives and avoiding the detailed control of overhaul and inspection periods, were the direct result of "focusing high-level attention on the internal decision-making process within the FAA."[89] But then, the ATA has always succeeded in stopping the FAA from issuing rules and regulations that the industry disliked. An ATA document dated June, 1968, states: "During the past few years cooperative work between the [ATA] Committee and the FAA has practically buried the idea that specific Federal Air Regulations are needed to define mechanic qualifications." Similarly, the ATA fought against the FAA requirements with respect to emergency arresting gear because of its high cost. After continuous discussion, the ATA reported, the FAA lost "some of its enthusiasm for this approach."[90]

The ATA has consistently defeated all programs of the federal government and the FAA for the abatement of aircraft noise. The ATA carriers strongly opposed the creation of a new federal agency to deal with aircraft noise, preferring the regulation of noise by the FAA. Even before the issuance of the rules, the FAA informally advised the ATA that the rules would be so flexible as to permit the 747s to operate without any restrictions as to payload. When the noise certification rules were finally issued, ATA was very pleased with them, because they "represented a great deal of industry effort."

CONCLUSION

The public's right to travel by air is subjected to censorship by the trade associations of airlines. These two extralegal associations, IATA and ATA, are the major instruments of aviation regulation, even though regulation of public utilities by private trade associations is neither contemplated nor authorized by the law. The CAB's role in the regulation of rates and services is only collaborative and supplementary. This CAB-IATA-ATA triumvirate, a cartel in the true tradition of that onerous term, has brought the airline industry to a state of stagnancy in the United States.

The effectiveness of the Federal Aviation Act has been much eroded by the distorted and industry-oriented interpretations imputed to its provisions by the CAB. Until the CAB reverses its policies concerning air fares, competition, mergers, and intercarrier agreements, its regulation of the airline industry will continue to constitute a fraud on the American public. Any regulatory agency that construes the public interest as the exclusive interest of the producer, or permits the producer to exact a price that is double the reasonable price, is a contradiction in terms.

The prospects of mass air travel in this country will remain remote until the Congress brings about drastic changes in the regulatory setup. At a minimum, Congress should investigate the monopoly practices of the airlines and their trade associations. The CAB should be deprived of its power to grant antitrust immunity to anticompetitive activities of the airlines, such as monopoly price-fixing, mergers, and joint actions through trade associations. Any change in the regulatory scheme should assure the right of the public and consumers to participate in the CAB proceedings in parity with the airlines.

POWER

7

Power for the People: Electricity and the Regulatory Agencies

MARSHALL BEIL

Most people consider the electric power industry—by far the nation's largest industry, with assets well over $100 billion*—to be a natural monopoly, regulated for better or, usually, worse by the state and federal governments. They reason that one Consolidated Edison is all New York City needs, or can put up with. Why two, they ask? Why three? And why a chapter on electric power in a book about economic competition?

It is true that more than one utility serving New York's, or any town's, residents would require duplicate sets of power lines and other equipment and thus be expensive and wasteful.[1] But it is not true that the company that *distributes* power to consumers must be the one that *generates* the power. Modern techniques of transmission are so developed that it may actually be cheaper for Con Ed not to generate all its "bulk power"—the millions of kilowatt hours generated for wholesale distribution—in its plants in and around New York City, but to buy at least some from

---

* The industry is also among the most profitable. The annual return on common equity for the major privately owned utilities averaged 12.5 percent in the last half of the 1960s, a 2 percent increase over the previous decade.

other sources. It could for example, go to the hydroelectric
plant at Niagara Falls, or to a company in the West that, because of time zone differences, has a surplus of power
when Con Ed's demands are greatest. Thus principles of
antitrust must guarantee Con Ed, and all retail distributors
of electric power, a broad range of choice among suppliers
of bulk power. Competition at this wholesale level can play
a significant role in keeping power costs down, and lowering the price the consumer pays for his electricity.

One example demonstrates the value of competition and
its beneficial effects on regulation. The city of Bartow,
Florida, has a municipally owned utility distributing power
to local residents. For many years Bartow purchased most
of its wholesale power from the Florida Power Corporation,
but thought Florida Power's rates too high. Along with
other municipal utilities, Bartow complained to the Federal
Power Commission, which regulates wholesale rates, and
a settlement was negotiated that lowered the price slightly.
But Bartow, still dissatisfied, sought to switch suppliers to
the neighboring, and cheaper, Tampa Electric Company.
Tampa would not deal with Bartow because of an agreement with Florida Power dividing the wholesale market
between them, and Bartow was in Florida Power's terri-
tory. But in mid-1968 the Justice Department filed an antitrust suit to invalidate this agreement. Florida Power, fore-
seeing the consequences, "voluntarily" lowered its rates to
customers (including Bartow) within transmission distance of Tampa to Tampa's level. (In 1971, the two
companies negotiated a consent decree with the federal
government outlawing territorial allocation of markets.)

To develop a competitive bulk power supply industry
requires an understanding of the technological revolution
that the industry has undergone in the past two decades.
The key phrase is economies of scale: the bigger the plant,
the cheaper the power. Several huge generators recently
installed by the Tennessee Valley Authority and the
American Electric Power Company produce ten times
more electricity than the largest generators in use in 1950,
at only a fraction of the cost per kilowatt hour. And new,
extra high voltage transmission lines can now carry power
economically over distances once hardly thought possible.

The new plants themselves are vastly more expensive to build than their predecessors. New plants cost

upwards of several hundred million dollars each, more than all but the largest utilities can afford. Transmission lines are also expensive, costing as much as $165,000 a mile, exclusive of land. And these plants and lines can be environmental monsters, consuming inordinate amounts of land, fuel, air, and water; if not properly constructed, the plants can disgorge huge quantities of pollutants in return. Yet 250 to 300 new plants, representing an aggregate investment of over $80 billion, will have to be built in the next twenty years to meet the growing demand for power.[2]

Clearly, the development and siting of new plants must be carefully planned to keep their number to the minimum necessary to maintain an adequate yet clean supply of power. And to achieve inexpensive power requires that attention be paid to competition between those who generate the power, those who transmit it, and those who distribute it, not permitting the efficiencies in large-scale generation to lead to consolidation over all levels of the industry.

The Industry

At first glance the industry looks unconcentrated, composed of almost thirty-five hundred electric systems of diverse size and ownership—public, private, and cooperative. These numbers are deceptive. Twenty-four hundred systems are small, private, municipal, or rural cooperative utilities that generate little or no electricity. They are predominately retail distributors of bulk power purchased elsewhere. Of the remaining companies, thirty-five separate decision makers—twenty independent companies and fifteen holding companies—control 70 percent of the assets of the industry's private sector, and four public systems control most of the public sector's assets and generation.[3] Altogether about one hundred systems generate nearly all of this country's electric power. Among these large companies there can be considerable competition for bulk power sales, as noted in the story of Bartow. They compete both to attract new customers into their areas and for actual customers when more than one generating company serves a region.

The Federal Power Commission (FPC) regulates the interstate bulk power (wholesale) business, which accounts for about 15 percent of the private sector's total sales.[4] But the FPC has neither the means nor the will to be an effective substitute for a competitive market to keep prices down. In the 1960s, when the rapid development of economies of scale kept reducing costs, the commission's staff settled most complaints by negotiating reduced rates. Those cases that were fully litigated, however, often took years and thousands of dollars in legal fees before the commission and the courts reached final decisions. In the past three years, when inflation has reversed the downward trend of costs, the number of disputed cases before the FPC has drastically increased. One former commissioner told a meeting of municipal utilities:

> [Y]our interest may be better served through bargaining with your supplier looking toward settlements than through the process of invoking the assistance which the law proffers you in proceedings before the FPC.*[5]

But if a large utility has a monopoly over the bulk power supply of a region, a small retailer will not be in a strong bargaining position. If the competitive market is to work, there must be several suppliers of generation in order to have competition among them in any one area. There are several ways to accomplish this. One is to have new companies build new plants in the region, which entails troublesome economic and environmental costs. A more preferable alternative is to use long distance, extra high voltage transmission lines to allow a company's plants to serve several areas. Then different companies in different places could compete for the same customers.

There is even no need to build more than one set of transmission lines if "wheeling' can be widely employed. Wheeling occurs when company A, for a fee, carries on its transmission lines bulk power generated by company B to B's customer, C. It could avoid the unnecessary construction of expensive and unsightly transmission lines. More important, its potential for increasing bulk power competition is immense. If power can be wheeled, supplier and purchaser need not be geographically contiguous, but can be as far away as transmission lines are long. Under tradi-

---

* Of course, this work load has forced the commission to rely solely upon complaints to ferret out unlawful practices. The FPC itself has not instituted a rate case on its own motion in almost nine years.

tional "bottleneck monopoly" theory, the company that owns transmission lines, which as a practical matter cannot be duplicated, must allow all comers fair and equal access to it. Hence an area's transmission grid should be available for use by all companies, regardless of whether they own the lines, up to, of course, the limit of the line's capacity.

In many areas of the country wheeling is already standard practice. But in other places, anticompetitive refusals to wheel are a commonplace tactic of the large companies, who own the lines, in their continuing battle with small utilities. In what former FPC Chairman Lee White said was a "painful" decision, the commission ruled in 1969 that it did not have the statutory authority to compel wheeling.[6]

Under pressure from several public utilities denied access to low-cost federal power by private companies that refused to wheel and from congressional public power advocates such as Montana Senator Lee Metcalf,* the Justice Department filed a test case against Otter Tail Power Co. to break "the tyranny of transmission." In late February of 1973, the United States Supreme Court issued a landmark decision which held that refusals to wheel could indeed be attacked by means of the antitrust laws. By a four to three vote, the Supreme Court affirmed a decision made by a U.S. District Court a year and a half earlier and ordered Otter Tail to cease its

> refusals to sell at wholesale or to wheel [practices which were employed] solely to prevent municipal power systems from eroding its monopolistic position.[7]

Wheeling assures that every generator of bulk power will have access to transmission lines, but wheeling alone is not enough. If only a handful of companies generate bulk power, all the wheeling in the world will not create effective competition. It therefore becomes necessary to have a great many bulk power generators, but this imperative seems to run dead into the wall of economies of scale. Most companies by themselves cannot afford to build the

---

* An alternative means of promoting wheeling has recently been revived by Senator Metcalf and others who have proposed the construction of a federally owned National Power Grid, which would transmit power for all systems, private or public.

large efficient new plants, the accompanying transmission lines, and the reserves necessary in case a generator should fail. The economic impact of these plants requires that they be built only according to carefully thought out, long-range, *regional* plans. Is it possible for the numerous systems that comprise the power industry to work together to plan and build new plants and lines, yet still retain enough competitive incentives to keep costs and prices down?

Some, like Donald C. Cook, former chairman of the SEC and currently chairman of the nation's largest private utility, American Electric Power Company (AEP), answer no. Cook believes that a competitive power industry of firms of diverse size and ownership will be unable to exploit technological advances effectively. Instead he proposes that the industry be reorganized into twelve to fifteen regional giants, each monopolistically supreme in its own region.[8] This proposal of course would eliminate bulk power competition. It would also mean the disappearance of small, locally controlled distribution utilities. But there is no economic justification for total vertical integration in the power industry. Few economies of scale exist at the retail distribution level. If wheeling is enforced to guarantee them access to low cost bulk power (wherever and by whomever generated), utilities that sell only to consumers at retail need not be very large. There is simply no justification for sacrificing local control to the deity of efficiency as Cook proposes.

Cook's scheme goes even further: it would effectively exempt the electric power industry from governmental regulation. Because each of Cook's companies would be a vertical monopoly generating, transmitting, and distributing all of a region's power, there would be no wholesale sales for the FPC to regulate. The regional size of the companies would defeat state attempts at regulation.

State regulation currently entails public service commissions regulating retail consumer rates on a cost of service basis. Retail sales—including sales to industry, which are generally unregulated—account now for over 93 percent of total revenues of electric utilities.[9] Because Cook's proposal would increase this to 100 percent, quality state regulation is essential to protect the consumer and limit the utilities' power.

Most states now are doing a very poor job. A recent

econometric study shows that regulation has not been effective in reducing prices; in fact, on the average, regulated rates of privately owned utilities are only slightly below what monopoly prices would be.[10] Some of the reasons were explained by Charles R. Ross, former chairman of the Vermont Public Service Commission for two years and a member of the Federal Power Commission for seven, who recently testified:

> [R]egulation of a large . . . utility system is a hard job at best, and in many cases State regulation, particularly, has been plagued with lack of funds, lack of staff, too many political appointments, and too few independent knowledgeable commissioners.[11]

Creating Cook's twelve to fifteen regional giants would finish off the state commissions' power; this loss would make the political task of their resuscitation (that they *have not* been responsive to the public interest does not mean they *cannot* be) all but impossible. It would be nearly impossible for any single state to determine which part of a multi-state operation was properly allocable to that state in order to determine what a just rate for that state's consumers would be. Already Cook's company, AEP, which operates in seven states, is essentially unregulatable by any one of them and is substantially free to set uniform, system-wide rates. As utilities grow larger, the states' problem would be even greater.

Moreover, these large utilities would then be politically untouchable. As former Commissioner Ross noted of today's large, privately owned systems:

> The best lobbyist is on their payroll; the important, and usually the best lawyers are retained by them; the best-known advertising agency is employed by them when needed. The industry's trade organization is constantly advising them as to the proper tactics in beating regulation.[12]

He should have added that the most prominent financiers and businessmen sit on their boards of directors. In Philadelphia, for example, ten of the eleven members of the board of Philadelphia Electric Company also sit on the boards of five leading Philadelphia banks. The boards of the four major New England utilities read like a *Who's Who* of the local business and financial community, with banks, insurance companies, investment brokers, and universities predominant among the affiliations of the board members.[13] It would be naïve to believe that these men did not add their own influence to their lobbyists' and lawyers' to protect their interests. Enlarging the size of the utilities would only add to the economic and political power that the companies and their directors wield.*

Cook's proposed reorganization would also eliminate two other forms of competition, generally grouped together under the rubric of "yardstick" competition. No two firms are identical; they each have different administrative, managerial, and technical practices that have different costs and benefits. A multiplicity of firms means a variety of practices, which can be compared by the regulatory agencies, the public, and the firms themselves to determine the most efficient.†

The second form of yardstick competition results from diversity peculiar to the power industry: the conflict between public and private ownership. Since the early days of the industry, the privately owned utilities, and local, state, and federal governments have waged almost continual battle over the government's proper role. Although the relative size of the two sectors has remained stable for more than a decade—private companies generate approximately 77 percent of all bulk power; federal projects, about 13 percent; state and local utilities, the rest[14]—the intensity of the ideological and political struggle has not diminished.

Some of this competition has been beneficial to the consumer, spurring different utilities to improve service and lower rates. The proximity of publicly owned utilities, whose rates are generally lower than their private counterparts,[15] has driven down the costs of private power. As *Fortune* magazine noted, "federal power projects, such as

* It is nearly impossible to determine precisely who owns the private utilities. Much of their stock is held by institutional investors on behalf of others, but present FPC and SEC regulations require only the listing of the institutional investor (the "street name") on ownership reports and not the real parties in interest. Senator Metcalf has strongly criticized this practice.

† To facilitate such comparisons, the FPC in late 1969 circulated the preliminary draft of a proposed new publication, "Performance Profiles," which lists basic data for the 216 major private utilities in thirty-seven different categories. As these statistics supply much of the raw data for intercompany comparisons, their regular and widespread publication is still long overdue.

the TVA, have had the healthy effect of lowering the prices, improving the efficiency and even raising the earnings of neighboring private utilities."[16] A TVA pamphlet confirms this statement. Using 1937 to 1963 data, it shows the rates of private companies increasing proportionally to the distance from TVA. It also shows that the earnings of private companies bordering on TVA have grown much faster than the national average of private utilities.[17]

Nonetheless, political battles are still waged over every proposed expansion or contraction of public power. And many private utilities continue to engage in wasteful and discriminatory practices against public power systems. For example, a recent SEC hearing uncovered a summary by a participant in a January, 1968, conference of private utility executives on various means to acquire public municipal systems. The process described was long-term and complex, involving good public relations, careful political and legal maneuvering, and calculated refusals to sell or wheel wholesale power at low cost. The object was to force the public system either to build its own inefficient generator or sell out to the private company.[18] The executives also discussed excluding municipals and rural cooperatives from the planning and ownership of new generators, thus perpetuating the public systems' dependence upon the private utilities for a supply of bulk power. Sometimes, when private companies actually do sell bulk power to municipals, they charge discriminatory rates or impose anticompetitive restrictions on the use of the power. These rate schemes have been the subject of extensive and lengthy litigation before the FPC, and generally have been struck down.

Nonetheless, the practices persist, and recent testimony before the SEC reveals that many large private systems use similar techniques against small private utilities. Privately owned companies are particularly vulnerable because in order to protect shareholders and attract investors, a company's earnings must increase over time. Because a utility's earnings are based on its capital assets (its rate base), private utilities prefer to invest in new generation and transmission equipment rather than simply purchase wholesale power. By denying a small system the opportunity to participate in the joint ownership of new units that the small company cannot afford to build by itself, a large company can do serious damage to a small one's long-term growth potential. This tactic effectively coerces the small company to sell out to the larger one while it can still command a good price.

The private utilities—big and little—have also engaged in intense lobbying efforts against extension of public power projects. For example, seventeen New England utilities reported to the FPC that they spent $567,000 from 1964 to 1968 in a successful, joint campaign to defeat the proposed federal Dickey-Lincoln School hydroelectric project in northern Maine. Their efforts were called by Senator Edmund Muskie, and several other congressmen, "the most vicious [lobbying we] have ever experienced."[19]

Cook's proposal would end all this competition and rivalry. Instead, he would substitute interfuel competition, especially between electricity and natural gas. But in many instances the two products are not interchangeable. As Amherst economics professor James R. Nelson testified before the SEC, "natural gas has always found its greatest strength in heating uses, and electricity in lighting and power." Furthermore, Professor Nelson argued that for interfuel competition "[t]o be effective . . . [it] would have to involve a number of different suppliers of each of the two energy resources." Thus, he concluded "that at best *inter*modal gas-electric competition is weak and *intra*-modal competition is a necessary prerequisite for effective intermodal competition.[20] Competition should not be eliminated in one area because it exists in another.[21] Our goal should be to foster competition wherever possible and Cook's proposed industry reorganization would do just the opposite.

What is needed is a reorganization plan designed to maintain institutional diversity, to preserve bulk power and yardstick competition, to assure equal access to transmission grids, and to protect local distributing companies; in short, a plan designed to preserve as many—not as few—companies as possible, consistent with the efficient exploitation of economies of scale.

Two major procompetitive alternatives to Cook's scheme have been proposed: the separation of generation and transmission from distribution, and the wide scale use of pooling.

Several experts, including S. David Freeman, former director of the energy policy staff of the Office of Science and Technology and a former FPC staff member, have revived Leland Olds's suggestion to separate generation and transmission companies from distribution utilities. Modeled after TVA and Bonneville Power Administration, the "G&T" companies would supply bulk power in large enough quantities to take advantage of scale economies, and would share a common transmission grid to which all systems would have access. The "G&T" companies would not distribute at retail; that would be left to numerous local utilities. The industry would be able to achieve economies of scale where possible without forgoing bulk power and yardstick competition, regulation, and local distribution.[22]

This proposal has considerable merit as a long-range plan to institutionalize a competitive, efficient power industry. Two important questions, which have been the subject of much disagreement among the proposal's adherents, must still be answered. How many "G&T" companies should there be and who should control them? First, as the number of companies in a region diminishes, rate and yardstick competition among them also decrease. The fewer the number of companies, the greater the need to protect against the danger of monopoly profits. And second, either the regulator (the FPC) must be considerably strengthened or the "G&T" company publicly owned. The latter is now the case with TVA and Bonneville and was recently recommended for New England. But even a publicly owned company, especially if given powers of eminent domain, raises additional problems of political accountability and responsiveness to local environmental and economic concerns. As Freeman stressed:

> it would seem wise to keep as many bulk suppliers in the business as are consistent with considerations of efficiency because even the prospect of a single G&T for each region raises problems of concentration of economic power which are a cause for concern.[23]

Nationwide adoption of Freeman's proposal would require congressional action, but its basic principles can be tested now. The FPC and the SEC, when ruling upon merger applications, should consider conditioning their approval upon a divestiture of distribution facilities and a guarantee of open access for any other utility to transmission lines.

The Federal Power Commission's *National Power Survey* in 1964 suggested the second alternative: a complex network of power pools in which all systems of diverse size and ownership would participate. Instead of a few large companies or thirty-five hundred isolated systems, the *Power Survey* envisioned a national system of many, fully coordinated, and interconnected regional power pools, each composed of economically independent companies. By means of interconnections (transmission links between utilities), several companies could share the costs and output of large generating units and pool the necessary reserves in case of breakdown. These pools would coordinate expansion and operations and allow staggered or joint development of new equipment; as a result, a fully interconnected industry could effectively exploit new technology with minimal damage to existing patterns of ownership, competition, and regulation.

Pooling itself has potential antitrust difficulties. By working together, pool members are able to take advantage of scale economies none alone could utilize to generate the lowest-cost power possible. But in the process the pool becomes the sole supplier of cheap bulk power in its area. Nonpool members are then at a significant disadvantage in competing with pool members for customers. Under classic antitrust concepts, such joint action would be prohibited unless necessary to achieve some desired goal (in this case, economies of scale) and unless its benefits were available to all competitors on fair terms. Thus membership in pools and participation in their coordinated operations and expansion must be open to all systems on equitable terms.

In fact, however, the large private companies appear to be systematically excluding small utilities from full-fledged pool membership, without significant government interference. Of the twenty-two formal power pools in operation in 1970, only four included public power systems. In the other eighteen, only eight of the participating private systems could be considered small. "One can only conclude," Dr. David S. Schwartz, assistant chief of the FPC Office of Economics, told a Senate committee in 1971, "that the small systems [public and private] have not been successful in finding an accommodation in the various formal power pooling arrangements."[24] One pool, the CARVA pool in Virginia and the Carolinas, recently disbanded because of internal disagreements and because of fear of an antitrust challenge by public systems denied membership.

Because pooling is based upon interfirm coordination, it involves more collusive activity than would normally be permitted under the antitrust laws. Much of this activity is necessary to achieve desired economies of scale, but the possibility of "more restrictive agreements than necessary" is still great.[25] What is required is careful governmental surveillance of pooling agreements. But as is noted below, such scrutiny has not been forthcoming.

On the whole, however, pooling appears to be an extremely effective, procompetitive means of exploiting new technology. Pushed by the FPC, the industry reacted favorably to the recommendations of the *Power Survey*. The number of formal power pools increased from nine in 1960, accounting for 23 percent of the country's total generating capacity, to twenty-two pools in 1970, accounting for 65 percent of generation capacity.[26] There is an even larger number of informal pools, coordinating and reliability councils, and backup interconnections. The major disappointment of the pooling movement has been the failure of the federal government to follow through on the *Power Survey*'s vision of a pooled and pluralistic power industry. To this story we now turn.

The Federal Power Commission . . . and Friends

The Federal Power Commission got off to a good start in the area of pooling but has since faltered. Its *National Power Survey* in 1964 popularized and stressed the concept as a means of preserving companies of diverse ownership and size. Under the chairmanships of Kennedy-appointee Joseph C. Swidler and Johnson-appointee Lee C. White, the commission promoted pooling with some success, but the scope of the commission's authority under its 1935 statute was uncertain. After two major blackouts in the Northeast, the FPC in 1967 petitioned Congress for plenary authority to regulate power pools and steam generation plants and to compel the full participation of all segments of the industry. In return the commission could grant antitrust immunity. Private companies, however, opposed any extension of the commission's authority and the forced inclusion of public power systems into pools; the legislation died in committee.

This opposition seems to have overwhelmed the present commission. Under Chairman John N. Nassikas, appointed by President Nixon, the agency has taken no formal steps to assure the full participation of all systems in technological advances. In 1970, for example, in establishing regional councils to promote inter-system coordination to increase reliability and control blackouts, the commission refused to require admission of all utilities to the councils. Instead, the FPC adopted a plan devised by the major private companies to forestall congressional action requiring more representative membership and closer governmental supervision. In its order the FPC specifically rejected a request by the American Public Power Association and the National Rural Electric Cooperative Association to require that the councils be open to all segments of the industry and not be left to the unfettered discretion of the large companies. The FPC did not even insist upon its own participation in the councils. It merely requested permission to attend in a nonvoting capacity.[27]

By stressing voluntary cooperation in the face of the major private companies' long-standing desire to eliminate small utilities, and in the absence of much real cooperation in the recent history of power pooling, the FPC effectively decided that competition and diversity of ownership are not important. Indeed, the commission has threatened to ask Congress for antitrust immunity powers if its voluntary cooperation scheme does not pass antitrust scrutiny.[28]

The commission's authority to regulate power pooling remains largely undefined. The Supreme Court recently affirmed the commission's broad authority to order pooling and set the terms and conditions of interconnections between systems.[29] Because all pooling agreements involve the purchase and sale of wholesale power, they are subject to the commission's general authority to regulate wholesale sales and "any rate, regulation, practice or contract affecting such rate, charge, or classification," under sections 205 and 206 of the Federal Power Act. Pooling agreements are in fact filed with the commission, but it has never exercised its authority to force modification of pooling agreements that unjustly or unreasonably discriminate against other systems.

Two antitrust challenges to pooling agreements are, however, pending before the commission and decisions in these cases could easily determine the future of broad-based pooling. In both cases the FPC accepted (after lengthy delays) agreements signed by the major private companies in New England and allowed them to take effect immediately over the objections of the municipals. At the same time the commission ordered hearings on the public companies' objections, but placed the case in a procedural setting in which the burden of proving antitrust or other violations would be on the objecting municipals, and in which only prospective relief could be granted. In the interim period before a final decision of the municipals' challenge—which could take years—the companies' agreements will be binding on all. The ruling, which will make it difficult if not impossible for the public systems ever to recover their damages should their challenge to the pooling agreements be successful, does not augur well for the future of pooling regulation by the Federal Power Commission.

The FPC has demonstrated its insensitivity to questions of competition in other ways. No one we interviewed could recall the FPC ever refusing a merger when its approval was required. In a recent case involving the merger of two Iowa utilities, the commission reviewed its competitive responsibilities: it would not require a showing of positive benefit to the public from the proposed merger nor would it examine alternative means of achieving the desired benefits, short of merger.[30]

The commission originally approved the Iowa merger over the opposition of Iowa Attorney General Richard C. Turner. When the case was in its final stages before the FPC, Turner filed a petition to intervene. He charged that the merger, which the companies had discussed intermittently for fifteen years, was the first step toward a planned consolidation of all Iowa utilities; this proposal would not result, he said, in the financial savings the companies claimed. In December, 1970, shortly after this petition had been filed, the commission approved the merger application. Turner moved for a rehearing and the commission

conducted a special hearing on his charges. At this point
the companies dropped their plans, citing the commission's
delay beyond their June 30, 1971, deadline.

The commission, in the December opinion, had rejected
staff suggestions that it order the merging company to
divest itself of natural gas distribution facilities in order to
deal solely in electric power. The staff argued that combination gas-electric utilities were inimical to interfuel competition. In Chairman Nassikas's words (although he
discounted these benefits as only a "possibility"),

> direct competition between gas and electricity may induce
> greater efficiency of performance and effort by each utility
> to economize on labor and capital and give better service.
> Competition may also provide more freedom of consumer
> choice and it will eliminate the danger that one service,
> either gas or electricity, will be neglected wherever there
> are advantages for a combination utility to promote one
> service at the expense of the other.[31]

The proponents of combination utilities argue that these
benefits are outweighed by the benefits of joint operation,
such as combined meter readings and joint service departments. But statistical studies by private and governmental
econometrists show that these savings are minimal at best.
In fact, customers of combination utilities generally have
to pay more for their electricity than consumers of single
utilities.[32]

In ruling on the Iowa merger, the commission ignored
these studies and said simply, without explanation, "substantial detriment would result from the divestiture of the
gas properties." A few months later, testifying before the
Senate Antitrust Subcommittee, Chairman Nassikas stated
that he opposed Senator Metcalf's bill requiring all major
combination utilities be split into two, one gas and one
electric. Noting that this bill would restructure about two-
fifths of the power industry, the chairman argued that "in
the absense of compelling evidence that the public interest
is not being served by the combination gas and electric
utilities, it is undesirable as a matter of Congressional
policy to mandate divestiture." Subtly, the chairman reversed the burden of proof implicit in the antitrust laws
and policy. No longer would competition be the primary
goal, to be moderated only when overriding considerations
dicate a different route. Under his analysis, the mere "pos-

sibility" of competitive benefits is insufficient to justify changing the status quo, even when statistical evidence does not show the noncompetitive status quo to be providing any significant benefits to consumers.

The staff's recommendation to approve the merger but require the divestiture of gas facilities was itself a compromise among various factions of the commission's personnel. Some were opposed to the merger entirely, arguing that the existence of a power pool and the possibility of a joint venture limited to new generation eliminated the need for a merger. Others were more inclined to accept the applicants' claim of administrative and managerial savings as sufficient, because there is no direct competition between the two firms. Discord among these factions and the absence of cooperation among the economic, technical, and legal staff specialists prevented the staff from making a strong showing at the hearings; they offered no witnesses, and limited themselves to cross-examination. As one pro-competition staff member summed up the case, "Iowa was a disaster."

Fortunately the FPC does not pass on antitrust issues in the electrical power industry in a vacuum. "Outside agitators" push and prod it in its judgments. These external stimuli include the courts, the Antitrust Division, and a private attorney named George Spiegel.

The courts have not applauded the FPC's efforts to ignore competition. In two leading cases, both dealing with the commission's regulation of natural gas but applicable in principle to electric power regulation, the courts have clearly reminded the commission of its antitrust responsibilities.

In the first case (part of the ongoing *El Paso* litigation), the commission attempted to immunize the merger of two natural gas pipeline companies that the Justice Department had filed suit to prevent. Two weeks after the suit was filed in U.S. District Court, the companies applied to the FPC for approval to merge. When this request was granted in late 1959, the companies immediately merged. The commission's decision was appealed to the Supreme Court, which ruled that while "evidence of antitrust violations is plainly relevant in merger applications" before the FPC, the commission has no power to grant antitrust immunity.

The court further held that when a court suit is pending challenging a merger, the commission should defer acting until the suit is decided. In a later decision, the Supreme Court unanimously ruled that the merger, which the FPC had approved, violated the antitrust laws.[38] But the companies, married with commission blessings, have yet to be separated because of the difficulty of framing an adequate divestiture decree.

In a more recent pipeline case—*Great Lakes*—the commission again ran afoul of the courts. *Great Lakes* involved a proposed joint venture by two potential competitors to construct a pipeline to transport Canadian natural gas through the large natural gas consuming regions of Minnesota, Michigan, and Wisconsin. Each of the companies originally had filed separate applications for permission to build the line, later withdrawing them in favor of a joint project. Both a competing applicant and FPC staff counsel George Lewnes attempted to raise antitrust issues at the hearing but were denied the opportunity to present relevant tesimony. The commission approved the joint venture and the losing applicant appealed.

The Court of Appeals for the District of Columbia ordered the commission to hear the antitrust evidence and weigh it along with other factors comprising the "public interest" standard that governed the case. After an extensive review of the fact situation, the court noted that the case "presents the most clear example of a joint venture lessening competition." The court reminded the commission:

> Even limited competition would seem to encourage suppliers of natural gas to become more aggressive in proposing new rates and services, and thereby increase the effectiveness of regulation by the Commission. . . . Unless the Commission finds that other important considerations militate in favor of the joint venture and that these considerations are more beneficial to the public than additional competition, the antitrust policies should be respected and the joint venture set aside.[34]

The case was sent back to the FPC for reconsideration. On remand, the Antitrust Division, which had claimed insufficient manpower to enter earlier, intervened to join the FPC staff in opposition to the joint venture. After a round of hearings on antitrust issues, the case once again came before the commission for decision. In oral argument the statements of the Antitrust Division attorney about potential competition and vertical foreclosure of future entrants were largely ignored; instead, the commissioners berated him for not entering the case the first time around. In its final opinion, issued July, 1970, the commission unanimously concluded that the proposal would not have serious anticompetitive effects, and reaffirmed its initial approval of the joint venture.[35]

The Antitrust Division's record in electric power matters is mixed but improving. The division's first two civil suits were successful. One, instituted in 1968 against the Tampa Electric–Florida Power agreement to allocate wholesale sales territories, ended in a consent decree forbidding such anticompetitive agreements and requiring the companies to modify all existing contracts and notify all electric utilities in Florida of the consent decree. *Otter Tail* was another, resulting in a strong opinion by the Minnesota district court that refusals to wheel in order to maintain monopoly power violated the Sherman Act; the Supreme Court affirmed the decision over the opposition of the FPC.*

On the major antitrust questions raised by power pooling, the division's response until recently has been less than satisfactory. Answering hypothetical questions posed by the *National Power Survey*'s Legal Advisory Committee, the then antitrust chief Lee Loevinger raised serious doubts whether pools with anticompetitive agreements to allocate service areas and customers would be valid under the antitrust laws. These answers did not please many in the industry who, contemplating one of the first major interregional pools, the Pacific Northwest–Southwest Intertie, were unwilling to risk division intervention. They convinced Senator Warren Magnuson, whose Senate Commerce Committee has jurisdiction over the FPC, to hold hearings in 1966 on a bill granting antitrust immunity to FPC-approved pooling arrangements.

Although the bill did not pass, the new assistant attorney

* The Antitrust Division has several other cases under investigation, one involving the efforts of a private utility in Louisiana to prevent the formation of a pool composed of municipals, cooperatives, and industry. The division declined an FPC invitation to intervene in the Iowa merger case, but entered two far more significant proceedings before the SEC, which are discussed shortly.

general, Donald Turner, gave the industry the reassurance it sought. Turner stated at the hearings that a "rule of reason" applies to the agreements and that "while agreements to refuse to deal with competitors or to divide sales territories are normally illegal, if the parties can show that they are necessary to secure the benefits of a desirable pooling arrangement, their agreements will probably not be invalid under the antitrust laws." The Justice Department, Turner concluded, was not intending "to launch a major antitrust effort in the electric power industry" and would pay considerable attention to an FPC determination that a particular agreement was reasonable.[36] Thus Turner effectively took the division out of power pool regulation. But by leaving the matter to the FPC, he removed antitrust enforcement as well.

There are indications that the Antitrust Division may be reconsidering this decision. A 1970 change in the Atomic Energy Act requires that all applications to the AEC for licenses to construct nuclear power plants must first be referred to the Justice Department for review. Sparked by a refugee attorney from the FPC staff, the division has interpreted its role under this amendment very broadly. From the "totality of Applicant's conduct vis-à-vis the smaller utilities" and others, the division decides whether to clear the application, sometimes imposing conditions, or to request the AEC hold hearings on the antitrust issues its investigation uncovers.[37] The division has asked for hearings in ten of the twenty-seven applications filed under the amendment so far. In nine others, division approval was granted only after the applicant had agreed to changes that eliminated the division's antitrust objections. The issues the division has raised run the full gamut of anticompetitive behavior, including refusal to admit small utilities to power pooling and joint ventures, refusal to wheel, and discriminatory rate and other contract provisions. Because most major utilities sooner or later ask the AEC's permission to build nuclear plants. AEC hearings (the first of which are now underway) and Justice Department review have enormous potential to eliminate antitrust activities in the industry.

The AEC review letters are signed by the assistant attorney general for antitrust; the attorney general's approval is not required. Were it otherwise the letters' content might be quite different, because, as *The Closed Enterprise System* extensively shows, attorneys general tend to resist aggressive antitrust enforcement.

The Antitrust Division's recent burst of activity in the electric power field is welcome. It comes after years of inactivity during which small utilities, seeking admission to power pools over the opposition of large private companies, were forced to adopt circuitous tactics to achieve their goals. The inventor and undoubted master of these techniques is George Spiegel, one of the few but growing number of Washington lawyers who regularly represent publicly owned utilities.

Practicing what one admirer called "guerrilla warfare," Spiegel has avoided expensive, all-out, risky rate cases or antitrust suits that big private companies could delay indefinitely. Instead, he has developed a new technique: intervention in agency actions brought by the big companies themselves for approval of a new project or financing request. As an intervenor, Spiegel raises antitrust questions, arguing that his clients have been unfairly excluded from participating in the proposed project. He petitions the commission to require the companies to purge themselves of these anticompetitive practices before approving the project.

Anxious to speed their plans through the agencies, the companies can either expedite trial on the antitrust questions, negotiate a settlement, or shut Spiegel out of the proceedings altogether. Attempts at the last alternative have not succeeded, as courts have upheld Spiegel's right to raise, and have hearings held on, antitrust questions. With this support, Spiegel, through negotiations and hearings, has educated the agencies regarding anticompetitive practices, and at the same time gradually secured favorable concessions for his clients.

Spiegel first intervened before the FPC in the *Northfield Mountain* case. In 1966 the three subsidiaries of the newly formed holding company, Northeast Utilities (NEU), applied for an FPC license to construct a one-million-kilowatt pumped storage hydroelectric plant on Northfield Mountain in western Massachusetts. The plant was to be the largest of its kind anywhere, and one of the largest of any type in New England. On behalf of his client, the

Municipal Electric Association of Massachusetts, Spiegel intervened in the license proceedings; he raised a number of issues, including two antitrust questions. He argued that the exclusion of the Massachusetts municipals from the private utilities regional planning council was a "bottleneck monopoly" or "collective boycott" that placed the municipals at an illegal competitive disadvantage in obtaining access to future sources of low cost bulk power. He also insisted that his clients be allowed to purchase power from the Northfield Mountain project on the same basis as private utilities.

The FPC staff attorneys agreed. Together with Spiegel they argued to the commission that approval of the project under section 10(h), the restraint of trade section of the Federal Power Act, be conditioned on the cessation of these illegal practices. Although the commission denied the exclusion from planning claim as "collateral" to the main issues in the case, it did set an important precedent by conditioning the project's license on NEU's promise to sell power on a nondiscriminatory basis to all, and to transport power to the limit of its transmission grid.[38] More significantly, during the course of the litigation, the private utilities agreed for the first time to let the Massachusetts municipals participate in a newly reorganized power planning council.

While this case was in progress, eleven of New England's largest private utilities announced the formation of two jointly owned corporations, Vermont Yankee and Maine Yankee. The new companies, hastily formed to preempt proposed state public power projects, would construct and operate two nuclear-powered generators in Vermont and Maine. These projects were planned to produce the cheapest electricity in New England. Before construction could begin, the AEC had to license the plant, and the SEC, because utility holding companies were involved, had to approve the financing of the joint venture. Arguing that their exclusion from these joint ventures violated antitrust law and policy, the Massachusetts municipals through Spiegel intervened and requested hearings on the antitrust questions before the AEC and the SEC. Both agencies, at the urging of the companies, denied this request and approved the projects. Spiegel appealed. In March, 1969, the Court of Appeals for the District of Columbia reversed the SEC and ordered the commission to conduct a hearing on Spiegel's petition. A few months later the same court upheld the AEC's decision to issue a construction permit but warned the agency that it would have to hear and decide the antitrust question before granting a final, operating license.[39] (Ultimately Congress changed the law in 1970 requiring an early referral to the Antitrust Division as noted above.)

Having successfully undone the commission's precipitous approval of the project, Spiegel turned the SEC hearing on remand into an extended negotiating session for his client, while at the same time exploring the companies' anticompetitive activities. Ultimately, a settlement was reached, guaranteeing the municipals and all other previously excluded systems an opportunity to purchase the plants' power. The companies once again agreed to wheel the power to the municipals over their regional transmission system.

The New England situation is significant because electricity rates are higher there than anywhere else in the continental United States, except New York City. As the Zinder Report to the New England Regional Commission stated, the average price per kilowatt hour paid by New Englanders in 1968 was 30 percent more than in the rest of the United States. One reason for these high rates is that the industry in this area is composed of 144 poorly coordinated utilities using small, relatively inefficient generators. In 1968, for example, the region had no nonnuclear steam generation plants capable of producing more than 750,000 kilowatts. In the rest of the nation, 37 percent of the generation capacity was in larger (and more efficient) plants.[40] But the New England utilities approach any limitation on their independence cautiously, making coordination difficult. It thus took several years of negotiations before the nine major private companies were able to reach agreement in December, 1968, to establish a comprehensive regional pool (NEPOOL) to coordinate generation and transmission facilities and to plan and build new units jointly.

But the agreement excluded the Massachusetts municipals, other publicly owned systems, and many small private companies. Flushed by the triumph in the *Northfield Mountain* case and hopeful that court appeals in the

Vermont Yankee case would be equally successful, Spiegel and the municipals threatened to intervene before the FPC to block approval of the power pool agreement. They also threatened a treble-damage antitrust suit against the companies. Rather than risk commission and court action, the companies reopened negotiations. This time representatives of all segments of the industry participated, including the municipals, small privates, and observers from the FPC and Senator Edward Kennedy's office.

Although the second round of negotiations appeared to bear fruit in an initial accord in May, 1970, the parties could never agree on final terms. On November 1, 1971, the major private companies agreed to establish a full-scale power pool, NEPOOL, on terms unacceptable to the municipals. As noted previously, the municipals formally objected to the FPC, which in September, 1972, allowed NEPOOL to take effect and placed upon the municipals the burden of proving the companies' wrongdoing. Pending the outcome of the hearings, the companies' agreement is binding upon all. Once again Spiegel has taken to the courts to undo this instance of the FPC's insensitivity to issues of competition.

Spiegel has also intervened before the SEC and FPC in three routine securities refinancing applications filed by the private utilities. The agencies refused to grant Spiegel and the cities a hearing on the antitrust issues they raised. Spiegel appealed the refusal and once again the Court of Appeals for the District of Columbia agreed with him and ruled that both commissions (and particularly the FPC) must consider antitrust issues even in connection with routine financial applications if there is "a reasonable nexus between the activities challenged and the activities furthered by the application."[41] The private utilities appealed to the Supreme Court, which has agreed to rule on the question just how much attention the FPC must pay to antitrust principles.

Mergers and the SEC

New England's major private utilities have not yet abandoned their policy of linking, wherever possible, agreements for joint construction of new generation with agreements to merge. In 1966 three companies, which for

many years had coordinated generation an[ ]
efforts while remaining independent as part[ ]
necticut Valley Electric Exchange, merged
holding company Northeast Utilities; this o[ ]
prior to their joint development of the North[ ]
tain project. Two years later, NEU, now the largest utility
in New England, solidified its dominant position in Western Massachusetts by swallowing up the small private
utility Holyoke Water Power Company, which had been
excluded from participating in the Yankee nuclear joint
ventures.[42]

The executives of two other small private utilities testified under subpoena at recent SEC hearings regarding
their efforts to construct the Seabrook nuclear plant. These
companies wanted the project to insure their long-range
independence by increasing their rate base and guaranteeing them access to low cost power. After expending over
$7 million on the project, the utilities were ultimately frus-
trated by the intransigence of the major private companies,
whose cooperation in the plant's financing and commitments to purchase power were necessary for a feasible
project. Without the participation of the majors, the project had to be abandoned.[43]

Several of the big private companies still do not appear
to consider NEPOOL a viable alternative to affiliation.
Three of the region's top seven, Boston Edison, NEES, and
Eastern Utilities Associates (EUA) have applied to the
SEC for permission to merge into a new holding company.
The proposed firm, Eastern Electric Energy System, with
combined assets of over $2 billion, would be the largest
utility in New England, with more than 36 percent of the
region's generating capacity and retail sales. It would
dominate the Massachusetts power market, with about two-
thirds of its generation and sales, and, in many categories,
would rank among the ten largest electric utilities in the
nation.[44] The proposal is before the Securities and Exchange Commission under the Public Utility Holding
Company Act.*

---

* In 1935, at the same time it gave the FPC wholesale rate regulatory power, Congress vested the SEC with authority to reorganize
the country's electric and gas holding companies that had collapsed
during the Depression. The SEC spent most of the next twenty
years breaking up the huge trusts into numerous smaller units.

Then three merger-minded New England utilities came to the SEC in 1965 seeking to form a new holding company, Northeast Utilities. The holding company technique was preferable to a straight merger because many state laws require that utilities be operated by a company incorporated in that state. Since the stock of the operating corporation can be owned by outsiders, a holding company, by owning the stock of several corporations, can operate in more than one state. This petition was unprecedented in two respects. No one in recent years had come before the SEC seeking to expand a holding company significantly or to create a new one by merging several utilities. Previously, all the SEC had done was to break up such companies. The industry's private sector, to reward their courage, gave the New England companies its prestigious Edison Award.

George Spiegel was the second precedent. On behalf of his client, the City of Holyoke Gas and Electric Department, Spiegel intervened in the proceedings, seeking to condition the merger on an order that the new company interconnect with and sell bulk power to his client. Holyoke was located in the area to be served by NEU and was in need of additional wholesale power. Spiegel argued that the merger, by increasing concentration, would decrease the city's competitive opportunities to secure a favorable interconnection agreement. No one had previously asked the SEC to order an interconnection; that was generally considered the FPC's business. But, as it was easier to give Spiegel what his client wanted than risk losing a court battle against him, the companies negotiated an agreement. Spiegel withdrew and the merger application was granted without opposition in 1966. Two years later, NEU was allowed to add a fourth company, Holyoke Water Power, to its holdings.

When Boston Edison, NEES, and EUA went before the SEC in 1968 with their own merger plan, they expected Spiegel to attempt to intervene. The one question mark was the Antitrust Division, which the companies had notified of the merger plans. On the last day of the Johnson administration, the division decided to intervene.

Not satisfied with the companies' prepared testimony, the division and the SEC staff counsel asked to see the relevant company files. Although routine in a division antitrust case, this extensive discovery was new to an SEC merger hearing. (It has yet to be tried at the FPC.) The companies responded by turning over twenty-six thousand pages of documents. As one attorney described it, the documents, when introduced in the hearings, ended the companies' "nice image" at the SEC. They contained evidence of the full range of anticompetitive behavior by the companies. They described the major private companies' plans to exclude the municipals and small privates from large-scale generation and from NEPOOL. The documents detailed the companies' joint efforts to defeat the federal Dickey-Lincoln School project and several state public power projects. They also revealed how the large companies attempted, sometimes successfully, to force smaller companies into merger by refusing joint ownership or cooperation in the construction of large generators. There was even an internal memorandum on the possibility of "buying Spiegel off" by giving him or his clients enough of what they wanted to keep them quiet.

Armed with this evidence, Spiegel, the Antitrust Division, and the SEC staff proceeded to pick apart the companies' claim that engineering and managerial savings would result from the merger. More importantly, during the twenty-month, nine-thousand-page hearing, they documented arguments that the proposed increase in the concentration of ownership in the New England power industry would have a substantially negative impact on NEPOOL and the government agencies' ability to regulate bulk power and yardstick competition in general. In a preliminary decision the SEC's hearing examiner approved the merger, modified to lessen its anticompetitive impact. The municipals, the SEC staff, and the Antitrust Division appealed to the full commission to disallow the merger entirely. The case is pending before the commission, and any decision it makes is likely to be appealed further to the courts.

Similar issues are being litigated in the other, major merger case currently pending before the SEC—the application of Donald Cook's American Electric Power to acquire Columbus and Southern Ohio Electric Company. In terms of installed capacity AEP is the nation's largest private utility. It had assets over $3.8 billion in 1971,

operating revenues of almost $750,000,000 for the same
year, yielding a 12.6 percent return on equity for its seven-
state operation.[45]

Without needing to enter into pooling agreements, AEP
by itself is able to take full advantage of all economies of
scale. It is already building the largest generators and the
highest voltage transmission lines possible. Columbus and
Southern Ohio, on the other hand, is a moderate-sized
company, whose total generation capacity is smaller than
one of AEP's new units. To achieve scale economies,
Columbus and Southern has entered into the "CCD" pool
with two other private Ohio utilities for the joint ownership
of new generation and transmission. The three-company
pool is roughly equal in size to AEP's Ohio subsidiary.

Although AEP has promised to honor Columbus and
Southern's commitments to the CCD pool until they expire, it is not in AEP's long-range interests to be tied to a
pool it does not need, one that would hamper its freedom
of operation. Recognizing this fact, the other members of
the CCD pool have announced that they are studying the
possibility of merger with six other private utilities, including all the remaining independent private companies in
Ohio. The new holding company created would be even
larger than AEP and Columbus and Southern combined.

The increase in concentration resulting from the AEP
merger is not necessary to achieve economies of scale in
generation or transmission. The existing power pools are
already capable of exploiting new technological advances.
AEP argues, however, that it is easier and more efficient to
have all the planning done by one centrally controlled,
fully integrated company than by a committee of several
utilities with diverse interests. Although it may be quicker
to have one man making key decisions, it is not economically more efficient. Replacing many with one eliminates
all checks on that one's exercise of power, checks such as
bulk power and yardstick competition, and effective regulation. While there may be some managerial savings achieved
by replacing a pool with a holding company—although
some economists testified there are managerial *dis*economies of scale—they are substantially outweighed by the
increased costs of monopoly control: the increased concentration of economic and political power, and the unchecked danger of monopoly profits, decreased supply, and

increased rates. Furthermore, as Commissioner Ross argued in opposition to the merger:

> Under the guise of efficiency, autocratic rule has been justified from time immemorial. In all cases, the public was led to believe that anything else was wasteful. In some cases, on a short-run basis, this has been true. In most cases, however, the larger the unit under such one-man rule, the more devastating the consequences when such a ruler becomes convinced he can do no wrong.[46]

Louis Roddis, president of Con Ed of New York, was subpoenaed by the SEC staff to testify on the benefits of pooling and the advantages of collective decision making. Roddis spoke most favorably of his company's recent experience as a member of the New York State Power Pool, and contended that a well-run pool could obtain all the benefits of a single company. This testimony of a fellow utility executive enraged AEP's Cook. According to a trade press, *Electrical World Week,* Cook was "livid over Roddis' testimony" and over the publicity it received by syndicated columnist Jack Anderson. "Cook characterized the staff's handling of the case as 'absolutely outrageous— positively the worst I have ever seen.' "[47]

Prior to Roddis's appearance at the hearing, Cook called two members of Con Ed's board of directors, William S. Renchard, chairman of the board of Chemical Bank, with whom AEP has a $10 million line of credit, and Richard S. Perkins, retired chairman of the executive committee of the First National City Bank, in an unsuccessful attempt to stop Roddis from testifying.[48] During Roddis's testimony, AEP's lawyers served him with a nine-page subpoena, requiring production of voluminous documents. (After Roddis and the SEC staff objected, AEP withdrew most of its requests, and the hearing examiner quashed most of the rest.) Finally, AEP cut off the exchange of technical information with Con Ed.

These moves to intimidate Roddis, and more successful maneuvers against other witnesses from industry that he intended to call, incensed chief SEC staff counsel on the case, Bernard Nash. He charged AEP with seeking to

> intimidat[e] all those within the electric utility industry who would otherwise disagree with certain views of the applicant company and would otherwise communicate those

views to the appropriate governmental authorities for us to use as evidence in this proceeding.[49]

Nash countered with a subpoena to Cook and to an AEP lawyer in Ohio, to testify and produce documents regarding the extent of their ex parte attempts to influence the proceedings. Nash argued that this was necessary to explore the relationship between economic and political power. But the commission, anxious to complete the case, quashed the subpoenas.

The AEP merger application is in its sixth year before the SEC. Initial briefs were filed early in 1969 after six months of hearings, but AEP moved to reopen the hearings. At that point, the Justice Department, which had taken a long time making up its mind, intervened. The second round of hearings finally closed in early 1972 with a record over twenty thousand pages long. Just prior to the filing of briefs, AEP and the Ohio municipals announced that the municipals had withdrawn their opposition to the merger in return for AEP's promise to sell them a generating unit and to wheel power from the unit to the municipals. This settlement, however, did not mollify the opposition of the SEC staff and the Antitrust Division, who filed lengthy briefs charging, as the SEC staff wrote, that "approval [of the merger] would necessarily reject viable alternatives to merger—such as joint ventures, power pools, and other cooperative ventures. The affiliation will substantially lessen actual and potential competition, [and] will adversely affect localized management and control and effective regulation. . . ." The case is awaiting decision.

The commission's decisions in the AEP and the New England merger cases could very well set the pattern for restructuring the power industry in the coming decades. In each case, the SEC faces in almost naked form a choice between pooling and affiliation, competition and concentration. The antitrust laws and the history of the Public Utility Holding Company Act support the competitive alternative. The commission should follow the lead of its staff and the Justice Department and adopt that course.

The Wrong Remedy

Ever since the SEC completed the task of reorganizing the holding company structure in the mid-fifties, various officials, including most recently the Ash Commission, have proposed to transfer the SEC's authority over utility holding companies to the FPC. Supported by both agencies, this proposal would seem to make a good deal of administrative sense. But its adoption would sound the death knell of a competitive power industry.

The SEC made its reputation by a single-minded devotion to competition and deconcentration in breaking up the holding companies. The commission explained in 1946, when denying AEP's earlier bid to acquire Columbus and Southern, the basic philosophy motivating its decisions:

> We cannot emphasize too strongly that an essential part of the spirit pervading the initiation and adoption of [the Holding Company Act] was the desire to arrest the processes of concentration of power characterizing the growth of holding company systems. The concentration of control *per se,* its localization in financial centers, and the tendency of large aggregates—by reason of their very size alone—to become unamenable to effective regulation and essentially local management are stressed and repeated in the documents constituting the legislative history of the Act.[50]

Although its approval of the Northeast Utilities merger in 1966 may indicate a movement away from these policies, the vigorous staff work on the two pending merger applications reflects the best traditions of the SEC. Furthermore, in the early 1960s, the commission adopted a policy against combination gas-electric utilities.* And recently, the SEC, after some wavering, issued a new decision prohibiting holding companies from becoming conglomerates and entering the housing market.[51]

Competition, on the other hand, is a rarely heard word in FPC offices. The FPC's expertise lies elsewhere—in technical questions, rates, and interconnections. The commission has failed to realize that competition supplements regulation and can be a valuable tool for a regulator. To many of its staff, questions involving competition are a

---

* It is instructive to note that the two Iowa companies, whose plan to merge was initially approved by the Federal Power Commission, first approached the SEC about forming a holding company. When the SEC staff told them that the commission would require a separation of the gas and electric operations, they dropped their application, and went to the FPC.

nuisance that interfere with more important work. The specter of such questions, continued Justice Department intervention, and additional adverse court decisions continue to plague the FPC. It appears to be making a major attempt to rid itself of these alien forces. Its chairman in recent speeches has requested power to grant antitrust immunity so that the commission may allow the power industry to take full advantage of the "substantial economic benefits to be derived from unified planning of generation and transmission, pooling of business and financial risks and the consolidation of managerial talent." He has made no mention, however, of the even more substantial benefits to be derived from competition, and deconcentration of economic power and local control.

The commission has also been negotiating with the Justice Department for several years for agreement on a bill that would undo the damage of the *El Paso* case to the commission's ego. The bill would permit the commission to immunize gas pipeline mergers, subject to some sort of prior Antitrust Division review. In an interview Chairman Nassikas said that he hopes to be able to send a proposed bill to Congress in the near future. The chairman is also working on a bill to give the FPC antitrust immunity powers in all its endeavors.

If history is any guide, giving the commission antitrust immunity power and holding company jurisdiction would be to relegate competition to darkness. With little exception the commission has consistently demonstrated that it considers competition to be one of its lesser responsibilities. It has shown time and time again that it simply does not understand what the fuss is all about. If the policies embodied in the antitrust laws and the Holding Company Act are to remain viable, they should not be left solely to the Federal Power Commission's jurisdiction. To be effective, they must be enforced by agencies whose *primary* concern is competition, agencies willing to challenge industry power. As an FPC staff attorney uttered during oral argument in the *Northfield Mountain* case: "Someone around here has got to get some guts."

PROCUREMENT

8

Defense Procurement: "Everyone Feeds at the Trough"

LARRY PAUL ELLSWORTH

The Pentagon creates more monopoly in one day than the Antitrust Division can undo in a year.
—*Professor Walter Adams*

In fiscal year 1950 defense expenditures were $13 billion, or about 5 percent of the Gross National Product; by 1969 they had jumped to more than $80 billion, about 9 percent of the Gross National Product and 44 percent of the total federal budget. For the last five years an average of about $40 billion per year has been spent on defense procurement, equivalent to about 25 percent of the federal budget and more than all federal expenditures in 1950. To an impressive extent, the government, and in particular the Department of Defense (DOD), determines by its procurement decisions whether there will be more or less concentration, whether power will be in the hands of the many or the few, whether we will have monopoly or competitive enterprise in many major industries.

Procurement decisions, however, have persistently been made without considering their competitive effects. Although the statutory and historically preferred method of procurement is formally advertised competitive bidding, the 1947 Armed Services Procurement Act includes seventeen exceptions to competitive procurement; it has not proved difficult to make the exception the rule. Only 10.6 percent of DOD procurement was formally advertised in the first half of fiscal year 1970 (the latest figure available) and the proportion decreases annually. Furthermore, although it has been shown that prices obtained by competitive means are approximately *25 percent lower* than those obtained on a single-source basis, only one firm is solicited to take part in the negotiations in about 60 percent of the contract awards.[1]

The development and production of advanced weapon systems in the United States is carried out primarily by private firms under contract to the Defense Department. Cost, time, and quality uncertainties are substantial, but the risks have been shifted to the government, now taking over the role traditionally held by the private entrepreneur. Most risk capital is put up by the government, and if a contract is canceled, a firm can recoup any investment it has made. Although there is some rivalry in sales promotion and product variation, price competition is minimal. DOD and a few large companies have built a close, continuing relationship that blurs much of the distinction between public and private activities. Defense contractors, as a result, have combined the comforts of socialism with the rewards of capitalism.

Concentration: The Big Get Bigger

Although the defense industry is composed of over twenty thousand firms, more than 70 percent of all prime contract awards (by value) go to the one hundred largest contractors. The largest twenty-five firms, alone, receive more than half the total awards and a mere five giant aerospace firms get more than 20 percent of the business. The share of business controlled by these few firms is on the increase. In fiscal year 1968, the one hundred largest defense contractors received 67.4 percent of the prime contracts; in 1969 that figure rose to 68.2 percent; in 1970 it increased to 69.7 percent; and in 1971 it was up to 72.1 percent, an increase of more than 1 percent a year.[2] Conversely, while small business received 20.3 percent of the prime contracts in 1967, that share fell to 18.4 percent in 1966, to 17.5 percent in 1969, and to 16.8 percent in 1970; it has plummeted to 14.6 percent for the first six months of fiscal year 1971. Based on such data, the Joint Economic Committee of Congress concluded: "Defense buying practices are reducing competition for Government contracts and increasing economic concentration within the defense industry."[3]

Similarly, the National Aeronautics and Space Administration (NASA) and the Atomic Energy Commission (AEC), both of which deal for the most part with the same firms as does DOD, have done all they could to help the big get bigger. NASA awarded 92 percent of its 1970 budget of $3.4 billion to its largest one hundred contractors. The AEC, with its smaller $1.6 billion budget gives its ten most favored contractors 70 to 75 percent of its funds.[4]

The most concentrated part of the defense industry is in the manufacturing of major weapons systems, such as aircraft, missiles, ships, tanks, and electronics. This sector alone accounted for over $20 billion in fiscal year 1970. Broken down into military product categories, one finds that the top eight firms account for more than 70 percent of the sales in twenty-two out of twenty-seven categories,* and in twelve of these, eight firms received 99 percent of the business (1967 figures). Thus, Murray I. Weidenbaum, former assistant secretary of the Treasury and now professor of economics at Washington University in Saint Louis, asserts that "military procurement tends to be highly concentrated, perhaps more concentrated than American industry generally."[5]

A handful of firms also received the majority of the $5.5 billion awarded in fiscal year 1970 for military research and development contracts—a dramatic fifty-five-fold increase from the estimated $100 million spent on research and development in 1950.[6] Here too, there is a positive relation between firm size and the value of government research contracts received.[7] Because the firm to get the

* These are "high seller concentration" industries under the stringent standards of Professor Joe Bain. Under the less exacting Kaysen-Turner standards, twenty-five of the twenty-seven categories fall into the classification of heavily concentrated industries—oligopoly—where eight firms account for at least half of the market.

R&D contract almost inevitably gets the follow-on production contract as well, this connection is especially significant.

The preference for large firms over small ones occasionally approaches the ludicrous. When the Air Force decided that Minuteman launching areas should have cots installed so that the areas could be manned at all times, Boeing received the contract—and duly designed and delivered eighty-two beds at a cost of $1,080 apiece. Comparable standard Air Force beds cost about $38 each.

Pentagon procurement, it must be emphasized, not only protects existing concentration by its choice of contractors, and inflated profits, but it also *creates* concentration—in computers, for example, which may be the most important technological development of this century and may someday, if not already, dominate our lives. The danger of having a monopoly in this line should be apparent to all and is part of the reason that the Antitrust Division of the Justice Department is now in court in an attempt to detach IBM from its market stranglehold. Yet much of IBM's growth in the 1950s was due to government favoritism in its contracting practices. The DOD practice of tailoring specifications for computer purchases to IBM products certainly made it easier to obtain these contracts. In 1967, Representative Martha Griffiths revealed that IBM employees sometimes helped to draw up federal procurement specifications to make sure that only IBM equipment could meet those specifications. Another government practice has been to buy complete computer systems rather than to take advantage of the substantial savings that could be had by buying, from smaller manufacturers, parts of complete systems called "peripherals," which can be plugged into the larger systems. Consequently, the Joint Economic Committee reported in 1968 that government procurement of computers was stifling competition by favoring larger computer manufacturers over smaller companies.

Unlike computers, most complex modern weapon systems are produced by a number of different manufacturers; the prime contractor buys system components from other firms, thus creating a tremendous network of subcontractors for components and auxiliary equipment. DOD estimates (based on 1957–1963 data) that approximately 50 percent of prime contract funds are subcontracted.

Small business is capable of supplying a variety of these goods and services. The Defense Department collects no overall data on subcontracting but, on the basis of sampling, it seems that about 40 to 45 percent of the work subcontracted goes to small business.[8] DOD's admittedly sparse statistics show that only about 20 percent of the money volume of prime contracts goes to small businesses as subcontractors. Although small business appears to fare somewhat better in the subcontracting arena than in the prime contracting one, it is not much better.

The Pentagon purports to answer this problem by including a clause in all prime contracts of over $500,000 requiring that the aggregate amount of small business procurement be recorded and that quarterly reports be submitted. It seems obvious, based on the low levels of small business participation, that this obligation is inadequate to promote greater competition unless the government acts on the data. That this further action is not forthcoming is apparent from the reply of the former general counsel of DOD, Paul Warnke, to our question of what these data are used for: "To answer inquiries from Congressmen." As early as 1955 economists Walter Adams and Horace Gray wrote that "the government cannot [continue to] abdicate its responsibility of assuring by *direct* action that subcontracts are diffused as widely as possible and that a broad industrial base is maintained and fostered. After all, can the fox, however amiable and gentle his disposition, be entrusted with stewardship over the henhouse?"[9]

The inadequacy of the data collected by DOD on subcontracting also leaves unanswered questions concerning the reasonableness of subcontrators' profits. Subcontracting can involve several tiers, so that a prime contractor may purchase a component from a subcontractor who, in turn, may purchase a piece of it from another company, and so on. There is, of course, a pyramiding of profits, with each company charging its own costs plus a profit. If done in moderation, there is not necessarily anything wrong with this pricing, as we would expect each firm to collect a reasonable return on its investment.

But that is a big "if." Examples of the profit pyramiding game are not hard to find. For instance, Western Electric was able to play the game to the tune of a 6,684 percent profit without doing any work. In the early 1950s, the Army needed launcher-loaders for its Nike missiles. Western Electric already had the contract for the Nike, so the Army gave the company the contract for the launcher-loader too. Western Electric then subcontracted the job to Douglas Aircraft. Douglas proved to be even more adept at the game than Western Electric. It gave a subcontract to Consolidated Western Steel Company, a division of United States Steel, which actually manufactured and delivered 1,032 launcher-loaders directly to the Army.[10]

Assuming that Consolidated correctly reported its costs (although this is not clear from congressional hearings), we start at the bottom of the pyramid with a figure of $13.5 million, including its profit. Then Douglas, which invested a grand total of $3,361 making plastic rain covers for the launcher, took its profit, $1,211,771—a 36,531 percent return on investment. It then became Western Electric's turn. Western Electric's total effort was $14,293 "for checking over the equipment at Army bases," but it based its profit on Douglas's "costs" of $14.7 million. Even so, it managed to take $955,396 profit on the $14,293 effort—a pyramided profit of 6,684 percent. The government, therefore, paid $16.4 million for $13.5 million worth of equipment and services, Douglas nosed out Western Electric in the game of pyramiding costs, and only the taxpayer lost.

It is not only the question of subcontractors' profits that are hampered by a lack of data but also the broader question of overall profit margins of defense firms. In fact, DOD cannot even accurately state the profit rates of the defense contractors. A General Accounting Office (GAO) report released in March, 1971, contained two estimates of defense firm profitability: based on replies to a questionnaire sent to seventy-four large DOD contractors, there was a pretax return on equity of 21.1 percent; but based on an actual study of 146 completed defense contracts, the return was 56.1 percent. In addition, even though firm, fixed-price contracts make up more than half of its total expenditures, DOD does not obtain complete data on them and, as a result, it must exclude them from its own annual review of profit rates negotiated on certain types of contracts. This omission would not be so alarming if defense contracting were a free competitive market, but it is not.

As noted, competition is the exception rather than the rule, which leads to the constant danger of excessive profits and wasted resources.

Another difficulty is the lack of agreement upon a definition of profits. In the past, surveys by DOD and GAO, among others, have dealt with profits as a percentage of costs of sales, but, as the March, 1971, GAO report acknowledges, these are useless and misleading criteria when speaking of the defense industry. The primary reason is that defense contractors, at least the larger ones, use large amounts of government supplied capital. In fact, about half of the total capital assets controlled by defense firms is government owned.[11] To illustrate, if there were a $100,000 profit on a $1 million contract, there would appear to be a 10 percent profit margin. But if half of the plant and equipment is supplied by the government for a nominal fee so that the company's investment is only $500,000, the $100,000 profit is actually a 20 percent profit (on investment).*

A final problem concerning profits on defense contracts is the defense procurement practice of computing profits as a percentage of estimated costs; that is, past or historical costs. This puts a premium on increasing costs. The more inefficient, the more wasteful a contractor is in the short run, the more he can increase his profits in the long run. In fact, the contractor who increases his efficiency, thus saving the taxpayers' money, may in the long run actually lose profit under the present system. To use our earlier example, if it costs $1 million to build a certain weapon and

---

* A similar difficulty has resulted from DOD's policy of granting so-called progress payments of up to 90 percent of incurred costs. Today, the Pentagon has over $9 billion outstanding in such interest-free payments, which are not necessarily related to the actual amount of work completed. They are in reality interest-free loans that inflate contractors' profits. Former Deputy Defense Secretary David Packard, on recommendation of a subcommittee of the Pentagon's Industry Advisory Council, directed important changes in this policy, although he did not end it. First, progress payments will no longer be made any more frequently than every two weeks; the panel had found that under the previous system large companies often got paid every few days while smaller companies received payments monthly. Second, "out-of-house" costs, such as materials and payments to subcontractors, will no longer be paid when the prime contractor lists them on his books but only when he actually pays his bills.

the DOD's prevailing profit margin is 10 percent, then the contractor will be paid $100,000 every time he does the job. But ironically, if he cuts his costs to $900,000, then the next time he will receive only $90,000 for the same job. Consequently, there is little incentive to do the job more efficiently; rather, there is a strong incentive to keep investment low and costs high. While the way to increase profits in the competitive market is to cut costs, quite the opposite is true in the defense market. A Senate subcommittee concluded that these and similar Pentagon policies created "a vast subsidy for the defense industry, particularly the larger contractors."[12]

Much of the reason for the many huge cost overruns of recent years—which reached $33.4 *billion* on sixty-one weapons systems as of June 30, 1970[13]—can be laid to gross mismanagement, inefficiency, and waste. A. Ernest Fitzgerald, the former Air Force deputy for Management Systems who first made public the $2 billion overrun on Lockheed's C-5A (and whose job was then abolished) has asserted that labor efficiencies of only 20 to 50 percent of normal are commonplace in the factories of the large defense firms, for they know that cost is no problem.[14] And Colonel A. W. Buesking (U.S. Air Force, retired) has revealed that many plants do not have control systems that are essential to prevent excessive costs. He estimates that costs in these plants are 30 to 50 percent in excess of what they would be under competitive conditions, and even this estimate has been called conservative by Admiral Hyman Rickover.*[15]

Although the Pentagon has long based future contract prices on past costs, it does not base future contract awards on past contract performance. So a firm may receive lucrative new contracts even though it performed badly on a previous one. This fact was revealed by a 1968 study done by Richard Stubbing, an official in the Bureau of the Budget, which disclosed a series of performance inade-

* In 1968, the Navy for the first time implemented its own cost control system. Called the "should-cost" approach, it is an attempt to determine what a project ought to cost if there were reasonable efficiency on the part of the contractor. On that first occasion the Navy chopped $100 million off the $1.2 billion price quoted by the Pratt & Whitney Division of United Aircraft Corporation for the TF-30 engine. One hopes DOD will expand the use of the should-cost method.[16]

quacies in high-risk electronics components for aircraft and missiles. He also examined the relationship of profits to performance, concluding that "the current special partnership which exists between government and the aerospace industry not only results in a very high incidence of delivered electronics systems with degraded performance, but there is no effective mechanism in existing contractual arrangements to reward or penalize contractor performance."[17]

It is no wonder that Gordon W. Rule, the ousted director of the Navy's Procurement Control and Clearance Division, concluded in a memorandum to his superior that the repeated failures by industry to produce quality products was the fault of the Pentagon's permissive attitude. "No matter how poor the quality, how late the product and how high the cost, they know nothing will happen to them." The problem is created, he said, by "representatives of the government who today are condoning the acquiescing in the failure of industry to perform as they should."[18]

In recent years, supposedly informed observers such as former Secretary of Defense Clark Clifford have pointed to the Renegotiation Board, an independent arm of the executive branch, as the public's safeguard. The board is supposed to recoup for the government any "excess profits" that a contracting company makes from defense procurement, although one of its own witnesses testified before the House Ways and Means Committee in 1968 that a return on investment of 573 percent might be found "not excessive."[19] As carried out today, renegotiation cannot be effective. Congress has diluted the governing statute so that large blocks of defense work are not covered. Second, the statute requires the use of Internal Revenue Service accounting rules, even though they are not designed for cost accounting. Third, the board accepts industry reports on profits at face value without auditing them, despite ample evidence of inaccuracies.[20] (One wonders what would happen if the IRS accepted all income tax returns at face value.) Fourth, contractors are allowed to average their profits over the entire amount of their government business, permitting them to make excess profits on contracts where there is no competition and bid low on contracts where there is competition. Finally, all the board's work is secret, which guarantees that evidence of profiteering is kept in strict confidence. Even if it therefore had the will, the Pentagon could not weigh the board's findings when awarding a new contract.

Nor does the Renegotiation Board have the legal protection of independent regulatory agencies. Its existence must be renewed by Congress every two or three years, and its members serve at the pleasure of the president. In fact, one DOD procurement official told us: "The Renegotiation Board is a farce, made up of a bunch of political hacks." Quality of personnel aside, its staff and funds are minuscule when compared to its immense responsibilities. While in 1953 its staff totaled 742, today it has only about 200 personnel, including clerical and administrative workers as well as professionals. There is no way that the board's seven headquarters accountants could have adequately reviewed the cost and profit statements of the 4,354 contractors they surveyed in 1968. Federal procurement from more than 23,000 firms now exceeds $60 billion; in 1970 the board returned $33 million. As Admiral Rickover put it, that "is about as effective as putting a band-aid on cancer."[21]

The net result of noncompetitive bidding, awarding contracts to traditional and huge firms, and the famous cost overruns is excessive profit for big firms. After comparing a sample of large defense contractors doing at least 75 percent of their business with the government, with similar sized industrial firms doing most of their business in the commercial market, Murray Weidenbaum concluded: "The higher turnover rates [of the former group] more than offset the lower profit margins. Hence, the defense companies' return on net worth—net profit as a percent of stockholders' investment—is considerably higher—17.5 percent versus 10.6 percent [for other industry] during 1962–65."[22] And, according to a study conducted by the Rand Corporation, profits in the aerospace industry rank second only to drugs among major American industries.[23] These conclusions may seem to contradict the financial problems aerospace firms continuously complain about. Indeed, due to the firms' inefficiencies they often are in trouble, but they have invariably been bailed out by the Defense Department—at a profit.

In sum, the defense industry is an example of oligopolistic power at its worst—created, aided, and abetted by the government. It is a highly concentrated industry, with high profits and low efficiency. The barriers to entry are great. As is usual in the absence of competition, more money is paid for less product. Given this situation, what have the Justice Department and the Department of Defense done about it?

The Role of the Justice Department

There is no regular coordination between the Justice Department's Antitrust Division and the DOD. Contact is ad hoc, informal, and very much dependent upon personal friendships. For example, the assistant attorney general in charge of antitrust during Johnson's presidency, Donald Turner, was a longtime friend of Paul Warnke; so when Warnke became general counsel for DOD, Turner spoke to him about problems created by DOD procurement practices. The Pentagon agreed to keep the division informed of what was happening with its biggest orders, but Warnke left DOD shortly thereafter and the liaison ended. Turner suggested to us that the only way anything can be accomplished in the defense industry is for the attorney general to go to the secretary of defense and "seriously and formally" urge a cooperative effort to reverse the trend toward concentration. But when Turner was asked whether he had ever approached his attorney general, Ramsey Clark, on this matter, he replied: "No, I probably didn't push this as hard as I should have."

What Turner did not know was that Clark, who himself felt that government contracting policies were crucial to keeping competition alive, had spoken to Secretary of Defense Robert McNamara. McNamara, a product not only of the Ford Motor Company but also the Harvard Business School, appeared both interested and willing to deal with the problem. But, as the former attorney general explained it, McNamara had too little long-range power. "The people at DOD were used to dealing with a small group of firms and they liked it that way. They have a historical incest with a few companies." Still, Clark does not think that the Justice Department can afford to give up, emphasizing that "our capacity to revitalize competition by contracting is better than by litigation."

The Antitrust Division has for some years opposed the DOD policy of paying the research and development costs of a contractor, and then allowing that contractor to keep the patent rights. There have been high-level meetings between Justice and Defense representatives on this subject, but neither side has budged. The antitrusters have, however, had some limited success in convincing DOD to redraw procurement specifications when they have been clearly written so that only one company can meet them. But the division only gets involved when it receives a complaint from a disgruntled businessman—which is unlikely if the businessman wants to continue to deal with the Pentagon. Again, there is no systematic approach. An attorney at the Antitrust Division simply calls the procurement officer in charge and tries to arrange a compromise. No attempt is made to stem such anticompetitive practices, according to former Antitrust chief William Orrick, where procurement agencies other than the DOD are concerned.

By statute, the heads of all agencies must report to the attorney general all bids received through formal advertising that appear to violate the antitrust laws. And, by executive order, all cases of identical bids on advertised procurements of over $10,000 must be reported to the attorney general. The division's economics section compiles this data and puts out an annual report. Unfortunately, that may be all they do with it. While a series of identical bids does not prove an antitrust violation, it should indicate what areas of procurement and which industries warrant detailed investigation. As it is, the economics section will send over *additional* information on identical bids *after* an attorney begins an investigation. One can only speculate on its utility; neither Lewis Marcus, the economics section chief, nor Alfred Jacobs, the assistant chief, would name any cases that had been generated from the identical bid report.*

* The division has worked out an agreement with the General Services Administration (GSA) and DOD whereby a bidder submits a certificate of noncollusion with his bid, certifying that all submitted information is true to the best of his knowledge, and that he is not colluding with others on it. If this were later shown to be false, he would be subject to criminal prosecution under the false statements section of the U.S. Code as well as under the antitrust laws.

Antitrust policy is also expressly applicable, under the Surplus Property Act of 1944, to the disposal of government property worth over $1 million. The statute requires the Defense Department (or any other executive agency) to seek "the advice of the Attorney General on the question whether such disposal would tend to create or maintain a situation inconsistent with the antitrust laws."[24] Because of the million-dollar minimum, the requirement applies mainly to the disposal of government-built, contractor-run plants. This has long been a point of contention between the two executive agencies.

Beginning in the early sixties, the Department of Defense began disposing of surplus plants to big defense contractors by negotiated sale—not to nondefense contractors by negotiated *bids,* as the statute suggests. The Antitrust Division, in its advisory capacity, began to challenge these dispositions as contributing to existing concentration in the defense industry. Also, "the sales price was always just a fraction of the acquisition costs," complained one division lawyer overseeing these cases. DOD was displeased by this criticism, fearing embarrassment in congressional hearings or the media if it became known that Justice thought it was violating the antitrust laws. A letter was sent by the Pentagon to Deputy Attorney General Nicholas Katzenbach in 1963, suggesting that the division mind its own business. Katzenbach hedged, expressing sympathy for their problems but also concern over concentration in the defense industry. The Pentagon's reaction was duplicitous. One drafted reply, never sent, admitted to a policy of surplus disposal to large contractors; in a letter that was sent, and in later interagency meetings, Defense officials denied that any such policy existed at all. "There was an absolute, unswerving course at Defense," said a prominent division official, who dealt with the Pentagon on these matters. "It didn't matter if it was the General Counsel or the Defense Secretary—the same policy came out. They disguised it, camouflaged it and lied about it. Nothing we did had any effect."

The disposal process can be an affirmative tool in discouraging monopolistic practices while fostering competition, as exemplified by the aluminum industry after World War II. Until that time Alcoa was effectively the only

aluminum producer in the United States. After the disposal
of surplus property there were two new fully integrated
aluminum producers in the market, Reynolds and Kaiser.
But such affirmative use of disposal has been rare. At the
same time that the aluminum disposals were taking place,
disposals in the steel industry were handled in such a manner as to reinforce and perpetuate its oligopolistic structure.[25] Today these plants are usually sold, or as many
critics would say, "given," to the contractor-lessee who has
been using the plant for years. Because only the largest
contractors are given the privilege (and bargain) of using
the government plants, this tends to concentrate the resources of the industry further. Again, the big get bigger
through government largess.

Except for a few personal contacts and some isolated
efforts, the antitrusters remain uninterested in DOD practices. They see themselves as enforcers who should bring
suit against individual violations of the antitrust laws—
after the fact—rather than take even limited preventive
steps. Professor John Cibinic, Jr., the director of the
Government Contracts Program at George Washington
University, said in an interview: "The Justice Department
aims at monopoly that the U.S. Government didn't create,
forgetting the ones that the Government does create." Part
of the Antitrust Division's rationale for its lack of effort is
its limited budget, already spread too thin. But it is exactly
for this reason that antitrusters should make some concerted effort to influence and, in effect, to educate the
Pentagon in the advantages of competition. The effects of
government procurement are so great that a slight amount
of success would certainly mean more to the economy than
the bringing of one or two more minor merger cases.

The Antitrust Division has at least attempted to stop the
largest of the mergers involving defense firms, although
without much success. The agency recommended action
against the merger of the Douglas Aircraft Company (then
the twenty-fourth largest defense contractor) and the Mc-
Donnell Aircraft Corporation (then the sixth largest).
Attorney General Ramsey Clark, however, after several
meetings with top industry officials, feared Douglas's bankruptcy and refused to allow the suit. The Pentagon sided
with the industry, saying that a merger would combine

McDonnell's capability in fighter aircraft with Douglas's in commercial aircraft resulting in "one strong competitor" in the words of Leonard Niederlehner, the deputy general counsel of the DOD. The Antitrust Division proposed a compromise: McDonnell could purchase the aircraft division but not the aerospace part, which was economically healthy and whose acquisition would have involved a serious loss of "potential competition" in a highly concentrated industry. Clark and the Pentagon rejected the plan.

The very next year, North American Aviation, Inc., merged with the Rockwell–Standard Corporation to become the North American Rockwell Corporation. Senator Stuart Symington of Missouri, among others on the Hill, urged the Johnson administration to permit the merger. The rationale for the merger was the usual one—North American was in financial trouble. Yet this argument is always available when there is the possibility of a merger involving one of these leviathans, for they are inefficient and dependent upon the good graces of DOD. Wards of the state who appear to be in constant financial trouble, they will stay viable only so long as DOD continues to subsidize them, and any contractor, merger or not, will be ruined when the Defense Department ceases to do so. As the recent Lockheed "bailout" revealed, some of these companies would be driven into bankruptcy if forced to meet their contractual obligations; nevertheless, they continue to receive large profits as long as the Pentagon favors them with large orders and even more expensive contracts.

One other merger serves to illustrate the Antitrust Division's difficulty in the defense area. In 1962, Ling-Temco, the sixty-first largest defense contractor, merged with Chance–Vought Aircraft, the thirty-sixth largest. Chance-Vought was then the leading producer of naval aircraft. Justice attacked the merger in an attempt to preserve some small degree of competition in the defense market. The division attorneys went to the secretary of the Navy, then John Connally, to persuade him or one of his subordinates to testify for them. Connally's reply was that he hoped they lost. They did, with DOD testifying for the defense.

Based on such losses, and on the ingrained habits of a defense establishment that prefers procurement without competition, many division attorneys agree with Robert

Wright's prognosis that the situation is "hopeless." Others concur with division economist Leo Finn: "We leave it to them, you see, to police the situation."

Who Polices Whom?

Thus left to itself, what has the Pentagon done?

The Armed Services Procurement Regulations (ASPR) contain many safeguards for competition. When asked how aware DOD procurement officers are of competitive considerations, Marx Leva, a former general counsel for DOD, replied to the author, "Not very. These are one of the nuisances they have to put up with. They know the law exists; why it exists they have no idea." Similarly, one former Navy general counsel admitted: "We just don't pay any real attention" to the antitrust laws.

Granted that DOD's habits are ingrained and it is difficult to know how much competition is possible, there are still strong indications that there could be much more competition than at present. While defending the low levels of formal advertised bidding, the Pentagon itself estimated in 1968 that 15 to 20 percent of Defense purchases could be made in this way;[26] yet its use has now fallen to less than 11 percent. And while most of the competition comes in technology, not prices, this is all too often a rivalry in promises rather than results. It will continue to be so as long as DOD accepts below-standard products.

There is a general lack of concern and understanding of the advantages of competition at all levels in the Pentagon, as a look at the debarment area makes evident. A company may be made ineligible to receive government contracts for up to three years for certain reasons such as fraud, unsatisfactory performance, violation of the Buy American Act, or an antitrust violation. While DOD debarred companies in 299 cases between 1954 and 1964, only one of those cases was for an antitrust violation.* In that sole case,

---

* Although NASA and the AEC were among the agencies with the largest procurement budgets, NASA had no debarments for any reason during this period, while the AEC had only one, for fraud. And, although the AEC has spent just a shade under $28 billion in the past decade on prime contracts, it has had "no debarments for any reason during that time," according to the assistant director of the Division of Contracts, AEC.

eight firms and eight individuals were put on the debarred bidders' list. (These firms and individuals cannot be identified because the Government Services Administration refused to supply that information to the Justice Department.) But during this same time period, the Antitrust Division brought fifty-four cases resulting in antitrust convictions where collusion over bids or proposals played a leading role. Approximately 206 corporate defendants and a similarly large number of individual defendants were involved. Also, neither the military services nor GSA have debarred anyone for an antitrust violation in over a decade, although the division reports all convictions to the GSA which, in turn, reports them to each government agency that should be concerned. The Pentagon's faith in this elite of giant contractors appears to be unshaken by a decade of cost overruns, shoddy weapons, and late deliveries. The Defense Department is still convinced that these dinosaurs have unique capabilities that enable them to produce practically anything they are asked for, if only they are fed enough money and given enough time to digest it.

To maintain this industrial base, an informal policy has grown up to protect these giants from competition. "In fact," one recent book, *The Pentagon Watchers,* noted, "there is a clear tendency for all large defense firms automatically to receive a share of military business."[27] One North American Rockwell official explained, "Everyone feeds at the trough, even though it's not planned that way. The great demand for programs by government keeps most stuff working. So when there is excess capacity, government will usually quickly go for it. Everyone gets in."[28] It is widely believed in Washington that this viewpoint is responsible for the award of the TFX fighter plane (now the F-111) contract to General Dynamics, which was then in serious financial trouble (and still is). The same rotation policy may account for the award of the B-1 bomber contract to North American Rockwell. Only a few favorites are eligible for the rotation, but each of these is assured of another contract when the company's needs call for it.

It is important to understand how far this teamwork between government and industry extends. The Pentagon does not merely come up with an idea or perceive a threat it must meet and then "buy" a weapon system from a contractor. Rather, as explained by President Moore of

North American Rockwell's Aerospace and Systems Group, the process is one of "joint parenthood; a new system usually starts with a couple of military and industry people getting together to discuss problems. . . . But it isn't a case of industry here and the government there. . . . They are interacting continuously at the engineering level."[29] One of Pratt & Whitney's marketing men boasted to an interviewer, "We spoon-feed them. We ultimately try to load them with our ideas and designs, but in such a way that when they walk away from the conference table, they are convinced it was their idea all along."

According to University of Michigan Professor F. M. Scherer, the result of this teamwork has been "window dressing competitions" where "a government agency invited many firms to bid, even though one or two firms were strongly favored . . . so that it was 80–90 percent certain that those firms would ultimately be chosen. . . . Invitations to bid were often disseminated widely largely to please Congress."[30]

Two recent reports indicate that both industry and the Pentagon intend to continue and, if possible, intensify this congenial relationship. The National Security Industrial Association, made up of over four hundred defense contracting firms, has published the *Defense Acquisition Study*. Among the thirty-five recommendations are proposals that DOD and industry "consult, to the maximum extent possible and well beyond that currently being accomplished," that the 1947 Armed Services Procurement Act be amended to eliminate the preference it gives to advertised bidding, and that the government "self-insure" against certain risks in the procurement process rather than require the contractor to provide insurance, as he would have to do in commercial markets.

The second report was prepared for the Navy at an expense to the taxpayers of almost $100,000. Its conclusion is that officials should develop "informal working relationships" with contractors. Columnist Jack Anderson uncovered a two-page confidential memo from Captain J. R. Ward to the Navy's personnel research director that pointed out the report's many deficiencies.[31] Besides "distortions of the responsibilities assigned to various agencies concerned with advanced shipbuilding" and the failure to contact some groups at an early stage, Captain Ward protested that the recommendations calling for more intimate relationships "is a violation of contract administration procedures." He further warned, "Contractor claims against the government in other shipbuilding programs can be traced to the same sort of relationship that the report calls desirable." When Dr. Edgar Shriver, the principal investigator on the report, was contacted, he was astonished at the controversy, contending that it "was only a statement of present policy."

One reason that these close ties are possible is that a large number of retiring military people immediately move over to top jobs with defense contractors. It often seems that the only real competition between defense contractors is over who's going to hire what retiring general. What these jobs may entail was uncovered by a special subcommittee of the House Armed Services Committee in 1959. Admiral William Fechteler, a former Chief of Naval Operations who went to work for General Electric after retiring, testified that his role with GE was that of a "convenient, glorified messenger boy" who arranged for company executives to meet important admirals. For this he received $38,500 in 1958, while he was still receiving his military retirement pay of $1,014 per month.[32] The relevant statute has since been amended to prohibit such conduct for three years after retirement, but an industry source revealed that "at least 90 percent of the retired officers hired for top-level positions by the defense contractors ignore that regulation."*[33]

The exchange of personnel between government and industry works both ways. Large numbers of civilian employees, at all levels of the Pentagon, move from business to government and back to business. In fact, it is difficult to see how this could be avoided; the government needs engineers experienced in advanced weapons technology, and they exist mainly in the corporate estate. The result, as one official in the Office of the Director of De-

* Some idea of the potential of the problem was revealed by Senator Fulbright in 1969. As of February of that year, the top one hundred contractors—ninety-five reporting—employed 2,072 former high military officers, or an average of almost 22 per company. This may be compared with a 1959 average of slightly more than 8 per company. And while in 1959 the ten companies with the highest number of former officers employed 372 of them, by 1969 this number had almost tripled to 1,065.[34]

fense Research and Engineering (DDR&E) estimated, is
that about one-third of the professional civilian staff leave
within two or three years.[35]

The facile interchange of personnel naturally leads to
conflicts of interest involving government officials rewarding their former firms. A Senate Investigating Committee
in 1970 accused former Deputy Defense Secretary Roswell
Gilpatric of a "flagrant conflict of interest"; he was an
attorney at General Dynamics' law firm (Cravath, Swaine
& Moore) before and after his government stint and he
was involved in getting General Dynamics its TFX contract. Willis Hawkins has also made the round trip from
firm to government and back to firm, leaving Lockheed in
1963 to become assistant secretary of the Army for research and development, later returning to Lockheed. During his stay his office awarded Lockheed the Cheyenne
helicopter contract even though the Army evaluation board
had rated rival designs superior. Later the costs tripled and
the helicopter's performance was so bad that the production contract was canceled.

The private industry bias is exemplified by the role of
Dr. M. J. Kelly, then president of AT&T's Bell Telephone
Laboratories, in connection with the Justice Department
action against AT&T in the mid-1950s. By his own admission, in testimony before the House Antitrust Subcommittee, he became an "advocate" for his company within
DOD while he was in the Pentagon's employ. In 1953 Dr.
Kelly served as chairman of the Ad Hoc Committee on
Continental Defense on a "without compensation" basis.
Bell Labs was actually paying his salary. While Dr. Kelly
was advising the secretary of defense about continental
defense, he was also urging the secretary to intercede with
the Justice Department, first to delay the pending antitrust
suit for divorcement of the Western Electric Corporation
from its parent, AT&T, and later to get the divestiture
requirement dropped. DOD several times advocated as its
own position that taken by AT&T—that the suit must be
postponed so as not to interrupt work of Western Electric,
which was vital to the national security during wartime—
without any attempt to reach an independent judgment.
Finally, on July 10, 1953, Secretary of Defense Wilson had
a letter hand-carried to Attorney General Herbert Brownell
advocating that the prosecution be ended. The subcommit-

tee reported that the letter, except for two minor changes, had been "ghost written" by Dr. Kelly, who was still in the employ of the Bell System. The House Subcommittee concluded:

> Here the Department injected itself into the very merits of the litigation, no longer merely seeking postponement of the trial. It is deemed significant that neither Secretary Wilson nor Deputy Secretary Kyes saw fit to counsel with other officials, more familiar with the case, concerning the nature of the legal issues or their public importance. Instead, on behalf of the Department, they uncritically adopted and championed the view of the public interest that was being urged upon the Government by self-interested, private parties defendant.[36]

But the Defense Department is not only intimate with industry; it also actively shields itself and its contracting firms from outside scrutiny. "The alteration and softening of a General Accounting Office report on defense profits," began a front page *Washington Post* article of March 17, 1971, "closely paralleled recommendations by the Pentagon and contractor trade associations, a congressional inquiry disclosed yesterday." Investigative reporter Bernard Nossiter then revealed the closed-door maneuverings. First, a month before the report's release, Barry Shillito, the recent assistant secretary of defense for procurement, had warned the GAO against "overplaying" the high profits figure (56.1 percent return on equity) because it would give "ammunition to the critics of this industry." As a result, other data reflecting only a 21.1 percent return were expanded from eight pages in the original report to twenty-six pages in the heart of the final report. Logistics Management Institute [LMI], a private think-tank that Shillito headed for six years, requested that the chapter order be changed to place the higher profits figure at the end of the report instead of at the beginning—which was done.

Shillito also urged the GAO to eliminate from the report a comparison of the high profits data with an LMI survey showing lower profits—which was also done. The final report dropped the last line of the first draft, which had warned against profits "greater than necessary, particularly with the huge unmet social needs of the country"; the Electronic Industries Association had suggested this change. Unlike the first draft, the final report suggested that the Pentagon consider "risk" as well as investment in fixing profit objectives in contracts, an addition proposed by the National Security Industrial Association.

The General Accounting Office, supposed independent government auditor and watchdog, had clearly been compromised. But it was not the first time. By the mid-1960s the Pentagon and defense industry were upset at critical GAO reports on individual contracts, which were replete with words such as *overcharge* and included actual company names. Representative Chet Holifeld (D.–Calif.), chairman of the military subcommittee of the House Government Operations Committee, held some hearings to clear up the embarrassing problem. His opening statement articulating the issue had the virtue of candor: ". . . great concern . . . has been shown in industry circles and, recently, in the Department of Defense, over the difficult and sometimes awkward situations created by the GAO audit reports." As reported by Nossiter, the result of the hearings was that the GAO promised to issue only "constructive" reports in the future. It would avoid language such as *overcharge* and *excessive pricing,* would make fewer recommendations, would "respect business privacy," would stop naming negligent officials, and would not disclose referrals to the Justice Department.[37] The deterrent impact of these reports and the public's right to know had been sabotaged.

A Case Study: The M-16

That DOD is "duty-bound" to award contracts to the lowest bidder only when the lowest bidder is the right bidder was made apparent in the 1968 awarding of contracts for the M-16 rifle to General Motors and Harrington & Richardson.[38]

The first significant procurement of the M-16 rifle was made in 1962 from Colt Industries, the owner of the patent rights. Colt had bought the exclusive manufacturing and patent rights on the forerunner of the M-16, the AR-15, in 1959 from the Fairchild Engine and Airplane Corporation, which had originally designed it. By 1967 the House Armed Services Committee had uncovered the fact that Colt was receiving huge profits while running behind on its deliveries.

Major General Nelson M. Lynde, Jr., U.S. Army, who approved the excessive prices negotiated with Colt in 1963, retired in 1964 to accept the position of executive consultant with Colt at a salary of $20,000 a year, which was in addition to his $12,000 Army retirement pay. Before leaving the service, General Lynde sought approval for his new job from the adjutant general, saying that he did not contemplate any activity with regard to the M-16 rifle. The adjutant general said that, based on this claim, there would not appear to be any conflict. Yet a House subcommittee found that Lynde's name appeared on distribution lists for intercompany memorandums involving the M-16 rifle and that he had requested from the Army, as a retired officer, a classified document comparing the effectiveness of the AR-15 with the M-14 rifles. The subcommittee concluded that General Lynde's conduct was "at least unethical."

Congress urged that the Colt patent rights be bought by the Army and that a competitive contract be awarded to set up a "second source." Finally, on September 1, 1967, the Army invited four firms, the Cadillac Gage Company, the Hydra-Matic Division of General Motors, Harrington & Richardson, and Maremont Corporation to submit proposals on a multi-year contract for 167,000 rifles. In early March the Army increased the quantity to 380,000 units and accelerated the rate of delivery. At about this time, a special subcommittee of the House of Representatives discovered that the Army was in the process of negotiating a special and secret contract with General Motors, alone, for 100,000 units with an exceedingly high tooling cost. The subcommittee met with representatives of the Pentagon and Army and questioned the justification of such action. The covert negotiations with GM then ended.

On March 29, 1968, shortly after the abortive attempt to make an award to General Motors and one week before the price proposals were due, the following unusual instruction (which was to have importance later) was added to the proposed contract: "Under no circumstances are the budgetary estimates to be provided to the Government until specifically requested." The assistant secretary of the Army, Robert A. Brooks, afterward told the subcommittee that this was not customary but rather "a particular feature of this procurement." On April 4, 1968, the four bidding contractors submitted their proposals, each indicating its ability to meet the accelerated schedule. Curiously, the Army refrained from asking any questions even concerning areas where it later claimed that it lacked sufficient information. Nor were requests made for pricing information, although the two firms that later testified before the subcommittee, Maremont and Cadillac Gage, said that they were prepared to submit it at that time.

The technical proposals submitted, the companies waited for the request for budgetary estimates. It never came. The "particular feature of this procurement" had taken its cost. On April 22, the Army announced to the press that it had awarded contracts to General Motors and Harrington & Richardson, each for the production of an identical 240,000 M-16s, at ceiling prices of $56 million and $42 million, respectively. The shocking disparity between these two figures alone tells only part of the controversy. The disparity was even greater, because Maremont and Cadillac Gage had each prepared, but not been permitted to submit, proposed ceiling prices of just over $36 million. And none of these figures included the royalty costs to Colt, which were 40 percent more for the high-cost bidder, GM, than for Maremont. Little wonder that Representative Peter N. Kyros (D.–Maine) concluded that "a conscious effort was made by the Army to prevent Maremont from submitting its price—knowing that Maremont's bid would be lower than General Motors—and to permit an award to General Motors at a $20 million higher price."

When announcing the awards, the Army sought to defend its actions by stressing that the prices were ceiling figures subject to downward negotiation. It cited Labor Department average wage scale statistics to blame part of the disparity on the "considerably higher" wage scales in "Detroit"[39]—although the GM Hydra-Matic Division is in Ypsilanti, Michigan. Of course the proposed prices of the two low bidders were also ceiling prices, but DOD would rather have people forget this. And it is foolish to assume that the average GM worker really makes over $14,000 a year more than an employee of Maremont Corporation, yet this would have to be the case if the Pentagon's claim is to be believed.

Bewildered why they lost the contract, Maremont asked the Army for a "debriefing" conference to ascertain the reasons. Berge Thomasian, vice-president of the New England Division of Maremont Corporation, testified: "We were specifically told that we were qualified to undertake the accelerated production but that the Army placed 'a lesser relative degree of confidence' in Maremont than in the successful offerers." Twenty million dollars of the tax-payers' money is a lot of confidence. After viewing the Army's report, Representative Kyros concluded: "The only criticisms [leveled against] Maremont are of such a nit-picking variety as to be ludicrous." For example, the Army argued that Maremont's targeting and testing facilities appeared to be of questionable capacity, but even if that were true, one might think it a better situation than GM offered, because, as the Senate report showed, it had *no* testing facilities or any other essential equipment. It all had to be built at considerable government expense, which was made possible by a special provision in the contract that did not limit the facilities to be purchased on government account. Perhaps the preference for GM was simply that GM is bigger, so it "must be" better. The Hydra-Matic Division's only previous experience in ordnance production involved the manufacture of four thousand small aircraft cannon. It had never made a small-bore rifle. On the other hand, Maremont had produced hundreds of thousands of quality small arms specifically for the Army and, in fact, was then the sole source of the Army's M-60 machine gun.

Representative Kyros asserted that "the only conclusion is that there is something rotten somewhere." It is difficult to level any more specific criticisms—such as against the government officials who made the procurement decision—because the size and inscrutability of the Pentagon discourages penetration and accountability. The Senate subcommittee headed by Senator Howard W. Cannon added in its formal report that the procurement was "a most inept performance," while the chairman of the House special subcommittee, Representative Richard H. Ichord, charged that "there were mistakes made in this whole program that a BB gun expert would not make." But the word *mistakes* is misleading. The fact is that DOD almost invariably chooses the big over the small. From a purely bureaucratic veiwpoint, the fewer firms there are, the easier it is to deal with them, and with a few big firms the close personal relationships that the military likes are easier to cultivate and maintain.[40] And the firms themselves—by lobbying, political clout, and cooperation with the Pentagon in covering up blunders—encourage such preferential selectivity.

The Alternatives

Besides the fact that a supposedly democratic system cannot afford corporate favoritism and private concentration of power, the economic loss to the country makes present procurement practices indefensible. Studies conducted by the GAO and the Department of Defense itself led Secretary Robert McNamara to state that upwards of a 25 percent savings could be secured by shifting to competitive bidding.[41] With one war now in progress, and with the constant threat of other confrontations as well as urgent needs at home,* we cannot afford to continue wasting billions of dollars to support wasteful oligopoly. As Ramsey Clark told this project, "If someone in 1950 was watching the Government contracting policy, trying to spread the contracts to encourage competition, we could have avoided many of our present headaches." These "headaches" include: defense contracts concentrated in the hands of a relatively few large firms; high profits and low efficiency; a generally unconcerned and ineffective Antitrust Division; and a defense "team" seeing little reason to foster competition, with the result that industry is often both player and umpire.

Many recommendations have been made over the years to increase competition for military business without retarding defense production or significantly increasing costs. Here, the recommendations of Dr. Weidenbaum merit attention:

1. Broaden the competitive base by encouraging defense companies to diversify into commercial markets and commercial firms to diversify into defense work.

---

* Senator Philip A. Hart, chairman of the Senate Subcommittee on Antitrust and Monopoly, pointed out that the savings that Secretary McNamara indicated could be generated by more competition "would almost equal all we are now spending on grants to education, job training, model cities, rent supplements, urban mass transit, Appalachia, youth summer jobs, basic water and sewers, and school lunches. As you recite that, you get an answer to why some people think our sense of priorities is utterly ridiculous."

2. Emphasize production rather than research and development as the major point of competition.
3. Break out more subsystems for competition.
4. Widen the participation in subcontracts.
5. Reduce the competitive advantage of using Government assets.[42]

Yet the real difficulty is not how to get more competition into the defense market, but how one can get the defense bureaucracy to press for it. One viable method would be to require that the procurement officer who approved the contract, sign the contract. Personal accountability—something relatively unknown in this mammoth and amorphous bureaucracy—should prove a valuable disinfectant. All know the engineer who built a bridge; if the bridge collapses, so does the engineer's reputation. Encouraging such personal responsibility is equally appropriate for procurement officials.

As several people, both critics and advocates of the large defense budget, pointed out to us, mere procedural changes are insufficient. Secretary McNamara's experience proved this. Fifteen years ago, professors Adams and Gray insisted that

the administrative bureaucracy must be imbued with a pervasive and fundamental competitive philosophy. It is futile for Congress to devise competitive procurement standards which shortsighted, incompetent, or corrupt administrators fail to apply intelligently, imaginatively, and conscientiously. . . . On every level of the executive branch, there is needed a philosophic reorientation—a recognition that a government which forsakes competition eventually becomes dependent on monopoly.[43]

It is admittedly difficult to change the philosophy of a giant bureaucracy, but that must occur if we are ever to reclaim any of the objectivity of the marketplace in defense procurement. Former Attorney General Nicholas Katzenbach suggested to us that the president give a strong, serious executive order reaffirming the country's commitment to economic freedom, and its opposition to privilege and monopoly in the defense industry. Such a formal declaration alone would not have much effect. It must be followed by a combined program of the Pentagon working with the Justice Department's Antitrust Division. The former must clean out the unimaginative, shortsighted, or

corrupt procurement officials who are responsible for creating the concentration that antitrust officials later attempt to
break apart. The latter must vigorously prosecute cases of
collusive bidding in this area and all merger situations that
have the potential of leading to greater concentration
among defense contractors. It should further scrutinize all
team bidding and buy-in situations for antitrust violations.

We have suggested that present government procurement
practices give us the worst of two worlds. The defense
market is a market of special privileges, neither regulated
nor competitive. Yet perhaps even executive pronounce-
ments, new DOD personnel, and Antitrust Division atten-
tiveness would prove inadequate to undo the concentration
created by the present procurement policies. Other models
then come to mind. The Government Printing Office is a
government agency but subcontracts much of its work to
private business. By focusing primary responsibility in an
agency, which then subcontracts to business firms under
careful guidelines, accountability and efficiency could both
be increased. One model for the defense firm is a public-
private corporation, with management and directors
equally split between government and business representatives. Building an uncorrupted voice into the fabric of the
decision-making authority would, to some extent, be an
improvement over what are now entirely private decisions.

Another alternative is the public take-over of large defense firms, a view whose best-known advocate is Professor
John Kenneth Galbraith. He has suggested that any firm
doing more than 75 percent of its business with the Defense Department over a five-year period is in reality a
public corporation; therefore, it should be reorganized as
such with all its stock held in public hands. Among many
points, Galbraith argues that: the government owns much
of their plant and equipment anyway; monopoly pricing
and inefficiency prevail; control of the military establishment would improve; falsely calling defense firms "private"
permits them to lobby politically for weapons expenditures;
and "[f]inally, it is possible that fully responsible public
firms would be more efficient. Not being judged by their
growth, they might be judged by their efficiency. But perhaps it is enough to contend that things could not be
worse."[44]

Public ownership of industry is common in most industrialized nations, usually extending to rail and air service, broadcasting, electric and gas utilities as well as telephone service. Important manufacturing industries, such as automobiles, steel, and aircraft, are also frequently in the public domain. Even in the United States the supplying of water and electricity, the maintenance of hospitals and schools, the postal service, production at naval shipyards and army arsenals, and several minor manufacturing endeavors are wholly or partially in public hands. In fact, $8.8 billion of Gross National Product was credited, in 1967, to government enterprises selling their products to the general public.[45]

But public ownership is not without problems. In a reasonably well working private economy, the competitive mechanism will automatically promote efficient managements and methods (and get rid of inefficient ones). But this is the biggest shortcoming of a public enterprise system. How do you give government managers the knowledge and incentives to make publicly desirable decisions? To insure "correct" decisions by constantly passing them up the decisional ladder would, as the Soviet experience has shown, lead to inflexibility and breakdowns. To proscribe a profit maximization criteria, as many Western nations and Soviet satellites recently have attempted, may lead not to greater efficiency but to higher prices fixed by government fiat.

There are three basic types of incentives: coercive, nonmonetary, and monetary. Coercion is, in most cases, inconsistent with a free form of government; and the worth of nonmonetary inducements, medals and the like, appears quaintly irrelevant in the money-oriented United States. That leaves monetary compensation for increased production or lower costs. But the history of military and civil service pay scales, not only in the United States but in all democratic countries, indicates the unlikelihood that a government-run enterprise will ever compete effectively against private enterprise for high-quality technical and management personnel. Thus, lack of proper incentives for efficiency under the present contract system is, of itself, hardly a compelling reason for change.

There are other difficulties. One might hesitate before greatly expanding the federal bureaucracy by adding millions of workers to the government payroll, although Professor Galbraith has argued with some reason that these people are in reality already in DOD employ. Further, as the experience with naval shipyards has shown, it is politically very difficult to reduce needless spending in government enterprises; liberals and conservatives alike complain when their state or district is involved in a cutback.

How the virtues and drawbacks of public and private enterprise balance is unclear. As Professor Galbraith has suggested, economic arguments alone are an insufficient basis for a decision because there are also important political and ideological considerations. But this is no excuse for avoiding the question. His argument deserves the close scrutiny of both public agencies and the private sector, not the irresponsible name-calling such a proposal traditionally excites. Key questions about defense procurement have gone unanswered because, for the most part, they have gone unasked.

9

Drug Procurement: High on Profits

IRENE TILL

The federal government is not only a supplier of services to its citizens. It is also a mass purchaser of goods. Military hardware, discussed in another chapter, is one example. Drugs is another. The federal government currently spends about $1.5 billion a year for drugs, usually on high-priced brand name products bought in the most costly manner. As any competent procurement expert will attest, buying in large volume is the best way to obtain low prices. This is particularly true where the buyer is dealing with an oligopolistic industry such as drug manufacturing; big buyers must countervail big sellers. Yet centralized purchasing accounts for less than $150 million, or about 10 percent, of all drugs purchased by the federal government.

A primary offender in this respect is the Department of Health, Education, and Welfare (HEW), the largest single buyer of drugs in the United States. Its total expenditures covering drugs amounted to $1.04 billion in 1971. About half of this amount represented actual product cost, and the remainder constituted "overhead costs" such as pharmacy fees for prescriptions, hospital expenses in drug administration, and the like. Yet HEW buys no drugs directly. Under the Medicare program, costing over $540 million, the agency has nothing more than a check-writing

function. The Social Security Administration simply pays
whatever bills are submitted by hospitals and nursing
homes through fiscal intermediaries such as Blue Cross and
the large insurance companies. Medicaid, a program complementary to Medicare, is administered through grants to
the states with no real supervision by HEW of how the
money is spent. (In addition to the $455 million contrib-
uted by the federal government, state and local governments paid out $446 million for drugs under the Medicaid
program in 1971.)[1]

The two agencies with experience in buying drugs directly from manufacturers in volume are the Department
of Defense and the Veterans Administration. The low
prices they pay indicate the significant economies that can
be achieved under centralized procurement. Only a portion
of their purchases, however, are made in this manner. A
substantial volume constitutes local procurement at high
prices either through purchases from drug wholesalers or
under Federal Supply Schedule contracts. This pattern is a
tribute to the drug industry's ingenuity in maintaining its
enviable reputation for high profits. Traditionally, it leads
all manufacturing industries in the rate of profits. In 1971
its return on investment, after taxes, was 17.9 percent. For
all manufacturing, the figure was 9.7 percent.*

Unless there is an overhauling of the federal government's buying practices in drugs, this profit situation will
continue indefinitely. The government is expected to play
an ever-larger role in buying or paying for drugs. When
Medicare is expanded to include the outpatient drug bills
of the elderly—those not in hospitals or nursing homes—
almost half of the industry's output will be accounted for
by government expenditures. And when a federal health
insurance program is enacted, covering the entire popula-

* This situation prevails year after year. For the ten-year period
1960–1969, its rate of return was 65 percent higher than for all
manufacturing corporations. During these years the major firms have
rapidly gone conglomerate. Because profits from nondrug operations
generally tend to be lower than in drugs, such acquisitions have the
effect of lowering their overall rate of profit. Industry representatives have been alert in pointing out virtuously that the profit gap
between drugs and all manufacturing has narrowed in recent years.
It is generally believed, however, that, if drugs were separated out
of the miscellany of conglomerate operations, substantially higher
profits on drugs would be shown.

tion, the federal government will foot virtually the entire bill for the products of the drug industry.

Changes in Marketing Structure

To understand the current pattern of government drug procurement, one must have some knowledge of the changing marketing structure in the industry. It was first examined by the Kefauver Committee in the early sixties.[2] The retail pharmacy business had then been captured by some twenty of the major drug firms. Their technique was to employ heavy saturation advertising of brand names to the country's prescribing physicians. As Senator Estes Kefauver pointed out, a unique characteristic of prescription drugs is that "he who orders does not buy; and he who buys does not order." The physician acts as purchasing agent for the consumer. As one doctor recently remarked:

> The physician in the process of writing a prescription or a drug order for a patient is placed in the enviable position of spending someone else's money. Such a situation is not conducive to concern about costs. Thus, arguments that one drug may be cheaper than another, while being equally effective, seem to carry little weight.[3]

Physicians' reliance upon high-priced brand name products, instead of the cheaper generic-named goods, arose out of a change in policy of the American Medical Association in the fifties. For many years the AMA exercised considerable effort to promote prescribing by generic name. In editorials it continually urged doctors to avoid the use of brand names on grounds of "scientific principles." Not only was this practice said to be consonant with the training in medical schools, but it also resulted in greater awareness of the characteristics of the compound being prescribed by the doctor. The AMA also argued that generic prescribing eliminated the necessity of the doctor's remembering a vast collection of brand names, with the possible confusion such multiplicity involved. Until 1950 only the originator of a product was allowed to use a brand name in advertising in AMA periodicals; all other marketers had to advertise under the generic name only. Since the *Journal of the American Medical Association* [JAMA] was heavily relied upon by doctors for information on drugs, this policy had substantial effect.

At that time the control of JAMA advertising was directly in the hands of the AMA Council on Drugs, composed of the country's leading medical experts. A company wishing to advertise in the *Journal* had to supply evidence of effectiveness for the drug. Advertising claims in AMA periodicals were limited to those specifically approved by the council. Manufacturers whose drugs secured approval received a Seal of Acceptance on these products; the seal could be used on packages and in their advertising. For smaller companies, particularly, this seal was of utmost importance, constituting a guarantee to doctors and pharmacists of high quality.

Then, within the next five years, this entire structure was dismantled. The AMA hired a Chicago marketing research firm to examine ways of increasing its advertising revenues. Ben Gaffin & Associates interviewed officials of the major drug firms and found them hostile to the entire AMA program. As a result of its recommendations, the control of advertising was moved from the Council on Drugs into a new advertising department. The emphasis on generic prescribing was muted; any company was permitted to employ brand names in advertising in the JAMA, and the Seal of Acceptance was abandoned. The effect was immediately to make the major part of the AMA's income—previously derived from membership dues—dependent upon advertising in its periodicals. And brand name prescribing by doctors became the dominant practice.

In 1953 the National Pharmaceutical Council, composed of the leading drug companies, was organized. It immediately embarked on a campaign to secure passage in the states of "antisubstitution laws." Until that time substitution in the drug trade meant the selling of an erroneous medicament—a tranquilizer, for example, instead of the antibiotic prescribed. Soon most of the states made it unlawful for a pharmacist to fill a prescription with any but the particular brand name product listed in the prescription. Thus, if it calls for Pentids, the pharmacist must supply only Squibb's product, even though he may have on his shelves the same dosage form of penicillin marketed by a competing firm at a substantially lower price. The effect has been to reduce the role of the pharmacist to a mere clerical function—that of, in the words of many pharmacists, "taking a few pills from a big bottle and counting them into a small bottle." Somewhat belatedly the American Pharmaceutical Association, the organization of the country's pharmacists, awoke to this situation. It is now fighting for the repeal of these laws on the ground that they stifle the exercise of the pharmacists' expertise in drugs. For the small firm, "antisubstitution laws" virtually eliminated it as a competitor in the retail market.

The institutional market, however, still provided some room within which the smaller companies could operate. Purchases by government agencies, hospitals, and other institutions were still largely in the hands of skilled buyers knowledgeable in the ways of the market. Many of these agencies used "formularies"—an approved list of drugs compiled by generic name; advertised bidding was widely employed, with the lowest bidder winning the contract.* In this environment smaller firms could prosper. Without the financial resources for massive brand name promotion of their products, they fought for business on a price basis.

Today this system has been radically altered. In their effort to capture the institutional market, the major firms strove to shift buying control from the skilled purchasing experts to the prescribing physicians—a feat accomplished in the past decade. The effort was aided by the widespread expansion of private health insurance programs. Hospitals lost much of the incentive for achieving economies in drug purchasing as private insurers—and ultimately the public—assumed the bills. The failure of the federal government to supervise drug expenditures under Medicare and Medicaid programs speeded the process.

Even in federal agencies engaged in centralized procurement of drugs, a marked change in practice has occurred. During the Kefauver hearings in 1960, the Military Medical Supply Agency (MMSA) and the Veterans Administration (VA) provided data revealing the vitality of price competition in drug purchases. On advertised bids a number of large and small firms participated. Even on contracts that were "negotiated"—informal solicitation from suppliers for price offers—many companies competed on a price basis.

* An official of the New York Hospital, which instituted these practices as early as 1816, estimated that annual costs would have increased 50 percent if the hospital had purchased on a brand name basis.4

An example or two will suffice. One of the most dramatic moments in the Kefauver hearings occurred in connection with prednisone, then widely used in the treatment of arthritis. While Schering's price to the druggist in 1960 was $170 per thousand (about $290 to the patient with the inclusion of the pharmacy markup), its bid on business to the military was $23.63 for the same quantity. It lost out to a small firm, Premo Laboratories, whose bid was $20.98. Schering retaliated on a later round with a price of $17.97 only to be beaten out by the same firm with a price of $11.79.[5]

A similar situation occurred with reserpine, still widely used in the treatment of hypertension. While Ciba's price to the druggist was $39.40 for one thousand tablets (about $65 to the patient), the pressure of competition made it bid $.60 to the military for the same quantity. At the time the president of Ciba's U.S. subsidiary appeared before Senator Kefauver, he expressed regret in offering this bid. He remarked, "When we bid 60 cents for bottles of 1000 here, we didn't anything like recover our out-of-pocket costs. . . . In retrospect it was perhaps a mistake that we did that." However, after his testimony, Ciba's bid on another procurement was $.58 and still later went to $.52 while the price to druggists remained at $39.40. In all three cases, the business was awarded to other companies bidding below Ciba prices.[6]

In contrast, testimony before Senator Nelson's Small Business Committee in 1971 reveals the situation today. The General Accounting Office had just completed a survey of government centralized procurement practices. Comptroller General Elmer B. Staats reported: "It is clear that the degree of competition obtained in the drug procurement area is less than competition obtained for many other Government supply items."[7] He pointed out that the centralized purchasing of both the Defense Personnel Support Center and Veterans Administration totaled about $94 million in fiscal 1970; yet only 7 percent, or $6.4 million, were awarded pursuant to formal advertising procedures. He added:

> Many procurements are made by brand name either because only one brand of a particular drug is available or because of the prescribing physicians' preference. For example, about 70 percent of the drug items centrally

stocked by the Veterans Administration have been designated for procurement on a sole source basis in order to
obtain specified brand name drugs.

As a result, the institutional market is crumbling for small
business enterprises. The comptroller general testified that
"competition through formally advertised procurements
seems to have a decided effect on the participation of drug
manufacturers classified as small business."[8]

The situation was different for negotiated contracts.
Under this method of buying, the government agency
directly solicits offers from selected sellers. If the agency
widely canvasses all segments of the industry, it can be a
device for stimulating competition. On the other hand, if
solicitation is confined only to major firms, negotiation can
be used to suppress competition—it all depends upon the
manner of administration. With respect to VA, Staats
remarked:

> Only 3 percent of the negotiated procurements for cen-
> trally stocked drugs were awarded to small business con-
> cerns. Since negotiated contracts constituted more than 96
> percent of the total [$25 million], small business received
> only about 4 percent of the total procurements of cen-
> trally stocked drugs.

The record for the Department of Defense was little better.
Of a total centralized procurement amounting to $71.6
million, only 7 percent went to small business. According
to Staats, $19 million were awarded "under advertised
procedures or negotiated with competition." Here small
business received 17 percent or a total of $3.3 million.

Where does this leave the little firms? They are largely
dependent upon the institutional market. With price competition virtually a lost art in the governmental segment of
the institutional market, however, their prospects are dim.
No figures are available on the present attrition rate, but
the smaller firms estimate that, within the next seven or
eight years, their numbers—now about one thousand—will
be greatly decimated. And their decline is hastened by the
merger drive that has absorbed the more profitable small
firms into the giant drug conglomerates.[9]

An independent factor contributes to the decline of
small drug firms: the restrictive regulations of the Food
and Drug Administration (FDA). Most of the drugs in use

today fall within the agency's category of "New Drugs," which require clearance by FDA before the company may engage in marketing. In the introduction of a new product, the agency quite properly requires detailed animal and clinical testing to support the company's New Drug Application (NDA). This can be a costly procedure, often running into hundreds of thousands of dollars. Such information is kept secret by the FDA. Any other company wishing to sell the same drug must engage in duplicative testing work—at its own expense—in support of *its* New Drug Application. The single exception exists when the owner of the data permits its testing data to be used in another firm's NDA, thereby saving the second firm the expense and delay of performing its own testing work. Normally, this occurs during a patent battle, as the contestants privately settle the patent dispute. An agreement is reached that all but one party to the interference will withdraw; the remaining company will secure the patent and license the others under the grant. Small firms, of course, play no role in these complex treaty arrangements among the major firms.

The NDA requirement perpetuates a barrier to entry into the market long after the patent has expired. In the meantime the drug has been used widely in the treatment of human patients, and there is now no need for duplicative animal and clinical tests. Yet it is still required. Because small firms cannot afford the expense of this testing work, they cannot secure an approved NDA. As a result, the FDA requirement has become a more formidable bar to competition than the product patent, which at least expires in seventeen years. Protection accorded by the NDA regulatory mechanism, however, can run on indefinitely.*

* In recent years the FDA has been repeatedly apprised of the economic consequences of its actions, and has been half-heartedly working on an abbreviated NDA procedure. But little of practical help has yet occurred. When the patent expired in 1970 on chlorpromazine (Thorazine, a potent tranquilizer used in mental hospitals), small firms were anxious to enter the market. Efforts were made to secure from the FDA the requirements necessary to secure an approved NDA. No one in the agency seemed to be able to provide an explicit answer, with the tentative replies varying from one official to the next. It was even uncertain whether the proposed abbreviated NDA procedure applied to so-called potent drugs, and indeed what drugs were regarded by the agency as

The disappearance of the smaller firms can cause injury to the public. These independent units have provided most of the price competition that exists in the drug industry. This is not to say that the twenty-odd major firms do not compete. They do. Such competition, however, by tacit consent, is almost exclusively of a nonprice character. Extravagant and mendacious promotional claims, with respect to effectiveness or absence of side effects, are a standard "competitive" practice.[10] Slight molecular modifications of a successful drug—often referred to as "me-too" drugs—are permissible and prevalent. Yet price competition is another matter. Like most highly concentrated industries, the "club" composed of the large firms regards price competition, as a device for securing business, both as dangerous and disloyal.

By their very existence the smaller firms have breathed fresh air into this closed environment. In an industry noted for the total irrelevance of costs of manufacture to prices charged, the small units provide a public yardstick for the reasonableness of pricing by the major companies. It is true that small firms cannot secure access to many of the highly promoted brand name products under exclusive patent control of a single firm. Such products are often marketed under monopoly conditions or, in the event of a patent conflict, by an oligopoly. But, with few exceptions, these drugs are slight variations on existent compounds whose patents have already expired. Consequently, under circumstances where price and drug efficacy are made subject to candid evaluation, small firms can play a significant competitive role in the industry.

The Case of the Veterans Administration

For fiscal 1970 the VA's total drug expenditures were $57.5 million. The central purchasing agency—the Marketing Center in Hines, Illinois—bought $21.3 million.[11] As indicated earlier, 70 percent of all its drugs were brand name products bought on a sole source basis from the

---

potent. As of January, 1973, one company had obtained an abbreviated NDA on this drug—Wyeth, a subsidiary of American Home Products, the largest drug firm in the country.

major drug firms.* Nevertheless, by purchasing in volume, substantial reductions in prices were secured, as shown in Table A.

The remainder was bought locally by the various hospitals, either through Federal Supply Schedule (FSS) contracts or directly from wholesalers. Altogether, about $36 million—as contrasted with $21 million centrally procured —was secured by the individual hospitals themselves. Table A shows the far higher prices charged.

FSS prices are negotiated on an annual basis by the Marketing Center and the supplying firms. Usually there is no element of competition involved. Prices are agreed upon between buyer and seller, and prevail for the next calendar year. Furthermore, these prices are effective not only for VA hospitals but govern as well all purchases made by any government agency using FSS contracts. For fiscal 1970, total FSS contracts exceeded $60 million.

The contract mechanism is simple. When prices are agreed upon, the companies publish and distribute them widely to all federal hospitals. The individual hospital simply orders directly from the manufacturer and is billed for such purchases. Most of the large companies selling direct to the VA under its centralized buying program also sell under FSS contracts.

As indicated earlier, the various VA hospitals also buy directly from local wholesalers. For fiscal 1970, these purchases totaled $11.8 million—more than half of VA's centralized procurement for that year. This is the most costly purchasing method for the hospitals. By trade custom the wholesaler receives a commission of 17 percent off the price to the druggist. In charging the VA customer he may take his full commission; in that case, the hospital pays the same price as the retail druggist. If the hospital's order is large, and if it is a frequent customer, the wholesaler may shave a bit on his margin.

An examination of FSS prices indicates that they are

* No figures are available on the concentration of orders with large firms for 1970. However, the VA submitted such data to the Nelson Committee for the combined years 1968 and 1969. The compilation shows that 70 percent of the total of $51.3 million—or $36.7 million—went to twenty large companies. Nine of these firms (American Home, Bristol, Lilly, Pfizer, Roche, Smith Kline & French, Sterling, Upjohn, and Warner Lambert) accounted for 60 percent. Three—Lilly, Roche, and SKF—had 40 percent.

TABLE A

PRICE COMPARISONS—VA CENTRALIZED PURCHASES, FEDERAL
SUPPLY SCHEDULE CONTRACTS, AND PRICES TO DRUGGISTS

	VA Centralized (Fiscal 1969)	Federal Supply Schedule (1970)	Price to Druggist (1970)
Ritalin (Ciba) 10 mg., 1000's	$ 17.34	$ 44.97	$ 54.51
Doriden (Ciba) 0.5 gm. 1000's	18.04	32.01	40.01
Placidyl (Abbott) 500 mg. 100's	2.09	4.84	5.00
Mysoline (Ayerst) 0.25 gm. 1000's	25.25	36.36	44.52
Compazine (SKF) 10 mg. 5000's	180.16	229.50	576.00
Griseofulvin (Ayerst) 250 mg. 500's	11.06	40.10	52.00
Coly-Mycin (Warner) 5 ml. (bottle)	1.73	1.99	2.40
Furadantin (Eaton) 100 mg., 1000's	75.537	199.992	270.00
Macrodantin (Eaton) 50 mg. 1000's	38.115	84.996	114.76
Thiosulfil Forte (Ayerst) 0.5 gm. 100's	3.24	4.61	5.64
Ismelin (Ciba) 25 mg. 100's	5.75	7.84	9.50
Peritrate (Warner) 20 mg. 500's	9.05	14.50	16.88
Maalox Susp. (Rorer) 6 oz.	.0934	.20	.59
Gelusil (Warner) 1000's	7.60	12.04	14.50
Rio-Pan (Ayerst) 400 mg., 12 fl. oz.	.20	.88	1.02
Choledyl (Warner) 200 mg. 1000's	21.26	26.89	32.40
Diuril (Merck) 0.5 gm. 1000's	20.90	44.69	48.45

Note: Prices shown for centralized procurement are the prices actually paid by VA as reported to the Nelson Committee. The Marketing Center adds a 9 percent markup to cover administrative expenses. Thus, in the case of Ritalin, the first item, the VA hospital was charged an additional $1.57 or a total of $19.11.

frequently similar to prices to wholesalers. In a word, buyers under FSS contracts are usually treated by manufacturers as wholesalers entitled to a 17 percent discount off the company's prices to retail drug outlets. Thus, if the latter pays $5 for a particular drug, the FSS price is generally in the neighborhood of $4.15. In this manner both the FSS structure of prices, as well as that for the wholesaler, is tied directly to the artificially high structure in the retail market.

What results then is a great disparity in prices between centralized procurement and local buying under FSS contracts or from wholesalers. So far as manufacturers are concerned, the low prices they receive in the first case are more than compensated for by the high prices—constituting the bulk of dollar sales—secured under local procurement. So far as VA is concerned, most congressional inquiries are happily directed to centralized procurement. The agency has little detailed information available on the local aspect of its procurement activities. Indeed, at the outset of the Nelson hearings, a VA official stated that no specific information was supplied on local purchases; "It would have taken too long for us to have gotten it to you."[12]

Why does a local VA hospital elect to buy locally at high prices rather than from VA's centralized stock? The answer lies in VA's expressed policy that physicians must be free to exercise their individual preferences. As the VA administrator of veterans' affairs informed the Nelson Committee:

> The administrative process does not dictate the selection of drugs which will be prescribed and dispensed in our Veterans Administration hospitals clinics. We consider that the judgment of the physician is paramount to all other considerations in the drug selection process.[13]

Because physicians' prescribing practices are largely determined by the brand name promotion of the major companies, brand name drugs are preferred. The effect negates the usefulness of a centralized procurement system. It would be impracticable for the Marketing Center to stock centrally the thousands of compounds now prescribed by VA physicians. The individual quantities purchased would be too minute, and the price reductions too slight, to compensate for the administrative expenses involved. In consequence, under the present policy of VA, the largest share of its purchases are handled through local channels. This means high drug costs.

Senator Nelson's critical examination of VA's drug procurement covered two broad fronts. One was the purchase of high-priced brand name items no more effective than less costly products. The other was directed to the continued purchase of ineffective drugs long after they had been recognized as worthless and, in some cases, actually dangerous to the patient. Fiornal, for example, is a combination of aspirin, phenacatin, and caffeine. Nelson pointed out that expert medical opinion agreed that its analgesic effectiveness lay in the aspirin alone.[14] Yet VA was paying $9.45 for Fiornal and $.70 for aspirin per thousand. Dr. Benjamin B. Wells, deputy chief medical director of VA, replied that the agency "would accede to the judgment of the physicians, even though it might be wrong."[15]

> SENATOR NELSON: Now, if the Veterans Administration is going to let itself be pushed around because of an irrational prescription by an individual physician, who is to protect the taxpayer's dollar or, indeed, promote good medical practice?
>
> DR. WELLS: This is a very difficult question, sir, but we are in the position not infrequently of having to accede to the demands of the physicians and their judgment on their patient. This is a tradition we must follow.
>
> SENATOR NELSON: So what you are saying is, if an individual physician, against the expertise of the best pharmacologists and clinicians in the country, still insists on prescribing a drug, then you will spend the money and let him have the drug?
>
> DR. WELLS: On a limited basis, sir. I think we do everything we can to discourage that, but we, under pressure, I suspect would succumb.

An illustration of VA's purchase of drugs dangerous to the patient is Panalba, now banned from the market. Senator Nelson pointed out that the country's leading experts in the antibiotic field as early as 1957 had published an editorial in the *AMA Journal* severely attacking the use of fixed combination antibiotics. In 1968 the National Research Council of the National Academy of Sciences had recommended that these combinations be removed from the market. Through all these years, and even after the

NAS/NRC had recommended the drug's removal, the VA continued to purchase the drug. Dr. Wells replied, "This, I think, is really a classical example of our whole problem, Mr. Chairman."[16] At a later session, Senator Nelson argued that

> . . . if you have a position that is universally held by the experts in the field, then somebody who is not an expert shouldn't be permitted, at least, in a Government hospital, to override the experts. You say to him, "Sir, all the medical experts in this country say this. You have a contrary position. You bring to us the controlled clinical studies or the evidence that overrides the position of the experts and we will accept the drug that you are using." All you have to do is to apply the rule of reason and science to the doctor. If he can't do it, you shouldn't permit the drug in your hospital and the taxpayers shouldn't fund it and the patients shouldn't have to suffer through it either.[17]

Dr. Wells replied that "at this point in time, I would simply not be prepared to make that kind of recommendation to the Administrator which would mean that we would indeed be administering the practice of medicine from Washington."

The issue was also raised with Dr. Jesse L. Steinfeld, the surgeon general. His response was of particular interest because his agency, HEW, currently accounts for the federal government's largest expenditures for drugs under its Medicare and Medicaid programs. In 1969 the HEW Task Force on Prescription Drugs had proposed consideration of centralized procurement as a device for reducing drugs costs under these programs.[18] Nelson put the issue frankly:

> Everybody admits that advertising and promotion is what sells the drug, not proven therapeutic superiority. So every time doctors say we cannot interfere with the doctor's independent judgment, who is interfering? The advertising and promotion. And since the responsibility of the profession is to the welfare of the public, a little interference with the doctor's judgment, which may be determined by advertising and promotion, would be in the best interests of the public, would it not?[19]

Dr. Steinfeld replied, "Yes, I think we have to determine the appropriate amount." In a later appearance before the

Nelson Committee, however, he took the view that the solution lay in "educating" the doctors. After agreeing that the hearings revealed serious weaknesses in the present system, he said:

> The Department [HEW] is taking the approach that continuing education is the best method of bringing about rational drug therapy. As you know very well, most people, especially physicians, resent edicts of "you shall" or "you shall not." We plan to appeal to the logic of the results of important published studies on individual drugs and classes of drugs.[20]

This, of course, is precisely the approach of the Veterans Administration, with all its attendant weaknesses and pitfalls.

Our national policy, as embodied in legislation, requires the use of advertised competitive bids on government purchases.[21] In this manner, it is believed, the government secures the lowest prices possible; at the same time it provides all suppliers a fair and equal chance to compete for orders. The law, however, specifically exempts "medicines and medical property"; in this area federal agencies are free to purchase through negotiation.

Where an agency such as VA purchases almost entirely on a negotiated basis, how can it determine whether the prices charged are reasonable? Congress has been specific on this point. The comptroller general is authorized to require cost information from companies involved in negotiated contracts. Until 1971, however, this provision has not been invoked for drug manufacturers. The VA has never on its own made a request to the General Accounting Office for such an inquiry; and the GAO apparently lacked sufficient information to proceed in the absence of complaint. When Senator Nelson inquired why VA had failed to act, the director of the VA Supply Service replied, "They [GAO] don't have to be asked. They can come in and do it at their own instance."[22]

> SENATOR NELSON: You are buying repeatedly, year after year, on a negotiated basis, as are other agencies, and the law authorizes GAO to go in and examine the company's production costs. It seems to me that it would be an obligation for you to request this.

MR. WHITWORTH: The fact remains, Senator, that I have
behind me the manager of our marketing center in Chicago and he tells me we have never done so.

The VA's record is one of total abdication in securing
cost information. Currently, it relies upon going market
prices as a standard for establishing the reasonableness of
the prices it is charged. Its contracts simply require the
seller to certify that its prices to VA are based upon market
prices of items "sold in substantial quantities to the general
public in effect as of the date of supplier's offer."[23] This,
of course, begs the whole question. Where prices are
"administered," as in the drug industry, the prevailing price
structure tends to have little relationship to the costs of
manufacture.

Indeed, in industries where the market fails to function
as a price regulator, some costs themselves tend to be a
reflection of the prices charged. The high profits enjoyed
by the major drug firms have enabled them to expend ever
larger sums for advertising, for example. The Kefauver
Committee estimated in 1960 that $750 million was an-
nually spent by the drug industry in promoting its products
to 250,000 physicians. Data submitted to the committee by
twenty-two major firms showed that twenty-five cents of
every sales dollar was spent on advertising, as contrasted
with six cents on research. Today it is estimated that total
advertising expenditures for drugs exceed $1 billion. By
accepting the established price as a standard of reasonableness, the VA helps to perpetuate this extravagance. It also
multiplies its own problems in procurement by, in effect,
subsidizing the heavy promotional bombardment that
spirals the multiplicity of brand name prescriptions of VA
physicians.

There is, however, another way to check the reasonableness of drug prices: securing price offers from firms operating in more competitive markets. For many years drug
prices in Europe have been lower than in the United States
because of differences in patent protection.[24] In most
European countries only *process* patents—those on methods of manufacture—are permitted on products essential
to the public health and welfare. If another firm develops a
different manufacturing process, it is free to compete in the
market. In the chemical industry (of which drug manufac-

turing is a part), this is often relatively easy. But in the United States both *process* and *product* patents are permitted on *all* types of goods. As a result, even if a drug company invents a more efficient method of production, it cannot market the product unless it secures a license from the holder of the product patent. Usually this request is refused.

In federal procurement, however, the patent barrier may be bypassed. In order to insure more competitive prices, Congress has decreed that federal agencies may disregard all patents in purchasing; injured patent holders may sue for damages in the U.S. Court of Claims.[25] Thus the VA could, if it wished, secure more advantageous prices by buying abroad. During the course of the Nelson hearings, VA officials made it quite clear that they had little knowledge or interest in prices in foreign markets. As one official stated, "It is just our practice not to bid in the foreign market." Senator Nelson wondered why:

> In your negotiating, since 80 percent of these contracts are sole source, wouldn't good sensible bargaining require that you have the world price on any of these drugs, and that in negotiation you make some comparison, and when you encounter an excessive price, you say, "We will not pay it"? Why shouldn't that be a built-in automatic policy of any Government purchasing agency in order to protect the tax payers' dollars?[26]

He received the evasive reply: "We are hard put to conduct the necessary inspections in domestic manufacturing, and so have no resources in foreign locations." However, the inspection service of the FDA is constantly engaged in examination of foreign plants for drug companies wishing to import drugs from abroad. Senator Nelson asked why the resources of this agency should not be used for government purchases as well as for imports by private firms. The reply: "We feel we do not have the resources to determine that we are getting the quality that we require."

The marked savings possible through foreign procurement are indicated in VA's own experience in the case of meprobamate (Miltown, Equanil). The price information submitted to the Nelson Committee for fiscal 1969 shows that this drug was the only one imported by the VA. The price paid A/S Syntetic of Denmark was $1.55 for five hundred tablets (400 mg.); for the same drug purchased in the same year from Carter, holder of the U.S. product patent, the VA paid $36.25 for five hundred tablets. A price difference of $1.55 as contrasted with $36.25 might be expected to serve as an alert to a buying agency interested in effecting economies. Despite this cost savings, no other drugs were imported in 1968 and 1969 and, according to VA officials before the Nelson Committee, no inquiry was made as to whether lower prices would be quoted by foreign sources.

The VA's indifference owes itself to an inordinate and unnecessary deference to physicians' prescribing practices. Obviously, physicians cannot be expected to keep abreast of prices for all drugs that they prescribe to their patients. In the interest of economy in government procurement, they should not be permitted to require a particular brand name product when the same drug, equally effective, is available at a lower price. And when physicians are misled by massive drug advertising on high-priced specialties protected by patent, account should be taken of the judgment of medical experts who are concerned with therapeutic utility rather than the enhancement of corporate profits. Until this policy change occurs, there can be little rationality in the government's purchase of drugs or in the achievement of economies in procurement.

There is another factor accounting for the VA's indifference. Every government agency with a continuing relationship in an industry develops a cozy fraternalism. This is especially true in procurement, where the purchasing agency has riches to award in the form of sizable orders. Interested sellers—particularly if they are large—have the kind of expense accounts to help their cause along. Often this takes the guise of expense-free seminars and conferences on industry problems—which more accurately might be described as indoctrination centers for government procurement officials. A subtle but pervasive element in the relationship is the possibility of lucrative job offers from companies themselves or from their allied trade associations. It is not entirely surprising that interviews with VA procurement officials leave the general impression that one has been conversing with representatives of the Pharmaceutical Manufacturers Association or the National Pharmaceutical Council.

The Case of the Defense Department

Unlike the VA, the military buys the bulk of its drugs through centralized procurement—about 70 percent, with the remaining 30 percent locally procured. For fiscal 1970, for example, total drug expenditures amounted to $102.4 million, of which $71.4 million was centrally purchased by the Defense Personnel Support Centers (DPSC). The remaining $31 million was purchased locally by the various military installations. Federal Supply Schedule contracts accounted for $21 million of local procurement; another $10 million represented buying directly from wholesalers. These local purchases were, of course, at substantially higher prices than those under centralized procurement. Comptroller General Elmer Staats stated that the GAO had compared prices under FSS contracts with the highest prices paid under centralized procurement over a two-year period and found that FSS prices averaged 63 percent higher.[27]

An examination of the prices submitted to the Nelson Committee for 1968 and 1969 indicates that DPSC's prices under centralized procurement are similar to those of the VA—often slightly lower. The prices listed in Table B, selected at random, are indicative.

While the extent of centralized purchases by the Defense Department is laudable, the general absence of advertised competitive bids is not. Detailed price data submitted to the Nelson Committee for 1968 and 1969 show that the practice is virtually nonexistent. Of total domestic purchases reported, amounting to about $87 million for both years, less than $2.5 million involved use of advertised competitive bids.

Traditionally, the military has relied upon negotiation for most of its drug purchases. As previously mentioned, if properly administered, negotiation can be an effective device for competitive procurement. At the time of the Kefauver hearings, for example, the price data submitted showed a large number of competitive price offers secured under negotiation. When price competition was clearly absent in the U.S. market, the Military Medical Supply agency, (MMSA, the predecessor of DPSC) investigated foreign sources. In the late fifties, the domestic manufacturers of tetracycline, an important antibiotic, presented a united

TABLE B
PRICE COMPARISONS—VA AND DPSC CENTRALIZED
PROCUREMENT, AND PRICES TO DRUGGISTS
(LATEST PRICES IN FISCAL 1969)

	Price to VA	Price to DPSC	Price to Druggist (Red Book, 1970)
Thorazine 25 mg., 500's	$19.21	$16.3075	$ 28.50
Compazine 15 mg., 250's	23.89	21.4975	35.80
Valium 25 mg. 500's	18.00	18.10	38.00
Darvon 32 mg., 500's	6.58	6.45	17.67
V-Cillin K 250 mg., 100's	2.44	1.472	8.95
Terramycin 250 mg., 100's	7.90	3.73	21.36
Chlormycetin 250 mg., 100's	5.41	4.71	22.68
Erythrocin 250 mg., 100's	3.11	3.73	26.39
NegGram .5 gm., 1000's	83.20	81.84	128.66
Gantrisin .5 mg., 1000's	8.50	8.40	25.30
Orinase .5 gm., 500's	13.775	13.895	39.49
Diabinese 250 mg., 500's	11.80	12.39	44.06
Diuril .5 gm., 1000's	20.90	19.24	58.14
Hygroton 100 mg., 100's	4.13	4.01	7.26
Lasix 40 mg., 500's	24.99	25.55	37.80
Hydrochlorthiazide	7.94	6.74	30.00

front on price. The agency reacted promptly. Plant inspections were made of interested foreign suppliers, and tests were performed for product quality in cooperation with the Food and Drug Administration. In contrast to a $17 price quoted by American Cyanamid, Pfizer, and Bristol for one hundred capsules (250 mg.), the MMSA bought the drug abroad for $8.15.[28] On later bids, foreign sources were offering the product at $2.50. So successful was this effort that MMSA cautiously began to expand its foreign procurement to other drugs under monopoly control in this country.

But foreign price competition on procurement was the last thing the American drug industry wanted. Pressures were immediately exerted upon selected members of Congress to halt the practice. Representative Richard L. Roudebush (R.–Ind.) demanded an investigation. A staff memorandum prepared by the House Military Operations Subcommittee traced the congressman's interest to the fact that Pfizer held the U.S. product patent on tetracycline, and "one of the company's manufacturing plants is in Terre Haute, Indiana, a part of Mr. Roudebush's district."[29] MMSA officials were called to Washington to explain the furor their actions had created within the American drug industry. Shortly after their appearance before the Kefauver Committee in 1960, rumors of impending changes began to circulate. Within the next few years an entire dismantlement of the MMSA operation took place. The headquarters in Brooklyn, New York, were shifted to Philadelphia, with a substantial loss in skilled personnel. The top management was totally recast. Some, including Rear Admiral William L. Knickerbocker, executive director, retired; others resigned; while still others were shifted to different posts in the military service. Those in key command became "marked men" whose subsequent activities were kept under surveillance by the drug industry.[30] At this time the name of the agency was changed to the Defense Personnel Support Center.

The more cooperative attitude of the new management quickly became evident. In speeches before the drug section of the Defense Supply Association, an organization of the major private contractors selling to the military, the changes in policy were stressed. Officials of the drug firms were assured that the emphasis was now on "drug quality" and that price played a secondary role. References were made to the misguided diligence displayed by previous procurement officials in sacrificing quality for lower prices.[31]

The policy change was also reflected in the number of

drugs designated as "sole source." Although several suppliers often exist for these drugs, the military purchases only the specified brand name product of a particular company. Since 1960 a dozen products have been declared sole source, with all but one being brand names of major firms. For fiscal 1968 and 1969 combined, about $7 million were involved in these purchases. For example, Dilantin (Parke Davis) and PhisoHex (Sterling Drug) were made sole source items, thus excluding a large number of competing sellers.[32] The asserted reason for designating these brand names was that military physicians find them more efficacious than their competitors' products. Other factors, however, appear to play a role. For example, tolbutamide has been sold exclusively in this country since 1956 by Upjohn under the trade name Orinase. The American company has sole marketing rights under a license from the German firm that originated the product. In 1962 a small American firm secured an approved New Drug Application from FDA on tolbutamide imported from abroad, offering the product to DPSC at prices substantially lower than Upjohn's. Immediately thereafter Orinase was declared a sole source item, and the incipient competition on this federal procurement was eliminated.

As in the case of VA, the bulk of DPSC's purchases are brand name items secured from major companies. Many of these items are bought on a de facto sole source basis because they are controlled under patents and marketed by a single supplier. A large number represent minor molecular differences of a basic chemical on which patents have expired or are about to end.

Like the VA, the military defends its purchases of duplicate compounds on the ground that its physicians must be free to indulge their prescribing preferences. Yet its rationale goes slightly further. According to Rear Admiral Etter, it is difficult to keep young doctors in military service. "If you try to keep them from prescribing in the way they think best, it certainly can be one added way to make service life unattractive and that man is going to leave the service."[33] Senator Nelson then listed a number of brand name purchases that, according to the country's leading medical experts, were no more effective than cheaper compounds. He cited several products bought that had been declared ineffective or even dangerous to the health of the patient. Admiral Etter's defense, he remarked, was akin to saying that the military physician must be allowed to "practice bad medicine because we do not want to lose him."

In consequence of its policies, small business participation in DPSC's drug purchases has been insignificant. Detailed data were supplied to the Nelson Committee on $87 million worth of drugs purchased from domestic sources in fiscal 1968 and 1969 combined. Only $2.5 million involved use of advertised competitive bids. On negotiated contracts—representing the great bulk of the purchases—small firms received $2.3 million out of a total of over $84 million, or something less than 5 percent.[34] As in the case of VA, most of the business was concentrated in a few firms. Close to 80 percent of all the purchases came from twenty major firms. Seven companies—American Home, Bristol, Lilly, Roche, Searle, Smith Kline & French, and Sterling—received $44 million, or over half of the total. Three firms—Roche, Lilly, and Bristol—secured $24 million or close to 30 percent.[35]

Limiting the Number of Suppliers

DPSC employs a variety of devices whose practical effect limits the number of approved suppliers. One involves plant inspection. Although the FDA has statutory authority for inspection of drug manufacturing plants, both the VA and DPSC maintain their own inspection services— with DPSC's practices being quite restrictive. While FDA and VA inspect a plant as a source of supply for the plant's entire range of products, DPSC performs the task for *specific products*. Thus a firm may be acceptable as a bidder for one drug but unacceptable for another. Its plant operations are subjected to examination by DPSC officials for approval on each separate product offered to the agency. For small firms this involves an interminable number of inspections by different inspectors with varying standards. Even if they make the changes required to qualify for sales of a particular product, there is little likelihood they will secure the contract. For 1968 and 1969, on which data are available, less than fifty small companies were awarded any business. For many of them, discouraging experiences led them to give up any attempt to secure orders.

The situation is quite different for the large firms. As regular suppliers shipping almost continuously, there is a presumption by the agency that quality standards are met without inspection on additional contracts. An examination of the records submitted to the Nelson Committee indicates that large firms are inspected infrequently. The general attitude of the agency is expressed in the testimony of Colonel A. J. Snyder, chief of DPSC's drug procurement, before the Nelson Committee:

> [A] firm whose name and reputation and continued success in business is dependent upon quality pays more attention to it than a firm that may be entering the market for a particular opportunity to produce for a specific contract. Now, these conditions are met by these firms that are regularly engaged in marketing a product by anyone who does business with us, but there are many firms who supply those products and do not meet these standards. This is not a universal condition. It is something that some people do and some don't. We try to do business with those that do.[36]

The problem of multiple inspection of drug plants has now reached a crisis stage. Under the 1962 Kefauver amendments to the food and drug law, FDA is required to inspect at least once every two years. According to FDA officials, inspection of drug manufacturing plants now is made every ten months. But such inspection is not enough to qualify for sales to VA or the military; firms must meet the separate requirements of these latter agencies. In addition, the various states and some cities maintain their own inspection services. The arrival of inspectors from one government agency or another is a frequent occurrence, particularly for small firms.

Are such multiple inspections really necessary? DPSC officials argue that there is a "difference in philosophy" between the inspection work of their agency and the FDA. As one put it, "FDA's inspections are plant-oriented and ours are product-oriented." But the end purpose, of course, in each case is to assure drug quality. A more sensible approach to the problem would be to place responsibility for federal plant inspection in a single agency equipped with staff and expertise to do the job. A single set of uniform standards applicable to all plants could replace the contradictory requirements that currently prevail. Dr. Charles C. Edwards, commissioner of Food and Drugs, has remarked:

> I think without any question, it is a waste of resources, it is a waste of money to have this triple duplication by these three agencies [FDA, VA, Defense]. It really is the responsibility of the Food and Drug Administration to assure the American public, be it the Federal public or the private public, that drugs are in fact safe and efficacious and to have two other agencies involved in this is utter nonsense.[37]

Another device used for restricting the number of suppliers of drugs to the Defense Department is "product specs." For each drug purchased, the Defense Personnel Support Center maintains an exhaustive list of specifications, many of which allegedly exceed the standards imposed for the civilian market.[38] These extra requirements, it was explained, are necessary because drugs of the military "go all over the world" and are used under the most adverse climatic conditions. Yet they are not limited to overseas shipments, but are applicable to all drug purchases—even those in U.S. military hospitals and installations. Furthermore, there are many countries, particularly those in Europe, where climatic and storage conditions present no special problem. Why, then, are they universally necessary?

The fact is that "specs" are also employed to eliminate competition. When a drug is placed on the approved list for the first time, DPSC has no way of knowing what specifications should be used. Quite naturally it turns to the manufacturer who is offering the drug for sale to the government. And quite naturally that manufacturer writes into the proposed specifications certain requirements that enable it to become the sole supplier. As a result, the military drug "specs" are riddled with "fine print" requirements—unrecognizable to the uninitiated—which assure sales by a single supplier.

During his hearings Senator Nelson asked DPSC officials if their specifications did not add substantially to drug costs for the military. The following exchange occurred with Max Feinberg, a procurement official:

MR. FEINBERG: I don't know that, sir. But generally speaking, the standards that we have are utilized by the companies in their commercial market, too.

SENATOR NELSON: Oh, so what you are talking about is
automatically done by them in their sales in the domestic
market anyway.

MR. FEINBERG: So far as we know.[39]

Consequently, it would appear that the detailed specifications of the agency are not in any way distinctive, but
merely reflect those used by the companies in their domestic, civilian market. In that event, what real function do
they serve except to preserve monopoly sources of supply?

Limiting Foreign Procurement

As in the case of VA, DPSC has elected not to explore the
possibilities of more competitive drug procurement from
foreign sources of supply. Indeed this effort, originally
started by MMSA, the predecessor agency, has all but been
abandoned. For fiscal 1968 and 1969, only three products
were purchased by DPSC from European firms. In each
instance, prices were also sought from U.S. suppliers, and
the contrast is striking.

In view of the marked price savings available, why has
DPSC failed to explore foreign prices for other drugs controlled by patent monopoly in this country? Its predecessor
agency had found that a mere expression of intent to do so
had a beneficial effect: American suppliers reacted defen-
sively with quotations of lower prices. DPSC officials say
they cannot act because of the Buy American Act. Under
this law government agencies are directed to buy U.S.

TABLE C

PRICE COMPARISONS—FOREIGN AND U.S. COMPANIES
ON DRUGS IMPORTED BY DPSC, 1969

Product	Successful Foreign Bidder	Lowest U.S. Price Bid
Meprobamate 400 mg., 500's	$1.68 (A/S Syntetic, Denmark)	$9.50 (Carter)
Tetracycline 250 mg., 100's	.90 (Carlo Erba, Italy)	2.09 (Pfizer)
Nitrofurantoin 100 mg., 1000's	18.50 (Zambon, Italy)	76.30 (Morton-Norwich)

products unless their prices are "unreasonable."[40] The executive order governing this provision defines an unreasonable U.S. price as one that exceeds 10 percent of the foreign price, exclusive of duty.[41] But then the Department of Defense adds another hurdle. This is the 50 percent "evaluation factor" contained in the Armed Services Procurement Regulations (ASPR).

Here an intricate computation is employed. A substantial portion of the drugs imported into America are benzenoids, a class of chemicals whose tariff is determined by the American Selling Price (ASP). The Tariff Commission estimates that over 40 percent of all medicinals by value, and 80 percent by quantity, have their tariffs determined in this manner. As a result, the higher the monopoly price charged domestically, the greater is the tariff barrier to foreign competition. The ASPR regulation takes this factor into account in determining the acceptability of a foreign offer. It provides that either the 50 percent "evaluation factor" may be used, which involves arbitrarily upping the bid quoted by half, or alternatively the calculation may be made by adding 6 percent to the foreign bid plus the import duty. Selection is determined by which process results in the higher price. As can be expected, this artificially created barrier by the Department of Defense is formidable.

There are still other hurdles. These center around the regulations of the Food and Drug Administration. No firm can qualify as a bidder on a particular product for DPSC —and also for VA—unless it has an approved New Drug Application. This involves inspection of the manufacturing plant as well as submission of acceptable data showing the drug's safety and efficacy. For foreign firms, plant inspection is no real problem. Many of the European plants are newer than those in the United States, and fully meet American standards. The real difficulty arises from the FDA requirement that animal and human testing data must include detailed studies conducted in the United States. Many of these drugs have originated abroad and have been marketed there for many years. In most instances they have also been sold in this country for an extended period; and detailed testing data were submitted in support of approved NDAs before marketing. Where a drug's characteristics are already well-known, competent

testers and clinicians are understandably reluctant to duplicate existent work. (This problem is also faced by
small U.S. firms anxious to market products on which
patents have expired.) Given the expense of such work,
foreign firms hesitate to embark on this expenditure in the
face of the clear lack of interest shown by government
procurement officials. What is needed, again, is a clearly
delineated, abbreviated NDA procedure within FDA that
will ease entry into the market.

Finally, it is customary for the major drug firms, just
prior to the expiration of an important product patent, to
bring out a slight molecular modification of the older drug.
In this manner effective patent protection can be continued
indefinitely. The new product is promoted intensively to
physicians as a significant technological advance; and they
respond by shifting their prescriptions to the new brand
name. Although there is little therapeutic difference, extended experience with patients is often required before
physicians recognize this fact. In the meantime the older
drug has fallen into disuse as obsolete.

For the European firm this is a real problem. The Italian
supplier of nitrofurantoin, for example, went to considerable effort and expense to secure an approved NDA for
sales to the U.S. government. (Because of the patent held
by Morton-Norwich, it could not sell in the U.S. civilian
market.) Just prior to the expiration of the patent, Morton-
Norwich shifted its promotion to physicians from Furadantin, its brand name, to Macrodantin. The latter represents a change merely in particle size, which allegedly
reduces the amount of nausea associated with use of this
compound. According to medical experts, the same effect
can be achieved with the older drug if taken with meals.
Physicians in military and veterans hospitals are, however,
prescribing high-priced Macrodantin widely in response to
its advertising. If the Italian firm wishes to compete on this
product, it must apply for a new NDA and present testing
data conducted in the U.S. Its ability to compete on a price
basis is reduced with these added costs, particularly because patents prevent it from entering the American civilian market. This whole combination of circumstances, plus
the unwillingness of DPSC and VA to seek out competition, discourages foreign suppliers.

With a different attitude by federal procurement officials, the problem could easily be solved. Government hospitals are routinely used by American drug firms for testing in support of their NDA applications. These facilities are made available at public expense; in effect, the federal government subsidizes this research. These same facilities could be employed for clearance of NDAs. Once chemical equivalence has been established for the foreign drug with its American counterpart, a limited amount of clinical testing in government hospitals, and at a minimum cost, should suffice. The mere knowledge that government agencies were prepared to take such a step in the interest of buying competitively would have a corrective influence upon monopoly pricing practices of the American firms.

Yet they have *not* been willing to take this step. The result is that the United States taxpayer foots the bill each year for unnecessarily high drug costs incurred by our federal government. But the ultimate effect extends far beyond government procurement, reaching the structure of prices prevailing for the general public. Were the federal agencies to insure competition in their purchases, these prices could serve as a yardstick for the reasonableness of prices charged in the civilian market. At the present time, the public is incensed over rising health costs as well as the prices they must pay for drugs filled under doctors' prescriptions. But in the absence of specific knowledge, there is little they can do about it. And, unless the situation is remedied, future consequences will be great. When a federal health insurance program is enacted, the government will purchase most of the drugs used in this country. If it continues its present obeisance to monopolistic practices in the drug industry, the cost burden to the public under the program will be intolerable.

PATENTS

10

The Legal Monopoly

IRENE TILL

An Historical Backdrop

Like many other laws on our statute books, the patent grant has been diverted to uses far different from those originally intended. While its purpose, according to the Constitution, was "to promote the progress of science and the useful arts,"[1] the patent today constitutes the leading instrument in our economy for the creation and maintenance of monopoly power. Simultaneously, the purpose expressed by the Fathers has been converted into a national mythology to cloud the capture of the patent system by large corporate interests.

The mythology has it, for one example, that the Constitution requires the issuance of patents by the federal government. In fact, the word *patent* is not used in the document. It merely states that the Congress "shall have power"—to be used *if* it sees fit—to "secure for limited times to authors and inventors the exclusive right to their respective writings and discoveries."[2] The real purpose was to take the matter out of the hands of the states and create a unified federal system; already some of the states had enacted patent laws varying widely in character.[3]

At the time of the writing of the Constitution, there was little enthusiasm for monopoly grants of any kind. Experience was too recent with the British monarchs' practice of granting "letter patents" (monopolies on existing products such as tea, sugar, playing cards) to court favorites. Strong arguments were made, instead, for the use of cash bounties or generous grants of land to compensate inventors for their discoveries. But such direct rewards required evaluation of the worth of the invention—always difficult to measure before it has been tested in practical use.

The first statute, effective in April, 1790, provided for the issuance of patents granting exclusive rights for fourteen years.[4] The odd time period represented the length of two apprenticeship periods. (Later legislation represented a compromise between those urging two and three apprenticeship periods; the issue was settled by making it two and one-half periods or seventeen years.) The secretary of state, the secretary of war, and the attorney general were authorized to grant patents for "sufficiently useful and important inventions." As secretary of state, Thomas Jefferson took the lead in the activities of the new "Patent Board." Patents issued were held to a high degree of ingenuity. In 1790 only three were granted; in 1791, thirty-three; in 1792, eleven; in 1793, twenty.[5]

In retrospect, it is easy to understand the genesis of such a statute. The Industrial Revolution was well under way in England; the American colonies had just refused to serve the Mother Country as another raw material supplier for British factories. If the new nation was to make its way in the world, it needed the spur of inventions and discoveries. At this time the country was primarily agricultural, with a narrow fringe of petty trade and small manufacturing plants along the seaboard. Invention was more an avocation than a vocation. Gentlemen such as Thomas Jefferson and Ben Franklin played with ideas and engaged in practical experimentation. Craftsmen, skilled in a particular art, were using their imagination to better existent processes. The modern corporate research laboratory with its group performance was beyond comprehension. It was a relatively simple matter to pinpoint both the inventor and the invention in the issuance of the patent grant.

And the theory underlying the patent law appeared to offer great promise. To secure a patent the invention would be made totally public; others would then have the opportunity to study it and stimulate additional inventions. In exchange for full disclosure, the inventor would be accorded a limited period for exclusive exploitation of his discovery. This provided an additional advantage. If the invention had real merit, the market would be the automatic judge of the extent of his reward. If it proved to be worthless, the public would not be the loser, as would occur in the grant of cash bounties or grants of land before the development was put to practical test.

But theory and reality soon conflicted. The business opportunities latent in the exploitation of monopoly rights were quickly recognized. By 1793 the strict standards imposed by Jefferson were eased by statutory revision. In anger at this drift away from the constitutional objective, Jefferson remarked, "I might build a stable, bring into it a cutting-knife to chop straw, a handmill to grind the grain, a curry-comb and brush to clean the horses, and by a patent exclude anyone from evermore using these things without paying me."[6] He saw what was coming.[7]

Inherent in the concept of a patent as a stimulus to invention are two closely allied assumptions. One is that the creative imagination is largely propelled by financial gain. But if history and experience provide any guide, many of the world's significant contributions have often come from individuals who, in their own lifetimes, received no pecuniary rewards and were subjected to ignominy for their inventiveness.[8] Clearly, they were governed by some inner drives of inquiry that had little to do with monetary gain. They marched to the sound of their own drummer, whatever the consequences.

A second assumption is that an invention is the work of a single mind. Occasionally a discovery represents a monumental advance by one individual; but far more commonly, inventions are an inevitable next step in a developing technology. For that reason it is not surprising that many inventions occur simultaneously in many parts of the world. Their time has come; and within the limits of existing knowledge, it is mere accident who reaches the goal first. Speaking on this subject at a congressional committee hearing, David Novick of the Rand Corporation stated:

> Perhaps the best illustration of this . . . is the now commonplace zipper. In 1912 patents for a zipper were requested by a gentleman in Switzerland, a lady in Belgium and a gentleman in the United States and all three patents

were filed in a period of 9 months. Subsequent investigation has made it clear that none of the inventors knew anything about the work of the others, and yet, curiously enough, all of them had in mind a common application, a placket for women's skirts.*9

Even in the early days of the Republic, it proved difficult to assign contributions to particular individuals. Robert Fulton is usually given credit for inventing the steamboat. But the success of the *Clermont* was preceded by a number of experiments that provided Fulton with a body of knowledge upon which he could construct his seaworthy craft. Yet his predecessors receive no credit for their contributions.[11] The supremacy of Ma Bell's reign today is usually explained by the inventive genius of Alexander Graham Bell. But Bell was simply one among many plowing the furrows that led to the invention of the telephone; another was Elisha Gray. The question of who was the first inventor was never settled by the courts because the Bell interests and Western Union (operating under the Gray patents) reached a private settlement during intensive litigation over the issue. A bitter legal fight ensued in the 1880s with an independent telephone company, operating under the patents of Daniel Drawbaugh, a Pennsylvanian rural mechanic. During the trial, evidence was produced that Drawbaugh had invented a telephone several years before Bell, but it had not occurred to him to make immediate application for a patent. The Supreme Court finally ruled 4–3 against Drawbaugh.[12] Had one other justice switched to the minority, the whole course of the telephone industry in this country might have taken a different route. Near his death, Elisha Gray said:

---

* In this situation, where more than one person applies for a patent, the U.S. Patent Office holds an "interference" proceeding to determine which was the first inventor. The extent of multiple simultaneous invention is indicated by the number of such proceedings. As of July, 1970, the Patent Office reports there were over 750 cases pending before the Board of Patent Interferences; and, for the fiscal year 1970–71, 367 more were filed. It is estimated that one interference is declared for every two hundred applications for patents.[10] (Many important developments have involved interferences, e.g., oil cracking, the telephone, radio and TV, plastics, the Bessemer steel process, tetracycline and ampicillin, and computers.)

The history of the telephone will never be fully written. It is partially hidden away in twenty or thirty thousand words of testimony and partly lying on the hearts and consciences of a few whose lips are sealed, some in death and others by a golden clasp, whose grip is even tighter.[13]

If Drawbaugh or Gray had succeeded, the telephone industry might have resembled the early days of the automobile industry when the Selden patent—covering the entire automobile—was struck down by the courts. This opened the way for a highly competitive period in the history of the automobile industry. The events preceding that era are of interest. Beginning in the early 1870s, a spirited contest took place on both sides of the Atlantic to develop a workable "horseless carriage." Much of this effort was conducted by practical tinkerers working in isolation, in basements and makeshift sheds and barns across both continents. Some won local renown; most carried on in total obscurity. Sometimes patents were secured on their improvements; often they were not even applied for.

George Selden, a patent attorney in Rochester, New York, saw an opportunity and seized it. He possessed some mechanical skill and had unsuccessfully puttered around with an automobile engine in his basement. In 1879 he filed a patent application on the *entire* automobile. For the next sixteen years he bided his time, waiting for others to do the work. In the meantime he embodied their improvements in amendments to his patent application, and engaged in delaying actions in the Patent Office until 1885. In that year's annual report of the Commissioner of Patents, the Selden patent was heralded as the "pioneer invention in the application of the compression gas engine to road or horseless carriage use."

Within the burgeoning automobile industry, and among inventors, the Selden patent was ridiculed. It was generally believed that the concept of the automobile was so widely known that it fell within the public domain. According to William Greenleaf's *Monopoly on Wheels:*

Inventors took scant notice of the Selden claims when the patent was published in *Horseless Carriage*. That journal reflected the viewpoint of most automotive experimenters when it observed: "Many have contended and still contend that no basic patents can be held in the application of a hydro-carbon engine to the propulsion of road vehicles."[14]

The technical director of a European firm characterized it as "antediluvian" in concept, and totally useless as a guide to the construction of an operable gasoline-propelled vehicle.[15] For some years it was ignored.

But speculative and financial interests in Wall Street saw in the Selden patent what technical experts did not. Early in the 1900s, the corporation holding the patent issued infringement notices to the thirty-odd auto manufacturing firms in the country. They were tossed in the wastebasket. According to careful legal strategy, lawsuits were filed first against the weaker firms who lacked the financial resources to sustain a court fight. One by one these succumbed to the Electric Vehicle Co.; the losers then either took licenses under the Selden patent or went out of business. The attack then shifted to the stronger firms who had formed the Manufacturers' Mutual Association for purposes of resistance. A small group of these companies, however, saw in the patent an opportunity to curb what they regarded as "excessive competition" in the youthful automobile industry. They agreed to recognize the validity of the Selden patent and pay royalties on condition that they be given the right to name all other firms to be licensed. This proposal was accepted, and ten firms became charter licensees in 1903.[16]

A short time later Henry Ford, engaged in the assembly of automobiles, applied for a license. He was refused. Faced with the choice of acceding and leaving the industry, Ford chose to challenge the patent. After one federal district court upheld the Selden patent, a federal court of appeals finally rejected it in 1911.[17] By 1921, consequently, there were over eighty companies in this country engaged competitively in the manufacture of automobiles. A product previously limited to the luxury trade was then brought rapidly within the price range of almost everyone.[18]

Government Role in Research

The constitutional provision and enabling statutes were based on an assumption that inventive activity would be financed and carried on by private effort. The government would only step in to insure, with a patent grant, that the inventor would be rewarded for his work in the market-place. Yet today the country's taxpayers are the largest direct contributors to research and development (R&D). Of the $25 billion spent annually, the government's contribution is $15 billion.[19] Besides spending $10 billion of its own funds, private industry receives about half of the $15 billion spent by the federal government. The preponderance of the federal R&D contribution to industry is spent by the Department of Defense (67 percent) and the National Aeronautics and Space Administration (22 percent based on 1969 figures).[20]

The way the government spends this money encourages the growth of private monopoly. The Pentagon's roster of major recipients contains the names of the country's corporate titans—not only the large aircraft firms but also Western Electric, RCA, Philco, Ford, Westinghouse, Sylvania, General Motors, and similarly sized others.[21] Furthermore, it is DOD's general policy to permit its private contractors to retain title to any patents arising out of government-financed research, reserving for itself only a royalty-free license, which is rarely used.[22] Some legislative restrictions have been imposed on NASA, but it still follows the same policy. As a result, most of the *public* funds spent for R&D go to the research laboratories of the country's largest firms, but these companies also enjoy the *private* seventeen-year monopoly rights on patents arising out of these inventions. The effect, according to Richard J. Barber, then a law professor, testifying before a Senate committee, is that "other companies—usually the smaller ones—and other industries which might put this new knowledge to good use, perhaps in unforeseeable as well as entirely expected ways, are effectively denied the requisite information."[23]

In recent years there has been an intensive corporate drive to secure exclusive rights on patents owned by the federal government. About $4 billion is spent annually by the government on its own in-house research.[24] It secures title to all patents resulting from this work. In addition, the government requires, by executive order and court decisions, title to patents on all outside research conducted under certain circumstances: either where the contractual arrangements with private parties do not include automatic assignment to them of patent rights, or where all or a major part of the research resulting in the invention has been carried on with government funds.

Under established practice in the past, all government-owned patents have been made publicly available on a nonexclusive, royalty-free basis. Because public funds had financed the invention, it seemed only reasonable that its manufacture and sale should take place in a competitive environment. In this manner consumers enjoy the benefits of lower prices for the product as well as improvements in quality arising out of the competitive effort of many sellers to expand their market.

But this policy potentially contained two mutually reinforcing tendencies: corporations saw the buried bonanza of getting private rights from publicly funded discoveries; and the government's commitment to competition in the face of monopoly is less than tenacious. The corporate drive to secure exclusive licenses on these patents began in Congress during the fifties. It was then widely believed that government agencies required express statutory authority to make exclusive grants.[25] The argument presented in support of granting private monopolies was that exclusive licenses are necessary to induce companies to manufacture and sell the product. But when Senator Russell Long, chairman of the Senate Monopoly Subcommittee, asked government officials for specific examples of useful developments that had not been commercially exploited in the absence of exclusive licenses, none could be produced. An official of the U.S. Department of Agriculture, the agency with the longest experience in the field, testified: "Our experience has shown that if the patent, or the process or the product covered by the patent, has sufficient promise it has been pretty well taken up."[26] Following the hearings, Senator Long introduced amendments to a dozen authorization bills requiring the government agency to make available for general use the inventions arising out of government-financed research. These were enacted into law by the Congress.[27]

When the drive for congressional revision failed, the effort shifted to the executive branch. In 1963, President John F. Kennedy's Statement on Government Patent Policy somewhat weakened the government's stand on title to patents resulting from private contract and grant research performed with public funds.[28] No change was made in the handling of government-owned patents, but the ground was laid for future revision. The Federal Council for Science and Technology (FCST) was asked to submit annual reports on the effectiveness of the Kennedy policy and to make recommendations for needed changes. A "patent advisory panel" was also to be established under the FCST to look into the matter of government-owned patents and to make recommendations.

With this mandate in hand, the drive gathered momentum. A patent advisory committee was formed composed of the top legal officers of several government agencies.[29] The working subcommittee was made up of government patent attorneys and contract officers, whose outlook was largely indistinguishable from that of the private patent bar and corporate executives. The result: in 1967 it recommended the grant of exclusive licenses of government-owned patents. After clearance through the full committee, the proposal was submitted to the White House and culminated in President Nixon's Policy Memorandum on Government Patent Policy of August 23, 1971.[30] Section 2 authorized the grant either of "exclusive or non-exclusive licenses" following regulations to be issued by the General Services Administration.[31] The asserted purpose was to speed up the commercial use of government-owned inventions—despite the already mentioned fact that, at earlier congressional hearings, no one could supply specific examples of useful developments that had failed to be commercially exploited under nonexclusive licenses.

Even before the issuance of the Nixon memorandum, two executive agencies had already moved to implement the new policy. In 1969 the Department of Health, Education, and Welfare revised its regulations to permit "limited exclusive licenses";[32] and in 1970 HEW announced its intention of granting an exclusive license for six years to CCI, a large conglomerate.[33] Though Baxter Laboratories immediately requested a nonexclusive license under the government-owned patent, the exclusive grant was issued to CCI in 1971.

The Department of Agriculture made the next move. In 1970 its regulations were changed to resemble those of

HEW; a year later it announced its intention of granting exclusive royalty-free licenses to Welch Foods and the Upjohn Co. In each case the licenses were for periods less than the full-term of the patent grant; in some cases, however, they were less only by a few days. By this gimmick the department maintained that its action did not constitute disposal of government property and did not conflict with the Constitution.

The Corporate Accountability Research Group (CARG) lodged a formal protest with the Agriculture Research Service in September, 1971. This agency delayed rejection of the protest until April, 1972; in accordance with Agriculture's procedures, appeal was taken to the secretary. A group of twenty-one U.S. senators and congressmen joined CARG in the appeal. Up to the present, the department has made no formal response; sources inside the agency indicate that its program is currently being "reconsidered." In the meantime the General Services Administration is finalizing its government-wide regulations on the licensing of government-owned patents. As of January, 1973, they had not yet been issued.

The Corporate Research Laboratory

Today the solo inventor is largely an anachronism. Almost all research and development work is conducted in the corporate research laboratory. The National Science Foundation estimates that there are 11,000 companies in this country engaged in R&D. Only 3 percent—less than 350 firms—with ten thousand or more employees account for 85 percent of all research performed. The next 200 companies, numbering employees between five thousand and six thousand, do 6 percent of all R&D. Of all firms doing research work, 20 alone perform 56 percent of all such work in American industry.[34]

One still cannot discount the role played by the lone inventor in major inventive achievements. The classic work of John Jewkes and others in *The Sources of Invention* indicates that, of sixty important inventions they examined, made from 1900 to the 1950s, over two-thirds were the product of independent innovators.[35] Only sixteen could be attributed directly to the large corporate laboratory; even then much of the antecedent work had been performed by independent researchers.

In 1965 the Senate Antitrust and Monopoly Subcommittee held extensive hearings on industrial concentration and invention. Economics professor Daniel Hamburg presented testimony indicating that nearly half of twenty-seven important inventions made between 1946 and 1955 originated with independent inventors.[36] Dr. Donald Schon, director of the Institute of Applied Technology, National Bureau of Standards, submitted a list of important inventions for military use. All of these, made within the previous fifty years, were the work of individuals working without organization support. Even in the present era of highly organized R&D, as he points out, the solo inventor working on his own has been responsible for "an extraordinarily high percentage of important, radical commercial developments."[37] In his book *Economic Concentration,* Dr. John M. Blair suggests that, given the present concentration of research in large corporate laboratories, these should be the source of most inventive achievements. Nevertheless, Blair writes, "There is little in evidence to support such a presumption."[38]

This should not be surprising. The function of invention is to disrupt the established ways of doing things; it is basically revolutionary in purpose. It has little concern with the inconvenience caused by rendering obsolete a plant with substantial investment in equipment and know-how. Its interest is focused on the untried, on new explorations in utter disregard of the economic consequences. It is in this milieu that the lone inventor functions best, and here he can never be truly dispossessed.

The corporate research laboratory, instead, is wedded to serving the profit strategies of private enterprise. A revolutionary development is viewed with suspicion and some alarm. It may jeopardize an established plant with its vast complex of machinery and assembled skills. Even if it promises substantial reductions in cost, the payoff will not be immediate. As observed by Victor Abramson, former economic advisor to the U.S. Treasury Department:

The patentee may have investments in competing technology or in competing lines of manufacture which make it temporarily unprofitable for him to employ an invention which his competitors would exploit immediately. More fundamentally, patentees, since they enjoy a degree of monopoly power, are unlikely to exploit inventions to the extent warranted by their usefulness to society, and may be overcompensated in terms of their costs.[39]

Particularly in oligopolistic industries, where firms move in lockstep, there is great unwillingness to destabilize the status quo. Speaking of the U.S. Steel Corporation, for example, George W. Stocking remarked:

> It was slow in introducing the continuous rolling mill; slow in getting into production of cold-rolled steel products; slow in recognizing the potentials of the wire business; slow to adopt the heat-treating process for the production of sheets; slow in tin-plate developments; slow in utilizing water gases; slow in utilizing low-cost water transportation because of its consideration for the railroads; slow to grasp the remarkable business opportunities that a dynamic American economy offered it.[40]

The development of the oxygen conversion process in steel, resulting in substantial reductions in capital and operating costs, was the work of a small Austrian firm. Large-scale commercial production began in Europe in 1952; in this country a small steel company built a plant using this process in 1954. Ten years later—in 1964—U.S. Steel and Bethlehem instituted the first use of the oxygen process in their plants.

Much of the work in the large corporate research laboratory is devoted to minuscule changes in the existing art. Here the payoffs are reasonably assured, and they are, above all, immediate. The bulk of the effort is addressed to *product application*—either new uses for known technology or some modifications in existing uses.[41]

The atmosphere of these laboratories restricts the free play of inventive imagination. A research employee must be willing to take orders and be a member of the "team." Often he or she must devote much time to cosmetic rather than substantive changes in the art. The environment may involve elaborate political maneuvering, if the head of the research laboratory prefers bureaucratic sycophancy to real inventive talent.

Though our patent system assumes an invention is the work of a single person, this is not the case in the corporate research laboratory. Usually it represents a joint effort. The work is broken down into small steps; each member of the team has a specific assignment. The result of their work may be a patentable invention. No rights of ownership in the invention is vested in the research staff. They are hirelings; at the time of employment they agree to turn over all rights to their employer. The commercial exploitation of the invention is solely the prerogative of the corporation; and the financial rewards—whatever their size— belong to the corporation.*

Thus the corporate laboratory is not always a happy place for the real inventor. After a while, the patent becomes a goal in itself, rather than a reflection of inventiveness. There is, for example, great emphasis put on the continuous flow of patent applications to protect and expand the corporate domain. Walton Hamilton has said:

> A large corporation seeks to blanket as much as possible of its technological processes with letters patent. For this purpose the process is broken down into parts, and letters patent are taken out on fractions, often minute fractions, of the whole process. . . . If the technology is not static, novelties and improvements are constantly coming along and for each of these a letter patent is sought. As time passes, therefore, item after item drops out of the portfolio, and item after item comes to rest there as new grants are made.[43]

Since priority of discovery is of basic importance, the first glimmer of discovery must be immediately recorded with the Patent Office for possible use in a later patent proceeding. In this bureaucratic arena, the expertise of the patent expert and the patent lawyer often counts more than the work of the research staff. In some instances, it is his verbal ingenuity that constitutes the real invention.

It is clear that the solo inventor with marketable patents

---

* Yet when corporations are employed under contract to do research work for the government, they demand title to the inventions made. This is in addition to reimbursement for all costs incurred plus a profit. As Vice Admiral H. G. Rickover has remarked:

> Now, the companies apparently take a different stand toward the Government than they do to their own employees. Their own employees must sign an agreement providing that the company takes title to the patents they develop. Apparently, the companies desire better treatment from the U.S. Government than they accord their own employees.[42]

confronts strong pressures to dispose of them. Usually, he lacks the financial resources to engage in manufacture and sale, as well as the business skills and know-how to launch a venture and maintain it on a profitable basis. Above all, if the area involves established technology, the chances are that the large firms in the field have patents bordering or appearing to border on his invention. In that event, there will often be an intensive patent battle in the courts with a corporate contestant. Even if successful, the inventor's financial and emotional resources can be exhausted—all of which creates a great temptation to turn over the invention at the outset for whatever he can get.

It is difficult to ascertain the number of patents held by the country's largest corporations. Patents must always contain the name of the real or supposed inventor; in some cases it also shows the name of the company to which it is assigned. Often, however, it does not. It has been estimated that independent inventors account for less than one-quarter of the patents issued.[44] No one knows how many of these ultimately come to rest in large corporations, either through outright sale or license arrangements.

Some idea of the concentration of patents in the hands of large corporations is contained in a report prepared by the Patent Office for the Senate Subcommittee on Patents, Trademarks, and Copyrights. Between 1939 and 1955, twenty-nine corporations received over ninety thousand patents.[45] The largest number, about eleven thousand, went to General Electric. Among others, American Telephone & Telegraph secured eighty-five hundred; Radio Corporation of America, eight thousand; Westinghouse, seventy-five hundred; Dupont, sixty-five hundred; and Standard Oil (N.J.) five thousand. During the period 1939–1955, total patents issued numbered about forty thousand annually, with a drop during World War II years but a corresponding rise at its end.

The U.S. Patent Office

The law provides that an invention, to be patentable, must meet two tests: it must be *new* and it must be *useful*.[46] In addition, in determining what constitutes an "invention," the development must be something more than would be "obvious at the time the invention was made to a person having ordinary skill in the art."[47] The U.S. Patent Office is empowered by law to make these determinations, with provision for subsequent review in the courts.

In the past this agency has been variously lodged in the State Department and in the Department of Interior. Since 1925, by executive order, it now resides in the Commerce Department, the recognized spokesman for business interests in the government. This locale is important in understanding the activities of the Patent Office, for a subordinate branch in any agency invariably comes to reflect the dominant policies of the top officialdom.

Since the start of the patent system, there have always been difficulties in determining whether an invention deserved a patent. Is an invention useful if, in the current state of the art, it is prohibitively expensive to market commercially? Or if it is so ahead of its time that ancillary technology must first be developed before it can be put to use? Or if it is merely an interesting curiosity to the research staff? Today there is a general presumption in the Patent Office that anything new must have some kind of utility. The merest assertion of utility in broad, general terms is usually enough to satisfy the agency.

The basic test of patentability is novelty. But the Patent Office seems incapable of objectively and consistently determining this elusive standard. One standard is: if the invention was "known or used by others in this country" or if it was "patented or described in a printed publication in this or a foreign country," it is not subject to patent.[48] But to apply these criteria involves a considerable amount of searching, not only of publications in this country but also those all over the world. Few patent examiners have an extensive knowledge of foreign languages. Ordinarily, there is an examination made of the foreign patents that have been issued, but there is little or no search of the foreign literature.

Judging "novelty" is further complicated by the agency's structure. The Patent Office is broken into a number of tiny segments for the purpose of analysis by the various examining groups. As a result, a patent examiner becomes familiar with only a small, specialized area, which often cuts across several industrial frontiers. He can get no real grasp of the flow of technological advance in an industry to determine whether a new step, for which a patent application is made, would be clearly obvious to anyone skilled in the particular art. A process may be in commonplace use in some areas, but because of the classification system used by the Patent Office, it may reach an examiner to whom it is new and therefore patentable.

There are other deficiencies as well. The Patent Office has no laboratory facilities for testing submissions. The applicant files a description of his invention with specific claims of its novel aspects. There is no practicable way for the examiner to determine whether the disclosure, as presented, really produces the alleged invention. This ignorance encourages obfuscation by applicants. It is the rare invention that is fully disclosed in the patent—"inadvertently" a step is omitted, a crucial temperature point is missing, something is left out. Another common practice is to list a number of possible materials that may be employed in a process. This has the advantage of expanding the coverage of the patent; it also fails to indicate clearly the particular substance that the patentee has found most suitable and will use for commercial production. Thus, though the purpose of the patent is to make full disclosure for the purpose of allowing others to use it for further inventive work, it rarely serves this purpose.

The patent examiner also operates within severe time limits. Although the Patent Office has asserted that no "quota system" is employed, examiners claim there is great pressure to take speedy actions on pending applications. If they delay too long in reaching decisions, they are "inefficient"; if their denials are too frequent, they are suspect. The whole system of appeal procedures in the Patent Office also tend to favor the allowance of patents. If the patent examiner approves the issuance of the grant, his function is completed. If he takes a negative position, he faces a series of applicant appeals, which take more of his time on that case.

Agency procedure, in addition, is sharply affected by private patent attorneys, who have easy access to the Patent Office on behalf of their clients. They drop in frequently to determine the progress of applications, quickly learning which examiners are "easy" and which are not. In friendly conversations with supervisors, these lawyers dispense praise or criticism of examiners—a factor examiners **cannot be unaware of. Also, simply by careful draftsman-**

ship, private patent attorneys can steer their applications into the right hands. Consequently, it is not at all surprising that many patent examiners candidly admit that it is easy to get a patent. "If an applicant's attorney puts enough detail into a claim or prosecutes his application vigorously," one examiner remarked, "he can get a patent on almost everything."

The 1971 Annual Report of the Commissioner of Patents hails with some pride its current speed. It points out "new records were again established" on the number of patent applications received and disposed of. Total applications for fiscal 1971 reached 104,160, a new high; but it reports that "this record number of receipts was more than offset by the completion of 109,245 applications"—thus putting them 5,000 ahead on their backlog.[49] The report states that today new applications come up for examination, on the average, less than twelve months from the date of filing. However, average pendency of applications—the period from date of filing to issue of the patent—is twenty-nine months.[50]

Since 1955, when the volume of patents issued ran around forty thousand a year, the number has steadily increased. For fiscal 1971, it reached what the patent commissioner termed a "record number"—over seventy thousand patents.[51] According to the agency, "patents are granted in the case of about two out of every three applications for patents which are filed."[52] But no breakdown is available on how many of the patents issued are *product* patents as contrasted with patents on *processes* of manufacture. A product patent entitles the owner to exclude all others from manufacture and marketing, even if an outsider develops a more economical and superior method of manufacturing. Here our present patent system loses all contact with the intent of the Constitutional Fathers. Instead of advancing the industrial arts, it becomes the instrument for throttling such advancement.

In fact, very few of the seventy thousand patents granted each year actually constitute genuinely novel and significant inventions. The vast bulk represent minor changes in the current art, fanciful gimmicks, molecular modifications, even plagiarized variations of other patents. Many of them are dictated by marketing strategies in the campaign for expanding sales. Even as ardent a supporter of the patent system as Dr. Vannever Bush, a leading authority in the field of scientific research, has stated:

> True, there are altogether too many patents issued on the trivial and the obvious. An appreciable part of the burden on the Patent Office, and on industry, is due to the fact that the standards of invention have not been held sufficiently high, and because a failure to file on a trivial matter may result in the appearance of an embarrassing patent in other hands.[53]

All of the parties directly involved have an interest in swelling the number of patents issued. The Patent Office enjoys an increase in size, structure, and prestige; currently there are proposals to confer upon the patent commissioner the title of assistant secretary of commerce. The large corporations benefit by strengthening their arsenal of patents for industrial expansion; and their retinue of patent lawyers are well paid for their mastery of the arcane complexities of the patent system. The parties that suffer are the smaller business enterprises and the public. The former lack the financial resources to hire high-priced patent experts to wade through the jungle of existent patents in order to ascertain the availability of current technology. Ultimately, the cost falls upon the public—not only in maintaining this bureaucratic structure but in the series of monopolies and higher prices created by the patent system.

The fact that the Patent Office issues a patent is no guarantee of its validity. In effect, a patent is no more than a paper writ permitting the patentee to sue others in the assertion of his monopoly rights. The ultimate determination of validity is made by the courts. Unfortunately, only a small proportion are subjected to judicial scrutiny. But some measure of the Patent Office's generosity in handing out these writs is indicated by the fate of those that do reach the courts. *About three out of every four patents are declared invalid.* During a hearing in 1969 on the nomination of William Schuyler to be patent commissioner, Senator John McClellan, chairman of the Senate Patents Committee, said that 72 percent of challenged patents are ultimately declared invalid by the courts. "Considering the amount of money that the government is spending on examining patent applications," he concluded, "it does seem that either we must improve the quality of issued patents or else consider following the example of other countries and adopt some modified and less expensive procedures."[54]

One reason a court rejects a patent is if it was procured by fraud. But the Patent Office itself can take no action to set aside a grant based on fraud. In the antitrust case against Hartford Empire Co., for example, a patent was secured by the submission of a faked article prepared by three patent attorneys. But action for cancellation of the patent had to come from the Department of Justice; subsequently, at least, the commissioner of patents barred the private attorneys permanently from practice before the agency.[55]

Patents: Instrument of Restraint

Harnessed to serve the ends of corporate enterprise, the patent has become a potent instrument for restraint of trade. The very language employed by patent experts gives a clue to current usage. There are "umbrella" patents, "dragnets," "blocking," and "fencing" patents, "forestallers," "nuisance value," and the like.* Particularly in industries where the technology is subject to change, they are basic weapons in corporate strategy for eliminating, subduing, or harassing competition.[57] Most large companies have vast portfolios of patents, to be used as the particular circumstances dictate.

Where a company has a patent, it may elect to exploit the invention on a monopoly basis. This is often the case in the drug industry. For example, Eaton Labs, a subsidiary of Morton-Norwich, has for years been the sole marketer of nitrofurantoin (Furadantin), used in the treatment of urinary infections. Just before the patent was about to expire, it introduced Macrodantin, the same drug with a

---

* Walton Hamilton defines an "umbrella" patent as a "grant written so broadly as to cover all future innovations within its ambit." A "dragnet" patent is a "grant so comprehensive in its sweep and so closely fashioned in detail that any impending invention will be caught up and sterilized in its finely meshed net." A "blocking" patent involves "an exclusive right at a strategic point to block advances which others might make in the art." A "fencing" patent connotes fencing out others from entering one's preserves. It can also mean fencing in one's competitors into narrower and, preferably, a vanishing domain.[56]

change in the particle size. This was protected by a new patent, thereby enabling the company to continue its monopoly position for another seventeen years. Following an intensive promotion effort on the country's physicians, Macrodantin is now the "drug of choice" by prescribing doctors. The new product is, of course, monopoly priced, while the price for the older drug, falling into disuse, has been reduced. When patent protection for Macrodantin nears its end, this pattern can be repeated.

The staggering of patents is one of the neatest inventions ever devised to continue monopoly protection beyond the seventeen-year limit. Once the basic discovery has been patented, patents follow upon improvements, and then upon improvements on the improvements, and so on indefinitely. The United Shoe Machinery Co. provides the classic example of a firm that had so mastered the art of "proper spacing of patents" that its monopoly position in the shoe machinery field was impregnable for nearly a hundred years. Most of the large firms listed as owners of vast patent portfolios in the Patent Office study, *Distribution of Patents Issued to Large Corporations,*[58] have undoubted skill in the art of pyramiding patents to extend their life artificially.

For a variety of reasons, the patent may be licensed to others. In the case of meprobamate, a big-selling mild tranquilizer, Carter-Wallace lacked the marketing facilities for full exploitation of the product, and elected to grant one license only—to American Home Products, which possesses a vast domestic and foreign marketing organization.[59] For some years in this country Miltown and Equanil sold at the identical monopoly price. Subsequently, when this arrangement came under antitrust attack, the company entered into a consent decree that required compulsory licensing to all qualified applicants. Price competition immediately followed.

Often, as in the case of the cracking process in the oil industry, there is a tangle of ownerships in the technology. Here the firms must reach some kind of accommodation with respect to patents; the alternative is a kind of strangulation with each checkmating the others in the use of the manufacturing process. In this case there was a "pooling" of the patents; to secure access to the strategic rights held by others, a firm had to share some or all of its own.

Patent pools also exist in the automobile and airplane manufacturing industries, with the latter pool presently the subject of a civil suit by the Justice Department.

In many cases the accommodation occurs very early, when the invention is still in the patent application stage. Take, for instance, the drug industry. Parallel research was under way in two or more research laboratories in connection with tetracycline, prednisone, tolbutamide, and other prescription drugs.[60] In each case the companies all filed patent applications and reached the finish line at approximately the same time. In this situation the Patent Office, as mentioned, declares an "interference."

Although it is the job of the Patent Office to determine who has been first in discovery, it is a common practice for the companies to make this decision themselves. Representatives of the various contestants meet, study the documents that have been submitted, and decide who was first with the invention. Based upon an agreement among the parties that each shall be licensed under the patent, all but one withdraw their patent applications. Now there is no controversy before the Patent Office, and the patent automatically issues; the "losers" usually are then granted patent licensing agreements by the successful patentee. This makes the work easier in the Patent Office. It also forecloses the opportunity for a full airing of the issues in an interference proceeding as well as subsequent publication of the record and the agency's findings.* Ultimately, the parties are more interested in sharing a piece of the monopoly than in the possibility of having none at all. In this manner the Patent Office, supposedly representing the public interest, is eliminated in the whole decision-making process.

While patent licensing arrangements are theoretically preferable to pure monopoly situations, often these agreements contain provisions designed to restrict competition. Increasingly these arrangements have become more sophisticated as the Justice Department's Antitrust Division has sought to confine the exercise of monopoly to the patent itself. In this effort, the government has generally secured the support of the courts. But the cases instituted by the

---

* At every stage—from the initial filing of the patent application to the issue of the patent—the Patent Office maintains total secrecy on the proceedings. Thereafter the file is publicly available.

Department of Justice have involved only a small number of industries. It is therefore impossible to say whether, in the many not investigated, blatant restrictions are still fully spelled out in licensing agreements or whether they have simply been driven underground. In both cases a comprehension of the restrictions contained in a license agreement requires knowledge, often extensive knowledge, of the operation of the industry and its trade practices.

The cases brought do reveal the ways monopoly can be extended beyond the patent grant. Licensing agreements have contained production and marketing quotas for licensees. Directly or indirectly they have served as vehicles for setting prices and establishing limited market territories as well as "fields of use."* "Tie-in" arrangements have been common; here the licenser requires the purchase of specified unpatented materials as a condition for granting the license. Patents have been licensed in package deals. In order to secure access to a few essential patents, the licensee is required to take the total package, paying royalties on some patents that are of no use to him. In the *Hazeltine* case,[62] when the total package was refused, the patentee demanded a higher royalty on nine patents than for the entire package containing several others. Discriminatory royalties have been used to exclude new entrants into the field or to destroy existent competitors.[63] Sometimes, in the interest of maintaining the structure of private control, the payment of royalties continues long after the patent has expired. For years the University of Toronto has acted as the administrative agent for the patent pool on insulin, the major drug in the treatment of diabetes. Its patent agreements have allowed licensees to exercise their preference in continuing payment of royalties on expired patents.[64]

Where a firm is in a strong bargaining position, it has imposed a "grantback" provision. To secure a license, firms have been required to divulge, and turn over, all advances made by them during the term of the agreement. Until reversed by the recent *Lear* decision,[65] the licensee had

---

* The latter practice is exemplified in the famous Hartford Empire case, where a patent pool was separately incorporated to hold and license all patents. Some firms were licensed to manufacture only beer bottles, others only wine or medicine bottles, still others only pickle or holy water bottles, and so on.[61]

to agree to accept the validity of the patents under licensing and promise that, whatever the future circumstances, he would not contest their validity in court. Thus the bulk of the patents issued never got tested in litigation. Most agreements today also contain a provision that, in the event of dispute over terms, the parties will not resort to the courts but will engage in arbitration. The proceedings of the arbitration tribunals are held in total secrecy. Their extensive use is defended on the ground that they save the time and effort of our already overburdened court system. But their effect is also to veil from public scrutiny decisions that may have substantial impact upon the pocketbooks of consumers, but which occur in a context where there is no opportunity for the public interest to be represented.

The use of patents to suppress or control competition has not, of course, been confined to national boundaries. Most countries—including the underdeveloped—have a patent system, many of them modeled on our own. Large firms, in obtaining patents, frequently move simultaneously in countries throughout the world. Licenses are granted to foreign companies under their country's patents, thereby automatically establishing geographical territories for licensees. Often a single firm is licensed under the patents of his country, and the same pattern is followed in all countries where the licenser holds patent grants. In effect, what is created is a system of private international government, more commonly known as a "world cartel." As Walton Hamilton remarks, "The elected or self-appointed overlord controls entrance into the trade, assigns to business units their distinctive domains, allocates quotas to the members, fixes the boundaries of the markets to be served by each, and establishes prices."[66] This international structure makes the problem of government enforcement of competition particularly difficult. Restrictive agreements are lodged outside of interested governmental jurisdictions; many of the parties cannot be reached in a litigative attack; the isolated bits and pieces of evidence available are inadequate for a successful prosecution of the case.

The drug hearings conducted by Senator Estes Kefauver over a decade ago disclose the intricate way patent agreements curb competition.[67] Ten years elapsed before the Antitrust Division instituted action to eliminate the trade restrictions contained in the agreements.[68] The result, ironically, has been a new thrust toward exempting many monopolistic patent practices from the antitrust laws. The so-called Scott Amendments, introduced by Senator Hugh Scott, are designed to defang the antitrust agency in the patent field. The effort to pass the legislation, strongly supported by the major drug firms, has so far failed in the Senate Subcommittee on Patents, Trademarks, and Copyrights. By the narrow vote of 3–2, the majority felt the effect would be to "create significant exceptions to the antitrust laws" and would "destroy the Government's case in *U.S.* v. *Westinghouse* as well as other cases against companies in the pharmaceutical industry."[69] That this was regarded as a merely temporary defeat is indicated by the formation of two new patent lobbies, well financed and each headed by a former commissioner of patents.[70]

Some Proposals for Reform

Our present patent system has become a major device for corrupting competition. It needs to be returned to the function for which it was originally designed—the promotion of science and the useful arts. Monopoly grants under patents constitute an exception to our national policy of maintaining a competitive economy; therefore, contractual arrangements for exploiting such grants should be as narrowly limited as possible. Instead, current moves such as the Scott Amendments seriously threaten a national policy already endangered by corporate size and conglomeration.

The Antitrust Division has made only episodic attacks upon patents in restraint of trade. Except for its recent drug cases and the foray in the late thirties by Thurman Arnold, then head of the Antitrust Division, most of its actions involving patents have arisen only in the course of investigation of specific outside complaints. It has never made a cross-the-board investigation of the role of patents in reducing competition. The Federal Trade Commission for the most part has steered clear of this vexing problem, its 1971 action against Xerox being something of an exception. As a result, little is known of the detail and extent of patent abuses in many segments of American industry.

As a first step in securing the needed information, the government should require submission of copies of all patent licensing agreements in effect, both national and international. It should be emphasized that such documents are understandable only in the light of the industry's organization and trade practices; a necessary concomitant to their effective use, then, is a competent staff of government economic analysts to decipher them. Such documents should be publicly available for examination. A major barrier to the development of skilled industrial economists has been the dearth of documentary evidence on industry practices.

More structural than procedural a recommendation is that the Patent Office should be taken out of the Department of Commerce. While it is lodged in the agency most responsive to corporate interests, it can hardly be expected to raise the level of its standards on what constitutes patentable inventions. The post of commissioner of patents has, in past years, been little more than a political reward by the party in power—to a private patent attorney in service to large firms both before and after his brief sojourn in the Patent Office. It has often proven difficult to distinguish between his function as a private lawyer and his function as a government official.

The *product* patent is one of the most baneful aspects of our patent system. And its proliferation continues unchecked. Once the original patent has expired, a new use can recreate the seventeen-year monopoly. For example, the chemical cycloheximide has been marketed for years as an herbicide and the patent has long since expired. With the discovery that it can cause ripe citrus fruit to fall automatically to the ground, it has been given a new lease (patent) on life. Proliferation in the drug area is especially extensive. Rauwolfia has been used for centuries in the Far East for many illnesses; some purification of the root material resulted in a U.S. product patent on the compound christened resperine. If an old compound is joined with others equally old—and the claim is made that the therapeutic result is greater than the sum of its parts—this marriage merits a product patent. Similarly, a new method of administration for an old drug—tablet, injectable, inhalant, whatever—qualifies it for another seventeen-year monopoly. Even a particular dosage form may receive the blessing of the Patent Office.[71]

There are also basic questions of policy respecting the unbridled exploitation of exclusive rights under product patents. High prices are virtually inevitable under conditions of monopoly or shared monopoly, and they affect the necessities and luxuries of life with equal impartiality. One manner of attacking this problem is to eliminate all product patents on items essential to the public health and welfare. Another is a compulsory licensing provision where patents are the basis for unreasonably high prices. Both of these alternatives have been invoked in other countries; where effectively administered they have resulted in greater competition and lower prices. A more novel proposal would directly serve the constitutional provision "to promote the progress of science and the useful arts." This would require the automatic compulsory licensing of the product patent whenever someone else has developed a new process or an improvement in the process of manufacture.

There is, as well, the need for more effective machinery for the cancellation of a patent obtained by fraud in the Patent Office. The problem is dramatically illustrated in the pending tetracycline case. In 1963 the Federal Trade Commission found that the product patent held by Chas. Pfizer & Co. had been obtained by misrepresentations in the Patent Office. It could not, however, act to secure cancellation of the patent, because the U.S. Supreme Court has said this is the sole prerogative of the Department of Justice.[72] FTC ordered general licensing of the patent to all responsible applicants at reasonable royalties. While the case was on appeal, Pfizer instituted dozens of infringement actions, most of which were successful. Some of the weaker companies simply went out of business; others negotiated consent settlements; still others lost in court. In 1968 the FTC was upheld by the Sixth Circuit Court of Appeals, the Supreme Court later deciding to allow that decision to stand.[73]

In 1969 the Department instituted a civil action for cancellation of the patent as well as for recovery of damages in government purchases of tetracycline.[74] The case was joined with many other parties, including seven states, seeking triple damages. Roughly, the amount involved is estimated to exceed a half billion dollars. Justice proceeded to gather evidence in support of its pleas for cancellation, and preparation was made for trial of the case.

Then suddenly, during a pretrial proceeding in September, 1971, an official of the Antitrust Division disclosed that a consent settlement was being negotiated under which the government would drop its plea for patent cancellation.[75] This news was regarded as catastrophic by the other parties in the case. Dropping the cancellation count would shift the burden of proof of fraud upon them in their damage cases, and the accumulated evidence obtained by the government would be quietly buried away. Moreover, because only the Department of Justice can take steps to secure patent cancellation, the defendants would avoid other serious hazards arising from cancellation. The attorneys participating in the commission of the fraud could be disbarred from practice before the Patent Office; contempt proceedings against the patentee could be instituted in the courts where the fraudulent patent was enforced. Injured parties, who have thus far refrained from legal action, could quickly recover damages. The most serious effect, however, would be the impairment of the work of the antitrust agency. In effect, dropping the cancellation count would be a signal to other firms that fraud in the procurement of patents can be carried on with impunity; that, if they get caught, the whole problem can be ended with a consent decree.

Corrective action should also be taken respecting title to government-financed research. The bulk of all research and development money today is contributed by the country's taxpayers, and goes to large corporations under government contract. Title to inventions, in most cases, becomes private property, and the corporations are free to exploit these discoveries as private monopolies. This policy is now even being extended to government-owned patents, where much of the work is conducted in government laboratories. It would seem obvious that, where the public pays for the research, it should enjoy the benefits of competition and lower prices.

The ultimate effect of the present policy extends further —to the direct livelihood of American citizens. In the international field, corporate recipients of such patent rights are equally free to exploit the technology to serve their own best interests. They may elect to establish their own plants abroad or, alternatively, to license foreign corporate allies to use the inventions and know-how. The result is that American taxpayers who foot the bill for the original research become deprived of jobs as the manufacturing facilities get established outside of the United States. Vice Admiral Rickover remarked that he saw little merit in the argument that "unless we give industry full rights to patents where the Government has paid for the work, our economic system would be hurt."[76] Indeed, the evidence seems to support just the opposite—that by granting such rights our economy does suffer.

In other countries it is a common practice for the government to take title directly and then license private firms on a reasonable royalty basis, thereby recouping some or all of the costs of the research. During the exchange between Senator Russell Long and Admiral Rickover, the latter said:

> I agree with you that companies in the employ of the Government should receive the same treatment from the Government as they give to their own employees. In Great Britain, as you know, there is a different system. There, the patent rights for work financed by the Government belong entirely to the Government; the Government licenses industry and even shares in the royalties industry receives from non-Government applications. In Russia, the Government, of course, owns all the patents.

The conventional argument for the grant of monopoly rights is that private firms must spend additional funds in making the invention commercially practicable. Where this is so, the responsibility for completing the work should lie with the government, which has already invested substantial funds. To do otherwise is to co-opt the government in the service of corporate bigness and private restraint of trade.

FOREIGN TRADE

11

The $20 Billion Import Protection Racket

HOWARD KNEE

[The] rising tide of protectionism . . . [is] funda-
mentally against the best interest of American con-
sumers. If . . . imports are severely limited by
quotas, the range of consumer product choices will
be narrowed considerably; consumer prices will be
appreciably higher, and the burden will fall most
heavily on those low-income groups least able to bear
the costs.
        —Andrew F. Brimmer, Member of the Board of
        Governors of the Federal Reserve System

Sugar is twice as expensive as it should be. Gasoline costs
five cents a gallon more. A $16.15 boy's wool winter coat
sells for over $20. Tomatoes are high priced and of low
quality. Meat costs more—especially hamburger and sausage—as does everything made with steel. And the corner
bicycle dealer cannot meet demand for low-priced models.

Protected by an umbrella of tariffs, quotas, administrative practices, and departmental regulations, American
businessmen will divert almost $20 billion from consumer
pockets into corporate coffers this year. This represents
$240 for every working man and woman in the United

States—enough to feed and clothe an average family of four for nearly a month.

Why this enormous subsidy? What are its techniques? Who are its beneficiaries? How is the consumer affected? These questions are the focus of the following inquiry into the invisible web of American protectionism.

The Pros and Cons of Import Restrictions

"How many more plants are we going to have to close before we are going to get some action?" Representative James Burke's plea for the failing Brockton, Massachusetts, shoe industry typifies the protectionist complaint. Finding it increasingly difficult to meet foreign competition, industry after industry is seeking congressional aid in the form of import controls. The unsuccessful Trade Act of 1970 (the Mills bill), for example, would have imposed quotas on textiles and footwear and could have brought 120 more items, with imports equal to $7 billion, under restraints. Even more broadly, the proposed Foreign Trade and Investment Act of 1972 (the Burke-Hartke bill) would roll back *all* competitive imports to their average percentage of U.S. production from 1965 to 1969, a 40 percent reduction from 1971 levels.

Protectionists marshal three arguments in support of import restrictions: they (1) preserve American jobs; (2) maintain a healthy balance of trade; and (3) equalize the impact of harsh foreign restrictions on imports of American goods.*

Employment. Because foreign labor is cheap, the argument runs, foreign manufacturers can sell products for less than their American competitors. As their sales increase, those of domestic firms decrease—and American workers are consequently laid off. " 'Made in America' is a vanishing signature," says the AFL–CIO's Committee on Political Education (COPE). "[Even] American flags manufactured in Japan have begun flooding the market here."[1]

---

* Protectionists further argue that import restrictions are needed to contain U.S.-based multinational corporations. These companies, it is alleged, "export" American jobs and exploit foreign workers. Although an initial Commerce Department study has refuted such claims, more research is necessary before public policy conclusions can be drawn.

COPE claims that as many as five hundred thousand to six hundred thousand jobs or job opportunities will be lost to foreign imports in 1972.

This "Save Our Jobs" theme has much direct appeal, especially with almost five million Americans unemployed. But labor's answer is deceptively simple. In fact, it ignores how free trade policies can spur domestic employment and, conversely, how import restrictions can discourage it. The reasons for this are threefold. First, reducing imports from foreign countries, especially countries that sell most of their exports to the United States, would leave them with less money to buy American goods. This in turn would decrease employment in our export-related industries. Because U.S. exports are on the average more labor intensive than U.S. imports—i.e., a dollar's worth of exports produces more jobs here than a dollar's worth of imports eliminates—the result would be a *net job loss*.[2]

Second, substantially raising U.S. trade barriers would lead to retaliation in the form of foreign import restrictions. Again, this would reduce our exports, lessen our domestic production, and hence, reduce domestic employment. When the restrictive Tariff Act of 1930 was passed, other nations were quick to raise their own tariff rates. As a result, the United States' share of world foreign trade fell almost 30 percent from 1929 to 1933. John Renner, director of the State Department's Office of International Trade, has publicly warned that foreign governments today would not, and politically could not, sit by idly if we cut their exports. Commenting on the Burke-Hartke bill, Renner estimated that if enacted, foreign retaliatory action would on balance *cost* eighty thousand American jobs and $700 million in foregone American income.[3] In world trade war, American labor would surely be the loser.

Finally, one cannot overlook the effect of import restrictions on consumer spending, which is of course an important contribution to domestic employment. When imports are cheaper than comparable domestic products, buyers have more money to spend on other items. For example, if a consumer saves $1,000 by buying a Volkswagen, he can spend that money on other desired but deferred consumer purchases, such as home appliances. This will stimulate increased employment in consumer-selected areas and add to total economic productivity. Federal Reserve Board

Governor Andrew Brimmer estimates that 360,000 jobs were created as a result of this extra disposable income in 1971—equal to the total government employment in our nation's capital.[4]

It appears that foreign imports have become the scapegoat for America's unemployment problems. Both organized labor, opting to protect existing jobs, and business, either unable or unwilling to meet foreign competition, have turned adverse employment effects of imports into a club to obtain restrictive legislation. There is no doubt that a great many workers have lost their jobs in the last few years. One cannot, however, attribute these losses to increased imports. Brookings' economist Lawrence Krause, for example, found that if increased unemployment in 1970 was caused solely by trade dislocations, the unemployment rate for that year would have remained stable instead of climbing almost 2 percent.[5]

The policy choice is then clear: should we protect unproductive job slots or should we strive for increased total economic productivity? To ask the question is to answer it. This is not to say that competitively displaced workers, especially those too old to acquire new skills, should be ignored in the free trade calculus. Enhanced assistance and manpower training programs for such workers must be an integral part of a concerted government effort to reduce all unemployment and underemployment no matter what the cause. Only then can America best utilize its limited economic resources and spur accelerated economic growth.

Balance of Trade. "I don't know much about the tariff," Abraham Lincoln is purported to have said, "but I do know that when I buy a coat from England, I have the coat and England has the money [and] when I buy a coat in America, I have the coat and America has the money."[6] Although the dynamics of international trade are infinitely more complex than in Lincoln's time, protectionists still persist in citing the value of import restrictions in maintaining a healthy balance of trade (the difference between exports and imports of goods).

In 1971, for the first time this century, the United States imported more goods from abroad than it exported. The deficit was $2 billion, and it climbed to over $6 billion in 1972. It is not insignificant, however, that this deficit coincided with rising prices and domestic inflation.

What happened is that we priced our goods out of world markets. Just as Americans have had to forgo consumer purchases because of high prices, so foreign purchasers of American goods have had to do the same. And as the Nixon administration recognized, restricting imports is not the way to handle trade deficits. Rather, it required a realignment of international monetary rates, including a devaluation of the dollar, to regain our foreign markets without lowering prices at home. In this way, American exports become relatively cheaper and American imports relatively more expensive, thereby helping to reduce the trade imbalance.

Further, it is not clear that a trade deficit is something this country must avoid at all costs, especially if it means inefficiently allocating our resources. As our economy becomes more and more service oriented, we might expect such deficits. Professor Paul Samuelson predicts that American management and capital may find that their most efficient use is to substitute foreign labor for traditional American activities. Washington, New York, Pittsburgh, and Denver are already becoming "headquarters cities," says Samuelson, and the United States a "headquarter economy," with an emphasis on services rather than manufacturing. "It would become normal for us to enjoy an unfavorable balance of merchandise trade," he writes, "reverting to the pre-1893 pattern in which the value of our merchandise imports exceeded the value of our exports. This trade deficit normally would be financed by our current invisible items of interest, dividends, repatriated profits and royalties."[7]

American Retaliation. Protectionists often point to foreign import restrictions as justifying stringent American restrictions. The fact is, however, that U.S. quotas on industrial products cover a relatively large number of items and relate to a higher volume of trade than any of our major trading partners, including Canada, the United Kingdom, the European Community, and Japan. Further, average tariff rates (weighted by total trade) on industrial products are very similar, with only three and a half percentage points separating the lowest (U.S. and Canada—7.5 percent) from the highest (Japan—11.0 percent*).[7]

* Japan has since cut tariffs by 20 percent on, among other items, all manufactured goods except those under quota limitations.

Even if U.S. trade barriers were lower than foreign barriers, advocating a retaliatory increase makes as much sense as saying that if Japan chooses not to buy our cheaper computers, we would be justified in not buying its cheaper textiles. What must be understood is that our restrictions harm *us* as well as foreigners. By limiting imports, we deny ourselves cheaper goods and inefficiently use our resources to produce substitute products. As long as Americans can buy foreign goods more cheaply than American goods, we gain by producing products we can produce relatively more efficiently and trading them for the cheaper foreign goods. This is the essence of *comparative advantage*. Just as a group of people with varying skills and resources can increase production by specializing, countries with varying availabilities of labor, resources, and transportation can maximize world well-being (and their own) by producing those products that each can produce at the lowest cost relative to others. The inanity of excluding cheaper foreign goods from domestic markets was satirized by the French writer Frederic Bastiat in an imaginary petition by French candlemakers to the Chamber of Deputies:

> We are subjected to the intolerable competition of a foreign rival whose superior facilities for producing light enable him to flood the French market at so low a price as to take away all our customers the moment he appears, suddenly reducing an important branch of French industry to stagnation. This rival is the sun.
>
> We request a law to shut up all windows, dormers, skylights, openings, holes, chinks, and fissures through which sunlight penetrates. Our industry provides such valuable manufactures that our country cannot, without ingratitude, leave us now to struggle unprotected through so unequal a contest.[8]

The beneficial impact of imports on domestic competition, and hence inflation, should not be overlooked. By challenging U.S. products in the American marketplace, imports stimulate price competition, nonprice competition (e.g., quality, design), and product innovation. Foreign competition, for example, has forced the U.S. steel and textile industries to modernize, has spurred Detroit to manufacture low-priced compacts such as Chevrolet's Vega and Ford's Pinto, and has attuned American fashion designers to the latest in fashion styles and fabric quality. And through imports from Japan, the American public was first introduced to transistor tape recorders, television sets, phonographs, and radios. That 60 percent of U.S. manufacturing occurs in oligopolistic industries argues for more and not less foreign competition. The cost of this economic concentration to American consumers is in the tens of billions of dollars, reflecting monopoly overcharges, misallocation of resources, and internal inefficiency.

By holding down consumer prices, imports serve to reduce domestic inflationary pressures. This is especially true in such basic industries as steel, where price increases usually trigger others in different industries. According to economist John Blair, "The [steel] industry has come to be regarded as affected with a public interest because, as the underpining of the economy, any increase in the price of steel tends to 'pyramid.' By the time it reaches the ultimate consumer an increase in the price of steel will have grown until it is a significant multiple of the steel price increase itself."[9] Moreover, price increases in the steel industry signal producers in other industries that the time is ripe to have their own prices. Not surprisingly, the recent spurt in domestic inflation coincided with the implementation of voluntary steel import quotas in 1969. These arrangements have allowed domestic steel producers to raise steel prices five times as much since 1969 as in the preceding eight years. In the first twelve months alone prices soared more than in the previous ten years combined.[10] Whereas steel sold for $132 a ton in 1969, the price climbed to almost $170 a ton in 1971. The economic significance of this rise is reflected in the fact that a $5-per-ton steel increase is reported to be transferred into a $50 increase in the cost of an automobile.[11]

Although high consumer prices affect everyone, they hurt the poor most. Even minimal increases in the cost of such items as sugar, meat, clothing, and shoes can mean deprivation for many of the over twenty-five million Americans living in poverty. In a recent study on the impact of tariffs, economist Norman Fieleke concluded that extra payments due to tariffs constitute a higher proportion of spending by low income groups than by high income groups and that as the quality of an imported consumer product increases, its tariff rate is more likely to fall than

to rise.[12] Since the affluent generally purchase better quality items than the poor, the poor lose on this latter
criterion as well as the first one. Even if import restrictions
were considered a reasonable consumer burden to support
certain industries, it is far from reasonable to place that
burden on those persons least able to bear the costs.

Quotas

"Quotas," says economist Robert Baldwin, "run directly
against the basic principle that underlies a free enterprise
system—the freedom of consumers to choose what to
buy."[13] Unlike a tariff or import tax, which indirectly
limits imports, a quota is an absolute quantitative limitation. Once it has been filled, the restricted product is
prohibited from entering our market. The result is to force
consumers to buy from higher-priced domestic producers
or to shift their purchases to other less preferable products.
The ones who gain from this arrangement are the protected
domestic industry; importers, who reap as windfall profits
the difference between the low world price at which they
buy and the higher domestic price at which they are able to
sell; and foreign exporters, who can demand more for their
artificially scarce goods. Under a tariff system this premium would go to the government as tax revenue.

There are four different kinds of quotas:

Legislated Quotas. Domestic sugar producers are protected by the Sugar Act of 1948. Based on estimates of
domestic demand by the secretary of agriculture, the act
allocates U.S. sugar requirements between domestic and
foreign producers. Domestic producers are reserved just
under two-thirds of the market, with specific quotas assigned to the sugar beet industry of the western states, to
cane growers in Louisiana and Florida, and to Hawaii,
Puerto Rico, and the Virgin Islands. Some thirty foreign
countries, including South Africa, each receive a fixed percentage of our remaining needs. Congress designed the
Sugar Act to meet three objectives: to assure U.S. consumers of an abundant and stable supply of sugar at reasonable prices; to permit friendly foreign nations to participate equitably in supplying our market for the twofold
purpose of promoting U.S. exports and assuring us a stable

and adequate supply of sugar; and to make it possible, as a matter of national security, for the United States to produce a major part of its sugar requirement domestically.[14]

There is little evidence that the present program is needed to meet these objectives. Sugar is not scarce—indeed, American and foreign growers annually request additional quota allotments; U.S. sugar exports to countries with quotas are not significantly higher than to other countries; and our national security, however defined, cannot be tied to tooth decay, obesity, and empty calories. What the evidence does show is that the Sugar Act is essentially a device to protect domestic growers from low-cost sugar imports. "Stable supply at reasonable prices" and "equitable participation" arguments are nothing less than euphemisms commonly used as a smoke screen to rationalize protectionist programs. At consumer expense, U.S. sugar policy serves to inflate U.S. sugar prices, prop up the domestic sugar industry, and put millions of dollars into the pockets of wealthy foreign sugar producers. By giving growers a sizeable premium (the difference between the U.S. and world market price), the sugar quota has cost American consumers in the neighborhood of $500 million annually.[15] The cumulative effect of U.S. sugar policy, which includes tariff protection and direct subsidies as well as quotas, is that over the last dozen years we have paid nearly twice the world market price for our sugar.*

Competition for the sugar quotas is intense. The roster of lobbyists seeking them, according to the *Washington Post,* is "like an old boys club of ex-federal officials." These "sugar daddies" include Harold D. Cooley, former Agriculture Committee chairman who chaired hearings when Congress last divied up allotments in 1965, representing Thailand for $15,000 a year and Liberia for $10,000 a year; Thomas H. Kuchel, former California senator and Senate Republican whip, laboring for Columbia at $200 an hour; De Vier Pierson, White House aide to Lyndon John-

---

* From 1961 to 1972, the average world price of raw sugar was four cents per pound, compared to the American price of seven and a half cents per pound. The American figure includes duty and shipping costs of just over one cent per pound. In addition, there is a half-cent per pound tax on all sugar, domestic and foreign, marketed within the quota system. Tax revenues slightly exceed the amount paid in subsidies to domestic producers.

son, representing Mauritius for $25,000 a year; Thomas
Hale Boggs, Jr., son of the late House Majority Leader Hale
Boggs and a candidate for Congress in 1970, working for
Costa Rica, El Salvador, Guatemala, Honduras, and Nicara-
gua for $36,000 to $50,000 a year; and Charles H. Brown,
former Missouri congressman, serving Fiji for $2,000 a
month. Lobbyists for the American industry include James
H. Marshall, former head of the Department of Agriculture's
sugar division, representing a united front of domestic
growers, and Horace Godfrey, former administrator of
USDA's Agricultural Stabilization and Conservation Service (ASCS) with jurisdiction over the entire sugar program, representing the American and Florida Sugar Cane
Leagues.[16] These are the men who perpetuate and exploit
a program that Congressman Paul Findley has called "the
worst outrage on the American taxpayers and consumers
being perpetrated by the Federal government."[17]

Voluntary Quotas. Unable to muster sufficient legislative
support for a quota, a growing number of American industries are seeking sanctuary under so-called voluntary quota
agreements. Voluntary quotas have the same effect as legislated quotas, i.e., foreign imports above certain levels are
excluded from U.S. markets. But, unlike limits set by Congress, which are approved (or rejected) after hearings and
expert testimony, voluntary quotas are negotiated in secret
and without participation by all interested parties.

Negotiating these agreements illustrates international
politicking at its best, or worst depending on how you look
at it. Quota advocates threaten foreign producers with the
possibility of stiff legislation. Typically, it is a measure
designed to show foreign producers what could happen if
they fail to curb their exports of certain products to the
United States. The 1970 Mills bill and the 1972 Burke-
Hartke bill are two examples. Public statements by industry, the administration, and congressional spokesmen
follow, increasing foreign fears. At this point, foreign
producers often acquiesce to "voluntarily" limit exports of
agreed-upon products to the United States. The quid pro
quo is abandonment of the quota legislation. Such agreements, says former Undersecretary of State George Ball,
"have had a demoralizing effect on both our government
and industry since, being too easy to work out, they have

tempted hard pressed government officials to yield to industry pressure."[18]

Just how many voluntary undertakings actually exist is unknown. Fearing possible antitrust reprisals, foreign producers act in secret. "If you can't produce documents," admits one Japanese trade organization official, "you can't prove antitrust violations." Theodore Gates, Assistant Special Representative for Trade Negotiations confirms their success: "We just don't know all the areas where there are unilateral agreements, and I'm trying to speak for the government."

The most expensive voluntary restraint affects steel, with an estimated annual cost to consumers of between $500 million and $1 billion.[19] Due to mounting competition from foreign imports, the domestic steel industry went to Congress to plead its case in the mid-1960s. The result: a 1967 bill, introduced by Indiana Senator Vance Hartke, calling for steel import quotas. Japanese steel industry representative Yoshihiro Inayama suggested instead that steel-exporting countries unilaterally limit steel exports to the United States. European producers indicated they too would consider such restraints.

By early 1968, Japanese steel producers twice offered to restrict their U.S.-bound steel shipments. The American steel industry rejected these offers, complaining that they did not go far enough. Discussions intended to make the quotas more restrictive continued between State Department and foreign and domestic industry representatives. Finally, in late 1968, agreement was reached. (Assistant Secretary of State for Economic Affairs Julius Katz has denied that domestic producers endorsed the specific terms of the arrangements.) By its terms, Japanese and European producers agreed to limit steel exports to the United States to a growth rate of 5 percent a year for three years. The agreements were recently extended for three more years and include commitments by producers in the United Kingdom. The new agreements are even more restrictive than the old, with annual growth rates limited to one-half or less than the previously allowed rates.

Hendrick Houthakker, a Harvard professor and former member of President Nixon's Council of Economic Advisors, portrayed the voluntary arrangement as a victory for the international steel cartel and realpolitik and as a defeat for competition and the public.[20] For the quotas were negotiated despite the noncompetitive, inefficient state of the U.S. steel industry. "For over 50 years," writes John Blair, "the major steel companies of the U.S. [four of which account for over 50 percent of national raw-steel output] have been noted for their unresponsiveness, if not hostility, to new technologies."[21] More specifically, economist Walter Adams concluded: "The major steel inventions in recent years—including the basic oxygen furnace, continuous casting, and vacuum degassing—came from abroad. They were not made by the American steel giants."[22] Further, a 1971 presidential task force on steel found that output per man-hour in the industry had leveled off in recent years.[23] Nevertheless, protected by Uncle Sam, steel prices continue to climb and incentive for innovation remains deficient.*

Consumers are overcharged another $350 million annually to support voluntary limits on meat imports. Under the Meat Import Act of 1964, the president can set quotas on imports of certain meats (mainly beef and mutton) that the secretary of agriculture determines will exceed a fixed level. The act further provides that quotas may be suspended if "adequate quantities of meat are not available at reasonable prices." In fact, the president has suspended the quotas each year since 1968, apparently because adequate quantities of meat were *not* available at reasonable prices. Each time, however, he has replaced them with negotiated voluntary limitations. The result is that American consumers have been denied access to large amounts of meat produced abroad. Most of the meat excluded is hamburger and sausage, both important diet items for middle- and lower-income families.[24]

Despite the Nixon administration's well-publicized commitment to curb inflation, these restraint arrangements

---

* Consumers Union has challenged the legality of the steel agreement in a pending federal lawsuit, alleging the president exceeded his authority in its negotiation. After finding that the President can enter into such agreements within private firms so long as the agreements do not violate laws like the Sherman Act, Judge Gerhard Gesell, in a January, 1973, decision, declared, "it is apparent on this limited record that very serious questions can and should be raised as to the legality of the [steel] arrangements under the [Sherman] Act."

were negotiated again in 1972, excluding some three hundred million pounds of salable meat from American markets. At the same time, our meat supplies were further constricted by rising demand and a decline in the slaughter of dairy cows, ironically due in part to high milk prices artificially caused by government price supports and milk marketing orders. Predictably, the cost of meat soared. In February, 1972, beef and pork prices at the farm were at their highest levels since the end of the Korean war. Rising prices were accompanied by speculation that a loosening of meat import quotas would be used to increase meat supply and lower meat costs. This strategy, however, was opposed by cattle producers' associations and by Secretary of Agriculture Earl Butz. Butz declared that farm price increases, including that for cattle, are justified no matter what their effect on grocery bills.

Capping four months of inaction and high meat prices, President Nixon, perhaps yielding to election year pressure, suspended the meat import quotas in June, 1972. What effect this belated gesture will have on consumer prices will not be known for some time. Anticipating a restricted U.S. demand, foreign producers have planned their meat production accordingly. These producers will substantially increase their volume for export only if they are convinced our markets will remain open.

At a time when bicycle demand is booming, Japanese bicycle producers are "voluntarily" restricting their sales to the United States. Again, the American industry went to Congress complaining that "We are threatened by imports, that unless some relief can be provided when we need it we will suffer serious harm."[25] In flat contradiction, however, is the declaration of a Schwinn Bicycle Company executive that "If we could have increased our production by 50 percent or even 100 percent, we couldn't have met demand."[26] The American company had, in fact, received orders for its entire 1971 production by May of that year. Nevertheless, the voluntary quotas are still in effect.

Government-to-Government Quota Agreements. Higher clothing costs reflect import restrictions as well, in this case government negotiated agreements regarding cotton, wool, and synthetic textiles. Campaigning in 1960, John Kennedy promised the textile industry protection in return for their political support. The result was the 1962 multinational compact (the Long-Term Agreement Regarding International Trade in Cotton Textiles), limiting imports of cotton products such as sheets, towels, and underwear. President Nixon, thinking Kennedy had out-promised him in the textile states in 1960, was determined not to make the same mistake again. He pledged further protection for the industry in his 1968 campaign. Like Kennedy, Nixon paid off, as the following chain of events indicates.[27] President Nixon convinced Representative Wilbur Mills (D.–Ark.), chairman of the powerful House Ways and Means Committee, to support quota legislation on textile imports (the 1970 Mills bill). Assured by Nixon that the threat of congressional action would induce major textile exporters, including the Japanese, to agree to voluntary limitations, and under pressure from his southern colleagues, Mills agreed. With the chairman's support, the measure worked its way through Ways and Means and then through the House. But the bill was killed during the final days of the session due to complex procedural maneuverings in the Senate.

Shortly after the defeat, Mills decided personally to solve the textile import problem. Meeting with American representatives of the Japanese industry, the chairman made it clear that if voluntary textile limitations were not worked out, similar to those already in effect for steel, exporters would face highly restrictive quota legislation. Japanese producers capitulated, and on March 8, 1971, announced voluntary export limitations on man-made fiber and wool textile products (e.g., men's suits).

President Nixon, however, viewed Mills's role as an affront to presidential prerogatives and the restrictions as grossly inadequate; he vetoed the plan outright. The White House then successfully proceeded to negotiate its own agreement. It was far more restrictive than the Mills agreement and was negotiated with the Japanese government rather than with Japanese industry. The three-year agreement was justified publicly as a means "to prevent an abrupt increase and to provide for orderly development of export trade in wool and man-made fiber textiles from Japan to the United States consistent with the healthy development of the textile economies of both countries." A similar agreement had already been hammered out with Malaysia, and has since been negotiated with Hong Kong,

Taiwan, and Korea. The total cost to consumers of both the 1962 Cotton Agreement and the Wool and Man-Made Fiber Textile Agreement is estimated to be $1 billion.[28] Mr. Nixon had indeed delivered.

National Security. The multibillion dollar oil industry receives special protection from Uncle Sam under the presidentially created Mandatory Oil Import Program. Paradoxically named, the program actually *limits* imports of crude oil into the United States. Its ultimate effect is to force consumers to buy products made from either high-priced domestic oil or allocated imported oil, rather than from foreign oil available at much lower prices. The cost of the oil program to consumers is now almost $6 billion annually and is expected to climb as high as $8.5 billion by 1980, according to President Nixon's Cabinet Task Force on Oil Import Control. Per capital costs averaged $24 in 1969, reaching as much as $39 in New Hampshire, $41 in Maine, and $45 in Vermont.[29]

The program is usually defended on the basis of national security. On the recommendation of the director of the Office of Emergency Preparedness (OEP), the president is permitted to limit imports of any article that is being imported "in such quantities or under such circumstances as to threaten to impair the national security." President Eisenhower in 1959 was the first to invoke this authority, and every chief executive since then has continued the program with slight variation. The alleged threat to American security is that large quantities of cheap foreign oil would force U.S. prices so low that inefficient wells would be forced out of production and domestic exploration discouraged. We would then, the argument goes, become heavily dependent on insecure foreign supplies to our possible military, political, or economic detriment.

Sherman Adams, adviser and confidant to President Eisenhower, candidly admitted that protection of the domestic oil industry was a major factor in the president's decision to limit oil imports. Yet the program's utter irrelevance to national security requirements has been made clear. In a painstaking nine-month study, President Nixon's Cabinet Task Force concluded:

> The fixed quota limitations that have been in effect for the past two years and the system of implementation that has grown up around them, bears no reasonable relation to

current requirements for protection either of the economy or of essential oil consumption. The level of restriction is arbitrary and the treatment of several foreign sources internally inconsistent. The present system has spawned a host of special arrangements and exceptions for purposes essentially unrelated to the national security.[30]

Even the Defense Department does not maintain that the program is necessary to protect U.S. military capability in time of crises. Barry J. Shillito, outgoing assistant secretary of defense, recently testified:

Despite the vital importance of oil to our military forces, the risk to security from interruptions of oil supply do not, in the main, concern any danger to the functioning of the nation's armed forces. The military needs of the nation in an emergency, even if all requirements had to be produced in the United States, are such a small fraction of total domestic consumption that oil supply for the armed forces is very unlikely to be placed in jeopardy.[31]

The program's treatment of Canadian and Mexican oil underscores the transparency of the national security rationale. Because Canada and Mexico are close and long-time American allies and because their contiguity with the United States allows for virtually uninterruptable overland oil shipments, one would assume that Canadian and Mexico oil is treated the same as oil from domestic sources. This is not the case. Oil imports from Canada and Mexico have been limited by quotas in one way or another since 1962.

The dual treatment of U.S. and Mexican oil has led to interesting but questionable activities. Prior to 1970, Mexican oil entering the United States overland was exempted from quota limitations. Because no pipeline existed connecting the Mexican wells with U.S. refineries, the oil was first shipped by water to Brownsville, Texas, and then transferred to trucks that crossed back over the Mexican border, turned around, and reentered the states. The ceremony was referred to as the "Brownsville loop." The oil was then put on tankers and shipped to the East Coast where it was allowed to enter unrestricted. At the same time, oil sent by rail from Canada to southern Alaska was subject to quota restrictions because a short island waterway happened to be crossed by rail ferry. If this oil had come completely overland, it too would not have been restricted. Ironically, this created Alaskan dependence on oil shipped by the same waterway from Washington State. The relevance of these policies to national security is opaque, if not nonexistent.

East Coast bound residual fuel oil, used mainly to power and heat large institutions and utilities, is also exempted from quota restrictions. As a result, imports of this oil to the East have climbed steadily, comprising 40 percent of the area's heating fuel market in 1970. Why have domestic producers allowed this competition? The answer is simple: it permits them to concentrate their production on gasoline, jet fuel, and other products that yield higher profit margins. "One may wonder," along with the President's Oil Task Force, "whether the security test should be different when imports do not threaten the profits of the domestic industry than when they do."[32]

In practice, the Mandatory Oil Import Program has actually encouraged the depletion of U.S. oil sources and hastened our dependence on politically unstable Middle Eastern and North African countries where most of the world's remaining oil reserves are located. Thus, to the benefit of only the oil industry, and at a cost of billions of dollars to consumers, the Oil Import Program has historically created the very dependency and risk to national security it was allegedly designed to avoid.

President Nixon, confronted by severe domestic oil shortages, has allowed foreign imports to increase in recent months. But at the same time he has indicated he will not follow the recommendation of his Task Force and permanently end the present program.* Economic reality and political reality are two different matters where the powerful oil industry is concerned. The number of top government officials from key oil states is impressive: Speaker of the House Carl Albert (D.–Okla.), House Appropriations Committee Chairman George Mahon (D.–Tex.), House Democratic Caucus Chairman Olin Teague (D.–Tex.), House Armed Services Commitee Chairman F. Edward Hebert (D.–La.), and Senate Finance Committee Chairman Russell Long (D.–La.). Contributions by oil interests to the president's 1968

---

* Yet due to a worsening U.S. "energy crisis," domestic producers are operating near full capacity and the quota system is beginning to crack. In January, 1973, Interior Secretary Rogers Morton said that the program might soon be overhauled.

campaign chest included $215,000 from the Mellons (Gulf Oil), $84,000 from the Pews (Sun Oil), and $60,000 from Robert O. Anderson (Atlantic Richfield). And it was revealed that in 1972 Mellon heir Richard Mellon Scaife gave $1 million to Nixon's Commitee to Re-Elect the President; Elisha Walker, Jr., a director of Petroleum Corporation of America, donated $100,000; and J. Paul Getty, chairman of Getty Oil Co. and reputed to be the richest man in the world, contributed $97,000. In short, the evidence solidly supports Hendrick Houthakker's charge that "the [oil] program as a whole remains a constant reminder of the reluctance of the Federal government, irrespective of party, to let national objectives prevail over the wishes of a politically powerful industry."*[33]

Tariffs and the Tariff Commission

In the early stages of America's development, the tariff aimed to shield infant industries from the rigors of foreign competition. Without protection, these industries would not have been able to compete with the more mature, well-established English firms. Not only would this have proved ruinous to many existing companies, but it would have discouraged new ones from entering the market, thereby retarding U.S. economic growth. Not surprisingly, the first bill introduced in Congress was a tariff measure, declaring in its preamble that "it is necessary . . . for the encouragement and protection of manufacturers, that duties be laid on imported goods." For almost 150 years, the trend was in the direction of higher tariffs, culminating with the Tariff Act of 1930. Better known as Smoot-Hawley, it set U.S. tariff rates at their highest levels ever. Thirty-four foreign countries and one thousand American economists, led by Professor (later Senator) Paul Douglas, protested its enactment. Under Smoot-Hawley's four-year reign, tariffs on dutiable imports averaged 54 percent, peaking at 59.1 percent in 1932.

* The oil import program has recently been challenged in federal district court by the New England Governor's Conference, the states of Connecticut, Maine, Massachusetts, New Hampshire, Rhode Island, and Vermont, Consumers Union, and Ralph Nader's Public Citizen, Inc. Plaintiffs are contending that the program is unconstitutional and violates the provisions of the Trade Expansion Act of 1962 and President Eisenhower's 1959 proclamation.

The Reciprocal Trade Agreements Act of 1934 (the Hull Reciprocal Trade Act) reversed the trend toward higher tariffs. To supplement domestic markets, which had dried up during the Depression, the act undertook to expand foreign trade by authorizing the president to negotiate reciprocal tariff reductions up to 50 percent of existing Smoot-Hawley rates. According to then Secretary of State Cordell Hull, "It was fully realized that it was necessary to open up the American market to imports if foreign countries were to be able to earn the foreign exchange needed to purchase our exports."[34] Incorporating "most favored nation" clauses in these agreements meant that reductions applied to all nations. By 1960, U.S. tariff rates had dropped to 12.2 percent. Recent Kennedy Round negotiations reduced this ratio to less than 10 percent in 1971.

The infant industry rationale justifying early high tariff rates is a widely accepted exception to free trade theory. Professor Paul Samuelson explains it as follows:

> According to this doctrine, there are activities in which a country would really have a comparative advantage, *if only it could get them started.* If confronted with foreign competition, such infant industries are not able to weather the initial period of experimentation and financial stress; but given a breathing space, they can be expected to develop economies of mass production and the technological efficiency typical of many modern processes. Although protection will at first raise prices to the consumer, once the industry grows up it will be so efficient that cost and price will actually have fallen. If the benefit to consumers at that later date would be enough to more than make up for the higher prices during the period of protection, a tariff is justified [Emphasis in original].[35]

America's protected industries can hardly be characterized as infants. More accurately, most are comfortably middle-aged and prefer not to have to compete with younger, more vital, foreign enterprises (e.g., steel), while others are plain old and refuse either to become competitive or to die (e.g., textiles). Each, however, is intensely aware of how tariffs can help them and is quick to seek congressional aid. Samuelson's observation is typical of statements by economists and politicians alike:

> The single most important motivation for protective tariffs is obvious to anyone who has watched the "logrolling" in

Congress when such legislation is on the floor. Powerful pressure groups and vested interests—both business and labor—know very well that a tariff on their products will help *them,* whatever its effect on total production and consumption. Outright bribery was used in the old days to get the necessary votes; today powerful lobbies exist in Washington to drum up enthusiasm for the good old crockery, watch, or buttonhook industry [Emphasis in original].[36]

Again, it is the consumer who pays for pressure group politicking. Tariffs directly add at least $2 billion a year to consumer purchases. The total cost of the tariff and the concomitant increase in the price of comparable domestic products has been estimated as high as *five times* that amount.[37] This means that each year the average New York family gives $36 to the Treasury Department as tariff payments, and pays an additional $100 to $150 to domestic producers in the form of higher prices. "As so often happens," notes Nahum Stone writing on tariffs, "the unorganized consumers fall easy prey to organized greed."[38] In 1971, a 29.2 percent tariff on clothing (more protection for the textile industry) netted the government almost a half billion dollars; an 11.3 percent tariff on footwear, $86.3 million; and a 10.4 percent tariff on radios, $34.7 million.[39]

Congress created the Tariff Commission in 1916 to provide objective information on tariff matters. Run by six commissioners serving staggered six-year terms, the commission assists Congress and the president as an advisory fact-finding body on tariffs, commercial policy, and foreign trade matters. Although the commission is politically neutral (no more than three members of a political party can serve on the commission at the same time), it is not unusual for politics to play an important role in the selection of commissioners. This is especially true of the Nixon administration. The present chairman, Nixon-appointee Catherine Bedell, is a former Republican congresswoman from Yakima, Washington. Mrs. Bedell replaced retiring Chairman Chester Mize, also a former member of Congress and a Nixon-appointee. Of the remaining five commissioners, only one (Will Leonard) had significant experience in a broad range of trade matters before appointment to the commission. Other members include a former cotton lobbyist (J. Banks Young), a former post office official (George Moore), the former chairman of the Poultry Industry's International Trade Development Board (Joseph Parker), and a New York City lawyer (Italo Ablondi).

Tariff Commission investigatory duties are twofold.*[40] First the commission performs what may loosely be termed quasi-judicial investigations, most importantly under the escape clause and adjustment assistance provisions of the Trade Expansion Act of 1962, the Antidumping Act, and Section 22 of the Agricultural Adjustment Act. The escape clause permits the president to raise tariffs or limit imports of an article if the Tariff Commission finds that trade agreement concessions are the major cause of increased imports and that such increased imports are the major cause of serious injury to the domestic industry. Because the national interest may outweigh the benefit to a particular industry, the president is not required to act on affirmative findings by the commission. From the enactment of the Trade Expansion Act in 1962, until 1969, the commission did not make one affirmative finding of injury. The commissioners reasoned that because the country was prospering, other factors must have caused whatever distress might have developed for marginal concerns in industries which as a whole had not been seriously injured by imports. In the last three years, the commission has found the requisite industry injury on numerous occasions, and protective relief has been granted the piano, glass (in which two firms control 80 percent of the market), and earthenware industries.

The Trade Expansion Act further provides assistance for workers and firms injured under the same criteria described above for escape clause relief. Assistance to workers can take the form of a trade readjustment allowance, vocational training allowances, and relocation expenses. Firms qualifying for assistance can receive financial and technical aid and tax relief. But stringent eligibility requirements for assistance were written into the act to mollify congressional fears of excessive costs. Consequently, less than

---

* The commission also collects data relating to U.S. foreign trade and performs other administrative tasks.

thirty-five hundred workers have received payments under the act during the period from January to August, 1972, and weekly checks have averaged less than $65. Firms receiving assistance have totaled only eight from the program's inception until May 1, 1972.[41]

Adjustment assistance for workers merits special attention. Appended to the Trade Expansion Act to gain congressional support, the program in effect discriminates against workers whose unemployment is not related to trade activity but nonetheless results from the operation of impersonal economic causes. Strong government programs, on federal and state levels, are neeeded to relieve *all* unemployment, whether caused by trade concessions, environmental legislation, technological advances, or the like. We thus encourage enlightened governmental policy making by shifting its burden from a few individuals to society as a whole.

A second quasi-judicial activity of the commission is to investigate whether an American industry is being injured by "dumping" or international price discrimination. If the commissioners find in the affirmative, a special duty, normally equal to the difference between the U.S. and home foreign market price, is imposed on the importer under the Antidumping Act. An extreme example would be foreign cartels financing low-priced sales in the United States out of monopoly profits made at home for the purpose and with the effect of injuring the American industry. Practically no such cases have been found to exist in the fifty-year history of the Antidumping Act. Still, antidumping duties have been imposed, without regard to any anticompetitive effects, to the detriment of bargain-minded consumers. The act itself permits of such a reading, an act described by one commentator as "a curious hybrid of traditional tariff ideas and price discrimination theories of antitrust law."[42] Consumers would benefit from an interpretation requiring that anti-competitive effect be found before dumping duties are imposed. Not only does dumping enable Americans to buy low-priced goods, but it can also increase domestic competition, especially when American prices are artificially high. This standard would still suffice to carry out the congressional intent to suppress predatory pricing in international markets.

The commission's final quasi-judicial task to be discussed involves the determination, under Section 22 of the Agricultural Adjustment Act (AAA), of whether imports are interfering with any price-support or other program relating to agricultural commodities administered by the Department of Agriculture. If the commission finds interference, the president may limit imports of the commodity in question. Currently certain dairy products, cotton, wheat, and peanuts are subject to Section 22 quotas.

The second major function of the Tariff Commission is to conduct industry investigations. By providing an impartial factual analysis, these investigations can play an important role in shaping U.S. trade policy. Former Commission Chairman Stanley Metzger credits them with creating a climate of discussion "which will be characterized by an awareness of the facts, rather than either conjecture or the haunting feeling that decisions concerning trade policy may be made on the basis of competing selected facts."[43]

The commission does not normally consider the impact that proposed policies have on consumers, either because it is not requested to do so, or because the status treats such considerations as irrelevant. "That is not our job," said Al Parks, director of the commission's Office of Trade and Industry, in an interview. "The nature of our work and the laws under which we operate are not consumer oriented." Nevertheless, the commission is not prohibited from including such data in its reports.

Marketing Orders—The Great Tomato Conspiracy

For the last three years, the Department of Agriculture has limited imports of high quality, low-priced tomatoes from Mexico by means of a marketing order (a device to regulate the handling of agricultural products). The order, adopted at the behest of Florida tomato growers, imposes more stringent size requirements on vine-ripened tomatoes than on gas-ripened tomatoes. Because Florida growers generally pick their tomatoes green and artificially ripen them with ethylene gas, while Mexican growers let their tomatoes vine-ripen, the effect of the order is to discriminate against Mexican tomatoes. The moving force behind this order is the Florida Tomato Committee, a group composed solely of representatives from the Florida tomato industry. The committee functions as sort of a tomato "brain trust," applying its expertise to problems besetting the tomato industry. This is done informally and by recommending appropriate marketing regulations to the secretary of agriculture.

In the late 1960s Florida growers became concerned over increased sales of Mexican tomatoes in the United States. Failing to secure tariff or quota protection, they struck upon the idea of a marketing order. Because Florida tomatoes tend to be inferior to Mexican tomatoes, the growers could not base their order on quality, but had to rely on size. Under the standard recommended by the committee, gas-ripened tomatoes had to measure at least 2 9/32″ in diameter to be marketed. Vine-ripened tomatoes, on the other hand, had to be 2 17/32″ across or a full 1/4″ larger than gas-ripened tomatoes. It is not a coincidence that popular salad-sized tomatoes measure 2 9/32″ in diameter, thereby excluding Mexican tomatoes from this market.

The Florida committee made no effort to hide the purpose of its recommendation. "The reason behind it is that we can cut out a lot of Mexican tomatoes," said Harold Willis, chairman of the committee's marketing subcommittee. "Let's face it, we are trying to cut out more of the Mexicans than we are of ourselves." Another member, Paul DiMare, boasted: "It will eliminate our competition and that's what we're trying to do."[44] Despite this candor, the secretary of agriculture chose Orlando, Florida, as the site for hearings on the proposed order—in the very building occupied by the Florida tomato industry. Thus, government and consumer representatives alike trekked to the tomato growers to hear their case. To no one's surprise, the Agriculture Department, in typical disregard for the consumer, decided to retain the marketing order—although it is presently under attack by a group of consumer organizations.

The impact of the Agriculture Department's marketing order on the consumer is substantial in terms of tomato quality, price, and selection. Most significantly, it forces the consumer to buy lower-quality ethylene-gassed tomatoes. "Uncontradicted evidence in the [hearing] record," says consumer advocate Richard Frank, "indicates that immature ethylene ripened tomatoes have less nutritional value than naturally ripened tomatoes in that they contain lesser amounts of vitamin A and vitamin C."[45]

Vine-ripened tomatoes also are more flavorful than ethylene-gassed tomatoes and have a preferable texture, color, and skin. This fact has not escaped the Florida Tomato Committee. At a 1971 meeting, Jack Peters, manager of the committee, noted that a University of Florida study "very definitely confirms the experiments you and I have been observing for many years; that is, much of the time we are shipping these green tomatoes while they are mature according to [government] standards but they are not really as mature as would be required to supply the consumer with a quality product.[46]

Tomato prices have climbed dramatically as well, 40 percent to 45 percent more than the price of all foods since 1968. Because consumers spent over $800 million on tomatoes last year, or about 1 percent of their food budget, this increase is not insignificant. The cost is exacerbated by the fact that excluded tomatoes are smaller and less expensive than larger-sized tomatoes.[47] It is little wonder the President's Regulations and Purchasing Board found that a modification of the tomato marketing order "could significantly reduce consumer food prices.[48]

Administrative Deterrents

During congressional debate on the Smoot-Hawley Tariff Act, a prominent protectionist offered to allow free traders to set tariff rates, if they would allow him to draft the administrative provisions. His suggestion was only half-joking, for customs classification and valuation are important determinants of actual duty rates. If shipments are consistently delayed or if imports are refused admittance for failing to comply with complex and arbitrary administrative regulations, the impact on trade can be as harmful as outright tariffs or quotas.

Classification is a procedure that establishes the amount of duty, if any, payable on an imported item. Its subtleties can be gleaned from this response to an importer's protest. The article in question is a walking golf ball:

> This article was classified by customs officers under the provision for toys having a spring mechanism in item 737.80, Tariff Schedules of the United States (TSUS). The

> protestant claims that it should be classified under the
> provision for practical joke articles, in item 737.65, TSUS.
> . . . It would seem . . . that a practical joke article is
> one used to effectuate a trick or to place a recipient at a
> humorous disadvantage. Based upon an examination of the
> instant merchandise, we are of the opinion that it is just
> such an article. As noted above, in appearance it resem-
> bles a standard golf ball and when first placed on the
> green, it looks real. After the switch is released by the
> golfer playing the joke, the ball will appear to walk by
> itself toward the cup or in any direction in which it is
> aimed, thus, surprising or startling the other golfer.[49]

On the basis of this analysis, the ball was classified as a
practical joke article rather than as a spring-operated toy.

After the applicable rate of duty is determined, the customs officer must select the appropriate valuation method.
Congress has given him nine such methods from which to
choose. Most imports are assessed at the price for which
they are sold in their home market for exportation to the
United States (export value). Congress, however, has
afforded special protection to a few items, most notably
benzenoid chemicals. These articles, which include rubber-
soled footwear, are assessed at the selling price in the
United States of the competitive domestic product (American selling price). The difference between competitive U.S.
prices and export value can be considerable, sometimes as
high as 25 percent. American importers are especially critical of American selling price valuation and view the
multiplicity of methods as "a major nontariff barrier in
that it complicates customs administration, creates uncertainty, and is retained for purely protectionist purposes."[50]

Conclusion

A turn-of-the-century American cartoon depicted small
European characters trying to hold back a huge wave of
"Uncle Sam's Goods for the World." The caption boasted:
"They cannot keep back the rising tide of American competition." That was 1901. Today the tide has turned. Now
it is American industry that is determined to keep out the
flood of foreign goods.

Protectionist rhetoric is appealing. What American can
ignore a worker's plea to "Save Our Jobs," or the patriotic

ring of "Buy American." The facts show, however, that protectionist rhetoric is just that—rhetoric. Restricting imports will not increase U.S. employment, will not benefit consumers, and will not cure our economic ills. At the expense of many, protectionism helps only a few. "Our political system," says Houthakker, "has developed an infinite solicitude for well-organized pressure groups—even very small ones—provided they hire the right Washington lawyers and make the right campaign contributions. By the same token the general public interest, especially the interest of consumers, is being given less and less weight."[51]

The stake of consumers in international trade is high. Import restrictions currently lead to overcharges of almost $20 billion each year and affect a wide variety of purchases.[52] We must take steps to reduce this impact. The consumer is entitled to government policies that save him money, bring him the largest selection of products, satisfy his need for goods not produced in the United States, and which maintain a competitive impact on domestic prices, product efficiency, and innovation. These are the policies of free trade.

NOTES

Chapter 1

1. M. Green, B. Moore, Jr., and B. Wasserstein, *The Closed Enterprise System* (1972) (see especially chapter 1 and notes).
2. *Wall Street Journal,* July 30, 1959, at 1.
3. C. Phillips, *The Economics of Regulation* 10 (1969).
4. F. M. Scherer, *Industrial Market Structure and Economic Performance* 519 (1970).
5. *Survey of Current Business,* July, 1970, at S-2.
6. M. Postan, "Why Was Science Backward in the Middle Ages?" in *A Short History of Science* (1951).
7. Phillips, *supra* note 3, at 52–54.
8. 94 U.S. 113 (1877).
9. 291 U.S. 502 (1934).
10. R. Smith, *Public Utility Economics* 229 (1941).
11. Discussed in Phillips, *supra* note 3, at 107. See also, *Humphrey's Executor* v. *United States,* 295 U.S. 602 (1935), and *Wiener* v. *United States,* 357 U.S. 349 (1958).
12. See *Interstate Commerce Commission* v. *Illinois Central Railroad Co.,* 215 U.S. 452 (1910), and *Federal Power Commission* v. *Natural Gas Pipeline Co.,* 315 U.S. 575 (1942).
13. J. Nelson, "The Role of Competition in the Regulated Industries," 11 *Antitrust Bulletin* 1, 3 (1966); see also, Posner, "Natural Monopoly and Its Regulation," 21 *Stan. L. Rev.* 598 (1969), *and* "Comments on the Regulation of Natural Monopolies, 22 *Stan. L. Rev.* 510 (1970).
14. Meyer, Peck, Stenason, and Zwick, *The Economics of Competition in the Transportation Industries* (1959).
15. L. Loevinger, "Regulation and Competition as Alternatives," 11 *Antitrust Bulletin* 101, 115 (1966).

16. H. Gray, "The Passing of the Public Utility Concept," 16 *Journal of Land and Public Utility Economics* 8 (1940).
17. J. M. Landis, *Report on Regulatory Agencies to the President-Elect*. Reprinted as a Committee Report by the Senate Committee on the Judiciary, 86th Cong., 2nd Sess. (1960).
18. Ibid., at 5–6.
19. P. MacAvoy, *The Crisis of the Regulatory Commissions* vii (1970).
20. For a description of official nondisclosure to the public when the agency *does* have data, see Fellmeth, "The Regulatory-Industrial Complex," in B. Wasserstein and M. Green, eds., *With Justice for Some* (1971).
21. *Congressional Record,* April 16, 1970, at S.5887–9.
22. *Federal Trade Commission* v. *R. F. Keppel & Bros., Inc.,* 291 U.S. 304, 314 (1934).
23. L. Kohlmeier, *The Regulators* 48 (1969).
24. W. Cary, *Politics and the Regulatory Agencies* 12 (1967); see also B. Schwartz, *The Professor and the Commissions* (1959).
25. Kohlmeier, *supra* note 23, at 53.
26. 430 F.2d 891 (1970).
27. *California Motor Transport Co.* v. *Trucking Unlimited,* BNA *Antitrust Trade Regulator Reporter,* January 18, 1972, A-1.
28. *New York Times,* December 31, 1969, at 1.
29. Kohlmeier, *supra* note 23, at 53.
30. Fellmeth, *supra* note 20, at 251.
31. F. Malchup, *The Political Economy of Monopoly* (1952).
32. Baker, "The Antitrust Division, Department of Justice: The Role of Competition in Regulated Industries," 11 *Boston College Industrial and Commercial Law Review* 571 1970.
33. 36 U.S. (11 Pet.) 420 (1837).
34. C. Wilcox, *Public Policies Toward Business* 476–77 (1966).
35. 52 Stat. 973 (1938).
36. 66 Stat. 472 (1948).
37. 374 U.S. 321 (1963).
38. 373 U.S. 371 (1963).
39. 310 U.S. 328 (1968).
40. 399 F.2d 953 (1968).
41. Scherer, *supra* note 4, at 537.
42. "Rate Regulation," reprinted in MacAvoy, ed., *supra* note 19, at 1.
43. The rates are largely within the discretion of the commission involved, courts being reluctant to overturn them by independent review. See *Federal Power Commission* v. *Hope Natural Gas Co.,* 320 U.S. 591 (1944).
44. Stigler and Friedland, "What Can Regulators Regulate?

The Case of Electricity," 5 *Journal of Law and Economics* (1962); *cf.* Posner, "Should Natural Monopolies Be Regulated?" 22 *Stan. L. Rev.* 510 (1970).

45. Jordan, "Producer Protection, Prior Market Structure and the Effects of Government Regulation," XV *Journal of Law and Economics* 151, 161 (April, 1972).

46. *United States* v. *Trans-Missouri Freight Association,* 116 U.S. 290 (1897).

47. *Georgia* v. *Pennsylvania Railroad Co. et al.,* 324 U.S. 439 (1945).

48. Jordan, *supra* note 45, at 167. See also, W. Jordan, *Airline Regulation in America* (1970); G. Kolko, *Railroads and Regulation, 1877–1916* 210–217 (1965); P. MacAvoy, *The Economic Effects of Regulation: The Trunk-Line Railroad Cartels and the Interstate Commerce Commission Before 1900* 25–152 (1965).

49. J. Blair, *Economic Concentration: Structure, Behavior and Public Policy* 398 (1972).

50. C. Edwards, *Regulating Competition* at chapter VII (1964 edition).

51. R. Noll, *Reforming Regulation* 25 (1971).

52. See W. Capron, ed., *Technological Changes in Regulated Industries* (1970), which says that the data is inconclusive to prove regulation restricts productivity and technology.

53. "The Economics of Federal Subsidy Programs," a staff study of the Joint Economic Committee (January 11, 1972).

54. T. G. Moore, "The Feasibility of Deregulating Surface Freight Transportation," a paper presented at the Conference on Antitrust and Regulated Industries, October 28—29, 1971, Brookings Institution, Washington, D.C.

55. Levine, "Is Air Regulation Necessary? California Air Transportation and National Regulatory Policy," 74 *Yale Law Journal* 1416 (1965), cited in Passell and Ross, "Mr. Nixon's Economic Melodrama," *New York Review of Books,* September 23, 1971, at 8.

56. Maritime Transportation Research Board, *Legal Impediments to International Intermodal Transportation* 42 (1971).

57. McGowen, Noll and Peck, "Subsidization through Regulation: The Case of Commercial Television Broadcasting," prepared for Joint Economic Committee, December 1971, at 35–40; to be expanded into a book, *Economic Aspects of TV Regulation* (Brookings Institution, forthcoming 1973).

58. The case for continued regulation of natural gas field rates rests on the following arguments: While the present market is not particularly concentrated, the relevant market should

be firms bringing in *new* supplies into the market, and here
the industry is quite concentrated (D. Schwartz, *Supply-
Technical Advisory Task Force-Regulation and Legislation*
[FPC Task Force Report, dissenting report, 1972]); FPC
decisions themselves have said that "there are serious market imperfections which preclude us from relying upon the
free operation of the market, as evidenced by arms' length
bargaining, to protect the ultimate consumer from unreasonable purchased gas rates" (*South Louisiana Area Rate
Proceedings,* 40 FPC 530 [1968]); pipelines, which require
substantial backup reserves, are at a competitive disadvantage in dealing with gas producers and cannot effectively
bargain to keep prices down; also, because pipeline costs
are automatically passed on by the FPC, rate regulation
has no incentive to keep prices low (Schwartz, *supra*); it is
false, according to these critics, that low prices discourage
natural gas producers from further exploration, since they
are now earning a return of 16%–18% on equity (*New
York Times,* December 13, 1972, at 34 [letter of Charles
F. Wheatly, Jr.]); investigator Robert Sherrill charges that
there is a coordinated campaign by members of the natural
gas industry to convince the public that there is a gas shortage, so that prices will be pushed up (Sherrill, "Energy
Crisis: The Industry's Fright Campaign," *Nation,* June 26,
1972); Secretary of the Treasury George Shultz, while testifying before Congress in 1970, testified that he thought the
oil and gas industry were capable of feigning a crisis in
order to bend government policy its way (cited in *ibid.*);
finally, the FPC cannot trust the self-serving gas reserve
estimates of the American Gas Association, yet the agency
lacks the will to conduct its own investigation (*Concentration by Competing Raw Fuel Industries in the Energy Market and Its Impact on Small Business,* Committee on Small
Business, 92nd Cong., 1st Sess. [1971]). Because he believes that deregulation would lead to unacceptably high
consumer prices, Sen. Warren Magnuson has proposed to
create a federal corporation, similar to the TVA, to explore
and drill for natural gas on government land (*Wall Street
Journal,* December 15, 1972, at 4).

The leading advocates for deregulation are Professors
Stephen Breyer and Paul MacAvoy. In a forthcoming book,
they argue that rate regulation has led to uneconomical
practices, and that "neither economic theory nor empirical
study can produce much evidence of any lack of competition
in field pricing." (*Austral. Oil Co.* v. *Federal Power Commission,* 428 F. 2d407 [Fifth Cir., 1970]; McKie, "Market
Structure and Uncertainty in Oil and Gas Exploration,"
74 *Quarterly J. of Eco.* 543 [1960]). Breyer and MacAvoy

argue that regulation has led to the present gas shortage, which hurts small consumers. The FPC Task Force Report agrees.

59. W. G. Shepherd, "Regulation and Its Alternatives," 22 *Stan. L. Rev.* 529 (1970).

60. H. Simons, *Economic Policy in a Free Society* at chapter 2 (1948).

61. *Wall Street Journal,* January 6, 1972, at 1.

62. W. Berge, "The Antitrust Laws: A symposium," 39 *American Economic Review* 691 (1949).

63. Reprinted in "Price Discrimination Legislation—1969," Hearings before the Senate Antitrust and Monopoly Subcommittee, 91st Cong., 1st Sess. at 23 (1969).

64. Ibid. at 3.

65. Quoted in A. Kahn, *The Economics of Regulation* II (1971).

Chapter 2

1. Address by Spiro T. Agnew to the Chamber of Commerce of Montgomery, Ala., *New York Times,* November 21, 1969, at 22.

2. Transcript of National Educational Television Network, "The President's Men" (December 3, 1969, 8:00 P.M.) at 7.

3. B. Bagdikian, *The Information Machines* 211 (1971) (expenditures added for motion pictures and electricity to power TV sets).

4. *Associated Press* v. *United States,* 326 U.S. 1, 20 (1945).

5. Flynn, Book Review, 1969 *Utah L. Rev.* 277, 278.

6. B. Rucker, *The First Freedom* 68 (1968) (data for 1966).

7. Hearings before the Antitrust and Monopoly Subcommittee of the Senate Judiciary Committee, "The Newspaper Preservation Act," 91st Cong., 1st Sess., at 256 (1969). In twenty-two other cities editorially independent papers were jointly operated pursuant to the Newspaper Preservation Act. See Bagdikian, "Why Newspapers Keep Dying," *Washington Post,* July 23, 1972, at B5.

8. B. Tuchman, *The Proud Tower* 178 (1962).

9. Rarick and Hartman, "The Effects of Competition on One Daily Newspaper's Content," 43 *Journalism Quarterly* 459 (1966).

10. Appendix A, Comments of the Department of Justice, FCC Dkt. #18,110 (submitted August 1, 1968).

11. Hearings before the Antitrust and Monopoly Subcommittee of the Senate Judiciary Committee, "The Failing Newspaper Act," 90th Cong., 2d Sess., pt. 7, at 2410 (1968).

12. Rucker, *supra* note 6, at 197–98.

13. Study by M. H. Seiden & Associates, FCC Dkt. #18,110 (submitted January, 1969); reported in *Broadcasting,* February 3, 1969, at 19, 21.

14. Rucker, *supra* note 6, at 8, 20, 21, 189, 193, 194–95, 196.

15. Johnson, "The Media Barons and the Public Interest," *Atlantic,* June, 1968, at 43, 48.

16. See John Poole Broadcasting Co., Inc., 16 FCC 2d 458 (1969) (dissenting opinion of Commissioner Nicholas Johnson).

17. Hearings, *supra* note 11, 90th Cong., 1st Sess., pt. 1, at 263, 264–5 (1967) (Testimony of Jack R. Howard).

18. "The American Media Baronies," *Atlantic,* July, 1969, at 91.

19. Johnson, *supra* note 15, at 49.

20. B. Owen, "Empirical Results on the Price Effects of Joint Ownership in the Mass Media," appendix to Rosse, Owen, and Grey, "Economic Issues in the Joint Ownership of Newspapers and Television Media," FCC Dkt. #18, 110 (submitted May 25, 1970). See also, National Association of Broadcasters financed rebuttal, RMC, Inc., Report UR–150, "A Quantitative Analysis of the Price Effects of Joint Mass Communications Ownership," FCC Dkt. #18,110 (submitted March, 1971), which was criticized in Rosse, "Credible and Incredible Evidence," FCC Dkt. #18,110 (submitted April, 1971).

21. Bagdikian, *supra* note 3, at 176–177.

22. See, e.g., G. Litwin and W. Wroth, "The Effects of Common Ownership on Media Content and Influence," July, 1969 (prepared for and financed by the National Association of Broadcasters); criticized in Barnett, "Cable Television and Media Concentration, Part I: Control of Cable Systems by Local Broadcasters," 22 *Stanford L. Rev.* 221, 260–268 (1970).

23. Breed, "Social Control in the News Room," 33 *Social Forces* 326 (1955).

24. Donohew, "Newspaper Gatekeepers and Forces in the News Channel," 31 *Public Opinion Quarterly* 61 (1967).

25. Kerrick, Anderson, and Swales, "Balance and the Writer's Attitude in News Stories and Editorials," *Journalism Quarterly* (1960). See also Bagdikian, *supra* note 3, at 178–180; Bagdikian, "Wilmington's 'Independent' Newspapers," 3 *Columbia Journalism Review* 13 (1964); Bagdikian, "Houston's Shackled Press," *Atlantic,* August, 1966, at 87; Hearings, *supra* note 17, at 25 (statement of E. Cervi), 113 (statement of J. Flynn), 387 (statement of W. Rivers); Johnson, *supra* note 15, at 47.

26. Barnett, *supra* note 22, at 268–73.

27. *National Broadcasting Co.* v. *United States,* 319 U.S. 190,

223–24 (1943). See Note, "Diversification in Communication: The FCC and Its Failing Standards," 1969 *Utah L. Rev.* 494, 506–509.

28. See Green *et al., The Closed Enterprise System* 54–55 (1972).
29. *New York Times,* April 3, 1971, at 9.
30. *Broadcasting,* August 17, 1970, at 26, 27.
31. Antitrust Division officials blamed an inept staff job for its belated entry into the proceedings, including its failure to participate in the September, 1966, FTC hearing. But Senate staffers attribute both the delay and Turner's ambiguous position to his typical academic obfuscation of potential competition arguments. See Green, et al., *The Closed Enterprise System* 88 (1972). In interviews they claimed that Turner was ultimately swayed by persistent prodding from a small group of congressional liberals led by Senators Nelson and Morse.
32. Landauer, "Justice Unit Likely to Take FCC to Court if ITT-ABC Merger Review Isn't Held," *Wall Street Journal,* February 6, 1967, at 3.
33. "The TV Networks Shrug Off New Competition," *Business Week,* March 27, 1971, at 90, 91.
34. N. Johnson, *How to Talk Back to Your Television Set* 11 (1970).
35. See Webbink, "How Not to Measure the Value of a Scarce Resource: The Land-Mobile Controversy," 24 *Federal Communications Bar Journal* 202 (1970) (and authorities cited therein).
36. Based upon the estimate of a ten-year set replacement cycle commencing from the 1972 effective date of the new FCC requirement for "click" switch UHF channel selectors on all new TV sets. Staff report to the Federal Communications Commission, "The Economics of the TV-CATV Interface" 10 (1970).
37. Ibid., at 9.
38. Address of E. William Henry to the National Association of Broadcasters, in Washington, D.C., March 23, 1965.
39. McGowan, Noll, and Peck, "Subsidization Through Regulation: The Case of Commercial Television Broadcasting," (Brookings Mimeo, December 1971) at 35. See also the authors' forthcoming book, *Economic Aspects of Television Regulation* (Brookings Institution, 1973).
40. Second Interim Report of the Office of Network Study of the Federal Communications Commission, "Television Network Program Procurement: Part II" 721 (1965).
41. Ibid., at 47.
42. Report and Order, FCC Dkt. #12782, at ¶7 (adopted May 4, 1970).

43. Figures computed from FCC *Annual Report* 152–164 (1970).

44. Still, nonnetwork stations reaped a 31 percent average return on investment and an 83.5 percent average return on depreciated assets in 1966. Rucker, *supra* note 6, at 103. The prospect of monopoly profits explains the wide gap between the market price commanded by station licenses and the value of the stations' tangible assets. For example, KSAN-TV, a San Francisco UHF, was recently sold for $1 million although the depreciated book value of its assets was only $55,671. According to FCC data, the average depreciated asset value of 489 VHF stations (not including the 15 owned by the networks) as of December 31, 1969, was slightly less than $975,000 each. While station asset value is substantially higher in the larger population centers, such stations often command a market value, or sales price, of $10 to $20 million and higher. See *Broadcasting,* February 3, 1969, at 21; Rucker, *supra* note 6, at App. Table 25. The basic FCC fee for a television license is $150.

45. Bagdikian, *supra* note 3, at 58, 64–68.

46. L. Brown, *Television* 362–363 (1971).

47. Ibid., at 16.

48. 1963 CBS Annual Report.

49. *Business Executives Move for Vietnam Peace* v. *FCC,* 22 P & F Radio Reg. 2d 2089 (D.C. Cir. 1971); *cf. Retail Store Employees Union* v. *FCC,* 436 F.2d 248 (D.C. Cir. 1970); *Friends of the Earth,* 244 FCC 2d 743 (1970) *rev'd and remanded,* 449 F.2d 1164 (D.C. Cir. 1971).

50. Hearings before the Subcommittee on Communications, Senate Interstate and Foreign Commerce Committee, 83rd Cong., 2d Sess., at 1018 (1954).

51. FTC staffers have been investigating network advertising rates since 1965. Discussions with them and others indicated the following practices, among others: (1) time is "not available" for regional advertisers; (2) advertisers who may not desire to use an entire thirty-second segment may not sell, or "piggyback," the remaining portion to some other advertiser (favoring the larger diversified or multi-product advertisers); (3) some sponsors can cancel their obligations when a program turns out to be a dud, others cannot; (4) larger advertisers may be favored, if not in the dollar rate per thousand viewers in having their messages allocated to programs that draw audiences particularly susceptible to purchasing the advertised product—an economically desirable result were it administered evenhandedly.

52. In its "prime time access rule" opinion, the FCC observed ". . . that networks net about $14,000 more per half hour from independent programs than they do from net-

work-controlled programs. This indicates that on the three networks at least $50 million per year could be made available without reducing network income for cost-justified discounts to encourage sponsors and others to relieve the networks of the 'heavy burden' of financial 'risk' of program procurement." Report and Order, FCC Dkt. #12782, *supra* note 42, at App. II, ¶22, n. 31.

53. Ibid., at ¶20, n. 26.
54. Further Notice of Proposed Rule Making, FCC Dkt. #18179, at ¶4 (adopted January 13, 1971).
55. There may be instances where the program owner can reap more profits through an exclusive showing to eager or wealthy viewers willing to pay higher prices than through nonexclusive showings to larger numbers of viewers at lower prices. But that usually occurs when the program producer, a motion picture company, for example, keeps its most demanded features scarce in order to create a better market for its less attractive offerings.
56. *Supra* note 54.
57. Report of the Committee on Interstate and Foreign Commerce, "Network Broadcasting," H. Rep. No. 1297, 85th Cong., 2d Sess., at 274 (1958).
58. Ibid., at 275.
59. *United States* v. *Associated Press,* 52 F. Supp. 362, 372 (S.D.N.Y. 1943), *aff'd* 326 U.S. 1 (1945).
60. The commission also prohibited networks from acquiring syndication rights in films independently produced and licensed for network showing—80.4 percent of all 6:00 P.M. to 11:00 P.M. network programs in 1968. What this means is that the nominally independent studios that produce network programs will retain the right to license reruns to independent VHFs, UHFs, and cablevision operators. But unless and until exclusivity is abolished, it will make little difference whether independent producers or the networks themselves are the syndicators of network reruns.
61. W. Comaner and B. Mitchell, "The Costs of Planning: The FCC and Cable Television," 15 *Journal of Law & Economics* 177, 184 (1972).
62. *T.V. Guide,* January 3, 1970, at 20–21, quoted in Note, "Regulation of Community Antenna Television," 70 *Columbia L. Rev.* 837 (1970).
63. Industrial Electronics Division/The Electronics Industries Association Response to the CATV Inquiry, "The Future of Broadband Communications" 32, Proposed Rule Making and Notice of Inquiry, FCC Dkt. #18397 (submitted October 29, 1969). The reader is cautioned that this long-range estimate of $50 billion is an order-of-magnitude figure. Precise calculations are of course not feasible on the

basis of present information. It should be noted, too, that
the organization making the estimate may be optimistic.

64. E.g., McGowan, Noll and Peck, "Prospects and Policies for
CATV," Report of the Sloan Commission on Cable Communications, *On the Cable* 213 (1971).

65. McGowan, Noll and Peck, *supra* note 39, at 43. See also
Report of the Sloan Commission on Cable Communications, *On the Cable* 219 (1971).

66. Hearings before the Subcommittee on Communications and
Power of the House Interstate and Foreign Commerce
Committee, *Cable Antenna Television* (CATV), 92d Cong.,
1st Sess., Transcript vol., 1 at 75 (July 22, 1971).

67. Based on data from Television Bureau of Advertising, TV
Basics No. 12.

68. See, e.g., Barnett and Greenberg, "A Proposal for Wired
City Television," 1968 *Washington U.L.Q.* 1, 16.

69. *Broadcasting,* December 9, 1968, at 29.

70. Rucker, *supra* note 6, at 181.

71. *Radio-Television News Directors Ass'n Bull.,* January,
1970, at 1–2.

72. Minasian, "Television Pricing and the Theory of Public
Goods," 7 *Journal of Law & Economics* 71, 75 (1964).

73. Other costs are associated with advertiser financing of the
mass media:

(1) Financing the cost of mass audience programming
is also an inefficient use of advertising. The mass advertiser
may encroach upon 98 percent of a mass audience though
only 2 percent are receptive to his message. Conversely,
the more specialized the program, the more easily can an
advertised product be tailored to the selective tastes of
the audience.

(2) To the extent that advertisers seek out programs that
appeal to population groups that are most likely to purchase their products, programs appealing to other groups,
such as the elderly, are excluded even though they might be
willingly purchased on a subscription basis.

(3) For many there is a certain amount of misery in
having to watch TV commercials. In 1967 the average
viewer, not just the "intellectuals," characterized 31 percent
of television advertisements as either "annoying" (27 percent) or "offensive" (4 percent). The percentages of "annoying" ads for other media were: radio (24), newspapers
(12), and magazines (9). R. Bauer and S. Greyser, *Advertising in America: The Consumer View* 243 (1968).

(4) In 1967 ten corporations controlled 78 percent of
all network television advertising—Procter & Gamble, Bristol-Myers, General Foods, R. J. Reynolds Industries, American Home Products, Colgate-Palmolive, General Motors,

Gillette, Sterling Drug, and Lever Brothers. These ten corporations control more time in the American consciousness than schools and churches. Bagdikian, *supra* note 3, at 296.
74. Memorandum Opinion and Order, FCC Dkt. #18397 (adopted June 24, 1970) (dissenting opinion of Commissioner Robert T. Bartley).

Chapter 3

1. $50 billion $\times$ .01 = $500 million, but assuming a 50 percent corporate profits tax rate, AT&T would have to increase revenues by $1 billion in order to keep $500 million for itself.
2. Assuming a $130 million revenue increase per 1 percent rise in the federal rate base, $7.25 - 6.0 = 1.25 \times \$130$ million $= \$162.5$ million, doubled to $325 million to reflect a 50 percent corporate tax rate.
3. J. Goulden, *Monopoly* 327 (1968). Economists refer to this type of overcharge as "regulatory lag," often praising it for producing cost reductions through the lure of higher profits. Yet the purpose of regulation is to secure such cost reductions without exceeding the allowable rate of return.
4. Address of Nicholas Johnson before the Digitronics Users Association Conference, Hotel Ambassador, Chicago, Ill., October 19, 1970, "Why I Am a Conservative, or For Whom Does Bell Toil?" at 7. As a result of the alleged bias manifest in this speech, which focused on the theme that several of the AT&T practices described herein were diminishing the returns to AT&T stockholders as well as increasing prices to consumers, AT&T unsuccessfully petitioned Commissioner Johnson to remove himself from all future FCC deliberations involving AT&T.
5. Johnson, "Why Ma Bell Still Believes in Santa," *Saturday Review,* March 11, 1972, at 57, 58.
6. A 15 percent profit before taxes being necessary for a 7.5 percent return after a 50 percent corporate tax, $50 billion $\times$ .15 = $7.5 billion; $45 billion $\times$ .15 = $6.75 billion; $7.5 billion $-$ $6.75 billion = $750 million.
7. Goulden, *supra* note 3, at 314. Note also the regressive 10 percent federal excise tax on interstate telephone calls. AT&T's continued use of straight-line depreciation on existing equipment is required by §411 of the Tax Reform Act of 1969.
8. This and other technological distortions and rate base expansion devices are noted by Shepherd, "The Competitive Margin in Communications," in W. Capron, ed., *Technological Change in the Regulated Industries* 86, 108 (1971).

Usually, though, Bell's introduction of new technology does not hasten the accounting depreciation of the old, for unless an entire group of existing facilities is completely wiped out by the technological advance—something which almost never happens—the old equipment simply remains in the rate base and slow depreciation continues to be taken.

Note that slow depreciation, by inflating the rate base, produces greater profits over the long term, but the immediate impact is to hold down depreciation expense and therefore to reduce the company's overall revenue requirement and its prices. Bell's present financial crunch, as it struggles to respond to new demand and competitive technologies, has led it recently to propose increases in depreciation rates and a shift to expensing certain previously capitalized items, *see* note 10 *infra,* which will probably soon result in substantial further rate increases to cover the "new" expenses.

9. J. Newfield and J. Greenfield, *A Populist Manifesto* 71 (1972).

10. As long as the installation cost remains in the rate base, consumers are charged for the actual expense of installation plus a rate of return expressed as a percentage of that expense. Moreover, the rate of return element is spread among all telephone consumers rather than being borne only by those responsible for the installation costs. *Montana Rural Electric News,* October, 1970, at 28.

11. See A. E. Kahn, 2 *The Economics of Regulation* 291–294 (1971) and *Los Angeles* v. *California Public Utilities Commission,* 497 P. 2nd 785 (1972).

12. See generally Averch and Johnson, "Behavior of the Firm under Regulatory Constraint," 52 *Am. Econ. Rev.* 1052 (1962); Alchian and Kessel, "Competition, Monopoly, and the Pursuit of Money," in *Aspects of Labor Economics* (National Bureau of Economic Research, 1962). See Shepherd, *supra* note 7.

13. See Lessing, "Cinderella in the Sky," *Fortune,* October, 1967, at 201; Silberman, "The Little Bird That Casts a Big Shadow," *Fortune,* February, 1967, at 108.

14. Shepherd, *supra* note 7, at 107; Posner, "Taxation by Regulation," 2 *Bell J. Econ. & Magt. Sci.* 22, 35–37 (1971).

15. Johnson, *supra* note 5, at 59–60.

16. *Congressional Record,* February 25, 1972, at S 2659.

17. Newfield and Greenfield, *supra* note 9, at 70–76.

18. "Senators Probe Power Rates," *Washington Post,* April 13, 1969, at F1, F3.

19. See Kahn, *supra* note 11, at 147. See also Melody, "Inter-service Subsidy: Regulatory Standards and Applied Economics," in H. M. Trebing (ed.), *Essays on Public Utility Pricing and Regulation* 170 (1971).

20. *Cf.* "Why Ma Bell Constantly Needs More Money," *Business Week*, March 25, 1972, at 57–58.

21. See Federal Communications Commission, *Investigation of the Telephone Industry in the United States,* H. Doc. 340, 76th Cong., 1st Sess., 218–220, 245–246, 584–585 (1969); Complaint, *United States* v. *Western Electric Company and American Telephone & Telegraph Company* (CA 17–49, D. N.J.1956).

22. Shepherd, *supra* note 7, at 111. For a general discussion see Kahn, *supra* note 11, at 140–145.

23. W. H. Melody, "Interconnection: Impact on Competition, Carriers and Regulation" (Paper delivered to International Conference on Computer Communication, Washington Hilton Hotel, Washington, D.C., October 24–26, 1972).

24. Goulden, *supra* note 3, at 148–149.

25. See F. M. Scherer, "The Development of the TD-X and TD-2 Microwave Radio Relay Systems in Bell Telephone Laboratories" (Weapons Acquisition Research Project, Harvard Business School, Oct., 1960); Beelar, "Cables in the Sky and the Struggle for Their Control," 21 *Fed. Communications Bar J.* 26 (1967).

26. See generally Kahn, *supra* note 11, at 129–136.

27. See Irwin, "The Computer Utility: Market Entry in Search of Public Policy," 27 *J. Ind. Econ.* 239 (1969). Melody, *supra* note 23, points to "Bell's revision of its 1980 data market forecast from $2 to $5–$6 billion, the creation of a specialized in-house group for computer-communications and data services, the speeding up of installation of its data transmission capacity as well as its manufacturing capacity on competitive equipment, and the filing of a 25% price reduction in certain data modems because of competitive necessity"—all as evidence that AT&T wants this market, also, exclusively for itself.

28. W. H. Melody, "Technological Determinism and Monopoly Power in Communications" (Paper presented at Annual Meeting of the American Economic Association, Jung Hotel, New Orleans, La., December 28, 1971). Other historical material is found in R. Gabel, "The Early Competitive Era in Telephone Communications Problems," 34 *Law and Contemporary Problems* 340 (1969); C. Phillips, *The Economics of Regulation,* chapter 17 (1968).

29. See L. Waverman, "The 'Natural' in Natural Monopoly: The Federal Communications Commission and the Regula-

tion of Intercity Telecommunications" (Paper presented at the Brookings Institution Conference on Antitrust and the Regulated Industries, October 28–29, 1971).

30. See M. Green, B. Moore, and B. Wasserstein, *The Closed Enterprise System* 38–41 (1972); Goulden, *supra* note 3, chapter 5; Hearings before the Antitrust Subcommittee (No. 5) of the House Judiciary Committee, "Consent Decree Program of the Department of Justice," 85th Cong., 2d Sess. (1958).

31. See M. S. Goldberg, "The Consent Decree: Its Formulation and Use" 37–48 (Bureau of Business and Economic Research, Graduate School of Business Administration, Michigan State University, Occasional Paper No. 8, 1962).

32. But see *International Telephone and Telegraph Co.* v. *General Telephone & Electronics Co.,* (D. Hawaii 1972), wherein it was ruled that certain of GT&E's acquisitions of local telephone companies illegally foreclosed IT&T from the equipment market, and divestiture was ordered.

33. On this issue see generally Kahn, *supra* note 11, at 295–305; M. R. Irwin, *The Telecommunications Industry: Integration vs. Competition* (1971); Sheahan, "Integration and Exclusion in the Telephone Equipment Industry," 70 *Q.J. Econ.* 255 (1956).

34. Irwin, "The Communications Industry," in W. Adams, ed., *The Structure of American Industry* 380, 407 (4th ed., 1971).

35. Independent equipment manufacturers, almost assured of no substantial market for their products and not attaining the aggregate size of AT&T for collateral, will have to pay higher interest rates for credit than Western, and would incur substantial sales and marketing expenses.

36. Kahn, *supra* note 11, at 300–301.

37. A point made by Shepherd, *supra* note 7, at 111–112.

38. Melody, *supra* note 28.

39. The following scheme is adapted from D. Rosenbaum, "The Structure Is the Policy" (Mitre Corp. M72–74, June, 1972).

40. *Cf.* Baumol and Klevorick, "Input Choices and Rate of Return: An Overview of the Discussion," *1 Bell J. Econ. & Mgt. Sci.* 162 (1970).

Chapter 4

1. The interagency memoranda and personal notes cited throughout this chapter come from the extensive private files of a former administration official who was actively involved in the subsidy issue.

2. *New York Times,* July 24, 1969, at 36.

3. "Building Ships Detroit Style," *Business Week,* May 30, 1970, at 106.

4. Department of Defense Working Papers of June 28, 1968.

5. Hearings before the Subcommittee on Merchant Marine of the Committee on Merchant Marine and Fisheries, 91st Cong., 2nd Sess., at 419 (1970).

6. The Nationwide Committee on Export-Import Policy, *The Cost of Becoming Competitive in Ocean Shipping* 6 (1966).

7. Hearings before the Subcommittee on Merchant Marine, *supra* note 5, at 680.

8. The 6 percent of the commerce carried by United States liners represents over 20 percent of its value. In other words, American ships carry the highest value goods. Any increase in carriage must therefore come from the hauling of cheaper and less profitable cargoes. The Department of Defense Working Papers point up another dilemma: "It is estimated that U.S. foreign flag ships under all registries carried over 55 percent of our petroleum imports. Thus, in attempting to increase the U.S. flag share of this market, we would be competing largely with U.S. owned companies."

9. During formation of the Department of Transportation in 1965, "pure political clout," as one Transportation official put it, "kept the Maritime Administration out of the DOT." The Maritime Administration was thus the only major, non-regulatory transportation function of the federal government that remained outside of the Department of Transportation. At the time of the Johnson bill, more than one hundred sympathetic congressmen had indicated support for an independent Maritime Administration.

10. Memorandum from Boyd's office to McNamara, Reynolds, Shultze, Califano, and Trowbridge, August 30, 1967.

11. Proposed Findings of Fact for Columbia Steamship Company, Docket No. S-244, Maritime Subsidy Board 96 (1971).

12. Hearings before the Senate Commerce Committee, 90th Cong., 2d Sess., at 96 (1967).

13. J. Lansing, *Transportation and Economic Policy* 351 (1966).

14. *New York Times,* March 18, 1970, at 46.

15. Proposed Findings of Fact for American Maritime Association, Docket No. S-244, Maritime Subsidy Board, V, at 46 (1971).

16. Hearings before the Subcommittee on Merchant Marine, *supra* note 5, at 427.

17. Proposed Findings of Fact for the American Maritime Association, *supra* note 15, at 46. The cost of these tax

benefits to the taxpayer, until the Nixon bill, ran between $15 and $20 million per year. This figure will certainly rise, although there appears to be no clear estimate of how much.

18. *New York Times,* Sept. 20, 1970, at 85. Despite all the tax-saving devices, the ship replacement fund has not encouraged much new building. A Maritime Administration survey found that two-thirds of the value of the shipping lines rests in their replacement funds. But despite the availability of funds, the ship replacement program of 1958 had fallen eighty-one ships behind its goal by 1968. In addition, the Nixon shipbuilding program fell seven ships short of its goal of nineteen new ships for 1971.

19. Proposed Findings of Fact for Columbia Steamship, *supra* note 11, at 47.

20. Department of Defense Working Papers. The proposed Findings of Fact for Columbia Steamship admit that one "cannot economically carry competitive non-preference cargoes in unsubsidized U.S. flag ships" (*supra* note 15, at 57).

21. Joint Economic Committee, *Discriminatory Ocean Freight Rates,* 89th Cong., 2nd Sess., at 41 (1965) [hereinafter cited as Joint Economic Committee].

22. Proposed Findings of Fact for Columbia Steamship, *supra* note 11, at 65.

23. Department of Defense Working Papers, *supra* note 4.

24. Department of Defense Working Papers. Industry backers point to a handful of incidents in which foreign ships refused to travel to Vietnam. But, as a Department of Transportation official countered, a couple of incidents grew out of previously simmering labor disputes, and several occurred on ships not chartered to the United States, but merely making a commercial stop in Vietnam. In reality, as the Department of Defense Papers point out, the nature and scarcity of seafaring jobs makes it "virtually impossible for crews to dictate on any significant scale whether or not ships will carry U.S. civilian or U.S. military cargo." For instance, the United States depended on thirty-four foreign flag tankers, in early 1968, to carry nearly 80 percent of our gasoline shipments to Vietnam.

25. Department of Defense Working Papers. Nevertheless, chartering costs for American lines were exorbitant. According to McNamara, "Chartering 23 U.S. flag small tankers has cost $39.7 million per year more than if we had used foreign flag tankers to meet all our needs, since foreign flag charters are available at 35 percent of the cost of equivalent tankers."

26. The Department of Defense Working Papers note that

Australia, which is completely dependent upon foreign shipping, has procured shipping in every time of crisis. The significance of foreign carriage to the GNP of countries such as Norway, combined with the dispersal of ship ownership among many nations, means that "there is virtually no risk that foreign shipping would be withdrawn from U.S. trade to the extent of disrupting the flow of U.S. oceanborne commerce."

27. Although seamen's unions stress that subsidies create jobs for American workmen, Jerry Landauer wrote in the *Washington Monthly* of October, 1969 that "foreigners eager to earn the higher wages paid aboard ships flying the U.S. flag make up a sizeable percentage of the crews."

28. Maritime Transportation Research Board, *Legal Impediments to International Intermodal Transportation* 415 (1971).

29. A. Ferguson, et al., *The Economic Value of the U.S. Merchant Marine* 470 (1961).

30. J. Landauer, "The Shakedown Cruise," *Washington Monthly,* October, 1969, at 55.

31. *The Wall Street Journal,* July 11, 1969, at 1.

32. Landauer, *supra* note 30.

33. See generally, "Labor; Cargo Problems Cloud Horizon as Shipbuilding Program Picks Up Steam," *National Journal,* July 24, 1971, at 1571.

34. *New York Times,* September 18, 1970, at 17.

35. Ibid.

36. Ibid.

37. *New York Times,* February 16, 1970, at 73.

38. *National Journal, supra* note 33, at 1572. Of twelve Maritime Administration decisions on subsidy affairs between 1967 and 1970, ten of these were overruled by the courts. More directly, the Maritime Administration has joined the fight against Department of Defense competitive bidding, suspended the publication of maximum "fair and reasonable" charges on charter rates for government bulk cargo carriage, and even forced one company to hire a lawyer more to its liking. Perhaps more importantly, the Maritime Administration has watched conglomerates move into shipping and reserve funds flow out despite warnings from maritime observers that the industry was being milked.

39. G. Hearn, "Cargo Preference and Control," 2 *Journal of Maritime Law and Commerce* 497 (1971).

40. *National Journal, supra* note 33, at 1567.

41. An operating subsidy may even reduce the total cost of the subsidization program. According to Samuel Lawrence, "direct payments to U.S. flag bulk carriers would actually

require a smaller outlay than the present indirect payment through cargo preference." S. Lawrence, *U.S. Maritime Shipping Policies and Politics* 351 (1966) [hereinafter cited as Lawrence].

42. In 1966, the Bureau of the Budget suggested an operating subsidy geared to the average industry performance on a given trade route. The cost-reducing American company on the route thus receives the payout. To enhance freedom of movement, trade route areas, transference restrictions, and sailing requirements can be eliminated.

43. *Thompson* v. *Cayser,* 243 U.S. 66 (1917).

44. House Merchant Marine and Fisheries Committee, *Report on Steamship Agreements and Affiliations,* 63d Cong., 1st Sess., at 418 (1914).

45. Joint Economic Committee, *supra* note 21, at 4.

46. 107 *Congressional Record* 19333 (1961).

47. *F.M.B.* v. *Isbrandtsen,* 356 U.S. 481 (1958).

48. House Committee on the Judiciary, *The Ocean Freight Industry,* 87th Cong., 2d Sess., at 119 [hereinafter cited as Committee on the Judiciary]. Around this period, forty-seven conferences, or 58 percent of them, had achieved rate stability without using the dual rate contract, including thirty-one conferences with independent competition. Ibid. at 217.

49. *Washington Post,* August 4, 1961, at D4.

50. Committee on the Judiciary, *supra* note 48, at 216.

51. Ferguson, *supra* note 29, at 380. In addition, sanction of the dual rate contract appeared to contradict other provisions of the Shipping Act, which "expressly prohibit a number of practices utilized to eliminate independent or non-conference competition because of their predatory nature." Committee on the Judiciary, *supra* note 48, at 285.

52. 107 *Congressional Record* 19346 (1961).

53. What is one man's rate war is another man's competition —except that large shippers and foreign liners receive the greatest benefits from the rebating and rate wars.

54. Maritime Transportation Research Board, *supra* note 28, at 42.

55. See Joint Economic Committee, *supra* note 21, at 20.

56. See Committee on the Judiciary, *supra* note 48, at 251.

57. See Joint Economic Committee, *supra* note 21, at 23.

58. *New York Times,* September 25, 1970, at 42.

59. See Committee on the Judiciary, *supra* note 48, 359.

60. *National Journal, supra* note 33, at 1569.

61. See D. Marx, *International Shipping Cartels: A Study of Industrial Self Regulation by Shipping Conferences* 132 (1953). "It is far from clear that the Commission's entire

regulatory doctrine, even if applied upon a proper record, is capable of producing rational results." Gordon, "Shipping Regulation and the Federal Maritime Commission," 37 *U. Chi. L. Rev.* 90, 257 (1970).

62. See Joint Economic Committee, *supra* note 21, at 22.
63. According to the head of the agreements section of the commission, the commissioners accept only about 5 percent of the lower staff's recommendations for hearings on questionable agreements.
64. See *National Journal, supra* note 33, at 1569.
65. See Committee on the Judiciary, *supra* note 48, at 172. With a revenue pooling agreement "American taxpayers may not only be subsidizing our own vessels, but the lines of foreign nations belonging to the pool as well."
66. Ibid., at 47.
67. Ibid., at 220.
68. Of ninety-six unsubsidized liners in the U.S.-flag fleet, eleven were transferred out of operation in 1970. Proposed Findings of Fact by Columbia Steamship, *supra* note 11, at 99.
69. Ferguson, *supra* note 29, at 404.
70. Gordon, *supra* note 61, at 135. In the *Saber Line* case (FMC 1083, 1967), the commission established an "out of pocket" cost test that enables conferences to set rates at levels sufficiently low to drive out the poor nonconference competition. Ibid. at 131.
71. Committee on the Judiciary, *supra* note 48, at 301.
72. Ibid., at 71.
73. Even an unafraid shipper may be, in one lawyer's words, "just plain ignorant" of the paths to relief. In the mid-1960s, the commission published a pamphlet entitled "Guidelines for Shippers' Complaints" and followed that up with a letter to many shippers. But the commission has done less in recent years. When asked about the commission's efforts to encourage complaints, Commissioner Barrett responded, "We make speeches," at which time the pamphlet might be distributed or the audience told "that all they have to do is write in and get them." According to the commissioners, the commission also sends the pamphlet to trade associations from time to time.
74. Ferguson, *supra* note 29, at 363. The large shipper may go to one carrier, promising all of his business to the liner in return for lowered rates. The complexity of the tariff structure often enables the carrier to obtain lowered rates on particular items, without the benefit accruing to other shippers or the other conference members discovering the full details.

75. *Consolo* v. *FMC*, 383 U.S. 607 (1966).
76. Federal Maritime Commission, *Investigation of Ocean Rate Structures between U.S. No. At. Ports and Ports in the U.K.*, No. 65–45 (1968).
77. Gordon, *supra* note 61, at 294.
78. Committee on the Judiciary, *supra* note 48, at 360.
79. *Nation's Business,* May, 1970, at 58.
80. Ferguson, *supra* note 29, at 381.
81. Ibid., at 467.
82. The containership trade, with its similarities of costs between carriers, may furnish a convenient jumping off point. The commission should also consider pressuring containerships to charge by space and cost, rather than by the economically unsound and mischief-producing commodity-by-commodity pricing.

Similarly, more adequate public disclosure of conference machinations might inhibit possible abuses, and would facilitate communication between smaller shippers as to shipping prices. To persuade the less-developed nations to forgo bilateral agreements, the United States could offer programs of technological assistance and an end to our cargo preference protectionism. As for the commission, economists should be absorbed into the decision-making process, task forces on specific issues established, and regular reports issued on progress toward particular goals. The commission might also encourage the transportation agency recommended by the Ash Commission.

Chapter 5

1. G. Kolko, *Railroads and Regulation, 1877–1916* (1965); G. Hilton, "The Consistency of the Interstate Commerce Act," 9 *Journal of Law and Economics* 87, 1966.
2. R. Fellmeth, *The Interstate Commerce Omission* 3–4 (1970).
3. L. Kohlmeier, Jr., *The Regulators* 48 (1969).
4. Fellmeth, *supra* note 2, at 18.
5. *New York Times,* August 24, 1969, at 1.
6. Statement of Benny Kass, U.S. Senate Commerce Subcommittee on Transport, March 18, 1970.
7. R. C. Cramton, "The Effectiveness of Economic Regulation, A Legal View," American Economic Review, Paper & Proceedings, May, 1964, at 188–189.
8. Letter of Professor Richard B. Heflebower of Northwestern University, dated July 7, 1970.
9. A 1967 dissertation by Andrew Gold at Northwestern University ("Commission Decision Making in Intermode Transport Rates Cases") makes this distinction in analyzing

commission decision making, and tests it by regression analysis, with generally favorable results.

10. T. G. Moore, "The Feasibility of Deregulating Surface Freight Transportation," paper presented at the Conference on Antitrust and Regulated Industries, October 28–29, 1971, Brookings Institution, Washington, D.C. *See also,* Friedlaender, "The Social Costs of Regulating the Railroads," LXI *Am. Eco. Rev.* May, 1971, at 234.

11. *Economic Report of the President,* January 27, 1966, at 126–7.

12. Friedlaender, "The Dilemma of Freight Transport Regulation," Brookings Institution Study, 1969, at 98.

13. Ibid., chapter 8, "Summary of Conference Discussion."

14. Fox-Smythe Transportation Company Extension Oklahoma, 106 ICC 1.

15. Robert A. Nelson, "Economic Structure of Highway Motor Carrier Industry in New England," in *Public Transportation for New England,* New England Governor's Conference, November, 1957, at 31–2.

16. Inventory of Motor Carrier Authority Study, ICC (not released), at 42.

17. Fellmeth, *supra* note 2, at 130.

18. Ibid., at 119–120.

19. See "Mergers and Concentration in the Trucking Industry," Report to the Senate Select Small Business Committee, April 21, 1968.

20. Meyer, Peck, Stenason, and Zwick, *The Economics of Competition in the Transportation Industries* 97 (1959).

21. J. C. Nelson, "Effects of Entry Control in Surface Transport," National Bureau of Economic Research, *Transportation Economics,* at 406.

22. W. Adams, "The Role of Competition in the Regulated Industries," XLVIII *American Economic Review* 533, May 1958.

23. Meyer, et al., *supra* note 20, at 243.

24. M. Peck, "Competitive Policy for Transportation?" reprinted in P. MacAvoy, ed., *Crisis of the Regulatory Commissions* 243 (1970).

25. See Nelson, *supra* note 21, at 410.

26. Friedlaender, "The Social Costs of Regulating the Railroads," LXI, *American Economic Review* 234 (May, 1971).

27. Friedlaender, *supra* note 12, at 98.

28. P. W. MacAvoy and James Sloss, *Regulation of Transport Innovation: The ICC and Unit Coal Trains to the East Coast* (1967).

29. A. Gellman, "Surface Freight Transportation," in William Capron, ed., *Innovation and Change in Regulated Industry* (1971).

30. See Fellmeth, *supra* note 2, chapter 7.
31. Walter Miklius, "Agricultural Exemption," unpublished Department of Transportation study.
32. Nelson, *supra* note 21, at 422.
33. Miklius, *supra* note 31.
34. R. N. Farmer "The Case for Unregulated Truck Transportation," *Journal of Farm Economics,* Vol. 46, May, 1964.
35. *Washington Star,* October 14, 1970.
36. *Economic Report of the President,* 1970, at 108.
37. Testimony of Commissioner Tuggle, Senate Commerce Subcommittee on Surface Transport Hearings, Review of ICC Policies and Practices, June 24, 1969, at 98.
38. *Baltimore & Ohio RR Co.* v. *United States,* 386 (U.S. 424 (1967) (concurring opinion).
39. E. G. Caudell, "Regulatory Policy, Railroad Consolidation and Transportation Efficiency," dissertation, American University, 1968, synopsis.
40. Exceptions of the United States to Examiner's Report and Order in Northern Lines Merger, FD21478, 79, 80. at 6–8.
41. 386 U.S. 424, 442 (1967) (Douglas, J. dissenting).
42. Charles A. Webb dissent, quoted in L. Kohlmeier, *The Regulators* 109 (1969).
43. *Time,* January 26, 1968, at 71A.
44. See *New York Times,* March 9, 1969, Section III, at 1.
45. R. E. Gallamore, "Railroad Mergers: Costs, Competition & the Future Organization of the American Railroad Industry," dissertation, Harvard University, 1968.
46. K. Healy, "Economies of Scale in the Railroad Industry," 1961. (study "update" by DOT staff).
47. Department of Transportation Staff Study, "Western Railroad Mergers," January, 1969, at 13.
48. Gallamore, supra note 45, at 308.
49. George Milton, "Ralph in the Roundhouse," *Trains,* November, 1970, at 44.

Chapter 6

1. *Kent* v. *Dulles,* 357 U.S. 116 (1958).
2. *CAB Handbook of Airline Statistics,* 1969 ed., at 523–30.
3. 72 Stat. 731 (1958).
4. Phillips, "Air Transportation in the United States," in *Technological Change in Regulated Industries* 157 (1971) (W. Capron, ed.).
5. W. A. Jordan, *Airline Regulation in America* (1970).
6. Section 1002 of Federal Aviation Act, 49 U.S.C. 1482.
7. *Moss* v. *Civil Aeronautics Board,* 430 F.2d 891 (1970); Cherington, *Airline Price Policy* 84–110 (1958).
8. *Moss* v. *CAB,* at 893.

9. W. A. Jordan, *Airline Regulation in America* 122 (1970).

10. Quoted in Jordan, *supra* note 9, from *Aviation Week and Space Technology,* May 1, 1967, at 27.

11. CAB Orders No. 71-4-59 and 71-4-60, dated April 9, 1971, at 3. This decision was made final by order 72-8-50, dated August 10, 1972. Before October 15, 1970, the CAB granted a 6 percent fare increase, and the legality of that increase is still under review by the CAB.

12. *ASTA Travel News,* March, 1971, at 30. The figure shows decrease in revenue passenger mile.

13. ICAO Circular No. 105-AT/26, April, 1971, at 39.

14. *Aviation Week and Space Technology,* September 6, 1971, at 33.

15. The seats are calculated by using the number of passengers enplaned and the reported load factor. Figures are taken from the *Air Transport World,* March, 1971, at 9.

16. See generally Barber, "Airline Mergers, Monopoly and the CAB," 28 *Journal of Air Law and Commerce,* 189, 210, 219–20 (1962).

17. Hale and Hale, "Competition and Control: Part II, Air Carriers," 109 *U. Pa. Law Review* 319 (1955); Fulda, *Competition in the Regulated Industries* (1962).

18. "The Anti-trust Laws and the Regulated Industries: The Doctrine of Primary Jurisdiction," 67 *Harvard Law Review,* 929 (1954); Barber, *supra* note 16.

19. *United Western Acquisition Case,* 1 C.A.B. 739, 741 (1940).

20. *Federal Maritime Commission v. Svenska Amerika Linien,* 390 U.S. 238 (1968); *Northern Natural Gas v. Federal Power Commission,* 399 F.2nd 953 (D.C. Circuit 1968).

21. Exhibit "B" in Exhibit EA-100 of Eastern Airlines in CAB Docket No. 23315, p. 7. (Supplemental memorandum of discussions, dated February 4, 1971).

22. Transcript of the ex parte conference, at 1–15.

23. *WKAT, Inc.* v. *FCC,* 296 F.2nd 375, 383 (D.C. Cir. 1961).

24. *Aviation Daily,* June 11, 1971.

25. *Travel Management Daily,* September 1, 1971, Vol. III, No. 165.

26. The department made a comprehensive study of Airline Merger Policy Criteria in 1969, in which it concluded: "Study of various factors involved in the regulation and the economics of the airline industry suggest a policy of continued competition in air carrier service in all sectors of United States air transportation." (at 14).

27. *Travel Management Daily, supra* note 25.

28. CAB Order No. 3728 (Agreement No. 389) dated June 5, 1945. The order contains only two short paragraphs. It states that the approval "shall not be effective as to any

United States air carrier party thereto, and named therein, until such air carrier has accepted the Articles of Association and filed concurrence therein with the Board as required by section 251.1 of the Economic Regulations."

29. 6 CAB 639, at 646.
30. 6 CAB 639, at 644.
31. 6 CAB 639, at 654 (see dissenting).
32. 6 CAB 639, at 644.
33. 6 CAB 639, at 642, 643.
34. 6 CAB 639, at 643.
35. *Slick Airways* v. *American Airlines,* 107 F. Supp. 199 (1952); *S.S.W., Inc.* v. *Air Transport Association of America,* 191 Federal Reporter, 2nd Series, 658 (D.C. Circuit) (1951); "Extraterritorial Application of the Antitrust Laws: A Conflict of Laws Approach," 70 *Yale Law Journal* 259 (1960).
36. *American Banana* v. *United Fruit Co.,* 213 U.S. 347 (1909); *U.S.* v. *Alcoa,* 148 F. 2nd 416 (1945); *Report of the Attorney-General's National Committee to Study the Anti-Trust Laws* 66–77 (1955).
37. CAB Order 70-11-35, November 6, 1970, at 2.
38. CAB Order 70-11-35, November 6, 1970.
39. CAB Order 71-8-15, August 3, 1971, at 7.
40. For instance, the presidents of North Atlantic air carriers held a meeting in New York on May 27–28, 1971, to discuss air fares. The board was not even informed of that meeting, not to mention the availability of any documents with respect to such meeting.
41. CAB Order No. E-23130, dated January 13, 1966.
42. CAB Order 5196, dated September 24, 1946.
43. The CAB letter to air carriers, dated July 16, 1968. The documents were released for public inspection in November, 1972, as a result of petitions filed at the CAB by the Aviation Consumer Action Project.
44. The minutes of traffic conferences contain only ridiculous statements such as: "A proposal to increase the normal fares was supported by 20 carriers, opposed by 5 carriers and 12 carriers abstained."
45. The air distance between New York and London is 3,442 miles while the distance between New York and Los Angeles is 2,587 miles. If the proportional fares are fixed in proportion to the one-way normal New York–London economy fare of $226, the proportional fare for NYC–LA, in proportion to the distance, should be $167. If the fare for NYC–LON is calculated on a fare per mile basis using the $126 proportional fare for LA–NYC, then the NYC–LON fare should be $167.

46. Section 404(b) prohibits discrimination by both domestic and foreign carriers.
47. William Patterson, "The Big Picture," *ASTA Travel News,* March, 1971, at 33.
48. This assumes that the American visitors used the airlines from the New York Port.
49. Exhibit No. 4001 of the Bureau of Economics in CAB Docket No. 21866-9, dated November 20, 1970.
50. *Wide Bodied Jet: Aircraft Operating Cost and Performance Report,* Vol. 5 (prepared by the Bureau of Accounts and Statistics, CAB), July, 1971, at 1–2.
51. A Review of the Economic Situation of Air Transport, 1960–1970, ICAO Circular 105-AT/26, April, 1971, at 42.
52. The agreement, for instance, increased the New York–London economy fare by 8 percent, the seventeen to twenty-eight day excursion fare by 9 percent, the twenty-nine to forty-five day excursion fare by 12 percent, the GIT fare by 24 percent, the forty-passenger affinity group fare by 10 percent, and the eighty-passenger affinity group fare by 17 percent.
53. See CAB Order 71-3-87, dated March 16, 1971, and the justification filed by TWA on December 29, 1970.
54. *Forecast of Scheduled International Air Traffic of U.S. Flag Carriers, 1971–1980,* study by Civil Aeronautics Board, September, 1971.
55. *Survey of Current Business,* No. 58, at 23.
56. At present ATA has thirty-one "operator" members and two associate members from Canada. All the thirty-three members are scheduled carriers.
57. The varied functions of the ATA are apportioned among its ten administrative departments. However, the most important activities of the ATA are carried out through the instrumentality of four conferences—the Air Traffic Conference (ATC), the Airlines Operations Conferences (AOC), the Airlines Financial and Accounting Conference (AFAC), and the Personnel Relations Conference (PRC). The ATA also maintains five regional operation offices to parallel the regional offices of the FAA. The board of directors of the ATA retains absolute financial and functional control over the ATA complex of departments, conferences, and regional offices.
58. The Airlines, Report of the Antitrust Subcommittee of the Committee of the Judiciary of the House of Representatives, 85th Cong., 2nd Sess., at 1328 (April 5, 1957).
59. Affidavit of J. W. Rosenthal (director of Carrier Relations, Bureau of Economic Regulations) in Docket No. 10281; Letter of the CAB chairman to Stuart Tipton, dated May 1, 1945—in Appendix C of the affidavit.

60. Memo from M. Robinson to J. W. Thompson (ATA-internal) dated Feb. 18, 1948 (in Rosenthal affidavit, *supra* note 59, at appendix C).

61. Memo of R. L. Turner, ATA–VP, to S. Tipton, ATA president, dated July 19, 1957 (Rosenthal affidavit, *supra* note 59, appendix C).

62. ATA Minutes, March, 1964; December, 1965; December, 1966.

63. ATA Minutes, April, 1968.

64. Interview by Sarah Chasis, ACAP volunteer (August 1971), with J. W. Rosenthal, former director of carrier relations, Bureau of Operative Rights, CAB.

65. Air Traffic Conference Travel Agents Handbook, Section 80, Resolution 80.10, at 3.

66. See the Petition of ACAP dated July 12, 1971, filed in CAB Docket 23542 (Investigation of the bylaws of the ATC).

67. *Civil Aeronautics Board* v. *Air Transport Association of America,* 201 F. Supp. 318 (D.C. District Court) (1961).

68. 49 U.S.C. 1377.

69. CAB Order No. E-20409, dated January 29, 1964.

70. Interview by Sarah Chasis, ACAP volunteer, with W. Gilliland, vice-chairman of the CAB, dated August 19, 1971.

71. Information obtained by ACAP from the Bureau of Operating Rights, CAB.

72. Interview with H. Thomas, CAB Agreements Division, July 26–August 3, 1971.

73. Such permission is necessary under the board's practice. See, for example, Agreement Between American Airlines, et al. CAB Order No. 70-11-35, dated November 6, 1970, at 2.

74. ATA Minutes, March, 1970.

75. ATA Minutes, June, 1970.

76. ATA Minutes, October 1970. In 1966, the Revenue Accounting-Passenger Committee recommended the establishment of a base rate for the whole industry, and for each city-pair market (Minutes, November, 1966).

77. ATA Minutes, June, 1968; March, 1971; October, 1968; June, 1969.

78. Final rule ER-417 dated September 18, 1964 (ATA Minutes, November, 1964).

79. EDR 146, September 25, 1968.

80. Airline Finance and Accounting Conference, Minutes, November, 1968.

81. Airline Finance and Accounting Conference, Minutes, November, 1965.

82. Exhibit "A" of the ATA Minutes, March 26, 1971, at 5.

83. J. F. McLeod, "Washington Window," *Washington Daily News,* July, 1971, at 13.

84. The ATA report on the discussion that took place on June 13, 1969, states that the "February, 1969 fare increase of only 3.8 percent was only temporary relief therefore."

85. Statement of G. James, ATA senior vice-president, (ATA Minutes, November, 1970).

86. ATA Minutes, October, 1970.

87. Interview by Sarah Chasis with employee of the Bureau of Aviation Safety of the National Transportation Safety Board (name withheld).

88. Report of ATA Engineering and Maintenance Advisory Committee, ATA Minutes, June, 1965.

89. ATA Minutes, June, 1965.

90. ATA Minutes, December, 1965.

Chapter 7

1. Despite the duplication in not very large communities, competition among retail distributors of electric power may result in lower rates, W. J. Primeux, Jr., "A Reexamination of the Monopoly Market Structure for Electric Utilities," a paper delivered at a Brookings Conference on Antitrust and Regulated Industries, October 28–29, 1971, Washington, D.C.

2. Energy Policy Staff, *Considerations Affecting Steam Power Plant Site Selection* (1968), at viii.

3. Statement of C. R. Ross at Hearings on Competitive Aspects of the Energy Industry before the Senate Antitrust Subcommittee, 91st Cong., 2d Sess., at 340 (1970). [Hereinafter cited as *1970 Energy Hearings*]. See also Table 4 of statement of D. S. Schwartz, at 570.

4. FPC, *National Power Survey* 17 (1964); *Federal Regulation of the Electric Power Industry* 5 (FPC, 1967).

5. Address of J. A. Carver, Jr., to the Annual Conference of Municipal Electric Utilities of Wisconsin, June 10, 1971.

6. *City of Paris, Kentucky* v. *Kentucky Utility Company,* 41 FPC 45 (1969).

7. *Otter Tail Power Company* v. *United States,* 41 U.S.L.W. 4292, 4296 (S. Ct. Feb. 22, 1973).

8. D. C. Cook, "Coordination and the Small Electric Power System," *Public Utilities Fortnightly,* November 23, 1967, at 19, 24. An economist more recently has suggested twenty to thirty systems. Hughes, "Scale Frontiers in Elec-

tric Power," in W. Capron, ed., *Technological Change in Regulated Industries* (Brookings Institution, 1971).

9. *Federal Regulation of the Electric Power Industry* 5 (FPC, 1967).

10. Moore, "The Effectiveness of Regulation of Electric Utility Prices," 36 *Southern Economic Journal* 365 (1970).

11. Direct Testimony of Charles R. Ross, New England Electric System, File No. 3-1698, (SEC 1970), D.J. Exh. 68, at 6.

12. Ibid., at p. 7.

13. See Hearings on S. 607 (Utility Consumers' Counsel Act) before a Subcommittee of the Senate Committee on Government Operations, 91st Cong. 1st Sess., at 153, 764–68, 774–80 (1969); *Standard & Poor's Register of Corporations, Directors and Executives—1971.*

14. *Statistics of Privately Owned Electric Utilities in the United States 1968* (FPC, 1969).

15. Moore, *supra* note 10.

16. Main, "A Peak Load of Trouble for the Utilities," *Fortune,* November, 1969, at 200. See generally L. Metcalf and V. Reinemer, *Overcharge* (1967) on the subject of public versus private power.

17. "TVA's Influence on Electric Rates," (TVA, 1965) reprinted in Hearings on Prelicensing Antitrust Review of Nuclear Powerplants Before the Joint Committee on Atomic Energy, 91st Cong., 2d Sess., at 367–81 (1970).

18. The document is summarized in Webster, "Companies plot take-over strategy," *Public Power,* August, 1970, at 12. See generally Utility Consumers' Counsel Act Hearings, *supra* note 13.

19. *Washington Post,* September 21, 1970, at A-2; *Providence Journal,* October 28, 1967.

20. Direct Testimony of J. R. Nelson, American Electric Power Company, File No. 3-1476 (SEC, 1971), at 18–21.

21. Even Cook *verbally* agrees with this principle. He has said: "The benefits of competition cannot be stressed too much." *Supra* note 8, at 24.

22. Testimony of S. D. Freeman, *1970 Energy Hearings,* at 107–10, 115–18. Others who have proposed separate "G&T" companies include Miller, "A Needed Reform of the Organization and Regulation of the Interstate Electric Power Industry," 38 *Fordham Law Review* 635 (1970), and *A Study of the Electric Power Situation in New England 1970–1990* (New England Regional Commission 1970) [hereinafter cited as *The Zinder Report*].

23. *1970 Energy Hearings,* at 117.

24. Statement of D. S. Schwartz, *1970 Energy Hearings, supra* note 3, at 552.

25. See L. W. Weiss's excellent paper for the Brookings Conference (*supra* note 1), "An Evaluation of Antitrust in the Electric Power Industry," for more detailed discussion of this problem as well as others raised generally throughout this chapter.
26. Statement of D. S. Schwartz, *1970 Energy Hearings, supra* note 3, at 552.
27. FPC Order No. 383-2, 35 Fed. Reg. 6121 (April 15, 1970), 45 FPC 515 (1970).
28. Hearings on Federal Power Commission Oversight Before a Subcommittee of the Senate Commerce Committee, 91st Cong., 2d Sess., at 65 (1970).
29. *Gainesville Utilities Dept.* v. *Florida Power Corp.,* 402 U.S. 505 (1971).
30. Opinion No. 590, Iowa Power and Light Co., 44 FPC 1640, 1645 (1970).
31. Statement of J. N. Nassikas, Hearings on S. 403 (Combination Gas-Electric Utilities) before the Senate Antitrust Subcommittee, 92d Cong., 1st Sess., May 13, 1971.
32. F. Cook, "Comparative Price Economies of Combination Utilities," *Public Utilities Fortnightly,* January 19, 1967, at 31; W. A. Collins, "The Social Desirability of Combination Gas-Electric Utilities," Hearings on S. 403, *supra* note 31, at 191; statement of J. D. Pace, *ibid.,* at 238, 247.
33. *California* v. *FPC,* 369 U.S. 482, 484 (1962); *United States* v. *El Paso Natural Gas Company,* 376 U.S. 651 (1964).
34. *Northern Natural Gas Company* v. *FPC,* 399 F.2d 953, 958, 967–68, 970, 971 (D.C. Cir. 1968).
35. Opinion No. 580, Great Lakes Gas Transmission Company, No. CP66-110 (FPC July 10, 1970).
36. Hearings on S. 3136 (Antitrust Review Amendment to the Federal Power Act) before the Senate Commerce Committee, 89th Cong., 2d Sess., at 58, 62, 71 (1966).
37. Letter from R. W. McLaren, assistant attorney general for Antitrust, to B. H. Schur, associate general counsel, AEC, regarding Consumers Power Company, dated June 28, 1971, at 5.
38. Western Massachusetts Electric Co., 39 FPC (1968), *aff'd sub nom. Municipal Electric Ass'n. of Mass.* v. *FPC,* 414 F.2d 1206 (D.C. Cir. 1969).
39. *Municipal Electric Ass'n of Mass.* v. *SEC.* 413 F.2d 1052 (D.C. Cir. 1969); *City of Statesville* v. *AEC,* No. 21,706 (D.C. Cir. December 5, 1969).
40. *The Zinder Report, supra* note 22, at 81 (footnotes omitted).
41. *City of Lafayette, La.* v. *S.E.C.,* 454 F. 2nd 941, 953 (D.C. Cir. 1971), *cert. granted. Gulf States Utilities* v. *F.P.C.,* 406 U.S. 956 (1972).

42. Documents relating to Holyoke Water Power Co. are reprinted in *1970 Energy Hearings, supra* note 3, at 438–440, 469–471.

43. Testimony of A. N. Gordon (Tr. pp. 5706–5979) and William C. Tallman (Tr. pp. 5347–5699), New England Electric System, File No. 3-1698 (SEC, 1970). See *1970 Energy Hearings,* at 440–444.

44. Applicant's Brief, New England Electric System, File No. 3-1698, (SEC, January 29, 1971), at 75–76; *Moody's Public Utilities Manual 1970* (for assets data).

45. "The 500 Largest Utilities," *Fortune,* May 1972, at 220.

46. Direct testimony of C. R. Ross, American Electric Power Company, File No. 3-1476 (SEC, 1971), at 30–31.

47. *Electrical World Week,* November 30, 1970.

48. Testimony of W. S. Renchard (Tr. pp. 16,441–97), American Electric Power Co., File No. 3-1476 (SEC, 1971).

49. Transcript p. 12533, American Electric Power Co., File No. 3-1476 (SEC, 1970).

50. American Gas and Electric Co., 22 SEC 808, 817–18 (1946).

51. *SEC* v. *New England Electric System,* 384 U.S. 176 (1966) (combination utilities); Michigan Consolidated Gas Co., SEC Holding Company Act Release No. 16763 (June 22, 1970) (housing).

Chapter 8

1. Military Prime Contract Awards and Subcontract Payments of Commitments, July–December 1970, Office of the Secretary of Defense at 39 (Figures on a volume basis). "Historically it has been shown that prices obtained through competitive means are approximately 25 percent lower than those obtained on a sole source basis." Subcommittee for Special Investigations, House Armed Services Committee, "Review of Army Procurement of Light Observation Helicopters," 90th Cong., 1st Sess. (Comm. Print 1967) (Quoting from an Army Cost Evaluation Report). Secretary of Defense Robert McNamara has testified to the same effect. See note 41, *infra.*

2. 100 Companies Receiving the Largest Dollar Volume of Prime Contract Awards, Fiscal Year 1971, Office of the Secretary of Defense, Directorate for Information Operations, October 29, 1971.

3. Subcommittee on Economy in Government, Joint Economic Committee, "The Economics of Military Procurement," 91st Cong., 1st Sess., at 4 (Comm. Print 1969) [hereinafter cited as Comm. Print 1969].

4. Source of NASA statistics is a letter from H. Pryor, Chief,

Staff Operations Division, Procurement Office, NASA, to the Study Group, December 23, 1970. For later AEC figures see United States Atomic Energy Financial Reports for 1969 and 1970 at 43 and 47 respectively.

5. Subcommittee on Antitrust and Monopoly, Senate Judiciary Committee, Hearings on Competition in Defense Procurement, 90th Cong., 2d Sess., at 21 (1968) [hereinafter cited as Antitrust Procurement Hearings].

6. Military Prime Contract Awards and Subcontract Payments of Commitments, July–December 1970, Office of the Secretary of Defense, at 28; *see also,* J. Peck and F. M. Scherer, *The Weapons Acquisition Process: An Economic Analysis,* (Division of Research, Graduate School of Business Administration, Harvard University, Boston, 1962).

7. I. J. Masse, *The Effects of Government Research and Development on the U.S. Economy,* dissertation, State University of New York at Buffalo, 1969.

8. "In fiscal year 1968, 886 large prime contractors awarded subcontracts worth $15.2 billion. Of this sum, $6.5 billion went to small business. . . ." Comm. Print 1969, *supra* note 3, at 7–8.

9. W. Adams and H. Gray, *Monopoly in America* 104 (1955).

10. For this and other examples, see Government Operations, Senate Report No. 970, "Pyramiding of Profits and Costs in the Missile Procurement Program," 89th Cong., 2d Sess., (1964).

11. Levine, "Pentagon Slows Payments to Defense Firms, Will Force Them to Seek Private Financing," *Wall Street Journal,* August 16, 1971, at 24.

12. Ibid., at 4.

13. "The Biggest Racket," *The Nation,* April 12, 1971, at 453.

14. Speech of A. E. Fitzgerald before the Smaller Business Association of New England Breakfast Club, Lexington, Massachusetts, March 18, 1970.

15. Comm. Print 1969, *supra* note 3, at 15.

16. "Should-cost is the new weapons test," *Business Week,* May 30, 1970, at 48.

17. R. A. Stubbing, "Improving the Acquisition Process for High Risk Military Electronics Systems," *Congressional Record,* February 7, 1969, at 1450.

18. Kaufman, *The War Profiteers* 53 (1970).

19. House Committee on Ways and Means, "Hearings on the Extension of the Renegotiation Act," 90th Cong., 2nd Sess., at 36 (1968).

20. Subcommittee of the House Committee on Government Operations, "The Efficiency and Effectiveness of Renegotiation Board Operations, Part I," 91st Cong., 1st Sess., at 61–3 (1969).

21. Ibid., at 81.
22. Antitrust Procurement Hearings, *supra* note 5, at 22.
23. Based on return on net worth for the period of 1957–64. I. N. Fisher and G. R. Hall, "Risk and the Aerospace Rate of Return," Rand Corporation RM 5440, 1967, at 6. And this remains true after adjusting for the amount of risk; *see* Fisher and Hall, "Risk and Corporate Rates of Return," LXXXIII *The Quarterly Journal of Economics,* February, 1969, at 79.
24. 63 Stat. 391 (1949), *as amended,* 40 U.S.C. §488 (1958).
25. See Adams and Gray, *supra* note 9, at 121.
26. "Two Myths About Defense Procurement," from office of Assistant Secretary of Defense (Installations and Logistics), June 14, 1968.
27. L. Rodberg and D. Shearer, eds., *The Pentagon Watchers* 230 (1970).
28. In this section, we are indebted to D. E. Sims, a graduate student at the Harvard School of Design, for allowing us access to his notes from several interviews conducted with officials of large defense contractors, as well as Pentagon officials in the summer of 1969. He is one of the coauthors of *The Pentagon Watchers, supra* note 27.
29. *Washington Post,* December 8, 1968, A-1.
30. Reply of F. M. Scherer to mailed questions of the Senate Subcommittee on Antitrust, July 2, 1968, Antitrust Procurement Hearings at 134.
31. Jack Anderson, "The Washington Merry-Go-Round," *Washington Post,* August 1, 1970, at C-11.
32. *The Pentagon Watchers, supra* note 27, at 245.
33. *Congressional Quarterly,* May 24, 1969, at 1160.
34. *Congressional Record,* March 24, 1969, S3072–81.
35. *The Pentagon Watchers, supra* note 27, at 256.
36. See Subcommittee No. 5, House Committee on the Judiciary, Report on Consent Decree Program of the Department of Justice, 86th Cong., 1st Sess., at 43–59 (1959).
37. B. Nossiter, "GAO Walks a Fine Line with Hill Factions," *Washington Post,* March 28, 1971, at B-1.
38. Unless indicated otherwise, the source of information and quotations in the M-16 section is Special Subcommittee on the M-16 Rifle Program, House Armed Services Committee, 90th Cong., 2d Sess., at 10975–11072 (1968). See also Special M-16 Rifle Subcommittee, Senate Armed Services Committee, 90th Cong., 2d Sess. (1968).
39. "Army Contracts for M-16 Rifles," *New York Times,* April 20, 1968, at 5. "Army is Paying Premium Prices for Rush Order of M-16 Rifles," *New York Times,* May 1, 1968, at 6.
40. As a direct result of the M-16 incident, the governing

statute, 10 U.S.C. 2304(9), has been amended to require the government to take price into consideration on negotiated contracts.

41. Subcommittee on Federal Procurement and Regulation, Joint Economic Committee, "Hearings on Economic Impact of Federal Procurement," 89th Cong., 1st Sess., at 12–14 (1965), and Subcommittee on Federal Procurement and Regulation, Joint Economic Committee, "Background Material on Economic Impact of Federal Procurements," 89th Cong., 2d Sess. (1966).

42. Antitrust Procurement Hearings at 22–23.

43. Adams and Gray, *supra* note 9, at 116.

44. Galbraith, "The Big Defense Firms are Really Public Firms and Should Be Nationalized," *New York Times Magazine,* November 16, 1969, at 50.

45. See F. Scherer, *Industrial Market Structure and Economic Performance* 418–422 (1970), and the articles cited therein.

Chapter 9

1. *Prescription Drug Data Summary,* Office of Research and Statistics, Social Security Administration, HEW, 1972.

2. Hearings on Administered Prices in the Drug Industry before the Senate Antitrust and Monopoly Subcommittee of the Judiciary Committee (1959–1961) (hereinafter the Kefauver Hearings). See also E. Kefauver, *In a Few Hands —Monopoly Power in America* chapter 1 (1965), and R. Harris, *The Real Voice* (1964).

3. Subcommittee on Monopoly of the Senate Select Committee on Small Business, *Competitive Problems in the Drug Industry,* Part 20, 8009 (1971) [hereinafter the Nelson Hearings].

4. Kefauver Hearings, *supra* note 2, Part 21, at 11566.

5. Report of the Subcommittee on Antitrust and Monopoly of the Committee on the Judiciary, U.S. Senate, *Administered Prices—Drugs* at 93 (1961).

6. Ibid., at 94.

7. Nelson Hearings, *supra* note 3, Part 20, at 8009.

8. *Ibid.,* at 8020.

9. The acquisition trend was illustrated in the course of the Nelson Hearings. (Part 18, at 7569–70). At the time that Rear Admiral H. S. Etter appeared on behalf of the military, he was asked specifically what small firms had successfully secured drug contracts. The question was referred to a subordinate who answered promptly, "The Endo Laboratory, Knoll Associates, the Strong, Cobb Arner Laboratories, Day-Baldwin—these have all been successful suppliers in the small business category, sir." However,

Colonel A. J. Snyder, chief of the Medical Procurement Division, hurriedly intervened:

> I would like to add, though, that each of those has been acquired by large business in the last 2 years. This is one of our great difficulties. . . . We are still buying, generally speaking, from these very successful small firms, but they have in the main been acquired by one of the conglomerates or one of the larger holding companies.

10. See M. Mintz, *The Therapeutic Nightmare* (1965) (*By Prescription Only,* paperback ed.); R. Burack, *The New Handbook of Prescription Drugs* (1970).

11. *Prescription Drug Data Summary,* Office of Research and Statistics, Social Security Administration, HEW, at 15, 1971.

12. Nelson Hearings, *supra* note 3, Part 18, at 7471.

13. Nelson Hearings, *supra* note 3, Part 18, at 7429.

14. The VA attempts to persuade physicians to accept "generically equivalent products" through use of standard prescription forms. If he places a check in the box indicating objection, the brand name preferred is purchased.

15. Ibid., at 7452.

16. Ibid., p. 7457.

17. Ibid., Part 20, at 8181.

18. HEW Task Force on Prescription Drugs, *Approaches to Drug Insurance Design* 21 (1961).

19. Nelson Hearings, Part 18, at 7680.

20. Ibid., Part 20, at 8107.

21. 41 U.S.C. 252.

22. Nelson Hearings, Part 20, at 8185.

23. VA contract provision relating to "Certificate of Established Catalog or Market Price."

24. For an interesting comparison of European and U.S. prices, see *Domestic and Foreign Prescription Drug Prices, 1970* in HEW Social Security Bulletin, May, 1971, at 16 ff. This shows, for example, that Lilly's price to druggists for Darvon (65 mg., one hundred tablets) was $7.02 in the U.S. Its prices in other countries to druggists were: Australia, $2.73; Brazil, $3.72; Canada, $5.29; Ireland, $1.66; Italy, $7.86; New Zealand, $2.08; Sweden, $3.33; U.K., $1.92.

26. Nelson Hearings, *supra* note 3, Part 18, at 7446.

27. Nelson Hearings, *supra* note 3, Part 20, at 8007.

28. Kefauver Hearings, *supra* note 2, Part 24, at 13791 ff.

29. *Defense Procurement of Foreign-Made Drugs,* Military Operations Subcommittee Staff Memorandum of the House Committee on Government Operations, at 1 (1962).

30. Personal interviews within the industry, conducted on condition that the interviewees remain anonymous.

31. In 1965 Colonel Jesse N. Butler of DPSC addressed the Medical Seminar of the Defense Supply Association. He stated:

> For the past several years a fine group of dedicated pharmacists, chemists and engineers within our medical directorate have valiantly fought to ensure the procurement of quality medical materiel. At times it appeared they were rowing against the current. Competition seemed to outweigh quality. Price seemed to be paramount. Medical care appeared to be secondary. For the past three or four years, the situation has changed. The importance of quality medical materiel has been recognized.

(*The Review,* published by Defense Supply Association, January–February, 1966, at 31.)
32. For full list see Nelson Hearings, *supra* note 3, Part 18, at 7652 and 7670.
33. Nelson Hearings, *supra* note 3, Part 18, at 7550.
34. Nelson Committee files.
35. Nelson Hearings, *supra* note 3, Part 18, at 7471.
36. Ibid., Part 20, at 8227.
37. Ibid., at 7991.
38. Ibid., Part 18, at 7582.
39. Ibid., Part 20, p. 8226.
40. 41 U.S.C. 10d.
41. Executive Order No. 10582, December 17, 1964, 19 Federal Register 8723, amended by Executive Order No. 11051, September 27, 1962, 27 F.R. 9683.

Chapter 10

1. U.S. Constitution, Art. I, Sec. 8.
2. See also *Deep South Packing Co.* v. *Laitram Corp.,* 92 S.Ct. 1700 (1972).
3. See *Graham* v. *John Deere Co.,* 383 U.S. 1 (1966).
4. Kingsland, "The U.S. Patent Office," 13 *Law and Contemporary Problems* 354 (1948).
5. W. Hamilton, *Patents and Free Enterprise,* Temporary National Economic Committee, Monograph 31 (1941) at 25.
6. Jefferson, *Works* (Liscomb ed.) Vol. XIII at 380.
7. Jefferson also soon became aware of another problem involved in the grant of patents. After he invented a hemp break, he wrote to a friend, "Something of this kind has been so long wanted by cultivators of hemp, that as soon as I can speak of its effect with certainty, I shall probably describe it anonymously in the public papers, in order to forestall the prevention of its use by some interloping patentee."

8. For a recent example see M. Lehman, *This High Man, The Life of Robert H. Goddard* (1963).

9. Hearings of Subcommittee on Antitrust and Monopoly, Senate Committee on the Judiciary, *Concentration, Invention, and Innovation* (1965) Part 3 at 1243.

10. U.S. Commissioner of Patents, *Annual Report,* Fiscal 1971 at 18; Federico, "Patent Interferences in the U.S. Patent Office," 2 *International Review of Industrial Property and Copyright Law* 25 (1971).

11. See *Atlantic Works* v. *Brady,* 107 U.S. 192 (1883).

12. *The Telephone Cases,* 126 U.S. 1 (1887).

13. Hamilton, *supra* note 5, at 88.

14. W. Greenleaf, *Monopoly on Wheels* 49 (1961).

15. Ibid., at 50.

16. They were Olds, Autocar, Pierce, Packard, Apperson Brothers, Searchmont, Knox, Locomobile, Haynes-Apperson, and Peerless. Ibid., at 97.

17. *Electric Vehicle Co.* v. *Duerr,* 172 F. 923 (1909); *Columbia Motor Car Co.* v. *Duerr,* 184 F. 893 (1911).

18. *Administered Prices—Automobiles,* Report of Subcommittee on Antitrust and Monopoly, Senate Committee on Judiciary, 1958, at 4.

19. The rise has been spectacular. For fiscal 1950 federal funds for R&D were $1.0 billion; they rose to $8.0 billion in 1960 and to $15.7 billion in 1970. For 1972 estimated federal expenditures amount to $16.3 billion. See National Science Foundation, *Federal Funds for Research, Development and other Scientific Activities, Fiscal Years 1970, 1971, 1972* NSF 71–35 (1971) at 3.

20. National Science Foundation, *Research and Development in Industry, 1969,* NSF 71–18 (1971) at 3.

21. Office of the Secretary of Defense, *500 Contractors Receiving the Largest Dollar Volume of Military Prime Contract Awards for Research, Development, Test and Evaluation Work,* issued annually.

22. *Patent Practices of the Department of Defense,* Preliminary Report of the Subcommittee on Patents, Trademarks and Copyrights of the Senate Committee on the Judiciary (1961).

23. Hearings of Subcommittee on Monopoly of Senate Select Committee on Small Business, *Economic Aspects of Government Patent Policies* (1963) at 47.

24. *Federal Funds for Research, Development and other Scientific Activities, supra* note 19, at 23.

25. This view stemmed from an opinion in 1924 of Attorney General H. F. Stone (later chief justice of the U.S. Supreme Court), 34 Opinions of Attorney General 320.

26. Hearings of Subcommittee on Monopoly of Senate Select

Committee on Small Business, *Patent Policies of Departments and Agencies of the Federal Government* (1959) at 347. See also this subcommittee's hearings, *Government Patent Policies in Meterology and Weather Modification* (1962) at 147.

27. See, for example, Coal Research Act of July 7, 1960, 30 U.S.C. 666 (1964); Helium Act Amendments of September 13, 1960, 50 U.S.C. 167b (1964); Saline Water Conversion Act of September 22, 1961, 42 U.S.C. 1954b (1964); Water Resources Research Act of July 17, 1964, 42 U.S.C. 1961c–3 (1964); Appalachian Regional Development Act of March 9, 1965, 40 App. U.S.C. 302e (1964 Supp. V); Solid Waste Disposal Act of October 20, 1965, 42 U.S.C. 3253c (1964 Supp. V).

28. See text in *Annual Report on Government Patent Policy, Combined Dec. 1969 and Dec. 1970,* Federal Council for Science and Technology (1971) at 10 (or Federal Register, October 12, 1963, at 10942).

29. One of its first acts was to contract out to Harbridge House, a market research firm in Boston, the task of studying government patent policy and making recommendations. The report was written in the peculiar jargon affected by many market research firms and was virtually unintelligible. The "Explanatory Comments" accompanying the Nixon policy memorandum state, "The Federal Council *believed* that the results of the Harbridge House Study demonstrate that, under certain circumstances, this type of invention will not be used commercially, and will, therefore, be unavailable to the public, unless some form of exclusivity can be granted." Ibid., at 155. However, the report was submitted in May, 1968, a year after policy had already been determined upon within FCST.

30. *Annual Report on Government Patent Policy, supra* note 28 at 148.

31. Section 2 provides: "Under regulations prescribed by the Administrator of General Services, Government-owned patents shall be made available and the technological advances covered thereby brought into being in the shortest time possible through dedication of licensing, either exclusive or non-exclusive, and shall be listed in official Government publications or otherwise."

32. *Federal Register,* October 7, 1969, at 15560.

33. Ibid., May 26, 1970, at 8246.

34. *Research and Development in Industry, 1969, supra* note 20, at 1 and 6.

35. J. Jewkes, D. Sawyers, R. Stillerman, *The Sources of Invention* (1958, revised ed. 1969).

36. Hearings, *Concentration, Invention, and Innovation, supra* note 9, at 1281.
37. Ibid., at 1208.
38. J. M. Blair, *Economic Concentration* 213 (1972).
39. V. Abramson, *The Patent System: Its Economic and Social Basis,* Subcommittee on Patents, Trademarks, Copyrights of Senate Committee on Judiciary, Study No. 26 (1960) at 7.
40. Quoted in Blair, *supra* note 38, at 233.
41. Hearings, *Concentration, Invention, Innovation, supra* note 9, at 1247.
42. *Conference on Federal Patent Policies* of Senator R. Long with Vice Admiral H. G. Rickover, Senate Monopoly Committee Print (1960) at 4.
43. W. Hamilton, *The Politics of Industry* 76 (Vintage ed., 1967).
44. *Statistical Abstract of the U.S.* (1971), Dept of Commerce at 518.
45. *Distribution of Patents Issued to Corporations, 1939–1955, supra* note 39 at 10, Study No. 31 (1957).
46. 35 U.S.C. 101 provides: "Whoever invents or discovers any new and useful process, machine, manufacture or composition of matter, or any new and useful improvement thereof, may obtain a patent. . . ."
47. *Ibid.,* par. 103 of chapter 10 re Conditions for Patentability; Non-Obvious Subject Matter.
48. The courts have been less lenient in this regard. See *Brenner* v. *Manson* 383 U.S. 519 (1965); *In re July and Warrant,* 376 F.2d 906 (1967); *In re Kirk and Petrow,* 376 F.2d 936 (1967).
49. U.S. Commissioner of Patents, Annual Report, Fiscal 1971 at 2.
50. Ibid., Fiscal 1970, at 2.
51. Ibid., Fiscal 1971, at 13.
52. U.S. Patent Office, *General Information Concerning Patents* 21 (1972).
53. V. Bush, *Proposals for Improving the Patent System, supra* note 39, Study No. 1 (1957) at 15. See also F. Machlup, *An Economic Review of the Patent System,* Study No. 15 (1958).
54. Hearing of the Subcommittee on Nominations of the Senate Committee on the Judiciary, May 2, 1969, Vol. 1, Ward & Paul Transcript at 12.
55. *Hatch* v. *Ooms,* 69 F. Supp. 788 (1947).
56. W. Hamilton, *supra* note 43, at 78.
57. See also *Inventors and the Patent System* (Gilfillan Report), Joint Economic Committee (1964).
58. *Supra* note 45.

59. *Administered Prices—Drugs,* Report of the Senate Antitrust and Monopoly Subcommittee (1961) at 143.

60. Ibid., at 114.

61. *Memorandum of Law by Department of Justice, May 11, 1967* in Hearings before the Subcommittee on Patents, Trademarks, and Copyrights of Senate Committee on the Judiciary on S.643, S.1253 and S.1255 (1971), at 483.

62. *Hazeltine Research, Inc.* v. *Zenith Corp.,* 395 U.S. 100 (1969).

63. *U.S.* v. *United Machinery Corp.,* 110 F. Supp. 295 (1953); *La Peyre* v. *FTC,* 306 F.2d 117 (1966).

64. Files of Senate Antitrust and Monopoly Subcommittee. Par. 5 of Art. 5 of the licenses to Eli Lilly, Merck and Squibb states:

> At the request of the Licensee this agreement may be continued as to any of the letters patent of the U.S. of America beyond its normal expiry date for such period as may be agreed by the parties and also at the request of the Licensee this agreement may be extended to apply to any letters patent of the U.S. of America relating to insulin not made from insulin crystals expired at the date of this agreement for such period as may be agreed by the parties.

Rates of royalty are then specified.

65. *Lear, Inc.* v. *Atkins,* 395 U.S. 653 (1969).

66. W. Hamilton, *supra* note 43, at 120.

67. For text of patent licensing agreements, see Appendixes to Hearings, *Administered Prices in the Drug Industry,* by Subcommittee on Antitrust and Monopoly of Senate Committee on Judiciary, 1959–1961.

68. *U.S.* v. *Bristol-Myers,* Civil No. 822–70 (D. C.C. filed 3/19/70); *U.S.* v. *Fisons, Ltd.,* Civil No. 69 C 1530 (N.D. Ill. filed 7/23/69); *U.S.* v. *Ciba Corp.,* Civil No. 791–69 D.N.J. filed 7/39/69); *U.S.* v. *Ciba Corp. and C.P.C. International,* Civil No. 792–69 (D.N.J. filed 7/9/69); *U.S.* v. *Glaxo Group Ltd.,* Civil No. 558–68 (D.D. C. filed 3/4/68).

69. Report of the Senate Subcommittee on Patents, Trademarks, and Copyrights, June 29, 1972, at 9.

70. Association for Advancement of Invention and Innovation, headed by E. J. Brenner, U.S. commissioner of patents, 1964–69 and Intellectual Property Owners, headed by W. Schuyler, U.S. commissioner of patents, 1969–71.

71. The patent on promazine (Sparine) contains a claim for "a therapeutic composition in dosage form useful in excitatory and agitated conditions . . . in an amount between about 10 to 200 milligrams, said salt being com-

bined with a carrier." A claim in the tolbutamide patent (Orinase) is for "orally administering an effective amount" of a known compound.

72. *U.S.* v. *American Bell Telephone Co.,* 128 U.S. 315 (1888); *Hazel Atlas Glass Co.* v. *Hartford Empire Co.,* 322 U.S. 238 (1943).

73. *Chas. Pfizer* v. *FTC,* 401 F.2d 574 (1968).

74. *U.S.* v. *Chas. Pfizer & Co. et al.,* Civil No. 1966–69 (1969) filed jointly by R. W. McLaren, head of the Antitrust Division, and W. D. Ruckelstraus, head of the Civil Division.

75. Transcript of Coordinated Pretrial Proceedings in Antibiotic Antitrust Actions, 4–71 Civ. 433, St. Paul, Minn., September 8, 1971.

76. *Conference on Federal Patent Policies, supra* note 42, at 4. He added, "One of the reasons the Russians have been able to make rapid progress is because they disseminate technical information faster than we. They probably lead the world in the thorough and rapid dissemination of scientific and engineering information."

Chapter 11

1. *Memo from COPE,* Feb. 14, 1972, at 3.

2. Even if the present trend toward high productivity, capital-intensive U.S. exports continues, our exports will generate higher wages than import-competing industries, such as textiles, footwear, and steel. F. Bergsten, *The Cost of Import Restrictions to American Consumers* (1972) (pamphlet published by the American Importers Association), at 5–6.

3. J. C. Renner, "The Employment Effects of the Quota Provisions of the Burke-Hartke Bill," remarks before the Columbia Society of International Law, April 28, 1972, at 2. Renner notes that his estimates are excessively conservative, partially by deliberate choice and partially because of data limitations.

4. A. F. Brimmer, "Imports and Economic Welfare in the United States," remarks before the Foreign Policy Association, N.Y., Feb. 16, 1972, at 16–17.

5. L. Krause, *Congressional Record,* Dec. 14, 1971, at E-13394. Krause concluded that if unemployment had increased only because of trade dislocations, the unemployment rate would have risen from 4.16 percent in the first quarter of 1970 to 4.18 percent in the first quarter of 1971, rather than to the actual 5.93 percent.

6. P. A. Samuelson, "Freud Fear and Foreign Trade," *New York Times,* July 30, 1972, at Section 3. Samuelson notes the political obstacles to the United States' becoming a

headquarters economy and observes that after we have moved our resources from manufacturing, it might turn out that nationalism "impairs the successful collecting of the fruits of our foreign investments."

7. J. C. Renner, "National Restrictions on International Trade," remarks at the Foreign Policy Conference sponsored by the Dayton Council on World Affairs, January 30, 1971, revised July, 1972.

8. Green et al., *The Closed Enterprise System* 229 (1972).

9. J. M. Blair, *Economic Concentration* 632 (1972).

10. "The Case Against Oil and Steel Import Quotas," *Consumer Reports,* Aug., 1972, at 529.

11. Blair, *supra* note 9. Blair cites *Iron Age,* April 25, 1963.

12. N. S. Fieleke, "The Cost of Tariffs to Consumers," *New England Economic Review,* Sept.–Oct. 1971, at 13–18.

13. R. E. Baldwin, "Nontariff Distortions of International Trade," in *United States International Economic Policy in an Interdependent World,* papers submitted to the (Williams) Commission on International Trade and Investment Policy, July, 1971, Vol. 1, at 644.

14. *The United States Sugar Program,* House Agriculture Committee Print, 91st Cong., 2d Sess., Dec. 31, 1970, at 45.

15. See Baldwin, *supra* note 13; Bergsten, *supra* note 2; and Brimmer, *supra* note 4.

16. S. Rich, "Sugar Act: Grower Prop or Consumer Swindle?" *Washington Post,* May 30, 1971, at A-1, A-4.

17. Testimony of R. A. Frank, on behalf of The Consumers Association of the District of Columbia, before the Committee on Agriculture, House of Representatives, 92d Cong., 1st Sess., Extension of the Sugar Act, at 684, quoting Congressman Findley.

18. G. W. Ball, *The Discipline of Power* 13 (1968).

19. *Consumer Reports, supra* note 10.

20. M. Mintz, "U.S. Defends Voluntary Steel Quotas," *Washington Post,* Oct. 1, 1972, at F-1.

21. Blair, *supra* note 9, at 233.

22. W. Adams, *The Structure of American Industry* 105 (1971).

23. *Report to the President on the Economic Position of the Steel Industry,* July 6, 1971.

24. A U.S. Tariff Commission Study found that in 1969–70 over 90 percent of aggregate imports of fresh, chilled, or frozen beef and veal were used in the manufacture of prepared products such as hamburger, sausage, and other food products. Only about 8 percent of the imports, on the other hand, were used to make table cuts such as steaks, chops, and roasts. "Uses of Imported Beef," U.S. Tariff Comm., Press Release, June 28, 1972.

25. Testimony of W. H. Hannon, chairman, Washington Affairs Committee, Bicycle Manufacturers Association of America, before the Committee on Ways and Means, House of Representatives, 91st Cong., 2d Sess., *Tariff and Trade Proposals,* at 3853.
26. M. Bender, "Bicycle Business Is Booming," *New York Times,* Aug. 15, 1971, Section 3 at 1.
27. The following discussion is based on J. Duscha, "The Ways and Means to Power," *Washington Post,* Sept. 12, 1971, at B-1.
28. Bergsten, *supra* note 2, at 3.
29. *The Oil Import Question,* A Report on the Relationship of Oil Imports to the National Security, Cabinet Task Force on Oil Import Control, Feb., 1970, 26–27.
30. *Ibid.,* at 128.
31. Testimony of B. J. Shillito, assistant secretary of defense, before House Committee on Interior and Insular Affairs, 91st Cong., 2d Sess., at 4–5.
32. Task Force Report, *supra* note 29, at 75.
33. H. S. Houthakker, "Free Markets Are More Needed Than Ever," remarks at a seminar conducted by the New York Coffee and Sugar Exchange, Inc., Washington, D.C., Oct. 28, 1971, at 5.
34. S. D. Metzger, "The Escape Clause and Adjustment Assistance: Proposals and Assessments," 2 *Law and Policy in International Business* 352, 354 (1970).
35. P. A. Samuelson, *Economics* 677 (7th ed. 1967).
36. *Ibid.,* at 671.
37. Bergsten, *supra* note 2, at 3, 10.
38. N. I. Stone, *One Man's Crusade for an Honest Tariff* 109 (1952).
39. *Highlights of Exports and Imports,* U.S. Department of Commerce, Dec., 1971, at 85.
40. See S. D. Metzger, "New Roles for the U.S. Tariff Commission," 1 *Law and Policy in International Business* 1 (1969).
41. Unpublished Labor Department study; Hearings Before the Subcommittee on Foreign Economic Policy of the House Committee on Foreign Affairs, 92d Cong., 2d Sess., at 252.
42. "The Antidumping Act—Tariff or Antitrust Law?," 74 *Yale L. J.* 707 (1965).
43. Metzger, *supra* note 40, at 5.
44. Brief for Plaintiff at 5, *Florida Tomato Marketing Order,* Docket A 265A3.
45. *Ibid.,* at 7.
46. *Ibid.,* at 8, 13.
47. *Ibid.,* at 9–10.

48. Regulations and Purchasing Review Board, *Progress Report,* Feb. 1, 1972, at 9.
49. PRD 71–1, *Customs Bulletin and Decisions,* Vol. 5, No. 17, April 28, 1971. This was the first decision under the new law providing for review within the Customs Bureau.
50. Statement on *United States Non-Tariff Barriers to Trade,* in connection with U.S. Tariff Comm. Investigation No. 332–66, March, 1972, American Importers Association, at 25.
51. H. S. Houthakker, "Competition Versus Controls," testimony before the Subcommittee on Antitrust and Monopoly of the Senate Committee on the Judiciary, Jan. 21, 1972, at 2.
52. The $20 billion figure includes the cost of tariffs ($10 billion in direct and indirect costs), sugar quotas ($500 million), voluntary steel restraints ($1 billion), meat import restrictions ($350 million), textile agreements ($1 billion), and the Oil Import Program ($5.9 billion), and a minimum estimate of $1 billion for unilateral restrictions, administrative actions, marketing orders, and trade restrictions not mentioned in this chapter (e.g., "Buy American" programs and in-state preference laws). Savings due to the present suspension of meat import quotas and liberalization of the Oil Import Program have not been subtracted from the total.

INDEX

ABC, 50; and ITT, 43–46;
    programs on, 52
Abramson, Victor, 299–300
Adams, Sherman, 333
Adams, Walter, 5, 231, 253
adjustment assistance, 340
Administrative Procedure
    Act, 12
advertiser financing of the
    mass media, 356n.73–357
AEP, *see* American Electric
    Power
AFL-CIO's Committee on
    Political Education (COPE),
    320–321
air fares, domestic, 160–162;
    international, 166–179
airline industry, stagnation of,
    189
airline mergers, *see under*
    mergers
Air Traffic Conference (ATC),
    182–183
Air Transport Association
    of America (ATA), 56, 57;
    anticompetitive actions of,
    180–183; and antitrust con-
    siderations, 185–186; investiga-
    tion of, 183–184; public rela-
    tions programs of, 187–188
Alcoa, 239–240
Alexander Commission of
    1914, 121
AMA Journal, 269; *see also
    Journal of the American
    Medical Association*
American Electric Power
    (AEP), 219–223
American Medical Association
    (AMA). 259, 260
American Newspaper
    Publishers Association
    (ANPA), 41
American Pharmaceutical

Association, 261
American Selling Price (ASP),
    283
American Telephone and
    Telegraph Company
    (AT&T), and antitrust
    considerations, 74–75;
    competition with, 90–91;
    divestiture suits against,
    91–94; as a monopoly,
    74–75, 78, 90–91; overcharge
    on equipment by, 86–87;
    patents secured by, 302;
    and Phase I, 79–81;
    and Phase II, 80, 81;
    profits of 75–76; rate base of,
    76–84; regulation of, 74–75,
    81–83, 94–99; tariffs of, 54;
    laggard technology of, 84–86,
    87–88; and television, 87–90;
    and Western Electric, 77, 78,
    90, 91–93; *see also* Bell
    System
American-Western Airlines
    merger case, 165, 166
Anderson, Jack, 153, 221, 244
antidumping laws, 340
antisubstitution laws, 260–261
Antitrust Division, 26, 40;
    and cable television, 66;
    and the Department of
    Defense, 238–242; and the
    electric power industry, 211–
    216; and ITT, 43–46; and
    mergers, 152–154, 156, 209–
    211, 240–242; and TV net-
    works, 58–59; and patents,
    312; *see also* Department of
    Justice
Antitrust Group, Nixon, 30
Antitrust Task Force, President
    Johnson's, 30
Armed Services Procurement
    Act, 228, 244